The Black Jews of Africa

The Black Jews of Africa

History, Religion, Identity

EDITH BRUDER

UNIVERSITY PRESS

2008

OXFORD
UNIVERSITY PRESS

Oxford University Press, Inc., publishes works that further
Oxford University's objective of excellence
in research, scholarship, and education.

Oxford   New York
Auckland   Cape Town   Dar es Salaam   Hong Kong   Karachi
Kuala Lumpur   Madrid   Melbourne   Mexico City   Nairobi
New Delhi   Shanghai   Taipei   Toronto

With offices in
Argentina   Austria   Brazil   Chile   Czech Republic   France   Greece
Guatemala   Hungary   Italy   Japan   Poland   Portugal   Singapore
South Korea   Switzerland   Thailand   Turkey   Ukraine   Vietnam

Copyright © 2008 by Oxford University Press, Inc.

Published by Oxford University Press, Inc.
198 Madison Avenue, New York, New York 10016

www.oup.com

Oxford is a registered trademark of Oxford University Press

All rights reserved. No part of this publication may be reproduced,
stored in a retrieval system, or transmitted, in any form or by any means,
electronic, mechanical, photocopying, recording, or otherwise,
without the prior permission of Oxford University Press.

Library of Congress Cataloging-in-Publication Data

Bruder, Edith, 1948–
The Black Jews of Africa : history, religion, identity / Edith Bruder.
   p. cm.
Includes bibliographical references and index.
ISBN 978-0-19-533356-5
1. Jews—Africa—History.   2. Africa—History.
3. Africa—Colonial influence—History.
4. Africa—Ethnic relations.   I. Title.
DS135.A25B78 2008
960'.004924—dc22   2007035833

9 8 7 6 5 4 3 2 1

Printed in the United States of America
on acid-free paper

Preface

In 1921 a band of self-proclaimed black South African "Israelites" drew up in formal military formations against armed white police: the "Israelites" were armed with knobkerries, assegais, one or two antiquated guns, and knives; the police had modern rifles as well as machine guns. Throughout the lengthy negotiations the Israelites were given the opportunity to surrender, but they refused, proclaiming, "We will fight and Jehovah will fight with us." The Israelites fought courageously, but the outcome was never in doubt. The massacre horrified both black and a good deal of white public opinion. Nelson Mandela, representing the ANC at the Conference of the Pan African Freedom Movement in Addis Ababa in January 1962, picked out the Bulhoek Massacre as perhaps the single worst atrocity in the history of South Africa. It is still remembered. A Bulhoek Massacre Heritage Memorial was unveiled with due ceremony on 27 May 2001.

The impact of "Israelite identities" upon Africans has not always been as dramatic as this. However, Black Africa, even now in 2008, contains a growing number of groups that identify completely with Jews or Israelites: in Nigeria, Ghana, Rwanda, Burundi, Uganda, South Africa, Zimbabwe, and elsewhere. In recent years the ancient narratives of such groups as the Beta Israel of Ethiopia and the Lemba of southern Africa have received wide popular and scholarly attention. The history of other Judaising African societies, the first manifestations of which date back to the beginning of the twentieth century, has received, up to now, scant academic attention.

Ideas connecting Africa and the Jews have been present for much of recorded history. The myth of the Lost Tribes of Israel over time penetrated just about every corner of the African continent. The use and reuse of this myth and connected myths about Jews served an immense array of ideological and spiritual needs and have had a striking impact on Africa. The spread of myths connecting Africa with the Jews has been spectacular. It arose primarily in the European and Middle Eastern imagination in the early Middle Ages and may be attributed in part to the ignorance of much of the world brought about by the breakdown of communications between the Islamic Middle East and Christian Europe. It became an axiomatic feature of medieval thinking about the world. It was used and reused, exploited and reinvented by colonialism in many distinct loci in Africa, where it served missionary and colonial interests.

This seminal and carefully researched work has looked at the history of Judaic and Israelite myths throughout Africa and has revealed the presence of networks of Judaising identities in the historical or imagined past and the lived present of a surprising number of African communities. In reviewing the major characteristics of the external and internal variables that shaped these group identities, this book will be a real contribution to a number of important disciplines and areas of research.

Tudor Parfitt
Professor of Modern Jewish Studies
School of Oriental and African Studies
University of London

Acknowledgments

This book is largely based on a doctoral thesis written under the supervision of Professor Tudor Parfitt of the School of Oriental and African Studies (SOAS), University of London. As a pioneer in the African Judaism field, he has been a great inspiration for my research topic suggestion. I am extremely grateful for his advice, invaluable guidance, constant encouragement, and enthusiasm over the years. Then there is the work of Professor Emanuela Trevisan-Semi of the Università Ca' Foscari, Venezia, on the sources of African American Jews' movement that also opened the way for my research and stimulated my thought.

I wish to thank Jacob Oliel, French historian of the Saharan people, who generously shared his time and knowledge and gave me access to his private archives and unpublished works on Saharan Jews. I particularly wish to express my gratitude for his helpful and astute criticism to Reverend Graham Shaw, who carefully proofread each page of the manuscript. Last but not least, I would like to thank my husband, Michel, for being a great source of encouragement and for giving me valuable comments in shaping up this work.

The elaboration of a work such as this book implies an intensive use of other researchers' work. The numerous notes and bibliographic references only partly attest my indebtedness to my predecessors in this field of research. Responsibility for the views expressed in this book, and for errors or omissions, is mine alone.

Prologue

One evening in March 2001 in my home in Paris, I switched on French TV and embarked on the greatest adventure of my life. On the screen, Professor Mathivha, leader of the South African Lemba tribe, a white Jewish skullcap on his head and a blue cloak covering his shoulders, was explaining that his people were one of the Lost Tribes of Israel. He solemnly said: "The Lemba are Jews. We are the descendants of Abraham, Isaac, Jacob, and the rest of them all. Those are our blood relatives." Tudor Parfitt's reportage on the Lemba—half researched history, half travelogue—struck me forcibly. I found myself transported to the northeastern corner of South Africa, where Parfitt was visiting traditional Lemba villages and witnessing customs such as circumcision and food taboos that did, indeed, seem Jewish. With fascination, I listened to a township Lemba, William Massala, an expert in the history of his tribe, claiming: "We came from the Israelites, we came from Sena, we crossed the sea, and we made iron and gold and pottery as we came down through Africa. We no way wanted to spoil our structure by carelessness, eating pig or marrying Lemba gentiles. We ask our ancestors to tell us what our nation is." The Lemba's food taboos and their ritual slaughter of animals, their circumcision rites and their endogamy clearly suggested an Israelite or Semitic ancestry. Distinctive cultural elements of their traditions and their saga of origins were of such a specific nature that they seemed to be rooted in historical experience. Was the Lemba elaboration of a Jewish identity the reflection of some unsuspected Jewish influence, centuries before, on the east cost of Africa? Or was it, in fact, the consequence of some particular social or religious interaction within the colonial context?

Ten months later, in January 2002, I had decided to embark upon a PhD at London University's School of Oriental and African Studies under Parfitt's supervision. Parfitt had urged me to attend a conference organized by the Lemba Cultural Association in Venda, near Tohoyandou, the region where most South African Lemba live. At first sight, the Bantu people I met there challenged my conception of Jewish identity. In the hackneyed phrase, "They did not look Jewish." However, during this two-day conference, the Lemba affirmed that they were the outposts of Israel in Africa and that they wanted to understand their diasporic history. My exchanges with them taught me that they invested heavily in their belief. At the same time, the Lemba had a strong sense of the "otherness" of their purported geographical origins and relied on that otherness to construct their own version of Jewish identity.

I was deeply intrigued by the issue. Who could think of lost Jewish tribes in Africa? Would there be other unsuspected putative Jewish claimants in the continent? Had the mythic image of the Beta Israel (Falasha), as the lost tribe of Dan in Ethiopia, produced echoes throughout Africa? If such peoples existed, their stories deserved to be told, not only to satisfy my curiosity but also to fill in some of the gaps in our understanding of the penetration of Jewish ideas in Africa. The paucity of academic studies on Judaism in Africa and the paradoxical dimension of an African-Jewish identity stimulated me to undertake the research on which this book is based. I decided to follow the footsteps of the Lost Tribes in Africa and to tell their story.

Contents

Introduction
Lost Tribes in Twenty-first-Century Africa, 3

PART I   Prehistory

1. The Lost Tribes of Israel, 11

2. Jewish Accounts and Christian Traditions, 19

3. The Mythography of Africa, 25

4. The Legend of Solomon and the Queen of Sheba, 29

PART II   Black Judaism: Genesis

5. Blacks and Jews the Archetypal "Others," 37

6. Encountering and Reinventing the Africans and the Jews in the Colonial Era, Fifteenth to Nineteenth Centuries, 51

7. Appropriating Jewish History by the African Diaspora, Nineteenth to Twentieth Centuries, 73

PART III   Africa, Judaism, and African "Jews"

8. Historical Narratives of a Jewish Presence in Sub-Saharan Africa, 97

9. African Jews in Western and Central Africa, 133

10. African Jews in Eastern and Southern Africa, 161

Epilogue
Ancient Myths and Modern Phenomena, 187

Notes, 195

Bibliography, 255

Index, 277

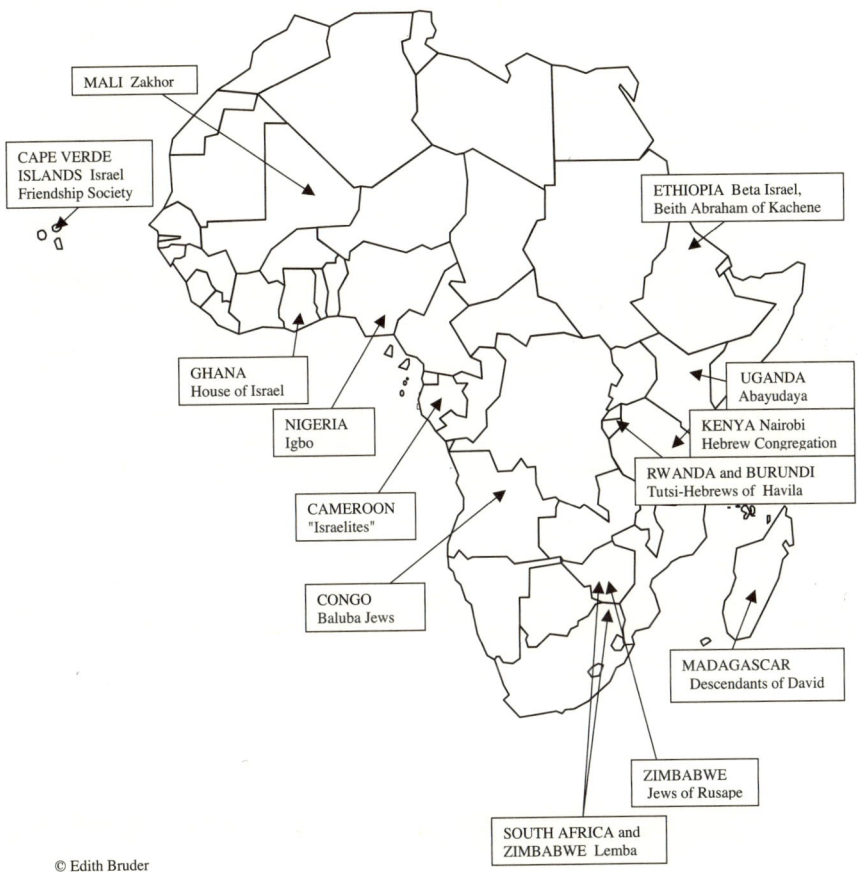

Africa's Jewish groups

The Black Jews of Africa

Introduction

Lost Tribes in Twenty-first-Century Africa

But, with this contempt, one would commit unfairness similar to the thoughtless rejection of the material of legends, traditions and interpretations of a people's prehistory. Despite all distortions and misunderstandings, it is through them that the reality of the past is represented; they are what the people formed from their original experience, under the control of once powerful and still efficient motivations, and if one could only, through the knowledge of all operating forces, cancel these distortions, one could be able to discover the historical truth behind this legendary material.

—Sigmund Freud[1]

Over the last hundred years or so, aside from the well-known case of the Beta Israel (Falasha), the so-called Jews of Ethiopia, different ethnic groups throughout Africa, without any specific link between them, have started claiming a Jewish, or Hebrew, or Israelite ancestry. Synagogues have been formed spontaneously in western, eastern, and southern Africa while various African groups proclaim that they are returning to long-forgotten Jewish roots and trace their lineage to the Lost Tribes of Israel. These forms of identification, not all of them strongly connected or indeed connected at all with the Jewish religion, have created a loose African network of apparently Jewish groups that together constitute a new kind of African Judaism.[2] Some are reworkings of biblical theology; others are the direct or indirect result of colonial interventions; some of them are derived from local or tribal traditions in search of a different form of expression.

The groups in question are located in different African countries. I refer in particular to the Zakhor movement of Timbuktu in Mali, the Igbo of Nigeria, the House of Israel of Ghana, the Tutsi-Hebrews of Rwanda, the Lemba of South Africa and Zimbabwe, the Abayudaya of Uganda, and others who claim mutatis mutandis to have a Jewish identity, in radically different ways over time and place.

Part of the intellectual background to this twenty-first-century discourse is an age-old fascination with the Lost Tribes of Israel. Every aspect of the history—and the very existence—of the Ten Tribes is no doubt fraught with controversy and epistemological difficulty. As the late Stanford Lyman observed: "Embedded in the esoteric history of the Judaeo-Christian civilisations of the Occident, the Lost Tribes continue to play their occasionally recognized and always intermittent role in both the praxes of modernity and in its postmodern epistemology."[3]

Interest in the subject has to some extent been triggered by recent events, not least the worldwide concern that the departure of the Beta Israel—from Ethiopia to Israel-generated in the 1980s and 1990s, and their subsequent history in the Jewish state. The exodus and the recognition of the Ethiopian Jews, identified as the lost tribe of Dan, have led to an interest to similar Lost Tribes identities developments in other parts of Africa.[4] Tudor Parfitt and Emanuela Trevisan Semi consider that "the implied universalism in such a construct has had the effect of stimulating a wider discourse in which the idea of universalistic Judaism has been prominent."[5] With the exception of the Rusape Jews in Zimbabwe, the Abayudaya in Uganda, and the Lemba in South Africa, none of the African groups considered in this study identified themselves as Jews before the 1980s. Alongside the Ethiopians' entry into world Jewish history, the Lemba of South Africa initiated a new web of ethnohistories and made up a wider myth of affiliation to an ancient Jewish Diaspora. The process leading to the emergence of "African Jews" was under way.

This book addresses the elaboration and development of Jewish identities by Africans. Africans have encountered Jewish myths and traditions in multiple forms and under a number of situations. The context and circumstances of these encounters produced a series of influences that gradually led, within some African societies, to the elaboration of a new Jewish identity connected with that of the Diaspora. The purpose of the book is to review the processes and the immensely complex interactions that shaped these new religious identities. It explores the ways in which Africans have interacted with ancient mythological substrata of both Westerners' and Africans' idea of Jews in order to create a distinct Jewish identity. It particularly seeks to identify and to assess foreign influences and their internalization by African societies in the shaping of new African religious identities. While these subjects are given detailed insight in the text, this survey does not intend to provide an exhaustive view of the wealth of the varied and dynamic religious experiences in motion among African Jews. It rather offers a network of theoretical suggestions for a more thorough understanding of them.

Because Africans have had so many explicit and implicit exchanges with Judaism, this book draws on concepts taken from ethnography, phenomenology, history, and religious and cultural studies. Recognition of the critical role of colonialism in shaping the relationship between Africans and Judaism has broadened my vision of the continuing effects of colonial and neocolonial intervention in Africa.[6] The role and effect of colonialism on these groups also situate this work in the framework of subaltern studies, but only marginally.[7]

When religion does receive scholarly attention, writers or academics generally tend to focus on mainstream groups and denominations. By contrast, the object of my research is the study of a micro-situation, what Carlo Ginzburg names the "paradigm of the clue."[8] Ginzburg pushes beyond the simple "clues" of historical evidences to tease out the information embedded in them and he challenges us to retrieve a cultural and social world that more conventional history does not record (as he demonstrated with his study of witchcraft). It must be said that the number of people involved in these African groups is, broadly speaking, insignificant in terms of the overall African population: the groups in question constitute a marginal phenomenon that may be seen as historically irrelevant. Moreover, due to the dynamic nature of religious shift, they are almost impossible to assess. In its broadest form, I consider socioethnic history to be a focus on groups whose general contribution to the broader history of a society has usually been ignored. Recent advances in the study of culture, as Renato Rosaldo has observed, have encouraged analysts to "look less for homogenous communities than for the border zones within and between them. Such cultural border zones are always in motion, not frozen for inspection."[9]

By exploring the ways in which Africans have identified with Jews ethnically and/or religiously, this book challenges existing Western racial ideas on what constitutes Jewish identity and ethnicity. *The Black Jews of Africa* raises basic questions about the meaning of Jewishness, but it does not purport to be a book on "Who is a Jew?" The Jewish identity theme and the essence of belonging to the worldwide Jewish community have a long history embedded in controversy about race and religion issues in general.[10] Due to the two distinct definitional standards at play in the Jewish community—religious and ethnic—there has always been a tension between the conflicting aspirations toward universalism on the one hand and particularism on the other.[11]

Over the past few decades, scholars from a variety of disciplines have increasingly questioned the existence of race as a meaningful scientific concept. If there is no race in any biological sense of the term, it is obviously rather meaningless to state that Jews are not a race.[12] For instance, in *The Myth of the Jewish Race* (1989), Raphael and Jennifer Patai forcefully argue that there is no genetic, physical, or biological Jewish specificity.[13] Ephraim Isaac insistently asserts that Jewish history is filled with interracial and intercultural mixing and that the popular vision of a single Judaism does not reflect any historical period: "Over two thousands years ago, the Jews were an ethnic group—but even then not a 'perfect' one.... The ancient Israelites were not a racial unit but a sacral association, called an amphictiony by some scholars. They were a people bound together by a common language, and common territory, similar historical experience, and common consciousness."[14]

Racial categories are, according to a growing consensus, socially and culturally constructed and the result of a variety of ideological and political factors, "not a biogenetic category but an ideology embedded in and expressed through specific relations of power."[15] However, within the body of Judaism, the belief that continuous descent from the patriarchs is the "sine qua non of Jewish identities" continues to survive alongside and in contradiction with claims of the essentially nonracial character of Jewish identity.[16]

From the twentieth century, the emergence of Jewish religious movements from Africa to Asia turned the generally accepted views upside down and expanded the debate. If groups of African Americans or Africans or Asians who were raised as Christians or Muslims or in traditional religions declared themselves to be Jews and formed new communities, did that make them Jewish?[17] In the United States, long-established communities of African Americans have been practicing Judaism for more than 150 years. Some of them have Jewish heritage, others identify with Judaism, some have converted to Judaism, and others are connected to Judaism through marriage or extended family. Chireau and Deutsch stress that "the identification of African Americans with and especially *as* Jews expands the parameters of this debate and highlights the issues of race ethnicity, and self-definition in determining who is a Jew."[18]

African Americans and Africans understood and experienced the Jewish religion, as they did for other religions, on their own terms. For the African peoples under study who identify *as* Jews, identification with biblical Israel assumes symbolic significance while almost totally ignoring the physical characteristics; they identify themselves as sharing a common descent with the members of the contemporary Jewish community. When identifying as Jews and with other Jews, they deny the existence of distinctive categories in popular concepts of Jews and subvert the racist image of blacks. Their self-definition lies in their collective historical and cultural experiences that have led them to assume a shared history with the Jewish people. The entry or reentry of these people into religious consciousness as Jews has necessitated a reshaping of the standard accounts of Jewish history and a rewriting of each group's version of its history. As Steven Kaplan notes about communities of "exotic" Jews, their narratives take on a circularity: "Since they are Jews, they must have participated in a shared Jewish history; since they participated in this shared history, they must be Jews!"[19]

Africa's great ethnic and cultural diversity is combined with an equally complex religious scene.[20] African Jews' recent religious identities were shaped by their participation in Christian, Islamic, or traditional African religions; moreover, many African groups and individuals that identify with Judaism also consider themselves to be Christians, Muslims, or members of African-based religions. Within the confines of this book, however, enumerating all the connections that have had an impact on African Jews' religiosity did not seem possible. Rather, I hope to illuminate one thread in the medley of race, ethnicity, and religion in the African religious experience.

The book is structured in three parts, each examining a different sequence of the genesis of African Judaism. The first part explores the prehistory of African Judaism. The emergence of an African Jewish identity appears to draw on a very long history. For thousands of years, myths have accumulated about the presence of Jews in sub-Saharan Africa. Directly—but never very directly—and indirectly—sometimes very indirectly—these mythic elements have played a role in the development of these communities. The myth of the Lost Tribes of Israel is one of them; the Solomon and Sheba legends, the issue of the biblical Children of Kush, and the mythic representation of Ethiopia and Africa in the Western *imaginaire* are others. It was essential to include a treatment of this mythic prehistory from which the reader may draw the necessary information to better understand the current manifestations.

The second part reveals the variety of interactions between blackness and Judaism from prejudices to reality. In chapter 5 and 6, special attention is paid to the Western representation of the racial "promiscuity" between Jews and Blacks, which became commonplace in the nineteenth century and has on occasion been adopted by the early twentieth-century anthropology. This part explores mainly the process of identifying and inventing Judaism in the New

World and in Africa by colonizers, which enabled local people themselves to get to know and have access to this religion. The impact on traditional societies of European missionaries and early ethnographers recognizing all sorts of similarity between ancient Judaism and primitive religion is questioned.

Chapter 7 focuses on the theories of Afrocentrism that provided the theoretical basis for Africans to appropriate the Jewish history. By trying to restore the primacy of African influence in the world, the Afrocentrist ideology has established a link of connivance with the most remote ancestors and asserted that Africans were the true original Jewish race. Following the history of these political texts, this part considers the precursors of African Diaspora identification with the Jewish Diaspora and the subsequent roots of African Judaizing movements: special attention is paid to African American Jewish movements. The symbolic role of Judaism in the religious imagination of the Hebrew-Israelites (in Israel) and the Rastafarian movement (in Jamaica) is also examined.

The third part reveals the historical background of Jewish traces or influence in Black Africa. Although direct sources supporting a Jewish existence in sub-Saharan Africa do not exist, several sources indirectly testify to the antiquity of a Jewish presence, in particular in western Africa, or to a Semitic presence in southeastern Africa. Based on these elements, this chapter provides a historical context for attempting to reconstruct the most ancient Jewish or Semitic influences on sub-Saharan Africa or to evaluate the extent of mythical realities (chapter 8).

Chapters 9 and 10 provide a survey of various African groups that self-proclaimed a Jewish identity and examine one by one the creative elaboration and development of their recent religious identities. This part explores how most of these societies work toward the construction of a mythical-genealogical connection from the Lost Tribes that would justify their claim of ethnic as well as religious Judaism. A section of this chapter assesses the impact of genetic research on group identity claims and the view of such claims by others.

In the epilogue, we turn to an overview of the catalysts for change. This final chapter examines the intricate tapestry of cultural, social, and political factors that could have led African religious traditions mingled with Christianity, and sometimes with Islam, to be superseded by a new Jewish cultural identity. Following Mircea Eliade, who states that the most important task in the study of religions is to "decipher" the "deep meaning" of religious phenomena, I shall suggest some hypotheses of the meaning and the benefits that these groups derive from their affiliation with Judaism.[21] Of course, the number of topics to which I could have devoted attention in this section would fill an additional volume. I hope nonetheless that these considerations will stimulate future debate.

PART I

Prehistory

I

The Lost Tribes of Israel

According to the Bible, the tribes of the kingdom of Israel's northern part were exiled in the eighth century BC, at which time they disappeared from the stage of history. Over time, a belief based on the Isaiah, Jeremiah, and Ezekiel prophecies took hold of the Jewish imagination, whereby the idea developed and survived: one day the Ten Tribes would be reunited, and this event would prefigure the messianic era. This strong myth influenced the Western world and its perceptions of the outside world from ancient times until the present day. Over 2,000 years, Jews, Christians, and to a lesser degree Muslims attached fundamental importance to the fate of these tribes and speculated on their exile and return. Theologians and exegetes, ancient and modern historians and geographers, ethnographers and missionaries of varied beliefs, and more recently geneticists contributed, through constructions, deconstructions, and imbrications, to the edification of the colossal and shifting knowledge of the Ten Tribes.

The lack of any evidence of their whereabouts left the way open for innumerable locations and innumerable geographical and spatial changes. Implicit interactions between legend, hearsay, and scientific geographical knowledge contributed to feeding the myth, as well as launching explorations of unknown regions to track the tribes. At times, the speculation over the location of the tribes played a role in new geographical discoveries, and at others geographical expansions inspired new speculation on the presence of the tribes on the world's map. Every continent in the world has thus been, at one time or another, designated as the place where the tribes took refuge, and various human groups, no matter how remote or unknown, were attributed the distinction—or disgrace—of descending from the Lost Tribes.

Through centuries the continued belief in the Lost Tribes showed no sign of abating. Unquestionable proof of their settling in Arabia, China, Tartary, Afghanistan, India, Denmark, and the Sahara was put forward by enthusiastic authors. By turns, it has regularly been asserted or claimed that the British, Irish, American Indians, Hottentots, Zulus, and Malagasy were of Hebrew ancestry. The theory positing that inhabitants of the British Isles and North America were descended from the Israelites was widespread in Europe from the seventeenth century up to the end of the nineteenth century. Millions of adherents considered that Great Britain and its empire together with America had inherited the covenant blessings given to Abraham.[1] From at least the seventeenth century, the Japanese royal family, like the British one, has been granted an Israelite ancestry, the samurai as well as a number of other groups having been dubbed descendants of the Lost Tribes of Israel.[2] A vast number of recent works by scholars as well as tribes seekers still attempt to prove the continued existence of the Lost Tribes.[3] But it would be reductive to limit the dimension of this tentacular myth to its fictional features. Alongside its imaginary aspect, the myth has been legitimated and has interacted with past and contemporary polities. From Africa to America, Britain to Japan, it has had significant cultural, sociological, and political bearings on the expansion of empires and on the colonized people of the world.[4] In recent decades the myth gave credence to contemporary policies and gave rise to theological-religious-based politics such as the recognition of marginal Jewish societies by the Israeli government. In 1985 and 1990, the repatriation of thousands of Ethiopia's Falasha to Israel under the "law of return" was legitimated by Israeli rabbinic authorities through their official recognition as descendants from the tribe of Dan.[5] In April 2005, the historic decision of Shlomo Amar, Israel's chief rabbi, to recognize India's Bene Menashe as descendants from Israel was legitimated by their appurtenance to the Menasseh and Ephraim tribes.[6] The recent DNA tracing of the nonimplausible "Jewish" descent of the South Africa's Lemba, the genetic data supporting the historical division of the tribes, and the dispersion of Levi's tribes among the other tribes are examples of the way in which modern science initiates its own contribution to the phenomenon.[7]

In the 1930s, Professor Allen Godbey, who taught Old Testament at Duke University, harshly disproved in a monumental academic book the fantasies about the Lost Tribes.[8] In this work, Godbey made repeated attacks against ethnographers' and missionaries' compulsions to discover Jewish tribes in every corner of the earth, severely refuting Westerners' fanciful identification of Hebrew or Judaic traces in remote ethnic groups. But at the same time, whether he likes it or not, Godbey emphasized the universal functions of the myth in the discourse about "otherness." In revealing the proliferation of ethnographic interpretations of supposed Lost Tribes, he opened the door for serious philosophical, psychological, and sociological considerations regarding the general significance of the tribes in world representation and experience. What Godbey's book finally brings to the fore is that the Ten Tribes' disappearance and finding are recurrent features of the world conceptualization carried by the biblical text. In other words, the Lost Tribes myth is a vehicle through which the world has been fundamentally imagined. The history of the Ten Tribes in its political and geographical dimensions goes alongside discoveries and explorations, expansions and wars, empires and colonizations and can be seen as characterizing Western modernity. As a cultural framework of reference, the "Ten Lost Tribes" offered a theological, sociological, and political infrastructure for all future speculations concerning unsuspected lands, different realities, and strange peoples. The utility of the myth rests on its paradoxical cultural functions for the understanding of the visible world.[9]

From the medieval ages, the story of the Ten Tribes produced a conceptual vision of the "other" in metaphorical as well as in concrete and representational terms. For the populations of medieval Europe, faced with a strange, faraway, and unknown world, the existence of the Lost Tribes in an unknown location represented a tool that provided the means to qualify and name both the incomprehensible and the fearsome. Up until the Crusades, which constituted the first expansion of Western Christendom, the imagination of the Western peoples prevailed over contact with reality. Albert Hyamson reminds us that the first known reference to the theories of the Ten Tribes by an English writer appeared in Matthew Paris's writings (ca. 1220–1259). When the Mongol hordes reached Germany in 1241, Matthew Paris spontaneously identified them with the Ten Tribes, "these Tartars of cursed memories who having forsaken the Mosaic Law followed the golden calves, and whom Alexander the Great endeavoured to shut up in the rugged mountains of the Caspian with bitumen covered rocks."[10] Emperor Frederic II made use of this assertion in a letter to Henry III of England: "It is said that they are descended from the Ten Tribes that abandoned the Law of Moses."[11] From the beginning of the fifteenth century up to the second half of the twentieth century, during the long era of the overseas empires, the Lost Tribes myth has been an essential part of the European colonial discourse.[12] From Africa to America, it was a critical element in the construction of the biological and cultural past for countless peoples and for the discourse about "otherness" One can say that it offered a conceptualization of the world divided into two different spaces, reality and fiction, history and messianic beliefs synthesized in a single event.

The biblical narrative, involving a "historical" background, plays a crucial role in the initial spread of the Lost Tribes myth. For centuries, the text provided authoritative proof of the tribes' exile history. As is well known, in recent times, an imposing array of critical analyses have regarded the Bible narrative as almost entirely fictional and have expressed radical skepticism about its historical value.[13] The various controversial suggestions questioning the historicity of the Lost Tribes are not really within the scope of this book, and the techniques of biblical criticism are rather far from its purpose. Indeed, I do not wish to make any claims about the disappearance of the Ten Tribes as a historical event. My interest is in the continuing importance of the myth that the narrative has created. The myth, as the "hard-worked and active force that never exhausts its meanings," which Bronislaw Malinowski writes about, is the present book's central pivot.[14] My aim is thus not so much to reconstruct the historical reality of claims to inclusion among the Lost Tribes by African communities as to follow the creative impetus of this myth in African mythology.

Let us now return to the Lost Tribes. What does the Bible teach us about the story of the Ten Tribes?[15] There were twelve tribes of Israel, descended from the twelve sons of Jacob. The Ten Tribes from the Northern Kingdom descended from Reuben, Simon, Levi, Dan, Naphtali, Gad, Asher, Issachar, Zebulon, and Joseph, and the tribes from the Southern Kingdom descended from Judah and Benjamin. According to the Bible, the Northern Kingdom was conquered by the Assyrian kings Tiglath-Pileser III in 733–732 BC and Sargon II in 721 BC, whereas Nebuchadnezzar exiled the population of the Southern Kingdom to Babylon after the destruction of the First Temple in 586 BC.[16] In both cases, the exiles were carried out in several stages, and the sources show that the kings of Assyria exiled parts of the Ten Tribes beyond the Euphrates (2 Kings 15).

We read in 2 Kings: "In the days of Pekah King of Israel came Tiglath-Pileser, King of Assyria, and he took Ion and Abel-Beth-Maacha and Janoah and Kedesh and Hazor, and Gileat and Galilee, all the land of Naphtali; and he carried them captive to Assyria" (15:29). The biblical narrative claims that all this happened because Israel had sinned against God, "therefore the Lord was very angry with Israel and removed them out of his sight" (2 Kings 17:18). Biblical passages documented the tribes' place of exile in Assyria "in Halah and in Habor on the river of Gozan and in the cities of the Medes" (2 Kings 17:6). Archaeological and documentary evidence from the regions shows that individuals with Hebrew names were still to be found in Assyrian army units in the seventh century.[17] Inscriptions of Hebraic names on a fragment of terra-cotta found in Halakh bear witness to the presence of Jewish craftsmen in the Assyrian city; also a Nimrod ivory bearing inscriptions in Hebraic letters, rather than Phoenician-Aramaic, was discovered in Halakh.[18] It is assumed that elements of the Ten Tribes, which had been exiled to Assyria, were absorbed by the local population and assimilated into Assyrian culture.[19]

This is when the Ten Tribes' history makes the transition to legend and is substituted by prophecies. The Ten Tribes' exile had very quickly assumed mythical importance, embodying symbolical features: on one hand, in the Bible (Amos 6) and in the Talmud (Tractate Sabbath 147), it was interpreted as the consequence of Israel's sins for worshiping idols; on the other hand, in the prophecies, the reunion of the Lost Tribes with the descendants of Judah's exile to Babylon characterized the messianic hope for redemption. Isaiah (11:11), Jeremiah (31:8), and above all Ezekiel's prophetic exclamations suggested that the tribes had maintained a separate existence and would be gathered in latter days with their brethren. In Ezekiel (37:21) we read that the Lord "will take the children of Israel from among the heathen, whither they be gone, and will gather them on every side, and bring them into their own land."

The continued existence of the Ten Tribes was taken for granted at the time of the Second Temple and the Talmud, but Adolf Neubauer points out that the Talmud is nearly silent on the existence of the Ten Tribes in Media and the adjacent provinces.[20] A metaphor alludes to it as "Babylon is healthy, Mesa is dead, Media is ill; Elam (and Gabai) are near to death," which is meant to express the purity of the families in Babylon, compared with those in Media, which were probably intermixed. The vague formulation of the Talmud leaves us to think that the sages of Babylon did not know of the existence of the tribes with certainty in the fifth and sixth centuries AD. They would then constitute a symbolic representation, already a part of the Jews' mythical patrimony.[21]

The Apocrypha perpetuated the story of the Lost Tribes by further developing it:

> [The tribes] formed this plan for themselves that they would leave the multitude of the nations and go to a more distant region where mankind had never lived, that there at least they might keep their statutes which they had not kept in their own land. And they went in by the narrow passages of the Euphrates River.... Then they dwelt there until the last times and now when they are about to come again the Most High will stop the channels of the river again so that they may be able to pass over. (2 Esdras 13:41–7)

Tobias, the hero of the book named after him, was described as a member of the Naphtali tribe, and a large part of the stories he relates took place in

Media (Tobias 1:14–15, 14:14). The Testament of the Twelve Patriarchs considers their existence as a fact, and in his fifth vision Ezra sees "a peaceable multitude...these are the Ten Tribes which were carried away prisoners out of their own land" (13:34–45). Flavius Josephus states as a fact that "the Ten Tribes are beyond the Euphrates till now, and are an immense multitude and not to be estimated in numbers" (Antiquities. 11:133).

Christianity simply integrated the myth of the Lost Tribes: James addresses his epistle to "the twelve tribes which are scattered abroad" (1:1) while Paul protests to Agrippa the charge made in his respect: "And now I stand and I am judged for the hope of the promise made of God unto our fathers: unto which promise our twelve tribes, instantly serving God day and night, hope to come" (Acts 26:6–7). The only opposition to this consensus is found in the Mishnah, where Rabbi Akiva (ca. AD 40–135) categorically expressed the idea that "the Ten Tribes shall not return again.... And ye shall be lost among the nations" (Sanhedrin 10:3), thus interpreting the exile as an annihilation.

The inability of the tribes to join their brethren was attributed to the fact that whereas the Judah and Benjamin tribes were scattered throughout the world (Gen. Rabbah 73:5), the Ten Tribes were exiled beyond the mysterious river Sambatyon (Gen. Rabbah 73:6), whose flow of sand and stones prevented its crossing six days of the week. Although the river stopped flowing on the seventh day, the laws of the Sabbath rendered its crossing impossible, which is why all trace of them was completely lost. On the Sambatyon riverbank, the tribes were thus cut off from immorality, the initial reason for their exile, and could virtuously keep Jewish laws in an ideal faraway place. This marvelous river, also mentioned in texts of Flavius Josephus and Pliny the Elder, became a key feature of the Lost Tribes notion, the symbol of a theoretical and ideal exile associated to an ultimate return.[22] The tribes were secluded "beyond the Sambatyon," waiting for the day the Jewish people would find its unity (Tanchuma, Nitzvim 1).

The location of the tribes constituted an immense subject of speculation, as well as an enigma for the commentators of the Old Testament. The Isaiah prophecy states that they could be scattered all over the world:

> And it shall come to pass in that day, that the Lord shall set his hand again the second time to recover the remnant of his people, which shall be left, from Assyria and from Egypt, and from Pathros and from Kush, and from Elam and from Shinar, and from Hamath, and from the islands of the sea. And he shall set up an ensign for the nations, and shall assemble the outcasts of Israel, and gather together the dispersed of Judah from the four corners of the earth. (Isaiah 11:11–12)

And he adds, "Behold, these shall come from far: And, these from the north and from the west; and these from the land of Sinim" (Isaiah 49:12). Jeremiah elaborates that the Ten Tribes are gathered in the north: "Behold I will bring them from the North Country and gather them from the coasts of the earth" (31:7).

However, according to the Jerusalem Talmud (Sanhedrin 10:6, 29c), the Ten Tribes were scattered in three exile locations: on the other side of the Sambatyon River, to "Daphnea of Antioch," and to another place where "a cloud descended and covered them." In other versions (Tractate Sanhedrin 94), the tribes were located in dark mountains: Mar Zutra claimed that they were exiled in "Afriki," which could be "Avriki" in the Caucasus mountains, a place recorded in the conquests of Alexander the Great, while Rabbi Hanina located them in the "Mountains of Sloog."[23] Later Rabbi Loew, maharal of Prague (ca. 1525–1609), noticed this discrepancy and considered these places as referring symbolically to the nature of the exile more than to specific locations.[24]

The theological significance of the dispersion of and the search for the Ten Tribes came out from these biblical foundations. It is from these crucial texts, through distortions, displacements, and reconstructions, that the symbolic structure of the Lost Tribes mythology took shape. One can say that the people of Israel became the paradigm of loss and wandering, their scattering shaping the notion of exile and Diaspora in Western consciousness. A spiritual dynamic in Jewish traditions took sustenance from the possible capacity of the tribes to preserve their identity and to ensure their redemption. That is not to say that keeping their identity was the condition of the redemptive process, but rather that the finding of the tribes had a potential of salvation attached to it. The psychological significance of the Lost Tribes as a vanished human group presumed to be present somewhere on earth puts forward a conceptual category stigmatizing what is at the same time missing and present, as well as an idea of eternal return. These notions came to be widespread values shaping a spectrum of forms as varied and complex as the conceptualization of exile and return. The emergence of the narrative of exile became the quintessence of the Diaspora concept and a frame for prefiguring subsequent events in Jewish history and the history of the world.

Biblical narratives and prophecies that mentioned the putative existence of Jews in the land of Kush (i.e., Africa) provided the scriptural foundations for subsequent complex connections between Jews and Africa. Isaiah's speculation over the location of the tribes (Isaiah 11:11–12) explicitly asserted the existence of a Jewish presence in the land of Kush, which he differentiates from Patros, the term for Upper Egypt, and he announces the final return of this Diaspora to Zion: "In that time shall the present be brought unto the Lord of hosts of a people scattered and peeled, and from a people terrible from their beginning hitherto; a nation meted out and trodden under foot, whose land the rivers have spoiled, to the place of the Lord of hosts, the mount Zion" (Isaiah 18:7). Zephaniah also, identifying Kush as a tribe's exile location, prophesies the rally of the Kush population to the Hebrew religion: "From beyond the rivers of Ethiopia my suppliants, even the daughter of my dispersed, shall bring mine offering" (Zephaniah 3:10). Various interpretations of these passages came to be critical components of the context in which the story of the Lost Tribes in Africa was cast and elaborated.

The book of Esther gives further information about the presence of Jews in the land of Kush. First, the biblical text makes a distinction between the land of Kush and India, which were often confused in ancient times: "Now it came to pass in the days of Ahasuerus which reigned from India, even unto Ethiopia, over a hundred and seven and twenty provinces," and states that there were populations that practiced Judaism in all the provinces of the kingdom, at the time of King Ahasuerus, in the fifth century BC, after the destruction of the First Temple in 587 BC (Esther 1:1). When Aman, Ahasuerus's counselor, spoke to Ahasuerus, he mentioned the presence of Jews, whom he sought to exterminate, in all the provinces of the kingdom, thus implicitly including Ethiopia: "There are a certain people scattered abroad and dispersed among the people in all the provinces of thy kingdom" (Esther 3:8). When the king took the Jews' side, thanks to the intervention of his wife, Esther the Jew, and that of her uncle Moordecai, the biblical text repeats that the Jews reacted by gathering in all the provinces of the kingdom. Similarly, when Queen Esther instituted the feast of Purim, it was implicitly stated that Jews were present in all the provinces of the kingdom, as far away as Ethiopia: "And he sent the letters unto all the Jews, to the hundred twenty and seven provinces of the kingdom of Ahasuerus, with words of peace and truth" (Esther 9:30).

A passage in the New Testament also seems to indicate a Jewish presence at the dawn of the Christian era in Meroe, near the enemy kingdom of Axum. One of the seven deacons, Philip, met an important personage who was in charge of the royal treasury of the court of Candace, queen of Ethiopia, returning from Jerusalem, where he had been to worship.[25] A religious dialogue with Philip informed him of the Messiah suffering and ended with the Christian baptism of this Ethiopian dignitary (Acts 8:27). Was this personage returning from Jerusalem to pray Jewish or Ethiopian or both? Was he white- or black-skinned? This legend allows us to imagine that a Jewish community, in which some members held high-level positions, existed in a region believed to be Ethiopia at the dawn of the Christian era, several centuries before the conversion of the Axum rulers to Christianity.

2

Jewish Accounts and Christian Traditions

Myriad interpretations of these passages framed the way for subsequent extrapolations connecting Africa with Jews. From this time, travelers and tribes seekers could plausibly suspect certain peoples of Africa to be remnants of the Lost Tribes. At the end of the ninth century, one of the most famous and most extravagant of travelers seeking the Lost Tribes was Eldad the Danite, a Jew who mysteriously came from eastern Sahara to carry out a religious mission in Tiaret, Fez, and Kairwan.[1] Eldad's experiences were legion and fanciful: he suffered a shipwreck, fell into the hands of cannibals, and whereas his travel companion was eaten, he escaped this wretched fate by being bought by a Jew from the tribe of Issachar. Eldad wrote an account in a somewhat archaic Hebrew, in which he explained that upon Solomon's death, four Jewish tribes, including his own, Dan, and the tribes of Naphtali, Gad, and Asher, settled in Africa. The tribes established an independent empire that dominated the country while remaining a nomadic people. Their kingdom was supposed to be in "Havilah," the country of gold, near Ethiopia, and the tribes, said to be of outstanding bravery, were constantly at war against their neighbours. Eldad also mentioned the existence of "sons of Moses," who lived nearby but were cut off from the world by the impassable Sambatyon.[2] "They are of perfect faith and their Talmud is all in Hebrew.... But they know not the Rabbis, for these were for the Second Temple and they did not reach them.... No unclean things are to be found with them, no unclean fowl, no unclean beast, no unclean cattle, no flies, no lice, no foxes, no scorpions, no serpents and no dogs. And they can speak only the holy tongue and they all take ritual baths and never swear."[3] What is to be thought of the material of *Sepher Eldad*? Half truth, half make-believe, it seems to be based on real historical characters and events—such as the conversion of the Arabian king Dhu Nuwas of Himyar and his subjects to Judaism (sixth century)—that were embroidered by the storyteller. Nonetheless, one can think that Eldad's account, with its numerous improbabilities (he locates the origin of the Halacha (Jewish law) in a Jewish community somewhere in Africa), had an underlying content.[4] Eldad's aim was probably to reinforce the Jewish faith by giving news of Israel's tribes that lived freely, and by contributing to the utopian dream of the Lost Tribes' return to Israel. The story of Eldad did not lack supporters in the tenth century, such as Rabbi Chisdai ibn Shaprut, the vizier of the caliph of Cordoba, whereas Ibn Ezra and Rabbi Meir of Rothenburg, in particular, considered him as an impostor. Much more recently, in the nineteenth century, P. F. Frankl denounced him too as a faker of Greek origin,[5] whereas H. A. Reifmann concluded that his account was a late forgery.[6] However, the Hebrew account of Eldad was widely disseminated. The earliest version of Eldad's account was published in Mantua in 1483, followed by a later version in Constantinople in 1519, and had a long-lasting influence on the Jewish and European imagination in the Middle Ages.[7] It reverberated in the imagination of both Jews and Christians the idea of the presence of Jews beyond the Sambatyon and reinforced the myth of the Lost Tribes exiled in some distant utopia.

In the twelfth century, Benjamin of Tudela (1165–1173), described as one of the greatest travelers who had ever lived,[8] undertook a journey of several years that took him as far as China to establish a sort of census of the Jewish populations he encountered.[9] He crossed France, Italy, the Greek islands, Palestine, Persia, and the Persian Gulf before returning home via Aden and Aswan. In Persia, he identified the descendants of the tribes of Dan, Zebulon, Asher, and Naphtali living in the mountains of Nishapur, in complete independence from the king of Persia and who told him, "We are Jews; we have no King and no gentile Prince, but a Jewish prince rules over us."[10] In a place he names Ibrig, which has been identified as Ceylon, Benjamin noted that the Jews, apparently those of Cochin, were black Jews: "All the inhabitants of the country are black (*shehorim*), the Jews as well."[11] He also provided important information about the presence of a small group of Jews in the Sahara, in a country he called Kush, specifying that they undertook fifty-day caravan journeys toward what is now Ghana, threatened by sandstorms, in order to bring back copper, salt, gold, and jewels. He described them as "Sons of Kush, who read the stars, and are all black in colour.... They know the law of Moses and the Prophets and, to a small extent the Talmud and the Halacha."[12]

Eldad the Danite and Benjamin of Tudela had famous successors, such as Patatiah of Ratisbon, in the twelfth century; Obadiah of Bertinoro, in the fifteenth century; the rabbis Eliezer ha-Levi and Moses Basula of Ancona, in the sixteenth century; and their contemporary David Reubeni. All claimed to have found the tribes in a number of different places from Arabia to Ethiopia and in others, often difficult to identify. Among these travelers, some reported encounters with black-skinned Jews. In a detailed description of Jerusalem, Obadiah of Bertinoro mentions pilgrims coming from the land of Prester John (i.e., Ethiopia) who told him about the Lost Tribes. He goes on to report on an encounter with black Jews, members of the Ten Tribes, captured in battle, sold into slavery, and brought to Egypt: "They are only somewhat black (*shehorim*) and not like the blacks (*benei kusi'im*)."[13] A century later, while Moses Basula described the land of Kush in an enigmatic way, a letter from the land of Israel from Israel Ashkenazi to Abraham of Perugia gives the account of a black Jew "almost like a black (*kushi*)" who was captured, enslaved, and redeemed by Jews from Alexandria. This description may be compared to that of the Italian traveler Ludovico Vartima, who described the Ethiopian Jews as "black rather than any other colour".[14] It is difficult to know whether these encounters took place with black Christians from Ethiopia, said to have come from Prester John's legendary kingdom, or black Jews, supposedly from the Lost Tribes. As to David Reubeni, who claimed to be the brother and emissary of the king of Khaibar who ruled the exiled tribes of Gad, Reuben, and Manasseh, he himself may have been of Falasha origin: a number of his contemporaries, for instance, Daniel of Pisa, described him as having a dark skin.[15]

Quite naturally, the travelers and scholars who dealt with the issue related to the country where the Lost Tribes were thought to be, and the people who lived there gave stereotypical descriptions of the nature and appearance of the Africans bound to geo-theological problems like the climate theory. Unlike Jewish scholars in the Islamic cultural world, those in lands of Latin-Christian culture in the late Middle Ages had virtually no contact with Africans except for travelers who, like Benjamin of Tudela and Obadiah of Bertinoro, reached North Africa and the Middle East and a few scholars active in the southern part of Christian Europe. Only in the mid-fifteenth century did black slaves from West Africa appear in Europe as a result of Portuguese conquests.[16] A recurrent antique link took place between the Lost Tribes and the presence, in the region where they were identified, of dark-skinned populations. One might assume that a surreptitious identification between dark-complexioned peoples and Jews was made in the background of the myth of the Lost Tribes.

Until this time traces of the Lost Tribes were sought in the conventional direction of Asia and Africa. Following the discovery of America, however, the search began among its native inhabitants and sustained the identification of the Lost Tribes with dark-skinned people.[17] In the seventeenth century, the myth of the Ten Tribes did not lose any of its strength. Menasseh ben Israel, who was then the rabbi of Amsterdam, demonstrated great interest in the fantastic account of Antonio Levi de Montezinos's journey to the New World.[18] He devoted a book, *Hope of Israel* (1650–1652), to the remarkable story of his encounter with Indians beyond the Cordillera passes.[19] When he returned in 1644, Montezinos declared that the Indians, who allegedly welcomed him by reciting the Shema Israel, had a few customs that reminded him of Jewish commandments. He thus identified this people—considered as somewhat "tanned" but in essence white—with the Lost Tribes. Menasseh accepted this account but rejected out of hand the possibility of identifying the lost Israelites with certain dark-skinned Indian tribes.[20] He refused the hypothesis raised by a few Christian scholars that the Canaanites, "black" according to the Midrashic tradition, wandered until they reached America after Joshua defeated them and expelled them from Canaan, and that the Indians were their descendants. He could, however, accept the argument, among others, that the Jews were originally light-skinned, but their complexions had grown dark as a punishment of their exile.

In the following centuries, the myth of the Ten Tribes did not lose any of its strength, and a number of Jewish travelers or Israeli emissaries (*shelulei Erets Israel*) brought forward proof that the desire for a confrontation between the present reality and the mythical past was actively being kept alive. We note that in the 1830s, one of these disciples, Israel of Shklov, leader of a group called the Kohel ha-Perushim of Safed, who wished to facilitate the reunification of the exiled communities, sent an emissary into the Arabian Desert to search for traces of the Ten Tribes.[21] In 1824, a disciple of the Gaon of Vilna, David D'Beth Hillel, began a long journey in search of eastern Jewish communities, which took him to Palestine and as far as India.[22] The sole reason that led David D'Beth Hillel to spend nearly ten years tracing the Jewish presence in the East was none other than to shed light on the existence and the status of the Ten Lost Tribes, who lived in freedom and virtuously. One might add that the messages of those travelers served the function of keeping alive messianic hopes in the face of general persecution of Jews in Europe and elsewhere.

An example of the amalgamation of Jewish and Christian myths and legends is the legend of Prester John, a supernatural personage who foreshadowed the return of the Messiah at the End of the Days. This legend dominated Western imagination for a long time during the Middle Ages and tossed another stone on the heap of the myth of the Ten Tribes in Africa. The account of the existence and the totally fictitious high deeds of this priest-king spread throughout Europe and forged the attitudes of the time.[23] How was this legend created? Around the middle of the twelfth century, the conquests of the Crusaders in Palestine were seriously threatened; the Saracens' power had significantly increased, and discouragement overtook the Christians. Prester John was known instantly in Europe due to a letter he ostensibly sent in 1165 to the Byzantine emperor, Manuel Commene.[24] In this letter, which was the basis of the legend for centuries, Prester John described himself as ruling in "India." The confusion that prevailed in the Middle Ages, in terms of geography, barely distinguished Africa from India, and the general ignorance prevailing transported Prester John to Africa that could be Asia. He went on to write that he was a Christian ruler and described his wealth, power, the great size and the diversity of his empire, and the botanical and zoological marvels that could be found there. Prester John's letter mentions also the presence of Jews nearby his states. His description strongly evokes the fabulous account of Eldad the Danite, "Between us and the Jews flows a river so rapid that no one is able to cross it except on Saturday, its day of rest. The Jews are twice as numerous as the Christians or Saracens, but the great King of Israel pays us a tribute of 200 horses loaded with gold, silver and precious stones."[25]

When Portugal began its maritime discoveries, Prince Henry sent emissaries to Ethiopia (Abyssinia), where they found a Christian king who, in some ways, displayed features already ascribed to Prester John. Vague ideas about remote religious doctrines, flourishing especially in Asia, contributed to the spread throughout Europe of the opinion that a powerful ruler, at the edges of earth, was professing Christianity. The legend of Prester John was assimilated by both Jewish and Christian myths and legends and constituted a reference for fifteenth- and sixteenth-century Jewish writings. Obadiah of Bertinoro affirmed in 1448: "Certain it is that a man has arrived from the land of the Prester John, which lies between great mountains, and extends ten days' journey, who says that there is the dwelling of Bene Israel and that they are in continuous warfare with Prester John."[26] In answer to this, another text known in Jerusalem in 1454 recounted that the Sambatyon had dried up and that the tribes were crossing it to wage war on Prester John.[27] We also note that the legend of Prester John drew on the medieval idea that the earthly paradise should be located somewhere in Africa. Later on, with the Portuguese interests being transferred to the Monomotapa empire, believed to be Ophir, assimilation was made between the Monomotapa and the myth of Prester John. This is how Vincent Leblanc, a French traveler, used golden columns and other architectural elements to describe the capital of Monomotapa as Prester John had depicted it in his famous letter.[28]

From the earliest times to the first conquests, the myth of the Lost Tribes and its plasticity gave weight to the world of interrelated representations, commonplace and stereotyped images, for laying out supposedly historical realities. The mental perception that resulted divided the world into categories in terms of these stereotypes. Closely tied in with ancient schemas of pagan or Christian origin that place at the frontier of known mankind models of perfection or barbarism, the myth contributed to a European propensity to a binary way of thinking. The persistence of the myth owed much to the tension aroused among Europeans by their encounters with the non-European, non-Christian. The myth gave birth, throughout these centuries, to a tendency to invoke the "Lost Tribes" to make sense of any unknown population. Isaiah's and Ezekiel's prophecies predicting the return of the tribes from the land of Kush provided an authoritative infrastructure for all future speculation concerning the presence of the Ten Tribes in Africa. For centuries, Western Christians have lived in ignorance of Africa. What and where this fabulous land was, was a matter wide open for speculation.

3

The Mythography of Africa

What did people in the early medieval times really know about Africa and Africans? Almost nothing. Through geographical errors and confusion between India and Ethiopian Africa, biblical traditions about the presence of Jews in the land of the Son of Kush, the legend of Solomon and the queen of Sheba, and the location of Ophir in Africa came to be set pieces in the repertoire of Jewish and Christian ethnography of Africa.

Use of the term *Aethiopia* up to the sixteenth century was characterized by geographical errors and confusion between India and Ethiopian Africa. India for geographers of the late Latinity was a land of Asia divided into three areas on the "two shores" of the Indian Mediterranean.[1] For Greco-Latin authors and their medieval successors, with such uncertain and inaccurate data, Aethiopia characterized the part of the African continent inhabited by dark-skinned people.[2] Aethiopia is thus defined by its population whose skin color would be essential for the elaboration of the images of the Aethiops.[3]

Through travelers, merchants, or missionaries, contacts with Africa other than North Africa were rare until the fifteenth century, due both to natural obstacles, such as sea and desert, and to the political and cultural barrier of Islam. In the high Middle Ages, the Eastern world beyond Islam was therefore practically unknown, and from the conquest of Egypt by the Muslims in AD 641, Africa and the Indian Ocean were beyond the horizon of Western Christians.

Their source of knowledge about Africa was therefore essentially books: the Bible and the classical writings, mainly Homer, Herodotus, Pliny, and Ptolemy, whose texts provided the medieval Christians with knowledge and interpretations about Africa. Some of the embryonic notions from which the Western imagination developed its myths about Africa were derived from these texts. Homer's assertion in *The Odyssey* that there were two Ethiopias—one in the west and one in the east, both at the extremities of the earth—was the basis for a number of later descriptions of Africa, beginning with Herodotus in the fifth century BC and continuing up to the fifteenth century. It introduced the concept of two Africas.[4] Homer's description, albeit mythical, was nevertheless inspired by two historical realities: the powerful Kushitic empire of Meroe on the Nubian Nile, whose inhabitants were perceived as being very civilized, "the admirable Ethiopians" of the east opposed to the nomadic tribes of the Saharan and sub-Saharan regions, who became "the other Ethiopians" of the west, and who were often represented as being savage, bestial, and treacherous. Homer's Ethiopians "who live . . . somewhere where Hyperion sets, and the others where it rises," were probably inspired by a historical reality on which the myth of the two Ethiopias was based in the ancient European image of Africa.[5]

This notion was taken up again by Herodotus, who followed the Nile to Aswan around 440 BC and described Meroe's Ethiopians as "the tallest and most beautiful men in the whole world," and as being cunning but peace-loving, whereas, far away from them, in the southwest, "live creatures with dog heads, creatures without heads, whose eyes, according to the Libyans are on their chests; and also wild men and women, and many less fabulous beasts."[6] In the first century BC, Diodorus Sicilus, who also visited Egypt, reinforced more schematically the division of Africa into two Ethiopias. He presented, on one hand, Meroe's Ethiopians as "the first to learn how to worship the gods," and those who "obviously enjoy the favour of the gods." On the other hand, he described Ethiopian tribes spreading out over the south and the west of Meroe's Ethiopia as "being of black colour and having flat noses and woolly hair . . . totally savage and exhibit a nature of wild beasts."[7]

Through a theory alleging the existence somewhere of the "antipodes of the West" and the "antipodes of the south," the church fathers reiterated the allegorical process used by the ancients and adapted it to their own vision of the world and to their theological concerns. In short, the known side of Africa was considered more or less an extension of Christendom, the unknown the epitome of barbarism.[8]

The lack of knowledge of Ptolemy's works seemed to have definitely associated the science of the stars and astral religion.[9] Cartography remained very dependent on such ideas and produced essentially a symbolic image rather than precise geographical information when mapping Africa. This vision is well reflected in the famous Hereford's *mapamundi* dated 1290, whose symbolic world reveals an allegorical vision of the Judgment and shows the damned being taken away to the southern end of a crescent-shaped Africa, toward monstrous creatures with a single foot or eye.[10] During the fourteenth and fifteenth centuries, these traditions were merged in the *portolans* produced by Arabian geographers for European monarchs. The maps of this period, as for example Martin Behaim's globe (1492), exhibit remarkable realism of the African coastlines, while simultaneously providing more symbolic representation of the interior of the continent.[11] It is not surprising to see that the Portuguese vision of Africa at the beginning of the fifteenth century was largely influenced by the notion of two completely distinct Ethiopias. Due to the strong tradition of the survival of a Christian kingdom at the sources of the Nile identified with Prester John's kingdom, Portuguese emissaries went in search of this great and remote empire, with the conviction that they were Christianity's witnesses. When the enterprise failed with the banishment of the Jesuits in the seventeenth century, the whole image of a fabulous empire was transferred, for a while, to Monomotapa's empire, with its abundance of gold and precious stones.[12] The notion of a welcoming paradise on earth coexisting with a barbarian Africa flowed through history and literature and can be found again and again in numerous fictional journeys, such as that of Mandeville, as well as in nineteenth-century adventure novels, such as those of Ridder Haggard or John Buchan. Malvern Van Wyk Smith writes: "Thus Homer's division, nourished by a European propensity towards binary thinking, continued to develop into the most powerful of European myths about Africa growing over the centuries into the elaborate ameliorative mythologies of a terrestrial paradise at the sources of the Nile, beyond the Mountains of the Moon; into the legends associated with Prester John and Abyssinia; of Monomotapa, of Sofala or Zimbabwe as King Solomon's Ophir."[13]

The literature produced by the colonization and exploration of Africa maintained dramatically this polarity of perception: Africa was reified both as a geographical topos and as an imaginary space. This is perhaps best typified in the evolution, in the course of the nineteenth century, of a myth known as the Hamitic hypothesis. In a familiar dualistic movement, this modern myth asserted that light-skinned people of Caucasoid origins had in times past spread across Africa, where they were capable of developing a high civilization. The myth maintained that they were dramatically different from the Negroid savage local people with whom they gradually interbred before degenerating. This was the explanation put forward by early ethnologists and historians for the apparent decline of a number of great African kingdoms such as the

Yorubaland or Great Zimbabwe. This view persisted forcefully into the twentieth century: the influential British anthropologist Charles Seligman, in his well-known *Races of Africa* (1930), maintained the difference between the "Negroid" agricultural Africans and the Europeans pastoral "Hamites." He was echoed by Leo Frobenius and various other anthropologists, paving the way to subsequent identifications.[14]

4

The Legend of Solomon and the Queen of Sheba

Traditions built around the biblical story of King Solomon have often been invoked to explain Africa's past. Who could even think of lost Jewish tribes in Africa without recalling the old belief that the gold-bearing regions of southeast Africa were none other than the biblical Ophir? As a source of dreams and fantasies, the biblical episode of Solomon and the queen of Sheba played a major role in the Western perception of the continent from Ethiopia to southern Africa, not only the country and its history but also, as we shall see, its inhabitants.[1] This myth, which serves as a myth of origin in African tradition, is referred to in the book of Kings and in Chronicles and mentioned the queen of Sheba's visit to Solomon in Jerusalem in the tenth century BC. "And when the Queen of Sheba heard of the fame of Solomon concerning the name of the Lord, she came to prove him with hard questions. And she came to Jerusalem with a very great train, with camels that bare spices, and very much gold, and precious stones: and when she was come to Solomon, she communed with him of all that was in her heart" (1 Kings 10:1–2).

There are only laconic allusions to Solomon and the queen of Sheba in the New Testament.[2] They contrast strongly with the various legends that developed in the Jewish, Ethiopian Christian and Islamic traditions. We know practically nothing about Sheba, this kingdom in southern Arabia, before the eighth century BC because there is no mention of a queen in Sabean inscriptions. On the other hand, there were queens in the north Arabian kingdom of Sheba during the eighth century BC, as attested by Tiglath-Pileser's annals.³ *Antiquities of the Jews* (VIII, 165) by Flavius Josephus, ascribes to the queen a great wisdom and make her the queen not of Sheba but of Egypt and Ethiopia, which led the Jewish historian to borrow from Herodotus the name of Nikaule and to ascribe it to this queen.⁴ However, in the Jewish tradition (Targum of Job), Sheba was identified with Lilith, Satan's wife, who lures innocent men into her net. Thus, the queen of Sheba was considered as a descendant of Kush while the Targum of Esther leaves her anonymous but ascribes to her the hairy foot of the demons.⁵

The meeting of Solomon, the ruler of Israel in the tenth century BC, with the queen of Sheba was described in more detail in one of the fundamental texts of the Ethiopian kingship, the *Kebra Nagast*.⁶ This text, having praised the two royal figures, recounts the conversion to Judaism of the queen of Sheba, who, after returning to her country, gave birth to Menelik I, the son of Solomon and founder of the Ethiopian royal lineage. The *Kebra Nagast* records that Solomon ordered a group of Jewish priests to accompany the queen of Sheba and charged them with the education of his son. Judaism thus allegedly became the religion of the royal family and aristocrats in Ethiopia until their conversion to Christianity at the beginning of the Christian era. After this, Judaism endured only in the small caste of Falasha. Until its extinction under Haile Selassie, this dynasty had adopted the "conquering lion of Judah" as its imperial emblem, which is also the emblem of the city of Jerusalem.

It is also in the book of Kings that the idea of Solomon going to Africa in search of gold with the help of Hiram, king of the Phoenicians, can be found: "And King Solomon made a navy of ships in Eziongeber, which is beside Eloth, on the shore of the Red Sea, in the land of Edom. And Hiram sent in the navy his servants, shipmen that had knowledge of the sea, with the servants of Solomon. And they came to Ophir and fetched from thence gold, four hundred and twenty talents, and brought it to King Solomon" (1 Kings 9:26–28).

Literature and art, both in the West and in the East, adopted the legend of Solomon's encounter with the queen of Sheba, to whom Islamic tradition gave the beautiful name of Bilqis. The Islamic world knew an abundance of legends about their encounter, of which Muhammad gave a shortened version (Sura the Ants, vv. 15–44), and which we find in more detail in texts by Arab historians such as Tabari.⁷ This implies that the legend of Solomon and the queen of Sheba originating in Ethiopia had reached Arabia before the rise of Islam.⁸ Solomon holds a prime place in the Muslim tradition: among the great leaders of people—Nimrod, Nebuchadnezzar and Alexander the Great—he is the most glorious, and the Arabic legend magnifies his actions and his wonderful magic powers. He thus is credited with having built, with the help of an army of jinn and other fabulous spirits from Arabic legend, the pre-Islamic temple of Marib for the queen in Yemen.[9]

Harry Norris claims to identify the first description of the monumental construction of Great Zimbabwe in a fourteenth-century Arabic text and demonstrated the long-standing nature of the assertion that it had been built by "King Solomon, the son of King David." Indeed, according to Norris, the Arab chanson de geste *Sirah Antarah* describes the conquest by the mythical hero Antarah ibn Shaddad of a stone-built African city, the Monoliths' Fortress, one of the capitals of king Humam. Antarah, the hero of this epic tale, gives a precise description of the city, including both the topography and the architectural outline of Great Zimbabwe:

> He [King Humam] had a city which was built of white stone. There was no other like it in that land. By report it was attributed to *jinn* builders who had raised it for our Lord Solomon, King's David son, peace upon him. Near to that city was a hill which (rose up) like a pyramid. It was covered with vegetation and impressively sown with every kind of tree and bush. In the middle of that hill stood an upright "sword" over which a bird constantly hovered. None could pass that "sword" save him who was clad in white raiment.[10]

This idea that Solomon acquired gold and wealth from Africa contributed to the notion that the location was Ophir the land of biblical gold, at the tip of Africa. It was both conveyed by the Portuguese navigators and confirmed by the Arabs they met there, which helped feed this myth that grew ever stronger through the centuries.

The earliest written information on the interior of this part of Africa came from the records of Portuguese explorers who established a trading post in Sofala, on the southeastern coast of East Africa in order to control the gold trade. Diego de Alçacova, in his letter dated 1506 to the king of Portugal, and five years later Antonio Fernandes described buildings made of stones with no mortar to join them.[11] Such buildings would not be reported again for nearly half a century, when João de Barros, in 1552, published the first *Decades of Da Asia*, the most complete and precise document on the Portuguese conquests. He wrote of ruins and mines:

> And these mines are the oldest known in the country, and they are all in the plain, in the midst of which there is a square fortress, masonry within and without, built of stones of a marvellous size, and there appears to be no mortar joining them.... The natives of the country call all this edifice Symbaoe, which, according to their language

means "court"....; and they say that being royal property.... When, and by whom, these edifices were raised, as the people of the land are ignorant of the art of writing, there is no record, but they say they are the work of the devil.... In the opinion of the Moors who saw it, it is very ancient, and was built there to keep the possession of the mines, which are very old.... it would seem that some prince who had possession of the mines ordered it to be built as a sign thereof, which he afterwards lost in the course of time, and though their being so remote from his kingdom; and as these edifices are very similar to some which are found in the land of Prester John, at a place called Acaxumo, which was a municipal city of the queen of Sheba, which Ptolemy calls Axuma, it would seem that the prince who was lord of that state also owned these mines, and therefore ordered these edifices to be raised here.[12]

It is clear that de Barros, disturbed by the peculiarity of the stone buildings, combined elements from different sources. We can recognize the successive probable comments of Swahili or Moorish traders of Sofala about the work of the Devil, perhaps the jinn of the Arabic legends, and the presence of the queen of Sheba and mention of the Western legend of Prester John. More than fifty years later, in 1609, João dos Santos, in his *Ethiopia Oriental*, adopted the descriptions of the "aged Moors" pointing out Solomon and the queen of Sheba, popular figures of Arabic folklore, as the builders of these ruins.

The natives of these lands, especially some aged Moors, assert that they have a tradition from their ancestors that these houses were anciently a factory of the Queen of Sheba, and that, from this place a great quantity of gold was brought to her, it being conveyed down the rivers of Cuama to the Indian Ocean.... Others say that these are the ruins of the factory of Solomon, were he had his factors who procured a great quantity of gold from these lands.... Not deciding this question, I state that the mountain of Fura or Afura may be the region of Ophir, whence gold was brought to Jerusalem, by which some credit might be given to the statement that these houses were the factory of Solomon.[13]

Ruined cities filled with gold, lost and unexplored lands at the far end of Africa, the visions of de Barros and dos Santos of Africa were colored by the hopes aroused by the great Christian kingdom of Prester John, and through knowledge of them that Ethiopia surely contained ruins of biblical kingdoms. Their descriptions and theories were repeated by European geographers for the two following centuries, acquiring the most fanciful additions through the particularly fertile intellectual speculations they aroused.

The intellectual context of those ideas shaped the pattern of thinking of our European forefathers and, as we shall see, had a considerable impact on the colonial past. For example, we find it in the works of the Italians Sanuto, in 1588, and Pigafetta, in 1591; the Englishmen Purchas, in 1614, Speed, in 1627, and Ogilby, in 1670; the Dutchmen Heylin, in 1656, and Dapper, in 1669; the Frenchmen d'Anville, in 1727, and Guillain a little later.[14]

Europeans' convictions that Zimbabwe ruins were erected by Solomon and that the ruins were of Semitic origin were adopted by the Dutch, who settled in the Cape in 1652 and dispatched several "treks" northward in search of King Solomon's mines.[15] This belief persisted well into the nineteenth century and was fully adopted by the newly settled Boers in Transvaal, who, strongly imbued with the Bible, thought that their new country might be adjacent to biblical lands, that they might join the promised land, and that they were "the chosen people of God."[16]

In the 1860s, Thomas Baines, a hunter and artist who traveled for years throughout Mashonaland, noted:

> The heaps of stones collected by the kaffir women when they clear a field for cultivation, and which remain long after that field has reverted to its primitive condition as part of the wilderness, were supposed (by the Dutch Boers) to be monuments piled up by the children of Israel.... The seaboard or Coast region was known under the name it still bears of "Sofala" which signifies in Arabic a plain or a low country.... Several ruins of ancient buildings are found still in this region which is drained by a river disemboguing on the east coast.... The memory of the Queen of Sheba is still preserved among the Arabs of Sofala.[17]

In 1862, Reverend A. Merenski, a German missionary in western Transvaal, undertook a search of Ophir and wrote that "in the land north and east of Moselikatse (Mashonaland), Solomon's ancient Ophir can be found."[18] His search was unsuccessful, but his convictions and ideas later inspired a German geologist, Karl Mauch, who took off in search of "the most important and mysterious part of Africa...the ancient Monomotapa or Ophir!"[19] Although Mauch was able to visit the ruins only three times, his notes, plans, and drawings provide us with the first real description of the ruins, without, however, offering any serious explanations regarding their origin. After examining wood taken from the lintel of the elliptic building's door, Mauch concluded:

> It can be taken as a fact that the wood which we obtained actually is cedar-wood and from this that it cannot come from anywhere else but from Lebanon. Furthermore only the Phoenicians could have brought it here; further Solomon used a lot of cedar-wood for the building of the temple and of his palaces; further: Including here the visit of the Queen of Sheba and considering Zimbabwe or Zimbaoe or Simbaoe written in Arabic, (of Hebrew I understand nothing), one gets as a result that the great woman who built the rondeau could have been none other than the Queen of Sheba.[20]

This apparent confirmation of the centuries-old tale aroused renewed interest in the region and revived the inspiration and imagination of those who were already familiar with the notion of an ancient Jewish presence there. Great Zimbabwe thus became the symbol of the wealth of Ophir, the biblical Havilah "erected in the time of Solomon by the South Arabian Himyarites, followed in the time of Solomon by the Jews and Phoenicians," and triggered a gold fever as well as abundant literature.[21]

The myth of the Lost Tribes of Israel has spawned legends that have been used to explain the origin of myriad of peoples in every part of the globe from ancient times until the present. While Jews and some Christians have attached fundamental importance to the fate of these tribes since medieval times, earlier episodes in the Bible and in Africa's mythology assumed particular significance, even if sometimes diluted, for interpretations of Africa as a Jewish homeland. All these elements together formed the mythological background for an expectation of Jewish traces in Africa's formative history. The connection between the Ten Tribes and Ethiopia and the lineage established by the legend of Solomon and the queen of Sheba made consistent the use of biblical imagery in the African oral cultural milieu. The convergence of these traditions from earliest times, often emerging in multifaceted and sometimes indirect combinations, contributed to the spread of an implicit connection of African inhabitants with the Hebrews. These allegorical associations converged to form the subterranean architecture of prejudices, beliefs, and ideologies in a collective memory shared by Africans as well Europeans.

PART II

Black Judaism

Genesis

5

Blacks and Jews the Archetypal "Others"

Otherness

The extensive travel accounts written by Hakluyt, Purchas, and Pinkerton in the seventeenth and eighteenth centuries, and the more intimate adventure stories of the nineteenth century's travel literature both brought focus to a broadened European ethnological knowledge. From the seventeenth century, travel literature presented native peoples in strange countries as both objects of conquest and subjects of representation.[1] Their discovery and invention reinforced and perhaps established the notion of Europe by focusing on it and surrounding it with a strange periphery.[2] As Mary L. Pratt put it, each "portrait of manners and customs" contributed to the formation of a "normalising discourse" intended "to fix the 'Other' in a timeless present."[3] The multiplication of travel accounts and their circulation among different European readerships gave rise to what has been named a "planetary conscience." The creation of Western identity was constructed in a certain way in opposition or relation to these "others." Susan Zantop has described how the Europeans, when absorbing the newly discovered lands in America, Africa, and the Pacific, both shaped and distorted, to their liking, the image of the "other." She wrote: "The connections between the 'other there' and the 'over here,' between the colony and home, the other and the self are of course at the heart of all 'colonial fantasies.' The 'other' is not just out there but forms an integral part of the self and its perception."[4]

What concerns us in particular is the encounter between European and non-European that lies at the heart of the questions of "difference" and "otherness."[5] While Michel Foucault proposed that the human sciences of life, work, and language produced a European ego that served as a universal reference for "Man,"[6] Edward Said analyzed the complex and subtle ways through which European subjectivity was confirmed and reinforced at the cost of the conquest, domination, and objectification of a world of colonized "others."[7] Both Foucault and Said concluded that a discourse produced by various representational practices, academic studies, exhibitions, literature, and paintings constitutes a form of racialized knowledge of the "other" ("Orientalism" for Said). An anthropological approach argues that the marking of "difference" is the basis for this symbolic order that we call culture. Mary Douglas, in referring to the work carried out by the sociologist Emile Durkheim on symbolic systems and to subsequent studies carried out on myths by the anthropologist Claude Lévi-Strauss, tells us that social groups impose meaning on the world by classifying and organizing things within binary classification systems. Paradoxically, however, this places more importance on "difference" and renders it surprisingly attractive, precisely because it is forbidden, taboo, and because it threatens one's cultural order.[8] A more recent approach of Anne McClintock and Robert Young used a psychoanalytical terminology for analyzing the social-political imagination of the colonists, adding that sexuality played a crucial role in the shaping of difference in colonial fantasies.[9]

The European attempt to articulate these new "others" became a key part of the colonial discourse. Prejudices, beliefs, and ideologies converged to describe the "primitive" within the scope of Western experience, establishing "a vital connection between Christianity and Western culture as a whole."[10] In a number of cases, the distinction between explorers, missionaries, and agents of the colonial development was blurred. The orthodox missionary discourse was supposed to be in harmony with the prospects of the political and cultural colonization of the empires.[11] On behalf of the Dutch East India Company, which had just established trading posts in southern Africa in 1652, Jan van Riebeeck proclaimed a colonial mission "in which the name of Christ may be extended, the interests of the Company promoted."[12] Similarly, the Virginia Company, created in 1607 for the colonization of North America, declared: "Our primary end is to plant religion, our secondary and subalternate ends are for the honour and profit of our nation."[13] Anthony Christopher noted rightly that "missionaries, possibly more than members of other branches of the colonial establishment, aimed at the radical transformation of indigenous society.... They therefore sought, whether consciously or unconsciously, the destruction of pre-colonial societies and their replacement by new Christian societies in the image of Europe."[14] In order to avoid a far too linear history of ideas, I wish to make it clear that, as the missionary strategies emanated from a very diverse Europe, they constituted contradictory and divergent myths that were only slowly aggregated to give form to the unknown "other."

However, many eighteenth-century explorers, nineteenth-century missionaries, and twentieth-century colonists used the same signs and symbols in their speech and acted in accordance with them. They generated an ethnological knowledge through their regular contact with local customs by adopting the missionaries' theory of history, which assumed that the language and culture of the "savages" would disappear with the implantation of Christian civilization.[15]

In *Orientalism* (1978), Edward Said alluded to the "battery of desires, repressions, investments and projections" that conspired with economic interests to the production of colonial mentalities.[16] Valentin Mudimbe, in order to define the development of discourse that came to be applied to Africa, used Frobenius's term "African genesis" (1937) to formulate his hypothesis about the epistemological locus of the African's invention and its meaning for discourses on Africans.[17] This should not imply that the Western inventors of an "African genesis" did not distinguish the different levels and types of interpretations of Africa. The internalizing of these myriads "others" through multiculturalism and increased mobility can be seen as heralding European modernity.

Medieval Christendom had known only two main kinds of "others," Jews and Moors, who personified two aspects of a little-developed—even bestial and degenerated—humanity. The Greek term *Mauri* was used at the time as both a poetical equivalent of *Aethiops* and a broad term that included black Africans.[18] As Parfitt wrote: "The archetypal 'others' of Europe—the essential religious and 'racial' others—the Moor and the Jew, whose relationship with Christian Europe had been forged from long centuries of religious and military conflict, were pressed into service. The immediate boundary between Christian and Jew or Moor was endlessly duplicated as Europe confronted the hitherto unknown parts of the world."[19] The two main vectors of the classification of the unknown "other" were religion and racialism, which were often inextricably intertwined. From Genesis to phylogenesis, the issue remains the same, even though it reflects the various social and scientific forms taken in the West over the centuries, and can be summarized as follows: it is the nature of the "other" and the study of his similarities and dissimilarities that enable me to determine the proximity of his race to mine.[20] The transformation that took place between the sixteenth and eighteenth centuries, as nation-states asserted themselves in Europe, not only led to the conquering colonial enterprise but also constituted the transition from biblical to racial theories, in other words, from the nearly intact heritage of medieval Christianity to the notions that gave birth to race theories.[21] One of the most crucial questions of the time was the unity of mankind, or monogenism, as opposed to the separate creation of races, or polygenism. At the end of the eighteenth century two views coexisted about Africans: the first one was that they were the result of "degeneration" due to different environmental conditions;[22] the second, the more widespread, was that they were a separate creation with subhuman characteristics.[23] In the eighteenth century, by asking questions about the situation of "negroes" compared with white men and apes, some Europeans in the name of science broke away from Adamic unity while others reemphasized the unity of mankind. The representation of difference through the body became the "discursive site through which most of this racialized knowledge was produced and circulated."[24] In fact, each of the major theoretical options specific to these periods has remained alive, each new option added to the former instead of replacing them. David Green discussed these views in relation to anthropology and ethnology, the disciplines that offered the most "scientific data" in that respect at the time:

> As the position and status of the "inferior" races became increasingly to be regarded as fixed, so socio-cultural differences came to be regarded as dependent upon hereditary characteristics.... Since these were inaccessible to direct observation, they had to be inferred from physical and behavioural traits which, in turn, they were intended to explain. Socio-cultural differences among human populations became subsumed within the identity of the individual body. In an attempt to trace the line of determination between the biological and social, the body became the totemic object and its very visibility the evident articulation of nature and culture.[25]

The set of views, opinions, beliefs, and attitudes regarding Africans and how they have been perceived has a long and complex development. Long-held and often unconscious associations preempted the encounter between parties involved in colonization and Africans. The assumed inferiority of black Africans, to which the myth of the Lost Tribes and its by-product in part contributed, was an essential characteristic of colonial discourse throughout the long period of colonial empires, from the first conquests to the beginning of twentieth century. As the history of Western perceptions of Africans has many contributors, so it would seem that African Jews are also the inheritors of a long-accumulating history.

The propensity to identify racial features common to Africans and Jews extended back to ancient times, through continuities and discontinuities. Through an amalgam of projections, similar traits were attributed to the two groups, including skin color and correlated characteristics. Surreptitious links between blackness and Jewishness were formed during the Middle Ages in Western society. A study of perceptions, symbolic associations, and ramifications will explore how dark-skinned people were perceived from ancient times, how negative associations attached to the color black were played out on the stage of history, and how connections between skin tone and Jewishness became embedded in Western culture. In this process, history and exegesis are intimately related with psychological projection, and the exegetical mirror provides a lens to focus on cultural needs.

The Blacks as Sinners

Frantz Fanon summarized the attitude of the West toward blackness:

> In Europe, the Black man is the symbol of Evil.... The torturer is the Black man, Satan is Black, one talks of shadows, when one is dirty one is black—whether one is thinking of physical dirtiness or moral dirtiness. It would be astonishing, if the trouble were taken to bring all together, to see the vast number of expressions that make the Black man the equivalent of sin. In Europe, whether concretely or symbolically, the Black man stands for the bad side of the character. As long as one cannot understand this fact, one is doomed to talk in circles about the "black problem." Blackness, darkness, shadow, shades, nights, the labyrinths of the earth, abysmal depths, blackens someone's reputation, and on the other side, the bright look of innocence, the white dove of peace, magical, heavenly light.[26]

Interestingly, in biblical scriptures, most references to Africans (i.e., *Kushim*) are descriptive and not judgmental.[27] The area south of Egypt descending into central Africa and extending east to the Red Sea was known to the ancient Near Eastern cultures as Kush in the Hebrew Bible, while in Greek writings the name for this land was Ethiopia. We also find the word *Nubians* in earliest sources, such as in Isaiah (20:4–6), and in time it came to indicate the originally African ethnic element of the Ethiopian population.[28] The inhabitants of Kush are frequently placed in a positive context as brave fighters, or they are merchants, and Kush is described as the land of precious stones.[29] In the Bible, the many references to Kushim may be divided into two literal and two metaphorical types: ethnic origins—in the genealogy of Noah's sons' offspring (Genesis 10); place—Kush is defined as a land lying south of Egypt (Ezekiel 29:10); a metaphor for a faraway place, at the ends of the Earth (Esther 12:1; 8:9); and a metaphor for another human situation referring to the black-skinned person designated as "other."[30] The word *Ham*, which in the History of Ideas came to define Africans, appears for the first time in Genesis.[31] In the Bible, Ham found Noah drunk and naked in Noah's tent. He told his brothers, Shem and Japheth, who covered the nakedness of their father, their faces turned away. When Noah awoke from his wine and knew what his youngest son had done to him, he cursed Ham's son Canaan, saying, "Cursed be Canaan; a slave of slaves shall he be to his brothers" (Genesis 9:18–25).

Some scholars have focused on the question whether Jews, Christians, or Muslims first connected the curse with black skin color, and it is a strange association indeed, for there is no reference in it to blacks at all. Some of them claim that this tradition grew out of a need of the Israelites to rationalize the dispossession of the Canaanite, pre-Israelite population.[32] Others argue that the interpretation of this verse was the cause of black enslavement for centuries.[33] Melamed comments, "The identification of Ham and his sons as dark skinned and naturally destined to slavery is post-biblical—the result of later historical and cultural circumstances—and is by no means to be projected anachronistically onto the Bible itself."[34] Many centuries later, in the sixth century AD, the Babylonian Talmud mentions that Ham, having supposedly emasculated Noah, was thus cursed and condemned to be black; Ham is described as a sinner and his progeny as degenerated, with negative moral and physical attributes:

> Now I cannot beget the fourth son whose children I would have ordered to serve you and your brothers! Therefore it must be Canaan, your first born, whom they enslave. And since you have disabled me... doing ugly things in the blackness of night, Canaan's children shall be borne ugly and black! Moreover, because you twisted your head around to see my nakedness, your grandchildren's hair shall be twisted into kinks, and their eyes red; again because your lips jested at my misfortune, theirs shall swell; and because you neglected my nakedness, they shall go naked, and their male member shall be shamefully elongated! Men of this race are called Negroes, their forefather Canaan commanded them to love theft and fornication, to be banded together in hatred of their masters and never to tell the truth.[35]

Thus, from time immemorial, Africans have been considered to be the descendants of Ham, carrying the stigmatism of Noah's curse, occupying a proscribed and inescapable place in biblical history. The interpretations of the Talmud and the Midrash of the curse of Ham were well known by Jewish authors in the Middle Ages, as evidenced in the following description of the south of Aswan by Benjamin of Tudela, the twelfth-century merchant and explorer: "There is a people ... who like animals eat the earth that grows on the banks of the Nile and in their fields.... They go about naked and have not the intelligence of ordinary men. They cohabit with their sisters and anyone they can find.... They are taken as slaves and sold in Egypt and neighbouring countries. These sons of Ham are black slaves."[36]

Frank Snowden analyzed antiquity's heritage concerning the basis of the relationship between Africans and racialism in order to understand how medieval Christians treated it.[37] Even if he concluded with certain optimism that, from an ideological point of view, antiquity and early Christianity did not demonstrate any notions of racial inequality toward Africans, it is difficult to deny that elements of a "white supremacy" existed. Early Greek culture and the Roman culture that followed it saw a link between physical beauty and moral perfection. Roman culture developed an entire science—"physiognomy"—on this basis and attempted to fit physical characteristics of the face and the body to spiritual characteristics.[38] A representation designating dirt and sin came, as a result of aesthetic norms and values, to mean dark color and to designate the black person. The Latin word *sordes*, which indicates baseness, later came to signify a dark complexion.[39] In later Hellenistic-Roman culture, ambiguous and even negative expressions made their appearance. On a basis of climate theory, the Romans assumed that the inferior psychophysical traits of the Africans in the south arose from harsh geographical and climatic surroundings.[40]

In early Christianity light plaid a large role—in the scriptures, Jesus is "the light of the world" (John 8:12, 9:5)—and its absence was associated with darkness. A clear tendency toward negative value judgments about Africans and about anyone whose skin was significantly darker than the norm emerged only slowly.[41] In the "black horse" presented in Revelation (6:5), Jerome, Césaire of Arles, and Bede immediately saw the symbol of a damned people.[42] Christian medieval iconography often juxtaposed the contrast between the black front of the synagogue and the white one of the church.[43] Similarly, all exegesis concerning verse 5:11 of the Song of Songs gives unfavorable treatment to the color black plausibly because of the accepted standards of beauty in Jerome's time.[44] Black appears as a metaphor for paganism, while "comely" is a metaphor for becoming a Christian, that is, choosing to do well in the verse: "I am black but comely, O ye daughters of Jerusalem, as the tents of Kedar as the curtains of Solomon. Look not upon me, because I am black, because the sun hath looked upon me" (Song 1:5–6). Paradoxically, as early as the Exodus, around the thirteenth century BC, an episode in the Bible mentioned that God condemned Miriam, Moses' sister, by inflicting on her "a leper as white as snow" (Numbers 12:10) for having criticized her brother who had married a dark-skinned woman. The sin was criticizing something concerning Moses' black wife, and the punishment was whitening the skin of the sinner, in contradiction to all stereotypes.

In the first century, the Hellenized Jewish philosopher Philo of Alexandria (ca. 20 BC– AD 50) was the first writer to attempt an allegorical interpretation of the biblical characters. Following Philo, in the third century AD, Origen professed an interpretation that made a major contribution to skin-color significance.[45] Without abandoning the traditional significance of the color black, he transposed the entire issue to the spiritual domain: blackness is not a flaw that is passively received or endured, but rather a feature that one acquires and for which one is responsible. Therefore, Origen assimilated blackness to Jews and pagans, which de-dramatized the physical question of skin tone.[46] Other Latin fathers, such as Augustine and Ambrose, also took inspiration from the allegory Origen had conceived about the Africans and created in his wake a typology for the subsequent ecclesiastical writers. To varying degrees, all the commentators consider the color black as being linked to sin, which must be "washed away" in order to return whiteness to the bearer, so as to ensure his salvation.[47] Following the same line, chroniclers took up the theme of the curse of Ham's descendants: Ham and the Aethiops were the predestined descendants of Noah devoted to the Devil. As descendants of Adam through Noah, they could only have a white ancestor, and therefore they became black through their own doing. The Christian exegesis combined with popular prejudices wove on this framework a recurring image wherein blackness became the symbol of evil.[48] Flodoard, in the tenth century, speaks very simply about "the Ethiopian people, black by sin and body."[49] One of the primary places where this Middle Ages Christian sentiment is evident is in religious iconography. For many centuries, black was the color of the Devil or of the executioner. The earliest testimonies known to date of the "blackening" of demons date to an eighth-century fresco in Santa Maria Antica in Rome, which shows Christ trampling a dark character underfoot during his descent into Limbo.[50] In an Italian manuscript of the same period conserved in Patmos, one can see traces of black paint on the anthropomorphic body of the demon.[51] Without specifying the exact color, the text of Perpetue's passion, written during the second century AD by Tertullian, was one of the earliest testimonials of the presence of an African executioner.[52]

Since the sixteenth century, the position of Africans in a universe enlarged by the European expansion was diversified and gave rise to a vision characterized by contradiction and ambivalence, but whose change of tone was obvious. This evolution can be attributed to the impact on attitudes caused by the discovery of America in 1492 and the rounding of the Cape of Good Hope a few years later, which obliged Europe to broaden its concept of the "other." A contrasting image of the African developed when the dark-skinned wise man appeared in Europe: Gaspard or Balthazar, depending on legend, which would be followed in the thirteenth century by Maurice, a more or less legendary saint, who became the first incarnation in the West of a sanctified African.[53] But laudatory traditions did not last long and did not carry much weight compared with negative representations. The habit, which followed for many centuries with the repetition of stereotypes anchored in medieval society, prepared the ground for the notion of cultural dominance that directed the interpretation of Africa and Africans from the "discoveries" up through the colonial enterprises.

The Jews as Blacks

Parfitt recalls that Amerigo Vespucci (1454–1512), in trying to define the strangeness of American Indians, only succeeded in doing so by referring to the Jew-Moor relationship: "They can be called neither Moors nor Jews, but worse than Gentiles."[54] Indeed, a long-lasting overlap of images of "otherness"—the Moor and the Jew—operated in medieval European culture.

The imagined Jews, in a way dichotomized with those who lived in European cities, played a hugely important role in Christian imaginations. From the Middle Ages, Western peoples, when they encountered a "crisis of representation," due to endogenous conflicts or to exogenous political phenomena, would call up the ambivalence in connection with the notion of the Lost Tribes.[55] One of the earliest invocations of the Jews as "others" was with respect to unknown and somewhat threatening populations of central Asia. For instance, Marco Polo (1254–1324) described a people "of excellent warriors, good archers and good soldiers in battle," and suggested the existence of Ten Tribes kingdoms in the East: "In Georgia, there is a king named David Melic, which in French means King David, who is a subject of the Tartar."[56] The legend of faraway Lost Tribes in Asia imprisoned by Alexander became almost commonplace in medieval literature for various European countries and, over time, underwent some interesting transformations.[57] In the *Jüngerer Titurel*, written about 1280 and ascribed to Albert von Scharfenberg, the red Jews are represented as shut behind mountains called Gog and Magog, according to the peoples of that name.[58] The presence of the Ten Tribes in the East was mentioned later on by Geoffrey of Viterbo,[59] then again in Quilichinus of Spoleto's text of 1236–1238,[60] then in *Konung Alexander*, which was written in medieval Swedish around 1380,[61] as well as in Rudolf of Ems's *Alexander*, written around the middle of the thirteenth century.[62] According to these authors, the Jews imprisoned by Alexander were not distinct from Gog and Magog, but in general they were attributed a hard and merciless heart, Judah's evil spirit and red hair. Indeed, people in those days thought that Jews typically had red hair.[63] From medieval Europe, a system of primordial associations was elaborated that makes out the supposed members of the Ten Tribes of Asia by the color of their hair or skin.[64]

Black-white symbolism necessarily transferred to social relations. The negative symbolism of the skin tone influenced how the European came to perceive the Jews. In the scriptures (1 Samuel 16:12) and since the Greek times, the harmony attributed to physical features was considered a sign of spiritual harmony. Anyone with alleged different features—the Jew and the African—was necessarily perceived as anaesthetic, that is, as not good. As Gilman observes, "The very concept of colour is a quality of otherness, not of reality, for not only Blacks are black in this amorphous world of projection, so, too are Jews."[65] The Roman historian Tacitus (*History* 5.2–5), in his famous criticism of the Jews and their customs, presents them as wallowing in superstition, sexually promiscuous, idle, and indolent, that is, exactly the same characteristics that were assigned to the Africans.[66] What was seen as their physical ugliness—long nose, flat feet, and hairy body—was merely a component of their "blackness."[67] As early as the thirteenth century, an expression of religious and ethnical hostilities toward Africans and Jews is represented in the overlap of Jew and black in the representation of Judas's treason where Judas is black.[68] Ancient writings already mentioned the Jewish appropriation of this self-image. In the *Nizzahon Vetus*, a treatise of the early Middle Ages answering the Christian discourse about the Jews, the author wrote:

> The heretics ask: Why are most Gentiles fair-skinned and handsome while most Jews are dark and ugly? Answer them that this is similar to the fruit; when it begins to grow it is white but when it ripens it becomes black.... One can respond further that Gentiles are incontinent and have sexual relations during the day, at a time when they see the faces on attractive pictures; therefore they give birth to children who look like those pictures.[69]

The argument for a degenerative Jewish nature coexisted easily with the belief that the Jews inherited distinctive personality traits. This view has a long history in European science. Some early Spanish writers of the seventeenth century were especially fond of arguments that connected racial heritage with behavior. Prudencio de Sandoval asked in 1604: "Who can deny that in the descendants of the Jews there persists and endures the evil inclination of their ancient ingratitude and lack of understanding, just as in Negroes [there persists] the inseparability of their blackness."[70] Seventeenth-century English travelers renewed the accepted stereotypes of Jewish racial otherness, including the belief that Jews were black-skinned.[71] When William Brereton noted his impressions of the Jews in the synagogue of Amsterdam in 1635, he observed that the "Jewish men are most black... and insatiably given unto woman," drawing on contemporary prejudices linking blackness and licentiousness.[72] The Scottish minister Robert Kirk, when he paid a visit to a synagogue in London in 1690, observed more than 200 Jews worshiping and noted, "They were all very black men, and indistinct in their reasoning as gypsies."[73] This point of view dominated the vision of the Jews so much that Adam G. de Gurowski, a Polish nobleman, "took every light coloured mulatto for a Jew."[74] By the end of the seventeenth century, François Maximilien Misson in *A New Voyage to Italy* (1714), moderated this opinion, considering that it is "a vulgar error that Jews are all black... it is only true of the Portuguese Jews, who, marrying always among one another, beget children like themselves."[75]

For the eighteenth- and nineteenth-century scientists, the blackness of the Jew was not only a mark of racial inferiority but also the external manifestation of a disease. The Bavarian writer Johann Pezzl, who visited Vienna in the 1780s, described the Viennese Jew as suffering somehow from "Jewishness":

> There are about five hundred Jews in Vienna. Their sole and only occupation is to counterfeit, salvage trade in coins, and cheat Christians, Turks and heathens, indeed themselves.... This is only the beggarly filth of Canaan which can only be exceeded in filth, uncleanliness, stench, disgust, poverty, dishonesty, pushiness and other things by the trash of the twelve tribes from Galicia. Excluding the Indian fakirs, there is no category of supposed human beings which come closer to the Orang-Utan than does a Polish Jew.... Covered from foot to head in filth, dirt and rags, covered in a type of black sack... their necks exposed the colour of a Black, their faces covered up to the eyes with a beard, which would have given the High Priest in the Temple chills, the hair turned and knotted as if they all suffered from the *plica polonica*.[76]

Beyond skin appearance, among English writers there was a persistent belief that a hereditary feature transmitted by Jews was their stench, the so-called *foetor judaicus*. For instance, James Howell writes: "As likewise that rankish kind of scent no better indeed than a stink, which is observed to be inherent and inseparable from most of them, above all other nations."[77] These exterior diseases of the Jews, associated with their unhygienic nature, are thus attributed to their moral state and reveal the Jew's very psychology. As late as the nineteenth century, the medieval humors were still occasionally invoked in this connection. James C. Prichard commented on "the choleric and melancholic constitution of the Jews, such that they usually have a skin colour somewhat darker than the English people."[78]

For the eighteenth- and nineteenth-century scientist, the blackness of the Jew was easily incorporated in the rhetoric of racialism. With specific political implication, the theories of Houston S. Chamberlain categorized the Jews in *Foundations of the Nineteenth Century* (1910) as "a mongrel race that had hybridised with the Africans while they were exiled in Alexandria."[79] Gilman asserts that by the middle of the nineteenth century, "being Black, being Jewish, being diseased, and being 'ugly' come to be inexorably linked."[80] It is, therefore, not only the color of the skin that enables the scientists to see the Jew as black, but the entire physiognomy. Associated anatomical signs such as the shape of the nose and prognathism supported the assumption of close racial relationship between Jews and Africans. At the end of the eighteenth century, the Dutch anatomist Petrus Camper analyzed the facial angle and its corollary, the nasal index, which corresponds to the line joining the forehead to the upper lip; the facial angle is calculated by relating this line to a straight line starting from the jawbone. Camper, by defining "fairness" as corresponding to a facial line with an angle of 100 degrees with the horizontal, connected the African and the Jew through the curve of their noses, considering that both African and Jewish nasal types reveal their inferiority.[81] Around the mid–nineteenth century, Robert Knox shared this analysis and wrote:

> The African character of the Jew, his muzzle-shaped mouth and face, removing him from certain other races ... the eyes long and fine, the outer angles running towards the temples; the brow and nose apt to form a single convex line; the nose comparatively narrow at the base, the eyes consequently approaching each other; lips very full, mouth projecting, chin small, and the whole physiognomy when swarthy, as it often is, has an African look"[82]

By the end of the nineteenth century, contradictory theses, such as that of Friedrich Ratzel, argued that skin color was a matter of geographical differences and could be modified by migrations of populations from one continent to another.[83] Other scientists went back to the previous works of Samuel Stanhope Smith (1787), president of the University of Princeton, who saw the Jews as a mutant people whose color was everywhere modified by the situation they occupied: "In Britain and Germany they are fair, brown in France and in Turkey, swarthy in Portugal and Spain, olive in Syria and Chaldea, tawny or copper coloured in Arabia and Egypt."[84]

Blackness as a common denominator of the inferiority of Africans as well as Jews has a long history in Western culture. It appears as the result of a system of primordial associations shared by Christianity and also by Judaism. The racial "promiscuity" of Jews and Africans became commonplace in the nineteenth century and came to be adopted as such by some twentieth-century anthropology, which declared on occasion that Jews were black. All this provided the rationale for the representation of "difference" and "inferiority," for both Africans and Jews, whereby the blackness of the Jew represented the synthesis of two projections of otherness according to the same code. Racialism could represent a more or less secularized version of some religious views and stereotypes of Jews and Africans; it could also represent a deliberately secular repudiation of a religious or sentimental account of the unity of mankind. In both forms it contributed to colonial policies throughout the world.

6

Encountering and Reinventing the Africans and the Jews in the Colonial Era, Fifteenth to Nineteenth Centuries

The Africans as Caucasoid

The Hamitic hypothesis, born in postmedieval Europe, is part of the "African genesis." It prevailed for many years and conditioned how reality was broken down by the various European players involved in Africa.[1] In particular, it would put Africans' genealogy to the test. A brief overview of the Hamitic hypothesis shows the importance of its influence for both Europeans and Africans themselves.

Basically, this theory argues that anything of value found in Africa was brought there by the Hamites, who were allegedly a branch of the Caucasian race. In the well-known work *Races of Africa* (1930), the English anthropologist Charles Seligman wrote:

> Apart from relatively late Semitic influence... the civilisations of Africa are the civilisations of the Hamites, its history, the record of these peoples and their interaction, with the two other African stocks, the Negro and the Bushman, whither this influence was exerted by highly civilised Egyptians or by such wider pastoralists as are represented at the present-day by the Beja and Somali.... The incoming Hamites were pastoral "Europeans"—arriving wave after wave—better armed as well as quicker witted than the dark agricultural Negroes.[2]

The notion of black Hamite, derived from the ancient tradition identifying the sons of Ham with Africans, was widely accepted by 1600. In one of the first postmedieval references, Leo Africanus, the great Arabian traveler, wrote about black Africans that they descended from Ham. The translator of the English edition, John Pory, added to the text his own commentary entitled "a summarised discourse of the manifold of religions professed in Africa," in which he underlined the punishment suffered by Ham and his descendants and thus reinforced the myth in modern times.[3] This interpretation remained familiar in Christian circles during the nineteenth century. Indeed, during the Vatican Council of 1870, sixty-eight bishops asked for the anathema weighing on the descendants of Ham to be lifted. This wish has remained unfulfilled.[4]

This mythical concept is both vague and complex. An analysis of the epistemological shift from the early Hamitic theory, whereby Hamites were allegedly blacks, to the later notion of a Hamitic race shows how the myth's survival can be attributed to its ideological usefulness, to which its ambiguity actually contributed.[5] As François-Xavier Fauvelle stressed, Ham is black when ideology demands the tangible mark of a curse that dooms him to slavery; Ham is white when ideology impresses the idea that only that which is white is civilized; "black" thus means "not to be civilized"; Ham is red when red evokes the first ages; black then means "without a past." [6] That the name of Ham is used for the "black" or the "white" individual in any case highlights the opposition between the two, an opposition that would be played out not only in the anthropological field but also in the religious, linguistic, social, political, and economic arenas.[7] Although derived from a religious source, the notion of black Hamites' inferiority traversed the seventeenth century to become, in the expansion of scientific research during the eighteenth century, the subject of great debate. Researchers of the end of this century and philosophers of the Enlightenment attempted to apply scientific methods to the study of man. Often in direct conflict with the scriptures regarding his origin, they broadened the debate.[8] At the end of the eighteenth century, two views coexisted about blacks: they were the result of "degeneration" due to environmental conditions, or as part of polygenism, they were a separate creation with subhuman characteristics. These ideas were compatible with some interests of the period, such as colonialism.

Napoleon's invasion of Egypt in 1798 prompted a new European interest in Egyptians and provided food for the Hamitic myth. Napoleon's scientists discovered the extraordinary fact that civilization began before Greeks and Romans. Their attention was drawn to the people who lived among these ancient splendors and who were believed to descend from the people who created them. It was a very mixed population, as it is today, with significant variations in physiognomy and "physical types" ranging from dark to black. French scientists concluded that Egyptians were Negroid. Vivant Denon (1747–1825), who participated in Napoleon's expedition, described them as follows: "a broad and flat nose, very short, a large flattened mouth... thick lips, etc." [9] He agreed on this point with the convictions of the count of Volney, who had spent four years in Egypt and Syria and had expressed a similar point of view.[10]

If the African descended from Ham, and Ham were cursed, how could he create a great civilization? The paradox of a Negroid people at the origin of the earliest civilization presented a challenge to the doctrine circulating in the West. Egypt had become the center of great interest among both scientists and a wider general audience. A number of works that were published about Egypt and the Egyptians, soon after the expedition of Egypt, tried therefore to demonstrate that the Egyptians were not black. William G. Browne, a traveler and typical exponent of this way of thinking, had the unusual idea of maintaining that the purpose of mummies was simply to leave a physical trace of the individual. The presence of mummies provided proof that these people were not black, and above all, that they wanted the information to be passed on: "Prescience of that people concerning errors into which posterity might fall, exhibits irrefragable proof of features and of colour of their skin."[11]

According to new interpretations of the Scriptures, the Egyptians became the descendants of Mizraim, one of the sons of Ham; the stories of the sons of Ham were debated, in particular, the curse. About this issue, Reverend Michael Russell wrote, "In the sacred writings of the Hebrews it (Egypt) is called Mizraim... the name which is applied to Egypt by the Arabs of the present-day. The Copts retain the native word 'Chemia' which perhaps has some relation to Cham, the son of Noah; or, as Plutarch insinuates, may only denote that darkness of colour which appears in a rich soil or in a human eye."[12]

Although this latter point did not meet with much success, the reading of biblical dictionaries of the period reveals the general acceptance of the new Caucasoid Hamites, who were not cursed and who were capable of developing a high civilization. The *Encyclopaedia of Biblical Literature*, published in 1846 by John Kitto, includes a long article entitled "Ham," which underlines that the curse of Noah was directed only against Canaan, while acknowledging the difficulty of tracing the history of the most important Hamitic nations—the Kushites, Phoenicians, and Egyptians—due to their mixing with foreign peoples.[13]

As the first decades of the nineteenth century saw a new development of the Hamitic myth, its "scientific" basis was also being strengthened. Craniology in the United States and in Europe led to the belief that the osteological characteristics of the Egyptians were Caucasian, which made it possible to explain their achievements on the basis of an innate racial superiority and to exclude blacks from any possibility of great achievements.[14] The young science of philology also added weight to the Hamitic theory, at a time when language and race were considered inextricably linked. Christian K. Bunsen, both a philologist and an Egyptologist, postulated that the Hamite or Egyptian had existed before the Semite and was antediluvian, which, according to him, was absolute proof that the Hamitic language belonged to the Caucasoid people.[15] This idea was widely accepted by travelers and theologians of the period.[16]

By the end of the nineteenth century, colonialism and modern racism had molded European attitudes toward Africa and Africans. Joseph de Gobineau gave the clearest expression of an ancient penetration of the African continent by a primary branch of the white race. This "primordial descent" of the superior race, described in epic terms, would have taken place around 5,000 BC: "Whilst the first conquest was difficult, due to the thickness of the attacked masses, and to their resistance—either furious or stupidly inert—the preservation of the States made possible by the victory required just as much effort."[17]

As a consequence, the ethnocentrism of travelers and colonists in the nineteenth century increased the standing of those who resembled them the most: these were declared to be Hamites or of Hamitic descent, endowed with a higher ability, and even exerted a positive influence on African groups. John Hanning Speke, the English traveler who discovered the source of the Nile, originated the Hamitic theory in its modern form.[18] When the kingdom of Buganda was discovered, with its complex political organization, he designated the Galla Hamites as the first bearers of culture in Africa, thanks to the intellectual superiority of all Caucasoids, while simultaneously putting forward that they could achieve real development only with the help of the white race. The existence of differentiated social categories, contrasting activities, and relatively diverse physical types in the kingdoms located between Lakes Victoria, Albert, and Tanganyika facilitated the extension of the hypothesis of foreign infiltration.[19] These ideas appear at the same time in Europe; for instance, the French traveler Pierre Trémeaux, whose work was awarded a prize by the Institut de France, explained that successive white waves were blackened by the climate.[20] In another version Martial de Salviac, a French Capuchin missionary, explained that the Galla were of Gallic origin because of an ancient expedition.[21]

The history of Africa was thus created through a succession of invasions, leading to various degrees of mixing, requiring ever more complex theories. For instance, Antoine de Préville explained in 1894 that a variety of the white race lived among the Africans and that this group could even be represented by "colored nations." In 1902, during the Eighth International Congress of Geography in Washington, a certain Romanet du Caillaud claimed in his lecture that the legendary founder of the kingdom of Buganda, Kintu, was the descendant of a group of Christians from Nubia who had been baptized by Saint Matthew, and that in 1307 these proto-Christians from Uganda had even sent an envoy to Beijing to ask for missionaries.[22]

Any cultural progress was thus linked to an invasion. "The Nouba population," wrote A. Lefèvre in 1892, "reddened by Asian and Libyan blood," was thus "awakened by contact with superior races."[23] The stereotype of the Asian myth dear to Gobineau would lead positivist authors, who continued to use the terms "Hamite" or "Chamite," to develop a theory about Asian invasions. Joseph Halévy, a French anthropologist, using craniology and linguistics as a starting point, invoked an article by Fulgence Fresnel about southern Arabian languages to conclude that "the settlement of Chamites in Asia dates back much further than their settlement on the African soil."[24]

This process presented a double advantage for colonial goals: it kept Africans in a position of inferiority while promoting the idea that civilization could be achieved only by the white race.[25] The ideological framework of colonial expansion was then set, and, as was observed by J. Barzun, "Politics and Race theories seemed natural allies" for colonial expansion and exploitation.[26]

Developed further and diversified at the beginning of the twentieth century, the confusions surrounding the Hamitic myth increased as new classifications searched for validity: linguistic typologies were built on racial types while the racial classifications themselves depended on linguistic definitions. The racial classification of Hamites included a wide variety of types from the fair-skinned, blue-eyed blond Berber to the black Ethiopian. The first racial typology was set up by Giuseppe Sergi in his book *The Mediterranean Race* (1901). In the chapter devoted to Hamites he claimed that these peoples settled originally in "the cradle of Mediterranean races in eastern Africa." He described Hamites as follows:

> "Some African populations occupied a large territory and exhibited a remarkable homogeneity as regards their morphological characteristics and, to a lesser degree, as regards their external characteristics, as well the languages they spoke in the past or still now. I wish to speak about populations known by the old word "Hamitic," especially because of their linguistic characteristics, which contributed to their classification and regrouping them together as a single race.... They still display the physical traits of their race, in spite of the incongruous and hybrid shapes which have shown themselves."[27]

Sergi insisted on the morphological unity of these diverse peoples, among whom were the inhabitants of the Sahara, the Berbers, and even peoples "who have wholly or partially lost their language," such as Egyptians, Watutsi, and the Masai. From 1880 on, the presentation of a Hamitic race grouping together the inhabitants of the Sahara, the Berbers, the Egyptians, the Abyssinians, the peoples of the Horn of Africa, and some groups of East Africa (the Masai and Tutsi-Hima) spread throughout Europe, and in particular in Germany, via the publication of *The History of Mankind* by Ratzel, the great anthropo-geographer.[28] In 1913, in England, Sir Harry Johnston, a great traveler and high-level official of the Crown, wrote in the same publication where Seligman had expounded his Hamitic theory a long article that defended the general theory that a high intellectual development necessarily signified Caucasian blood.[29] The Hamites discovered in sub-Saharan Africa were described as pastors, with blacks allegedly being farmers. Moreover, the particular fate reserved for the "Cafres," the Bantu-speaking peoples of southern Africa, in midcentury geographical science is striking. In France, Dr. Jean-Jacques Virey, who included in this denomination all the peoples of eastern Africa, noted that these peoples are prouder and more handsome than the "real Negroes" and that they are "naturally pastors" and "builders of empires."[30] As underlined by Sanders, pastoralism and all its attributes became endowed with an aura of cultural superiority, conferring on some groups a third dimension: a cultural identity.[31]

Historians such as Anson P. Atterbury in *Islam in Africa* (1899) and John W. Gregory in *The Foundation of British East Africa* (1901) began to compile writings on Africa, accepted all these elements as proven and indisputable facts, and presented them as historical explanations of Africa's past.[32] Roland Oliver argues in *The Missionary Factor in East Africa* (1952) that this mechanism provided the fodder for missionaries who wanted to learn more about general ethnology and whose work complemented ethnological research of the period.[33] In a book by Armand de Quatrefages published in 1889, a drawing of the king of Lesotho's son, Moshesh, dressed as a Victorian bourgeois man, was accompanied by comments about the crossbreeding of the Sotho with superior races and constituted a picturesque example of the mentality of the period. Biology was supposed to justify the diversity of ethnological situations.[34]

A large majority of anthropologists supported the Hamitic myth. Each trace or sign of what was called "civilized" in Africa was attributed to foreign origins, primarily Hamitic. Thus, ironworking was considered as having been introduced to Africans by others, along with complex political institutions or irrigation systems.[35] Important archaeological discoveries were also attributed to external influences and kept Africans out of their own cultural history. For example, Dutch and English colonists who encountered only bushmen or Hottentots had no reason to believe that the ancient greatness of Great Zimbabwe could be attributed to Africans and so oriented their researches and studies exclusively toward foreign origins.[36]

The Hamitic myth was challenged by only a few critics. Henry Spencer, in the introduction to *Sociologie descriptive des races africaines* (1930), denounced the supporters of this theory of racial prejudice and ethnocentrism.[37] Joseph Greenberg also attacked the entire Hamitic myth by suggesting that the term be abandoned; he referred to the fact that "non-Semitic languages of the Hamitic-Semitic family do not form a linguistic unity as do the Semitic languages. The term 'Hamitic' which is reserved for this use is not supported by any valid linguistic unity."[38] Despite such criticisms, St. Clair Drake could still conclude in 1959 that "the Hamitic myth is so anchored in common thought, as is Caucasian superiority, that it could only be eradicated through patient efforts," including among scholars of African origin.[39]

Eventually, the ideology carried by the Hamitic myth lost ground after World War II, even though its influence persisted in later works. Even Basil Davidson, a pro-African, antiracist author, advanced in his book *Old Africa Rediscovered* (1959) a version of the Hamitic hypothesis by identifying a racial African group called Hamites, while simultaneously fighting against the racist assumptions made by the myth.[40] As African nations gained their independence, some scholars began to cast doubt on the Hamitic hypothesis as they rejected colonial ties and discovered the indigenous achievements of the past.[41] The Hamitic myth, however, had instilled the mixing of the Black by the white at the same time as the concept of a "white with a black skin" and authorized the "detection of invasions," which, according to Chrétien, "became the mannerism of African ethnology."[42] In the African ethnology of the beginning of the twentieth century, such concepts led to the idea that the continent was inhabited by two groups, the Caucasoids and the Negroids, as well as mixtures of the two. Caucasoid and Negroid "types" were considered as absolute and universal, represented in the same way in biology, linguistics, and the cultural and political aspects of the black individual.

Although the academic dimension of the Hamitic hypothesis has fallen into disuse, the word *Hamite* still exists and now carries a mythical meaning. The vague fusion of Hamitic/Semitic notions would come to constitute the basis of a pattern of thought, which, after having conditioned European colonists, would also shape Africans' interiority up to the present. In a course taught in March 1960 at the Burasira seminary in Burundi, one could read, "According to the most widespread theory, the cradle of Hamites is western Asia. These Asians went to Africa eons ago by the way of the isthmus of Suez, and especially the Bab el-Mandeb strait, on their way from southern Asia, where they had already been subjected to Semitic influences."[43]

Reinventing the Jews in the New World and in Africa

In his first accounts of the native populations of the New World, Christopher Columbus noted in a letter, the content of which was spread all over Europe, that the Arawak Indians "do not hold any creed nor are they idolaters." Amerigo Vespucci in his *Mondus Novus* confirms this point: "Beyond the facts they have no church, no religion and are not idolaters, what can I say?"[44] Similarly early accounts on Africa often noted an absence of religion. In the sixteenth and seventeenth centuries, travel accounts frequently associated the lack of religion with the absence of other characteristics defining humanity, such as the institution of marriage, a system of law, or any formalized social or political organization. During the eighteenth century, when a trade zone opened up on the west coast of Africa, the Portuguese, Dutch, and English Christians, Arabs and African Muslims, African Christians, and African followers of local religions set up a relationship for social and economical exchanges.[45] It was then that some practices, such as fetishism, came to represent in the eyes of eighteenth-century traders an additional example of their absence of religion.[46] Later on, this absence of religion was confirmed by Richard Burton in the Great Lakes region of Central Africa,[47] by James Grant, in his *Walk across Africa*,[48] and by René Caillé, in his journey to Timbuktu.[49] It was also noted repeatedly in southern Africa by explorers, colonists, missionaries, and civil servants throughout the nineteenth century.[50] Only in Ethiopia, a Christian country, inhabitants were considered, since Greco-Roman antiquity, to be pioneers as regards religion.[51]

These European observers clearly based their reactions on the Christian model of religion that was the most accessible to them, and which provided a radical orientation for their interpretation of native customs.[52] However, they also drew analogies between indigenous customs and the religions known to them. During the seventeenth and eighteenth centuries, Europeans assumed that there were four religions in the world: Christianity, Judaism, Islam, and paganism, the latter being often subdivided into ancient, barbaric, and devilish forms. They had no trouble extending the scope of religious diversity to include the cultivated and sacerdotal religions of India, China, and Japan because the identification of written and ritual traditions in Asia provided sufficient analogies with forms of religion that were familiar to them.[53] By virtue of a similar process, the beliefs and practices of indigenous peoples were considered as being derived from ancient sources, in most cases, Hebrew religion. In North and South America, as in Africa and Australia, this vision of the world easily gave rise to historical hypotheses that native peoples were descended from the Hebrews and the Ten Tribes. Parfitt has shown how the Hebrew language played a crucial role, since the Middle Ages, together with the myth of the Ten Tribes, in European imagination. He analyzed "the pivotal role of Hebrew as an 'invented language' in colonial discourses," showing how many of the languages encountered by Europeans were interpreted as being related to Hebrew or other Semitic languages.[54] The fact that Jews and native peoples were similarly stereotyped in Europeans' minds contributed to the development of the theory that American Indians descended from Jewish stock. After all, the religious practices of both these groups provided objects of contrast for European understandings.

Colonial Fantasies in the New World

The propensity to see similarities between ancient Judaism and the religion of the "savages" was partially the result of stereotypes held about both contemporary "savages" and contemporary Jews in European minds from the sixteenth to the seventeenth century. Being anti-Christian, the two categories were described as only half human and posed the same problem, that is, how could they be converted? European authors used the same language and images to describe the religious practices of contemporary Jews and those of the New World "savages."

Spaniards had long experience of prejudice about Jews. When Columbus arrived in the Americas in 1492, he believed he had arrived in certain islands off the coast of Asia while paradoxically he thought he had discovered a biblical land.[55] In 1511, when he recounted how Columbus identified Española as Ophir, Pedro Martir de Angleria suggested the possibility of a Jewish origin of the inhabitants of the New World.[56] If Española were Ophir, Solomon's sailors could have left behind the ancestors of the Indians. This opinion was readopted by many Spanish authors, and in 1540 a manuscript of Dr. Roldàn attempted to demonstrate that "the Indians of India, of the Islands and Inland and of the Ocean Sea, presently under the rule of the kingdoms of Castile, are Hebrews descended from the Ten Tribes of Israel."[57] One of the reasons evoked by Roldàn to support his thesis is the similarity of customs between Indians and Hebrews, "They practice circumcision, daily and abundant ablutions, in sea, rivers, springs and lakes; they are forbidden to touch the dead;... their caciques and high leaders often have many wives, as is written about certain Fathers of the Old Testament."[58]

Roldàn's thesis was taken up again and further developed some years later by the Dominican father Diego Duràn in his work *Historia de las Indias de Nueva España e Islas de Tierra Firme* (1867), which saw in the destiny of the New World populations the accomplishment of all biblical curses. Indeed, stresses Duràn, there could not be "greater authority and reasons to make us understand that those Indians are Jews and that they descend from them."[59] In 1607 the Dominican Gregorio Garcia, who became Grand Inquisitor, collected the many different theories that the Indians were literally of Jewish stock into a famous book, *Origen de los Indios del Nuevo Mondo* (1729).[60] He wrote, "Many have supposed, the Spanish generally who reside in the Indies believe, that the Indians proceed from the Ten Jewish Tribes who were lost in the captivity of Salmanazar, king of Assyria."[61] Garcia insisted that the Indians seemed to retain some aspects of the Mosaic Law, that the Incas had a ceremony similar to Passover, that the Indians of the Yucatán practiced circumcision, and that the Mexicans and the Incas maintained eternal fires, as did the Jews.[62] This theory also appeared in the Spanish-controlled area and in northern Europe with the publication in 1567 in Antwerp of the work of Joannes Fredericus Lumnius, *De Extremo Dei Iudicio et Indorum Vocacione*, which also introduced obscure theological arguments in support of the Hebrew origin of the Indians.[63]

The dissemination of these theories aroused significant controversy. Thus, José de Acosta devoted a full chapter of his *Historia Natural y Moral de las Indias* to the demonstration that the "widespread opinion according to which the Indians are of Jewish lineage is false," pointing out the fact that, unlike the Hebrews, the inhabitants of the New World do not know how to write.[64] Similar disproval of the hypothesis of the Jewish origin of the Indians was voiced by Juan de Torquemada in his work published in 1615.[65]

The earliest printed work supporting the thesis that the Native Americans were of Hebrew descent was *Chronographia*, published in 1570 by Gilbert Génébrard, a French theologian and Hebraist. Génébrard refers to the account of one of his contemporaries, the cosmographer-monk André Thévet, who had reported the discovery in the Azores of gravestones with inscriptions in Hebrew letters, using it as an argument to confirm that "the Hebrew people were not only present in the land of Judaea but throughout this great universe."[66] English authors also analyzed common elements between the Hebrew religion and that of the American natives. The missionary John Eliot, in *A Brief Narrative of the Progress of the Gospel amongst the Indians in New England in the Year*

1670, adopted the view that the Indians were descendants of the ancient Jews and considered that his work of conversion of the "American Jews" would contribute to the coming of the end of the world.[67] Thomas Thorowgood, in *Jews in America or Probabilities That Americans Are of That Race* (1650), argues that the Indians must be descendants of the Jews because "the rites, fashions, ceremonies and opinions of the Americans (Indians) are in many things agreeable to the custome of the Jewes, not onely to the prophane and common usages, but such as be called solemn and sacred."[68]

In response to Thorowgood's book, Hamon Lestrange in 1652 wrote *Americans No Iewes, or Improbabilities That the Americans Are of That Race*, without denying all the arguments of the former, but recalling that these customs also existed among other peoples, who were clearly not of Jewish origin.[69] In the same way, Lescarbot, who thought that it was Noah's descendants who had populated America, established, among other things, parallels between the practice of exclusion of menstruating women in the Mosaic Law and among the Indians.[70]

The book of Father Lafitau, *Moeurs des sauvages amériquains comparés aux moeurs des premiers temps*, published in 1724, represents the culmination of the tradition comparing the practices of ancient Jews with those of Native Americans. Lafitau, in presenting Native American populations as having been separated from the rest of humanity before the revelation of Moses, attempted to demonstrate that the similarities between Indian and Jewish practices represented proof of their common religion since Adam.[71] As Eilberg-Schwartz notes, "Anthropologists and ethnologists have already emphasized the way in which Lafitau anticipated many crucial developments in the emergence of their disciplines.... He goes well beyond the other writers of his day recognising all sorts of similarity between ancient Judaism and primitive religion."[72]

It is clear that, over the course of history, the genealogical origin of Indian religions was distorted, whereas the genealogy of the Old Testament provided the fundamental vocabulary for identifying the religious roots of beliefs and practices of the native peoples. There is no single or simple explanation for this phenomenon. The invention of Jewish identities for remote people in some cases was a means of integrating strange places and societies into a divinely ordered religious scheme of history. European emissaries used the tribal and pastoral elements of the Old Testament to make sense of the strangeness of exotic societies while confirming the biblical paradigm. This knowledge fell within the scope of what Renato Rosaldo called "rhetoric of control," a discourse about others that reinforced colonial barriers as well as a global control of the entire development of human history and geography.[73]

Colonial Fantasies in Africa

Western, Central, and Eastern Africa

By the beginning of the nineteenth century, Hamitic hypothesis theories were widely accepted as authoritative among missionaries. The myth was launched. It filled a generalized explanatory function that no contradiction could weaken. Anatomical differences, combined with aesthetic impressions and cultural specificities, determined the physical or cultural observations of European missionaries and colonists. Within this prevailing total confusion of ideas, the beliefs and practices of African peoples were considered by colonists and missionaries, through a new semantic shift, as deriving from the religion of the Hebrews. In 1879, a French missionary, Father Girault, noted, "I have been told that Cham's tomb is nearby; this tomb is venerated by the Blacks; it is forbidden to kill anything there; it is a place of refuge for slaves. According to the Waganda, Cham, whom they call 'Vitu,' came in this country in his old age.... In the Ounyoro, Cham is called Ham."[74]

Once the colonists started the long process of giving meaning to Africa, existing literature began to filter into the collective European imagination, and "Jewish arrangements" began to play a role in decrypting and understanding the continent. Mixed in with medieval Jewish travel accounts such as those of Eldad the Danite, Benjamin de Tudela, and Obadiah of Bertinoro, historical hypotheses that placed the existence of a Jewish community on the African seashore and interior from the earliest times, this body of data gave rise to a number of hypotheses. The discourse that identified traces of the Hebrew language and religion in Africa were strongly supported by the emergence of evangelical Christianity. Protestant missions—the London Missionary Society, founded in 1795 (which significantly changed its name to the Church Society for Africa and the East in 1812), the Church Missionary Society (1799), the Wesleyan Methodist Missionary Society (1813), and the American Board of Commissioners for Foreign Missions (1810)—rushed in and set up operations in the African countryside.[75] The British and Foreign Bible Society, originally created for publishing Bibles in Gaelic, was converted in 1804 to the promotion of "the most extensive circulation of the Holy Scriptures both at home and abroad." Africa was soon inundated with Bibles, which could only modify the course of its future.[76]

In the missions, one could observe an ambiguous wavering between the possible Hamitic, Semitic, or Nilotic origin of Africans. In the 1900s, Father Van der Bugt, a Dutch missionary in Burundi, went into ecstasy over the "Jewish faces" he believed he perceived in Rwanda and Burundi, asserting that the Batutsi were "close relatives of the handsome Pharaohs of the Nile valley."[77] To support these statements, he specified that Africa had been inhabited by ancient Cainites and Kushites, then infused by successive waves of Semitic-Hamitic immigrants from Asia, of mixed-race people who, for him, made up the Hamites. It was claimed that the late Hamitic conquerors had had contact with their Semitic "cousins" in Mesopotamia or Arabia. This idea about the Galla, expressed as early as 1862 by the French traveler Tremoux, and later by Monseigneur Le Roy, became widely assumed in the missions, in particular among the White Fathers in the Great Lakes region.[78] Monseigneur Gorju more or less legitimized it in his work published in 1920 that, "The Bahima are 'Hamitized Semites' of western Asian origin who descend from cross-breeding among this 'bunch of peoples' who had concentrated in the Ethiopian mountains."[79]

Some decades later, a study carried out by the German africanist Adolf E. Jensen attempted to establish that biblical influences had reached black Africa through the so-called Nilotic cultures. Nilotic cultures, according to Jansen, constituted a unit at linguistic and cultural levels. They occupied an area to the east and west of the upper Nile, of which the Masai constituted the most southern group. Jensen explained the similarities between Nilotic and biblical cultures as follows:

> Biblical culture developed upon an old substratum which has been preserved in present-day Nilotic culture. In other words, in relatively early times, which undoubtedly preceded the development of the Egyptian high culture, one uniform culture must have held sway over the very similar geographical areas of western Asia and North-Eastern Africa, and this culture must have closely resembled the present-day Nilotic cultures.[80]

From parallels between biblical and Nilotic rituals, such as the practice of sacrificial covenant, "the covenant between pieces" (Genesis 15: 17–18), blood sprinkling practiced by Nilotes and ancient Hebrews, or the interdiction on eating pork among Kushitic peoples, Jensen concluded that "a precursor of the culture of the Old Testament was related to the Nilotic culture of North-East Africa. This is the explanation of the fact that wherever the Nilotic culture penetrated, and especially in South Africa, Old Testament type influences can be observed."[81]

The case of the Masai was studied by M. Merker (1904), a German officer who perceived significant parallels between this group of shepherds from Kenya and northern Tanzania and the myths and customs of the Hebrews of the Bible. After studying the history of the creation of the world, the fight between God and the Dragon, the Flood, the history of Moses (whom Merker identified with the Masai Marumi or Musama), and the Ten Commandments, Merker concluded that the Masai and the "oldest" Hebrews had the same origin.[82]

Joseph Williams, a Jesuit and member of the Royal Geographical Society and of the American Geographical Society, published *Hebrewisms of West Africa: From the Nile to the Niger with the Jews* (1930) with the help of eminent scientific personalities, historians, anthropologists, and colonial officers. In this work, he listed the largest possible number of native groups identified as exhibiting Semitic influences or identity, from Jamaica to central Africa, including eastern and southern Africa.[83] Williams endorsed the view of a full-blooded Israelite theory of the Ashanti, described by the British as virile, courageous, and patriotic. In a detailed study, he affirmed that he identified the supreme being of the Ashanti with the Yahweh of the Old Testament and concluded:

> Thus far, we have shown certain cultural elements common to the Ashanti and the ancient Hebrews such as Ob cult, religious dances, use of "Amen," vowel value, patriarchal system, parallel symbolism of authority in "stool" and "chair," endogamy, cross-cousin marriage rite and the part that wine plays in the ceremony, uncleanness after child-birth, purification ceremony, menstrual seclusion; besides Ashanti loan words of apparent Hebrew origin.[84]

When, in the beginning of the nineteenth century, Europeans explored the basins of Senegal and Niger, they discovered Peul societies, little known up to that time, that took interest in their origins and seemed to be superior to the neighboring agricultural groups. The collection of information on the Peul went with the search for the sources of Senegal and Niger rivers and the exploration of Timbuktu by French colonists.[85] In France, philologists and geographers, together in the Société de Géographie (1821) and then in the Société ethnologique (1839), linked with this hypothesis the idea that the Peul, light-skinned and of oriental origin, was superior to black natives. This idea actively supported the ideology of colonial conquest and was easily integrated within the thinking pattern of the French soldiers based in western Africa.[86] Theories, according to which the Peul were descendants of ancient Jews, became widely known thanks to the works of Maurice Delafosse (1870–1926), who was a French colonial administrator, historian, and ethnographer. He argued in *Haut-Sénégal-Niger* that the legendary ancestors of the Peul, the Foudh, were Judaic-Syrians whose branches scattered through Egypt and

Cyrenaica up to western Africa. They generated dynasties that were at the origin of the states of Ghana and Tekrour.[87] A second migration from Cyrenaica to Air, probably around AD 80, followed by another wave in the middle of the second century in Awkar (near Nema, in today's Niger), would have given birth to the empire of Ghana.[88] Delafosse explained, "Driven from Ghana by the Soninkes of Ouagadou in the ninth century, the Jewish-Syrians took possession of Futa, Whites and Blacks mixed with their flocks; a large number of blacksmiths were with them. Their chief was named Ismael.... The people dispersed themselves among the tribes of the conquerors: the Jewish-Syrians were become the Peul, 'the dispersed.'"[89]

The hypothesis of the Jewish genealogy of the Peul, the cornerstone of Delafosse's reconstruction scheme of western Africa, took root in the descriptions of Africa in France and elsewhere. His researches, which were supposed to gather what the French knew to date on the history and ethnography of the populations of the Senegal and Niger basins, had numerous followers. Charles de La Roncière, in *La découverte de l'Afrique* (1924), tried to place Peul as follows: "Others see in the Peul the Leucoaethiopians or White Ethiopians whom Pliny placed to the south of the Getulians of Mauritania, the Pyrriaethiopians of Ptolemy. The latest data of anthropology and linguistics, in connecting them with the Semite races, make them Jewish immigrants who came from Palestine to the Sudan by the way of Egypt."[90]

Racial considerations and morphological comparisons were mixed with historical hypotheses and stereotypes on Jewish phenotypical traits by the colonial theorists of the Peul. Edmond D. Morel, who dedicated a whole chapter to the Semitic origins of the Peul in his *Affairs of West Africa* (1902), supported this idea by citing Verneau's study of the skulls of five Fulani chiefs from Fouta Djalon, which allowed him to identify them as being of the same type as the ancient Egyptians.[91] Morel speculated that after Hyksos shepherds were expelled from Egypt, many of them could have found their way to Africa's interior by passing through Cyrenaica, and he noted, "The Hebraic flavour, if one may put it so, which seems to permeate many of the Fulani customs, especially among the less contaminated elements of the race, has been recorded by careful observers."[92]

In the same years, Herbert C. Hall noted that when the Fulani men grew old, "their aspect becomes wonderfully Jewish and venerable quite bearing out the idea they were originally of this race."[93] Dr. Blyden, too, is quoted as saying, "On entering a Fulah town, the first thing which strikes a stranger is the Caucasian cast of features, especially among the older people; yet, every now and then, in the children of the parents having all the physical traits of the Semitic family, there recurs the inextinguishable Negro physiognomy."[94]

In respect to Fulfulde the language of the Peul, Morel added, "Fulfulde cannot as yet be definitely classed among the languages, but as far as our knowledge extends, it has Semitic antecedents."[95] Captain de Giraudon, who published a handbook in Fulfulde, stayed for several years in Senegambia, and built up relationships with the Peul. In the lecture he delivered in 1886 before the Seventh Congress of Orientalists, he was struck by their particular knowledge of Jewish history. He considered that the Peul evoked Hebrew characters from the Old Testament with familiarity and knew the events described therein, talking about this period as if it were their own history: "It would seem that the Fulani, even if they did not themselves profess the Jewish faith, which I should have a tendency to assert more than to deny, were at least in permanent contact with the Jewish people in ancient times and that, influenced at one time or another by the Israelites, they directly received the legends of the Old Testament."[96]

For the neighboring groups such as the Yoruba or Masai, even though different circumstances prevailed in each area, the use of a Hebrew or Israelite model seems to have penetrated every corner of Africa. European colonists developed a repertoire of comparative procedures—genealogy and morphology—to account for religious resemblance and diversity. This amalgamation played well with the guidelines of the official Christian ideology, which was hostile to theories of evolution and rather favorable to migration schemes, connected with the biblical story. The superior "Hamites" or "Chamites," related to the Semites, exhibited marks of degeneration in comparison with their supposed superiority in previous centuries or millennia, which suited well the redeeming intentions of colonial and missionary politics. In the rivalry that existed between Arabs and Protestant and Catholic missionaries, this theory favored the Christian cause against Islam.

Southern Africa

In southern Africa as well, as we shall now see, whatever natives' religions were, they were interpreted by Europeans according to similarities with ancient Hebrew rituals and became the object of the most contradictory European fantasies. A "theory of degradation" from an earlier, higher religion—the South African version of the Hamitic hypothesis, frequently appeared in reports about southern African religions. A more diffuse and unpredictable cultural consequence of this was a theoretical dissemination of Judaism in an area where it had been totally absent. Upon his arrival in the Cape Colony in 1819, Reverend John Philip, who was in charge of the London Missionary Society, established a kind of "theory of progress," identifying the natives' potential to evolve from the ignorance he saw to a revealed religion brought by the missionaries.[97] In contrast, other missionaries suggested that the superstitions observed among these groups were the expression of a lost religion. Using morphological and temporal comparisons, by means of language and culture analysis, these missionaries drew imaginary paths of the degeneration of a religion down to its ruin, maintaining that the African tribes they met came from the ancient Near East.[98]

Peter Kolb, a German living in the Cape Colony in 1705, claimed he had discovered the historical roots of the religion of the Hottentots, whom he considered the children of Abraham. They allegedly had preserved, in a distorted manner, religious traditions dating back to ancient Israel.[99] Kolb reported that the Hottentots kept an oral tradition dating back to their remote ancestors Nôh and Hingnôh, who strongly evoked the biblical story of Noah. Insofar as they did not preserve a memory of Abraham, Kolb argued that it was more probable that the Hottentots descended from the Troglodytes, the children of Abraham by his wife Keturah (Genesis 25:1–4), who "not only observed all or most of the customs in which the Hottentots agree with the Jews, but likewise many other, observed by the Hottentots to this day."[100] On this comparative basis, it appeared to him likely that the Troglodytes were the ancestors of the Hottentots of the Cape of Good Hope and that their religion derived from a variety of Judaism.[101] As Chidester pointed out, "This comparison also required a redefinition of Judaism as a religious tradition that resembles the practices of Hottentots."[102] A striking element of Kolb's analysis consisted in establishing a link and comparing the resistance of Jews and Hottentots to Christianity and to deduce that Hottentots were "stiff as Jews."[103] Kolb's fantasies, however, had proliferated in all subsequent writings, and the French François Le Vaillant complained, "I have never read any voyage to Africa, in which the absurd dreams of Kolben [sic] have not been more or less introduced."[104] Well after the period of the first colonizations, this construction still endured. It was still current in 1914, when Sidney Mendelssohn, a mining magnate, wrote an essay entitled "Judaic or Semitic Legends and Customs among South African Natives," which was published in the *Journal of the Royal African Society*. Two centuries after Kolb, Mendelssohn put forward a multitude of details about the formal analogies and common descent of the Jews and the native peoples of southern Africa. Looking at the workers in the gold and diamond mines, he wrote, "In the great sea of black faces I have seen men of such an unmistakably Jewish cast of features that I have most felt inclined to greet them as strangers in a strange land."[105]

The theory of the degeneration of an older and nobler religion was a recurring theme in the studies of Xhosa-speaking peoples.[106] Xhosa were usually referred to by the word *Kaffir*, which means "unbelievers," as the expression of a religious judgment based on an ancient Chaldean root integrated in Jewish and Muslim discourses.[107] The Kaffirs were considered to be "a people who had once a much greater degree of civilization than they now possess."[108] At the beginning of the nineteenth century, the Glasgow Missionary Society asked its correspondents in South Africa to carry out research for the purpose of comparing their traditions and customs to those of the Jews. The only answer to this request was an "Essay on the Antiquity of Circumcision," proposed by William R. Thomson.[109] Later on, Reverend Francis Fleming identified the Xhosa as "wandering Arabs of the Desert," dating their origin to Ismael, the son of Abraham and Hagar, based on the tombs with Arabic inscriptions from the Koran that had been found in the area.[110] In the 1830s, the English colonist Thomas Philipps, who had a certain sympathy for the Xhosa, observed, "They have Mahometan and Jewish rites" mixed with idolatrous practices. Along the same lines, Robert Godlonton, a spokesman of the colonists, in his book *A Narrative of the Kaffir Hordes Irruption* (1835), insisted that the Xhosa language exhibited "traces of its eastern origin in the frequent occurrence of words which are plainly of Arabic or Hebrew extraction."[111]

The customs of the Zulu, like those of the Hottentots and the Xhosa, were compared to those of the Jews. In the beginning of the nineteenth century, Shaka, the chief of a small Nguni Zulu-speaking clan, founded the Zulu empire by violently subjugating surrounding tribes. In 1843, with the British annexation of Natal, European commentators identified the Zulu, albeit with hesitation, with Arab-Semites, as was the case for the Xhosa, and more categorically with Jews.[112] It must be said that in the 1820s, Allen Gardiner, a Royal Navy sailor, in conducting a survey among a group of Zulu prisoners, had discovered the knowledge, lost over time, of the existence of a Supreme Being or Chief (Inkosi pezûlu).[113] Following that, G. R. Peppercorne, who was a magistrate, underlined the moral qualities of the Zulu of Natal, and the European experts of the Native Affairs Commission repeatedly reinforced the comparison with the Jews: "A general type of customs of the Ama-Zulu may be found in the early history of Hebrews, until they became a nation under a settled monarchy."[114] Zulu life was therefore organized according to an ancient Israelite scheme, that Peppercorne described as premonarchic and a most perfect contradiction, with the importance attached to the king and his role among the Zulu. Indeed, Europeans who wanted to know the Zulu religion could refer directly to the Bible. There, they would find Zulu polygamy in the stories of patriarchs, their wedding customs in the book of Ruth, and their relationship with work in Genesis in the story of Laban and Jacob.[115]

This comparison between Jews and Zulu was reinforced by data provided by Henry F. Fynn in the 1820s. Fynn supplied an inventory of the most striking likenesses, war offerings, sin offerings, propitiatory offerings, festival of first fruits, the proportion of the sacrifice given to the *isanussi* (witch doctors), periods of uncleanness on the decease of relatives and touching the dead, circumcision, rules regarding chastity, rejection of swine's flesh. Because of "the nature of semblance of many of their customs to those of ancient Jews, as prescribed under the Levitical priesthood," Fynn concluded, "I am led to form the opinion that (Zulu) tribes have been very superior to what they are at the present time."[116]

In 1853, John W. Colenso, the bishop of Natal, who spoke Zulu, undertook a study of their religion through long conversations with people of Natal and Zululand.[117] His findings led him to the discovery of the belief in a Supreme God, the Almighty, and Prime Essence, which allowed him to ascribe a natural religion to the Zulu. Colenso asserted that their religion was in reality close to revelation because the two words they used for God reflected "the very ideas contained in the Hebrew words Elohim and Jehovah." As ancient Israel had two names for the same God, insisted Colenso, the same was true of the Zulu; and in the interpretation of Colenso, uNkulukulu, the Almighty, was Zulu Yahve, the Creator of the world, whereas umVelinqangi was Zulu Elohim, the Essence of Existence.[118]

Although the foundations of the comparison between Zulu and ancient Israelites had already been suggested by former observers, Colenso went further by asserting that the similarity of their ways of life provided a basis for comparison that was rich in teachings about ancient Israel: " 'Zulu' mode of life and habits, and even the nature of their country, so nearly correspond to those of ancient Israelites, that the very same scenes are brought continually, as it were, before the eyes, and vividly realised in a practical point of view."[119]

While doing this, Colenso developed a new way to read the Bible—in terms of the scheme and rhythms of African life—rewriting the Bible not only in the Bantu language but from the perspective of a comparative study of religions that included Zulu religion among the religions of the world. Colenso's interpretations had a real influence, since they were resumed and developed by William R. Smith in his *Lectures of the Religion of the Semites* (1889) and largely adopted by the Zulu themselves.[120]

By the beginning of the twentieth century, the comparison between Zulu and Jews had been fully internalized by the Zulu in their own religious legacy. In 1901, during theological discussions between the magistrate and linguist James S. Callaway and a learned Zulu, Lazarus Mxaba, they referred explicitly to the precedents of Israel and ancient Greece to rebuild an ancient history of the Zulu religion. Mxaba cited certain customs—both ancient Jews and Zulu slit their earlobes, burned frankincense during ceremonies, burned the bones and cut the meat of sacrificed animals in a similar way—as evidence of a previous historical contact between the two groups. Mxaba and his friends were convinced that their lineage dated back to the Lost Tribes of Israel.[121] Five years later, in 1905, another of Stuart's interlocutors, Dinya, reasserted this affirmation of their Jewish descent: "We are anxious to find out where we came from. These Jewish customs of ours are evidence that we came from the north, for this evidence was in existence before we came in contact with Europeans."[122]

From western to southern Africa, missionaries, while supplying the Old Testament and identifying the African groups they encountered with the ancient Hebrews, brought to them new ideas about the history of their origins.[123] The deployment of the myth of Lost Tribes and myths about Jews penetrated every corner of the African continent, serving both religious and political interests. How did the African themselves react? Interpretations of the Hebrew Bible provided the substance for many of the innovations that led to the evolution of Africans' sacred world. Although they underwent a process of representation of Europeans, Africans were certainly not merely passive. Nowadays none of the southern African groups concerned accept a Jewish origin, but some of the western and central Africa groups I have described currently claim a Jewish descent and declare themselves to be Jews. As Jean and John Comaroff pointed out about southern Africa, colonization during the nineteenth century can be seen as an intercultural exchange in which African and European subjectivities were negotiated and renegotiated. A new consciousness emerged among Africans who discussed, argued, and reconfigured their identities in new religious languages that modified their understanding of themselves.[124] With its changing aspects the myth of a Hamitic race, forged by Egyptologists, linguists, and theologians, persisted. It generated a silent adherence to a system of biblical values the assimilation of which can be seen in the traditions of groups with which this book is concerned. Either degenerated compared with its origin, or perpetuated from time immemorial, the African religion as defined by colonists was in search of analogies and ancestors. Deep mental structures were mobilized within African societies, with, on the one hand, the nostalgia of one's origins and, on the other, the resonance of the Aryan myth generating the concept of "white with a black skin." During the process of defining the nature of African religions, by identifying and reinventing world religions in Africa, theorists of religions made the knowledge about these religions accessible and available to Africans themselves. This fanciful genealogy of religions was used in such a way that it both transferred the Middle East to Africa and dispersed, in a conceptual way, the native populations of Africa to the Middle East.[125]

In a more general way, the question of origin and precedence appears as the epicenter of the problematic of identity and religion of the Africans, as expressed by Europeans. At the time of decolonization, Africa, through the voice of its intellectuals, undertook to reclaim the center of any discourse pronounced about it. It was therefore by tracing an overly defined path about their origins that Africans began to appropriate their history. A slow, difficult, and unavoidable takeover of African history by African themselves ensued, influenced by African American thinkers and Afrocentrists. As defined by Molefi Asante, Afrocentrism "literally places African ideals in the centre of any analysis involving the culture and the behaviour of Africans."[126]

7

Appropriating Jewish History by the African Diaspora, Nineteenth to Twentieth Centuries

Afrocentrism and the "Black Blood" of the Hebrews

Afrocentrism is the intellectual movement that contests the dominance of European interpretations by writing Africa's history from an African point of view that serves both the political and psychological needs of Africans and their Diaspora.[1] This movement expresses the rupture with Western ideological and cultural tutelage and is an emblem of the creation of a collective African memory unified and based on Egypt, Nubia, Ethiopia, and other African civilizations. Afrocentric thought asserts that humankind developed first in Africa not only biologically, as is now accepted, but also in terms of civilization. These ideas were not new: Herodotus, among others, thought that Greece's knowledge came from Egypt, and in his *Voyage en Egypte et en Syrie* (1787), the French philosopher Constantin-François de Volney (1757–1820), whose memory is revered by Afrocentrists, put forward the idea that ancient Egyptians were black.[2]

The historiography of a glorious African past, as assertions of identity, was elaborated first among African American authors. The first African American texts, that seem to date back to 1790, already included themes that would create an echo during the following decades.[3] From the 1830s, a variety of popular texts or religious sermons and books, glorifying ancient Africa and especially Egypt, provided disparate sources of new traditions: identification of ancient Egypt as a great black civilization, at least partially created by "Ethiopians,"

"Kushites," or "Sons of Ham"[4]—a belief that civilization was born in Africa and transported to Greece and to the entire world—the veneration of Africa for its past greatness as a source of racial pride and hope for future achievement.[5] Indeed, the appropriation of Africa's history by African Americans followed the path of a search for origins that provided total rehabilitation after the experience of white supremacy and discrimination. From the mid–nineteenth century to the early twentieth, the numerous writings of African American writers—a high proportion of them clergymen—contain these themes, which were to reecho through all subsequent decades.

Drawing mainly on the Bible, these works of impressive autodidact scholarship argued that ancient Africa was the birthplace of civilization and point to Egypt, Ethiopia, and Carthage as great ancient African civilizations. The Egyptians, who were a "negro" population, had taught the Greeks, and African-derived knowledge had passed on to Europeans via Greece and Rome. David Walker, in *Appeal to the Coloured People* (1829), suggested: "When we take a retrospective view of the arts and sciences (we see) the wise legislation— the Pyramids and other magnificent buildings—the turning of the channel of the river Nile, by the sons of Africa or of Ham, among whom learning originated, and was carried thence into Greece."[6] James Pennington's *Text Book of the Origin and History of the Coloured People* (1841) disputed on numerous theological grounds the notion that Africans were "the children of Cain" or subject to "Noah's curse." Indeed, Africans were the descendants of Kush, which meant that there was biblical support for the idea of their consanguinity with ancient Egyptians or Ethiopians: they were "cousins."[7] John William Norris's tract *The Ethiopian's Place in History* (1916) ran through the standard litany of biblical explanations of African descent and asserted that the wisdom and religion of the Jews were also of African origin.[8] While supporting the primacy of African civilization, the precursors of Afrocentrism during the nineteenth century shared a view of history defined in racial terms and were inclined to reappropriate the racial dichotomy, insisting in turn on natural and cultural differences to prove the "Negroid" character of ancient Egypt.[9] This led some of them, such as A. B. C. Merriman-Labor, to exclude "Copts, Berbers, Kaffirs and Hottentots" from this scheme because of their yellowish or brownish skins.[10] Many of the texts already mentioned included brief discussions of ideas drawn from racial anthropology to support their arguments or to attack the European anthropological tradition. William H. Ferris, who held degrees from both Yale and Harvard in philosophy and theology, thus combined in his work *The African Abroad* (1913) Sergi's theory of the "Mediterranean race" with familiar themes, while denying that it could be white. He described Egyptians, Ethiopians and Nubians, and blacks as being three distinct yet related groups, but without any white origin: "The Ethiopians... were neither Negroes nor Egyptians. But they were a mixed colour race the same as the coloured people of America. They represented a blending of the Hamites, a Caucasian race who settled in North Africa and Egypt, and Negroes; or they were a branch of the Mediterranean race from which the Negroes were an offshoot."[11] Samuel Crowther (ca. 1807–1891), Martin R. Delany (1812–1885), and James Africanus Horton (1835–1883), "the father of modern African political thought," must be included among the major figures who echoed these notions, which came to be the common currency of Afrocentrism.[12]

During the nineteenth century, Edward Wilmot Blyden (1882–1912) was probably the most important thinker of these circles. Blyden's semimystical message, impregnated with ethnic nationalism, founded and foreshadowed the current ideas that are nowadays at the heart of Afrocentrist movements. He believed that "every race... has a soul, and the soul of a race finds expressions in its institutions, and to kill these institutions is to kill the soul... no people can profit be or be helped under institutions which are not the outcome of their own character."[13] His views were generally less exclusive than those of many later nationalists, and he expressed positive attitudes toward Islam as well as Jews.[14] It is worth noting that Blyden's positions were consistent with an understanding of Judaism as a religion with a special appeal to African American people.[15] But it was probably William Edward B. Du Bois (1868–1963), thinker and activist, who had the greatest influence on African Americans' feeling of self-identification and their vision of Africa.[16] In line with the general theory, Du Bois—considered the initiator of a political movement in the twentieth century—adhered to more universalistic and rationalist philosophies, and had a great impact on subsequent activists such as Marcus Garvey or Malcolm X. Influenced by communist ideas as well as by the Hamitic hypothesis, although not entirely convinced by the whole idea of a distinct "Hamitic" race being responsible for Africa's major cultural achievements, Du Bois developed in his later writings what Anthony Kwame Appiah considers to be a racialist-romantic message:

> The actual ties of heritage between the individuals of this group vary with the ancestors that they have in common and many others, European and Semites, perhaps Mongolians, certainly American Indians. But the physical bond is least and the badge of colour relatively unimportant save as a badge; the real essence of this kinship is its social heritage of slavery; the discrimination and insult; and its heritage binds together not simply children of Africa, but extends through yellow Asia into the South Seas. It is unity that draws me to Africa.[17]

Traditions of Afrocentrist mythography nurtured a great number of African American religious movements such as Ethiopianist movements, black Jews, and Rastafarianism. Earlier Afrocentrist texts provided the theoretical basis and the recurring themes for the black Jews doctrine during its formative period. The identification with a great Egyptian or Ethiopian civilization provided the paradigm and the impetus for the eclectic strategies that were utilized by African Americans in their search for a historical heritage and the creation of new traditions. The assertion of "great cultural heritage," claiming ties to an exclusive lineage, led to the assimilation of Judaism as a source of black identity. The claim that people of African descent should rediscover common sociocultural traditions derived from their shared origins interacted with the religious encounter of symbols and images of Judaism in myriad forms. One can trace diasporic images of Africa asserting a specific cultural ethos and destiny for African Americans, a form of cultural nationalism, at least as far back as Blyden or, before him, in Martin Delany's and David Walker's writings from the pre–Civil War years. However, the most influential cultural expressions of these views came from the francophone Caribbean *noirisme* and from the West Africa's educated minority with the 1930s *négritude* literary movement.[18] The declarations of its leadings figures, Aimé Césaire, Léopold Sedar Senghor, and Léon Damas, set the tone for ethnic identity construction.[19] Through the mediation of what became known as "ethno-philosophy," a complex ideology of absolute cultural "otherness" spread. Ethno-philosophy, involving shared traditions and attitudes to life mythologized "African personality" and prepared the ground for the first metaphorical associations produced by African Americans attracted by the Judaism model.

One can see the influence of this structure of ideas on the following generations of African American chroniclers of the beginning of the twentieth century, who were in large part of West Indian origin. Authors from the Caribbean currents such as Marcus Garvey, J. A. Rogers, George G. M. James, and later figures as diverse as Yosef Ben-Jochannen, Ivan Van Sertima, and Louis Farrakhan, put these conventional themes in more polemical and more popularly accessible form.[20] Within the process African Americans' "Africanization," the reality of a link between Africans and Ethiopians or Egyptians, through almost exclusively biblical and creationist frameworks, became a familiar theme. For example, L. F. C. Mantle, a mysterious character who appeared on the Jamaican scene in 1935 claiming to have served the British army in Palestine, to have traveled in Ethiopia and Tibet, to have graduated in divinity, and also to be a rabbi, asserted the dual identification of all black people as Ethiopians, and of Ethiopians, in their turn, with the Jews of the Bible. The ancient Ethiopians from whom New World blacks descended had been the originators of civilization. They traveled down the Nile to Egypt and from there to Greece, Rome, and hence to all European cultures. Even if Mantle vanished from view quickly, as Ken Post comments, "'his hidden secrets,' reinforced by the contributions of others, produced a quite formidable body of doctrine."[21] Using European creationist beliefs mixed with polygenist ideas of some nineteenth-century European racial theorists, Mantle argued that Europeans, including the whites who falsely claimed the title of Jews, were descended from Adam, who was created only in 4004 BC, while the Ethiopians had existed more than 3,000 years before.[22] Some of these themes claiming black "priority" with regard to the imposture of the Jews were to be found echoed more than forty years later in the assertions of Yosef Ben-Jochannen and Jose Malcioln.

Marcus Garvey's ideas reflected the various themes of black and African history expressed earlier and distilled them into a mythologizing but extremely influential synthesis.[23] Between 1920 and 1935, Garvey, who was nicknamed "the black Moses," founded a Pan-Africanism, close to an African Zionism aimed at the masses, and proclaimed that all Africans were Hebrews.[24] The liberation message of Garvey's movement, the Universal Negro Improvement Association (UNIA), with the well-known concepts of emancipation, black pride, and identity based on race, could only generate followers among the poorest African American citizens.[25] According to Garvey, African history should be a source of inspiration and emotional uplift to blacks, associated with a systematic derogation of European claims for the past. Garvey, like many of the earlier promoters of past African greatness, proposed a broadly attractive vision of history, in which Africa had once led the world, had lost its primacy, but would now regain it thanks to the efforts of Garvey and the UNIA.[26]

This selection of suggestive influences points out how African Americans' understanding of Judaism were informed by the political orientations of black people in the United Sates and were often embedded in African Americans' response to discrimination. Having traced an overview of origins and influences on black reconstruction ideas about Africa, we now turn to their contemporary manifestations in relation to racial identity. The wider argument identifying the Hebrews of the Bible with a black nation came to be a dominant feature of pan-African movements in their formative period. Mantle, Garvey, and Albert Cleage, among many others, identified themselves with the claim that Jesus was black, which had been recurrent for well over 150 years. In Cleage's book *The Black Messiah* (1968) Jesus was "the non-white leader of a non white-people, struggling for national liberation against the rule of the white nation." He was "trying to rebuild the Black nation Israel," the original Jews being "a black nation intermingled with all the black peoples of Africa," which also included the Egyptians, the Canaanites, and the Chaldeans, from whom Abraham came.[27] The denial of white supremacy that led to the contestation of the veracity of white Jewish origins was required for the creation of a new racialized identity for many African Americans. The assertion that Judaism was solely suited to black people supported the belief that white Jews were religious impostors. Echoes of the same views sustained by Louis Farrakhan's anti-Semitic rhetoric and the deterioration of relationships between Jews and blacks were to be heard in contemporary Afrocentric academic circles.[28] Spokesmen of modern Afrocentrist ideas that Howe qualifies as "wild afrocentricity," such as Leonard Jeffries, Frances Cress Welsing, Yosef Ben-Jochannen, and Jose Malcioln, repetitively pursue ideas about the Egyptian, and therefore black, origins of civilization. They convey the thesis of the biblical Hebrews' identification with a black nation in an extraordinary mixture of ambivalent interpretations expressing alternately accusation and spiritual identification with Jews. Frances Cress Welsing, a pseudoacademic well known for her sensationalist declarations, claimed that "skin whiteness is a genetic mutation. Black people can produce white people. White people can only produce white people. White are mutants of Black people."[29] Having laid out this context, she considers the blacks' extermination as inevitable, with the destruction of Jews by Hitler representing the first phase of this process and Jews being "the products of the genetic mixture produced when white Greek and Roman soldiers invaded Africa and raped women, who of course were black, Semite is the same as the word mulatto. Thus they were considered to be half-black and half-white or genetically colored people."[30]

Yosef Ben-Jochannen, a longtime activist in Harlem's nationalist associations, claimed to be of Ethiopian Jewish origin[31] In his book *We the Black Jews: Witness to the "Jewish Race" Myth* (1993), he vehemently asserts that white Jews are historically impostors and that the cultural legacy that they claim belongs exclusively to black Africans.[32] The argument propagated by Ben-Jochannen, among others, was recently taken up again by another American Afrocentrist writer, Jose Malcioln, in his book *The African Origins of Modern Judaism: From Hebrews to Jews* (1996).[33] Malcioln argues that Judaism and later Christianity and Islam derive entirely from Egyptian sources. What he says is not based only on some tenuous similarities between a few biblical and Egyptian texts, but also on supposedly similar religious practices, such as circumcision and the taboo against eating pork. The insistence of these recurrent beliefs is interpreted by such critics as Schlesinger and Hughes, as either a compensatory therapy or a movement similar to the development of a new religion.[34]

In the period from the 1800s to the 1930s, Afrocentric ideas generated distinctive rhetoric that played a significant role in the development of new religious traditions for African Americans. They expounded their own myths, which had specific religious application to the situation of black people in the United States. As stated by Edwin Redkey, "American Blacks, cut off from most of their African memories and immersed in a nation that refused to acknowledge that Blacks could have a cultural background, have had a difficult time fashioning a cultural identity other than the tradition of oppression."[35]

The birth of the Black Muslims and that of the black Jews have much in common. In both cases, these movements arose from the metamorphosis of religious fact into an identity weapon against white supremacy: the need to create a new identity that broke away from past discriminations and was linked to the search for an ancestral and mythical place of origin.[36] The Black Muslim and black Jew movements were born against the background of the Great Depression of the 1930s, in the wake of the syncretic sects and para-Christian churches that addressed a common need for their members to recover an identity and a history. Profoundly heterodox compared with the standards of Islam, the Nation of Islam movement, founded in Detroit in 1930 by Elijah Muhammad and subsequently represented by Malcolm X, then by Louis Farrakhan as of the 1970s, denounced African Americans' integration in white America and condemned American society for its exploitation of African Americans since the period of slavery. In his book *Message to the Blackman in America* (1965), Elijah Muhammad explained that the African Americans are descendants "of the tribe of Shabbazz which, 66 billion years ago, stayed on earth after a great division had separated our planet in two parts, on one side earth, on the other side the moon." He adds, "Us, tribe of Shabbazz, were the first ones to discover the best part of our planet: the rich Nile valley in Egypt and the present site of Mecca in Arabia."[37] As Emanuela Trevisan Semi suggested: "The search for a historical heritage to which to refer and the possibility of recovering a past rich in traditions and symbols, whether Islamic or Judeo-African, certainly appealed to a people attempting to redefine itself and to find sources of pride to present to other communities. Judaism, the religion of the Book par excellence, with its tradition and intellectual vocation represented also the recovery of a written tradition."[38]

The Black Jews in the United States

No doubt the words of Theodor Herzl, a pioneer of Zionism, found an echo among the earliest Afrocentrist leaders who fought for the emancipation of their people when he wrote, in *Altneuland*, around 1900:

The problem of oppressed peoples, which only a Jew can measure the extreme horror, is not yet solved and has no solution to date: It is the problem of Negroes. Think about the atrocities of the slave trade. Men, because they were black, were captured like animals, deported and sold. Their descendants have lived far from their country, hated and despised, because they were of another color. I am not embarrassed to say, even if people make fun of me, that after having lived through the homecoming of the Jews, I would like to help to prepare the homecoming of Negroes.... This is why I am working to heighten the value of Africa. All men should have a homeland.[39]

Comparing Jewish and black aspirations for nationhood, Blyden referred to their parallel struggles: both communities, whose histories were marked by suffering, had developed what he called "their spiritual dimension," and he suggested that they could propagate "an international religion."[40] The achievement of the bimillenary dream of the Jewish people has thus strongly influenced the African American encounter with Judaism. In 1920, Garvey stated in a meeting that "a new spirit, a new courage came to us at the same time it came to the Jew. When a Jew says, 'We shall have Palestine,' the same feeling comes to us when we say 'We shall have Africa.'"[41]

In the eighteenth and nineteenth centuries, the appropriation of Jewish history by African Americans followed the path of a search for origins that gave them back a history and allowed them to overthrow American racism's hierarchy of values.[42] Unlike Jewish immigrants, the African peoples sent as slaves to North America did not own a common spiritual heritage or myth of origins.[43] Melville Herskowitz, in *The Myth of the Negro Past* (1941), underlined that the loss of their own African past and traditions contributed to an uncertain self-image among African Americans searching for a shared history and perspectives.[44] Convergences in the experiences of blacks and Jews—exile, common histories of dispersion and exclusion—facilitated the adaptation of Judaism within black religious aspirations and assumed particular significance. In an early stage, images, characters, and interpretations from the Hebrew Bible were powerfully invested by African American religion as a source of black American identity.[45] Parallels in their respective histories, interpretations of the black Diaspora and Exodus, analogous to the Jewish experience, appeared in African American writings as early as the nineteenth century.[46] They were conceptualized later on in academic literature. St. Clair Drake wrote, "In both the Jewish Diaspora and those of the African peoples, an unknown portion of those who were dispersed were 'lost' so to speak through the combined interaction of two processes: cultural assimilation as the end point of the acculturation process, and amalgamation or biological absorption due to miscegenation."[47]

The reading of the Old Testament, specifically the Psalms, Proverbs, and Prophets, influenced the formation of the cultural framework upon which black people began to construct a collective identity.[48] The religious songs of the slaves, the spirituals forged in the oral culture environment, made consistent use of Old Testament imagery. As Harold Courlander demonstrated, songs about Moses and Joshua came to be the "oral Bible" of the slaves.[49] From the early 1900s, folk preachers were conversant with the Holy Scriptures, and had spread the doctrine that "the so-called Negroes were really the lost sheep of the House of Israel."[50] This vision reflected the thoughts of enslaved black Christians when they wondered about their fate and captivity.[51] The slaves believed themselves to be the oppressed Hebrews of the Bible and projected their own lives into the narratives of Israel's formative history. North America came to be their "Egypt," and the same God who had led the Jews in the promised land would guide them.[52] Slave rebellion leaders like Gabriel Posser, Denmark Vesey, and Nat Turner all took inspiration in the Bible.[53]

In addition to biblical reference was the determining factor of the "Jewish model" developed by black leaders, such as the writer Booker T. Washington, who developed a model for freed African Americans that recommended imitating the Jews' behavior. In 1884, Washington wrote:

> We have a brilliant and striking example in the history of Jews in various countries. No other race has suffered as much in America and in other parts of the world, but they remained united. They kept their unity, their pride, their love for their race and their importance grew through the centuries even in those countries where they were despised. And it is above all because they maintained their faith and their destiny. If the Negro does not learn to imitate the Jews in these areas, then he cannot hope to succeed.[54]

In countering their experience of exclusion, the notion of being the chosen people and the identification with the biblical Jews took deep roots in African American imagination.[55] The appropriation of this religious sentiment combined with the multiple interpretations and meanings of the biblical prophecy of Psalm 68:31, "Princes shall come out of Egypt and Ethiopia shall soon stretch forth her hands unto God," provided fuel for the definition of an exceptional redemptive destiny. By the end of the nineteenth century, the doctrine of Ethiopianism posited that Africans were the people chosen by God for the redemption of the black race. From the sufferings of African Americans would come the restoration of the greatness of Africa and the spiritual and social uplift of African people.[56] From the Civil War to the 1950s, a multitude of African American churches and missionary associations proliferated, combining elements inherited from the African traditions, Protestant religion, and Ethiopianism. Ethiopianism was adopted by various movements of Caribbean origin, such as Garvey's UNIA or Rastafarianism in Jamaica.[57] The "chosenness" doctrine in Ethiopianism led to a racialist discourse asserting the identification of all black people with Ethiopians, and of Ethiopians, in their turn, with the Jews of the Bible. This characteristic rhetoric prepared the ground for Black Nationalist action and militant antiwhite dimensions in the century to come.[58] For example, in 1915 in Philadelphia, the prophet F. S. Cherry, leader of one of the first black Jewish cults, The Church of the Living God, the Pillar Ground of Truth for All Nations, elaborated a racial theology asserting the primacy of blacks in Judaism.[59] Prophet Cherry assured his followers that, in a vision, God had called him to bring the message that the true descendants of the biblical Hebrews were African Americans. Citing confused and sometimes contradictory interpretations of the Old Testament, Cherry concluded that God and Jesus were black and that blacks were the true original Jewish race. The Church of the Living God's followers, who preferably had had a vision or a spirit possession, believed in a black Jesus and, like Orthodox Jews, covered their heads and studied Hebrew.[60]

The first organized community of black Jews arose in 1896, with the street preaching of William Saunders Crowdy in Lawrence, Kansas. Crowdy, a railroad employee and a Baptist preacher, had begun to have visionary experiences that suggested to him that Christian churches were not pleasing to God, and that a return to Judaism was required.[61] To that end, he founded a Hebrew-Christian community among former slaves with the name Church of God and Saints of Christ. Crowdy adopted various rituals and symbols in which Old Testament traditions were mingled with Christian principles, to form a ritual synthesis. Members of the Church of God celebrated Sabbath and Jewish Passover and performed circumcision of newborns while also incorporating New Testament traditions and practicing Christian baptism. Later on, the adoption of components of Judaism integrated with Christian principles formed the pattern for a number of groups in the early establishment of black Jewish communities in the United States. Interestingly, Crowdy's experience is meaningful even now, for the present-day Jews of Rusape, Zimbabwe, who chose components of Judaism mingled with New Testament principles and who claim to be his followers.

At the turn of the twentieth century, additional social and political elements contributed to African Americans' identification with Judaism. After the Civil War, the dual migration of African Americans from the countryside toward cities and from the South to the North brought the two groups closer and provided meeting grounds for blacks and Jews.[62] The identification of African Americans with the Hebrews of the Bible was taken for granted among complex and multifaceted black Jewish religious communities. As Landing points out, "The terminology is as varied as their numbers, some referring to themselves as Israelites, others as Jews, Hebrews, Canaanites, Essenes, Judaites, Rechabites, Falashas and Abyssinians. Although the terminology differs, all such groups perceive themselves as lineal descendants of the Hebrew Patriarchs."[63]

In 1909, with the foundation of the National Association for the Advancement of Colored People (NAACP), rabbis and Jewish social workers, along with Du Bois and white liberals, who were heirs of the abolitionist movement, signed a call for action to act against racial hatred.[64] At that time, Harlem, which had been a largely Jewish immigrant district, underwent considerable transformation and major social changes. A large part of Harlem's Jewish population thus migrated toward new areas, and African Americans moved in. While half the Jewish population left (from a peak of 178,000 at the beginning of the century to 88,000 in 1927), the inflow of black residents to Harlem represented half of New York's black population (165,000 of New York's 328,000 blacks).[65] In the 1920s, thousands of Jews of Askhenazic and Sephardic origins still lived in the ghettos of New York. The geographical proximity of Jews and early black Jewish groups also contributed to the elaboration of their Jewish identity by the latter.[66] Yvonne Chireau notes, "In many of these new black-Jewish religious groups, not only were the symbols and images of Judaism employed allegorically, but Jewish practices led to the construction of new identities by which blacks literally *became* Jews."[67] For example, some African Americans from the ghettos occasionally worked as *shabbos goyim* (non-Jews employed by Jews) to perform tasks such as the lighting of synagogues during the Shabbat.[68] The exposure of black Americans to Judaism probably contributed to their assimilation of this religion and its practices.[69] Ulysses Santamaria used the expression "mimetic conversion" to explain this appropriation of Jewish religion by African Americans from the ghettos.[70] It is possible that the arrival of black migrants from South America and the West Indies carrying Jewish beliefs and practices also contributed to the proliferation of black Jewish groups in the cities. We know that in the seventeenth century, for example, Jews from Spain, Portugal, and the Netherlands had settled in the northern regions of Latin America, Central America, and the Caribbean. Intermarriage between these Sephardic Jews and blacks, either slaves or free persons, was not unusual in these areas; these unions gave birth to some of the first African American affiliation to Judaism in the New World.[71]

The black Jewish communities with structured ideologies appeared around 1915. Many of these early groups encouraged a rupture, distancing them from white Judaism, and at the same time rejected the use of the terms *negro* or *black*. Wentworth A. Matthew, a black from Harlem who would later be known as Rabbi Matthew, described how, according to the Bible, "Jacob was a black man because he had smooth skin."[72] The black Jews considered that American blacks were in fact African Hebrews torn from their origins and religion by slavery who had lost the knowledge of their ancestral heritage: "During slavery they took away our name, language, religion and science, as they were the only possessions the slaves had, and they were pumped full of Christianity, to make them more docile."[73] A new definition of themselves as "Hebrews of Ethiopian descent" was proposed by Rabbi Matthew that pointed to a common origin and reunification. This phenomenon was accelerated by the spread of information about a black Jewish Diaspora in Ethiopia, the Falasha. Jacques Faitlovitch—"father of the Falasha"—played a major role in the recognition of the Falasha. His presence in Harlem, in the 1920s and 1930s, even if ambivalent toward the black Jewish movement, speeded up the elaboration of Jewish identity among African American society by bringing documentation on the Ethiopian Jews.[74] Brotz emphasized that the knowledge of the existence of the Falasha was "the missing link," which for some African Americans symbolically settled the question of their Jewish identity in response to critics who had expressed serious skepticism about their claims.[75] Trevisan Semi wrote:

> The possibility of sharing a mirrored Diaspora—Blacks in America and Jews in Africa—linked obviously by the condition of slavery, exile, discrimination and a keen hope of redemption, gave rise to new myths of origin in which Ethiopia became a shared locus and the process of identification took the form of what we may call "Falashisation." As the country known in the Bible as Cush and associated with the glories of ancient Egypt and the Queen of Sheba, Ethiopia was well suited to represent a common birthplace.... Through this two-way route, both ideal and concrete, of "back to Ethiopia" and "back to Jewish America," some American Blacks hoped that the new Falasha identity would aid the integration process in the great Jewish American Diaspora.[76]

As for the Rastafarians, Ethiopia's emperor Haile Selassie became a major symbol in these groups' ideology, whose members claimed to be of Ethiopian Jewish extraction. The assumption that the original Israelites were Africans was substantiated by the existence and the ancient pre-Talmudic practices of the Ethiopian Beta Israel. Cultural elements considered common to the Africans and the ancient Hebrews were identified on the theme of Africans' Hebrew origins, Africa was mythologized as the cradle of Judaism, and conjectures about the Hebrew origins of African culture were advanced as "Hebrewisms."[77] Outside black American religious circles, a chain of "Hebrewisms" of African derivation was established by Williams in his academic book, *Hebrewisms of West Africa* (1930). Williams established numerous parallels of sub-Saharan tribes' cultural traits with Hebraic influence dating back to legendary times.[78]

Between the 1920s and the 1930s, several African American Jewish synagogues were built in the cities of New York, Washington, D.C., Philadelphia, and Chicago. The first black Jewish congregation, the Moorish Zionist Church (1924), was formed in New York by Arnold Josiah Ford, born and raised in Barbados, who claimed an Ethiopian and princely origin. Once in Harlem, Ford, who had left an evangelical sect led by his father in Barbados, completely rejected the Christian doctrine, and his anti-Christian sentiment seems to have found an outlet in Judaism.[79] He soon left the Moorish Zionist Church, created the Beth B'nai Abraham (the House of the Sons of Abraham), and six years after its creation became a member of the Commandment Keepers, the group led by Rabbi Matthew.[80] His multiple involvements contributed to pulling together the eclectic trends of an emergent black Judaism. Ford, who served as choir master at UNIA, Garvey's movement, encouraged the systematization of the myth of a glorious Ethiopian past by creating hymns and songs honoring Ethiopia, "the land of our fathers."[81] After studying Hebrew and Yiddish under the tutelage of some white liberal Jews, Ford claimed a hereditary right to the office of rabbi. He then declared himself the guardian of the Hebrew knowledge of Africans and gathered evidence of the close similarity between the Hebrew language and the Ethiopian and African ones. In 1930, Ford was sent to Ethiopia by his congregation for the coronation of Emperor Haile Selassie. Resettling in Addis Ababa over the following three years, Ford was followed in Ethiopia by some other members of Beth B'nai Abraham. They undertook to settle territory in an area north of Lake Tana for the black Jewish community, but Ford died in 1934 without having succeeded in establishing a black Jewish homeland.[82]

Harlem's most important congregation, the Commandment Keepers Congregation of the Living God, affiliated with the Royal Order of Ethiopian Hebrews created in 1919, largely contributed to the vision of an Ethiopian-based Judaism.[83] Wentworth A. Matthew, its leader, born in West Africa in 1892 and having spent his youth in the West Indies, like many other members of the community, claimed an Ethiopian origin. Albert Ehrman observed: "In the early twenties, Matthew learned of the romantic story of the Falashas and immediately discovered that he was a Falasha himself."[84] Once in New York, Matthew practiced various activities that brought him into contact with Jews, met Ford, who "ordained" him, and became Rabbi Matthew.[85] He and Ford shared the point of view that "the so-called Negroes were really children of the House of Israel." In a book entitled *The Anthropology of the Ethiopian Hebrews and Their Relationship to Fairer Jews*,[86] Matthew legitimated the Jewish heritage of African American Jews in expounding that as kin of the Jews of Ethiopia, black Americans descended from the royal lineage of King Solomon and the queen of Sheba related in the biblical account of 1 Kings 10 and 2 Chronicles 9. Matthew, who had acquired a slight knowledge of Hebrew from a Jewish immigrant, established his synagogue and the Ethiopian Hebrew Rabbinical School of Religion to train rabbis. He intended to give his followers both a moral and a religious education, honoring traditional moral values and probity. The group grew from about a hundred members, mainly women, in 1929 to 175 members in 1930, including 6 white Jews. Thereafter, the number of members increased continuously, reaching 800 in 1949 and 1,100 in 1957, according to Matthew himself.[87]

A myriad of heterogeneous black Jewish movements grew from the 1920s to the 1930s. While relying on the unanimous assertion of an originally black Jewish faith for their ideology and beliefs, they were decentralized and utterly diversified for half a century. This seems to change from 1995, when a charismatic character, Rabbi Capers Funnye from Chicago, decided to launch a new national organization, the Alliance of Black Jews. The aim of the alliance was to establish a permanent forum in which black Jews could share their experiences and foster a sense of common identity "to bring together people of African descent who believe in Torah and its mandates and/or who are culturally affiliated to Judaism."[88] Funnye's congregation descended from a self-proclaimed black Jew movement that formed in the 1920s and 1930s, rejecting Christianity as the religion of slavery. He was ordained in 1985 by Rabbi Levy Ben Levi, who succeeded Matthew after his death in 1973. Funnye's Beth Shalom B'nai Zaken Ethiopian Hebrew congregation is thus a direct descendant of Matthew's Commandment Keepers.[89] In Funnye's view, white Europeans have no monopoly on Judaism, and he affirms, "There never has been such a thing as the Jewish race and race never had any role in antiquity, as far as restricting an individual from coming into the House of Israel."[90]

These views existed in Jewish circles from the 1940s and 1950s and were shared by some white Jews. The creation in the United States and in Israel of proselyte associations, the Lost Tribes Committees, supported by such influential individuals as Yitzhak ben Zvi, the founding president of the State of Israel, or Nahoum Slouschz, a pioneering Zionist and great traveler, strengthened the tendency toward a universal Judaism.[91] Although from different Zionist backgrounds, these organized proselyting movements legitimized the return of those "lost" to Judaism that "they considered to be, with different nuances, an open religion, one which made no distinction between peoples and skin color, rather than an 'ethnic religion,' the expression of a single people."[92] A missionary movement of this type, named the Mosaic Law for One World, was formed in New York in 1944 by David Horowitz, and Eliezer Schindler succeeded in propagating the universalistic message of the Mosaic Law for One World among the black Jewish communities of Harlem and other areas.[93] It gave black Jews' communities more incentive and contributed to the strengthening of Jewish identities among groups of already receptive African Americans. Even if the conversion policy of the Lost Tribes Committee was not fully supported by the rabbinate and Jewish public opinion, their utopian tendency to a universal Judaism gave rise to several contemporary organizations that assist "lost" Jewish communities elsewhere in the world.[94]

The Hebrew Israelites from Chicago to Israel

Issues of biblical interpretation and the creation of new traditions were experienced by various groups that adhered to Judaism in the mid–twentieth century, throughout the United States. From the 1960s, Chicago became the home of emergent black Jewish communities, with five large congregations and half a dozen smaller ones. At the beginning of 1967, the United Leadership Council of Hebrew Israelites (ULCHI) was created by four black Jewish groups whose rabbis had earlier formed, with the help of some white rabbis, the Chicago Fellowship of Racial Jews in order to provide teaching for the communities of black Jews.[95] Among these diverse "camps," as they were known by their participants, was a group formerly called the Abeta Hebrew Israel Cultural Center, whose central ideology was a belief in African Americans' repatriation to the land of their ancestors. Carter Ben Ammi, the spiritual leader of these "Hebrew Israelites," had a divine revelation according to which Africans were descendants of the Judah tribe exiled in Africa during the dispersal period, and that the time had come for them to return to their homeland.[96] Ben Ammi's theory claimed that the America of whites had always lied about African history and the social-economic situation of Africa, and therefore rejected vigorously the whites' political power. In May 1967, three Abeta leaders, including Ben Ammi, flew to Liberia, the country formed by American slaves, to settle in the African continent.[97] They were rapidly followed by around 200 Hebrew Israelites who left the United States with a pioneering spirit and the arduous project of becoming farmers. The experiment lasted only two years due to economic difficulties and integration problems. In 1969, the community regrouped in Israel and claimed the right to Israeli citizenship under the law of return.[98] The Israeli government ruled that the Hebrew Israelites did not have legitimate claim to Israeli citizenship and denied them state benefits. After some negotiations between American and Israeli governments about their legal status, Hebrew Israelites settled in the cities of the Negev Desert, Dimona and Arad, where they practiced a system similar to that of the kibbutz. They developed a specialized school that combines education in modern Hebrew, science, math, and Israeli civics with Hebrew Israelite spiritual tenets.[99] Around a set of symbolic conceptions, the ideology of the community maintains that the Jews of Israel are not Jews by heredity, even if they share certain religious principles with the Hebrew Israelites. Upon his arrival Ben Ammi asserted that the black Hebrews, not the Jews, were the "true inheritors of Israel" and that only Blacks were true Hebrews, the black race being the only original Hebrew race. He explained: "Our customs are different from yours. We believe only in the Torah, not what was added later."[100]

From disparate motivations and experiences, the Hebrew Israelites have developed a religious vision that combines traditional African American identification with biblical Israel and Pan-African doctrine. They characterize their history in biblical terms and depict their journey from the ghettos of the United States to Israel as a reenactment of the Israelites' Exodus from Egypt.[101] The distinct identity forged by the Hebrew Israelites, visible in their beliefs, rituals, and lifestyle, fuses their particular interpretation of biblical religion with aspects of African American culture. For example, the community has a strict vegan diet that derives from its exegesis of Genesis 1:29 "And God said: Behold I have given you every herb-yielding seed, which is upon the face of all the earth, and every tree, in which is the fruit of a tree yielding seed—to you it shall be for food." Following the biblical example, Hebrew Israelite men are allowed to have more than one wife, and women follow the biblical rules concerning menstruation.[102] The hierarchy of the community, whereby the heads are called princes, evokes the way of life of a sect, and a vast list of punishments of disobedience has been included in a "National Guidelines" of what was called the Black Hebrew Israelite Nation.[103] In other words, black Hebrew symbols represent a "world of salvation" for followers and provide willingness and motivation to undergo dramatic life changes. As defined by Merrill Singer, "In short, Black Hebrews symbols weave simultaneous webs of signification and mystification."[104]

In 1996, Ben Ammi proclaimed that Hebrew Israelites had transformed their opinions concerning Jews and attributed part of the change in perspective to the political agreement that has eased their living conditions. Today, with their status in Israel at least temporarily resolved and with social and economical integration, Ben Ammi preaches a common heritage for African Americans and Jews.[105] Due to continued recruitment by Hebrew Israelite missionaries, in addition to the 3,000 people settled in Israel there are also other communities and numerous followers in Chicago, South Africa, Ghana, and other African countries who read the New Testament, do not study the Talmud, and observe Jewish festivals and religious practices. Overall, Ben Ammi's Hebrew Israelites have the distinction of being an international organization with roots in both Israeli and African American soil, including a number of non–African American members. As pointed out by Ethan Michaeli, "The Hebrew Israelites appear to be successfully navigating between African American groups such as the Nation of Islam, American Jewish organizations, and the Israeli government—groups that are often in conflict with one another. Moreover, the Hebrew Israelites have demonstrated that all borders are porous by adding Israeli political and cultural views to their core of African American religious beliefs."[106]

The Hebrew Israelites also find kinship, common doctrine, and musical sympathies with Rastafarians, who refer to many of the same biblical associations and traditions.

The Rastafarians in Jamaica

The Rastafarian movement, born in Jamaica, has many deep connections with Judaism. From the 1930s on, the Rastafarian movement acquired great moral authority in Jamaica owing to its pioneering approach to the questions of racial identity and skin color, as well as its important role in Jamaican culture. As in the United States, resistance in Jamaica was characterized by religion and by proposals modeled on those of Zionism. The need for a physical identification led Rastafarians to a personal rewriting of biblical history, in which they spread the subversive image of a black God, and to declaring the Jewish ancestors of the emperor—Solomon, Moses, and Jesus—as also being black.

The Rastafarian current arose from the metamorphosis of religious fact into an anticolonialist weapon underlying most Jamaican revolts. One century after the abolition of slavery in Jamaica (1838), the social reality of Jamaicans remained quite unchanged. During the Great Depression, Jamaica experienced multiple strikes and riots;[107] in addition, following the religious reawakening

(Great Revival) of the 1860s, a multitude of syncretist sects and para-Christian schisms appeared.[108] Up to the 1950s, expressions of so-called Revivalist cults existed in Jamaica, which combined elements inherited from African traditions and Protestant religion.[109] As noted by Boris Lutanie, "the climate of social dispute constitutes a 'religiogenic' factor in which the diversion from official religion must be considered as an attempt for emancipation."[110]

This movement derived its name from the term *ras Tafari*, which referred to Prince Tafari Makonnen, who became Haile Selassie, the new emperor of Ethiopia in 1930. His coronation in front of a gathering of kings, princes, and rulers of Western countries held great significance for the Africans of the continent and elsewhere. Since the Middle Ages, Ethiopian nobility claimed to be descendants of King Solomon and the queen of Sheba. The new emperor, by assuming the titles of "King of Kings" and "Conquering Lion of the Tribe of Judah," reaffirmed the ancient roots of Ethiopian civilization and its independent place in Judeo-Christian traditions—not to mention the fact that the Conquering Lion of Judah was the image used by the prophet Isaiah to name the Messiah. In 1916, in a Jamaican church, Garvey had implored his people to "look to Africa for the crowning of a King to know that your redemption is nigh," a prophecy he updated in 1927 upon returning from Jamaica to the United States. Consequently, the crowning of Haile Selassie fulfilled Garvey's prophecy, and Ethiopianism acquired a revolutionary dimension in Jamaica.[111] About the birth of the movement in the 1930s, Chevannes wrote:

> Looking to Africa, looking also to the Bible, a few followers of Garvey concluded that Ras Tafari must be the Messiah come back to redeem his people. The titles he bore, the homage paid by the White world through the heads and representatives of state, the antiquity of Ethiopia, and its mention in both Old and New Testament of the Bible, the Solomonic claim—like so many rivulets building up into a mighty river, all swept them away with the powerful conviction that Ras Tafari was none other than Jesus Christ and he was Black. Now did the Song of Solomon (1:5–6) make sense: I am black but comely.[112]

From a theological point of view, the impulse of the Rastafarian movement was based on the representation of a black God, the circulation of pious images representing a black Christ in street meetings, which triggered adherence and "conversion" to the movement. God was not only black but lived physically among them, and because blackness was a divine attribute, all Africans shared this divinity. Socially, the message found a fertile ground among urban masses as well as country folk and spread as a result of mass immigration toward

Cuba and the United States.[113] From the movement's beginning, the sacred wearing of "dreadlocks," considered as being based on biblical principles, the use of marijuana (ganja smoking),[114] and a Rasta language (Rasta-talk)[115] became the symbols of Rastafarianism, while musical messages inciting rebellion of the black supremacy type can be mixed with this.[116] Three men, Leonard Percival Howell, the pillar of Rastafarianism, Archibald Dunkley, and Joseph Hibbert, were, independently of one another, the architects of the Rastafarian movement. They relied on Garvey's "back-to-Africa" message and supported the divinity of Haile Selassie.[117] Evoking the return to the promised land, Garvey's slogan gave birth to numerous failed attempts at "repatriation," such as the one carried out by Reverend Claudius Henry in 1959. Henry, who proclaimed himself the "Moses of the Blacks," sold thousands of cards, for one shilling each, that made it possible to return to the homeland, and on which was written, "Pioneering Israel, scattered children of African origin, back home to Africa. This year 1959, deadline date–Oct. 5th; this new government is God's righteous Kingdom of Everlasting Peace on Earth.... No passport will be necessary for those returning to Africa."[118]

Lacking any organization or hierarchy, these groups shared professions of faith that mixed interpretations of the Bible, links with the history of the Jewish people, and faith in an Ethiopian Saviour God, who would liberate them and deliver them from the oppression they now suffer, in the "Satanic Babylon under White domination."[119] In Rastafarian worship, logical and theological rigor is less decisive than the commitment to faith: sources of religious evocation are mixed, and doctrinal discrepancies are frequent. While the name of Jesus might be mentioned in some groups, and a selective reading of the gospel is sometimes practiced, there are ceremonies in which "Jerusalem My Happy Home" is sung. In some groups elements of Hebrew-based worship, close to Falasha's heterodox Judaism, are introduced, such as the purification of women, fasting, and the interdiction to touch the dead.[120]

In the 1968s, a group composed of urban middle-class Jamaicans and including a few white members proclaimed itself the Twelve Tribes of Israel. The founder was Vernon Carrington, called Gad (in Jamaican, "a" is pronounced "o"), who had been a member of the Ethiopian World Federation, a Revivalist and a Rastafarian at the same time.[121] Carrington undertook a systematic study of the Bible, in parallel with books on Judaism and Egyptian and Ethiopian religions. He consequently developed a personal synthesis of Judaism and Christianity, mixed with cabalistic numerology, genealogy, astrology, and Rastafarianism. The members of this group revere Carrington as a prophet and consider Haile Selassie as the new Messiah. More organized than other Rastafarian communities that believe in total individualism, this group distinguishes itself by a number of practices and beliefs such as the mandatory daily reading of the Bible and the attribution to each member of the name of the tribe corresponding to his or her month of birth, according to the zodiac used by the ancient Hebrews. The return to the promised land of Rastafarians remained nonetheless a discreet event: in 1968, Carrington founded the only Rastafarian community of Ethiopia, bringing with him twelve men and twelve women chosen to symbolize the Twelve Tribes of Israel.[122] In October 2004, when I met this group settled at Shashemene in Ethiopia, the community comprised 150 families, for a total of 400 members, either descendants of the founders or others who arrived more recently from the United States, Great Britain, or Australia. Brother Bunny, who arrived twenty-eight years ago from Jamaica, said to me that Rastafarians were the only descendants of Abraham, Jacob, and David, the keepers of the Ark of Covenant, which was located not far from there in Debre Zion.[123] Answering my question about the religious practices of the group, he told me that the service, which the representatives of the Twelve Tribes of Israel attended, was led by the "Levites."

Among black Jews, Hebrew Israelites, and Rastafarians, the ideology of black Judaism has offered a set of powerful symbols concerning the genuine identity and divine mission of people of African descent. These conceptions stand in contrast to the damaging messages that were incorporated in the racist devaluation by white society. The new identity that asserts lineage from the biblical Hebrews is free of the effects of the social past and cultural deprivation. As part of this process, as defined by Clifford Geertz, the prior emotional state of suffering of members is placed "in a meaningful context, providing a mode of action through which it can be expressed, being expressed understood, and being understood, 'endured' or even transcended."[124]

The broad lines of the construction of these movements in the United States give us insight into the genesis of African Jewish movements. African encounter with Judaism exhibits a range of interactive influences and shares major emotional and theoretical characteristics with the African American model, including circumstantial adaptations. The Bible that brought African Americans the narrative account of the Hebrews' destiny is central in the formation of Africans' sacred world. All these movements partly rely on the central narrative of the scriptures as a form of resistance to a feeling of oppression and on a common need to recover identity and history. By claiming that all Africans were Hebrews, Garvey put in place a modern theology, which operated effectively and enabled African Americans to establish a link, via the Kushites or the Sons of Ham, with the most remote ancestors of the Old Testament. The physical identification of African Jews as the descendants of the Ten Tribes of Israel is the contemporary version of the nineteenth-century black American Christians' metaphorical identification with the enslaved Hebrew children.

The construction of the myth of origin of African Judaizing movements draws on structural characteristics of African American Jewish currents. The characteristic rhetoric of these movements owes much to Afrocentric ideas about the past, even if Afrocentrism does not have exactly the same definition among continental or "nondiasporic" African intellectuals.[125] Thus, the Judaizing process among some African societies follows the history of African American movements, which provided the theoretical basis for the identification of Africans with Ethiopians, the latter embodying the Jews of the Bible. In examining the process of Falashisation of the African Americans, we have seen that the black Diaspora in the United States could seek its reflection in an alleged Jewish Diaspora in East Africa.[126] In a circular motion, the affiliation to Judaism of African societies derives in part from the legitimization of African American Jews in the United States and in part from conjunction with the existence and the recognition of the Falasha. Present-day African Jewish identity construction is situated at the crossroads of a double legacy: that of Black American Judaism in its various forms, and the real or imaginary historical contacts of Judaism, in ancient times, with African peoples.

PART III

Africa, Judaism, and African "Jews"

8

Historical Narratives of a Jewish Presence in Sub-Saharan Africa

From Mythical Realities to Historical Metaphors

The Judaizing societies of Africa carry with them the dream of a genesis outside Africa. Beyond realistic generational chains, they revert to an ancient past, which celebrates the name of an original ancestor. These "genealogical dreams" stage their arrival in Africa through elements of an original "otherness" that is both geographical and religious, the primary function of these genealogies being to define the group as non-African.

In the absence of recorded African history, the myths of origin of these societies propose a version of their past based on the historical presence of Jews in Africa. Since the early Middle Ages, legends disseminated among Jews as well as non-Jews, claiming the existence of Jewish kingdoms in eastern and western Africa, gained in popularity and influence. Such genealogies uncovered by the travel accounts of Eldad the Danite in the ninth century, or Benjamin of Tudela in the twelfth century, which still have relevance and resonance for a surprising number of people, are claimed by those in search of a new identity. The accounts of their origin—and particularly their links with Judaism—are fed by mythical narratives according to which their ancestors were the descendants of Abraham and Jacob. The remarkable recurrence of some narrative patterns, such as the theme of the Lost Tribes of Israel or the arrival of Jews in Egypt following Jeremiah after the destruction of the First Temple, represents a complex search for origins, involving multiple dimensions (i.e., ethnic, religious, spatial, historical, social, mythical, linguistic, and more recently genetic). At the same time, these symbolic constructions have proved capable of continuous invention and development in response to new circumstances.

Myth constitutes one of the central mechanisms contributing to the elaboration of these genealogies.[1] Following Mircea Eliade, I am using the concept of myth, which reveals a living pattern rather than a pure fiction, "as a sacred history, and therefore a 'true history,' because it always refers to 'realities,' and at the same time, reveals the irruption of the sacred into the world."[2] In a way, the myth even precedes reality. The psychologist Rollo May writes in his study of myths in the United States, "Myth refers to the quintessence of human experience, the meaning and significance of human life.... The myth is a drama which begins as a historical event and takes on its special character as a way of orienting people towards reality. The myth, or story, carries the values of the society: by the myth the individual finds his sense of identity."[3]

The notion of belonging to the seed of Abraham is a leitmotif in the discourse of groups throughout the world claiming Jewish or Hebrew ancestry or origins. Most marginal Jewish communities, in order to legitimize themselves, make some attempt to show that they have always been Jews and are connected with ancient events and movements of people. So Yemenite Jews maintained that they were the offspring of Jews who migrated to southern Arabia before the destruction of the First Temple (586 BC).[4] In India, Judaizing natives of Kashmir, as well as those of Afghanistan, claim that they descended from the tribe of Judah or Menasseh sent east by Nebuchadnezzar and that many of them spread through India and the surrounding countries.[5] Judaizing Japanese sects claim that their origin is directly traceable to the Land of Israel as descendants of the lost tribe of Zebulun.[6] According to the most widespread Bene Israel tradition, their ancestors had been shipwrecked near the village of Navgaon on the Konkan coast of western India in 175 BC after they had fled Palestine during the persecutions of Antiochus Epiphane.[7] The central myth of origins of the Falasha evokes, in common with Christian Ethiopians, a descent from King Solomon and the queen of Sheba.

The eminently malleable accounts of lineage developed by African Judaizing movements have been attached to the earliest historical hypotheses on the arrival of Jews in Africa. Historians of Africa often write about the place of myth and history in African societies: "Myth ruled history and was responsible for justifying it."[8] The earliest Jewish Diasporas of Africa can easily provide a foundation for the imagination and identity of these Judaizing communities. As Hirschberg points out,

Jewish history in Africa, west of Egypt, begins with some wondrous tales: of the promise of the land of Canaan to the children of Israel, of the withdrawal of the Tyrians and Sidonians, who had controlled the approaches of Egypt to Africa after being expelled from Canaan in the days of Joshua; of David's victory over the Philistine ("Berber") Goliath; of Joab the son of Zeruiah, who pursued the Philistines to the western and southern ends of Africa; of the ships of Tarshish, i.e., Africa; of an ancient synagogue erected in the days of King Solomon; of a stone from the Temple of Solomon which was inserted in the *Ghriba*, the legend-enwreathed synagogue of the island of Jerba-folk traditions and stories collected and recorded on ancient times both by Jewish and Gentile (i.e., Greek and Arab) scholars or transmitted and written down only in recent generations.[9]

I do not intend to enter into historical details over such a long period and over such a vast region. I have selected, from a confusing array of traditions, those events that contributed to the understanding of a collective memory. My ambition is to disentangle—in regions with little written history—the true from the likely and the unlikely. If we consider these mythic genealogies that recount an ancient presence of Jews in Africa and their progression into the interior of the continent as a whole, the dispersion from Egypt constitutes one of the major narrative patterns claiming a Jewish presence in Africa.

The diffusion from Egypt was variously said to have taken place in the time of the Exodus, when some Jews went south along the Nile instead of toward Israel with Moses, or after the destruction of the First Temple in 586 BC, in the wake of Jeremiah, traveling up the Nile through Sudan to Ethiopia. The book of Jeremiah (44:1) mentions several settlements of Jewish colonies in Egypt: Migdol, on a branch of the Nile Delta; Daphne, the former camp of Greek mercenaries; Memphis, the capital city; and, last but not least, "the Country of *Ptrws*" the Egyptian term for "country of the south," the southern province whose capital was Elephantine.[10] The first historical report of the presence of Jews in the area west of Egypt occurred in the context of the controversy of Flavius Josephus against Appion. Josephus notes that during the third century BC, 100,000 Jews were deported from Israel to Egypt; from there, they went to Cyrenaica and probably other countries in northern Africa.[11] The harsh repression of the Jewish rebellion against Roman rule marked the end of the spread of Judaism in Cyrenaica. The Jews scattered; some probably wandered toward Djebel Nafussa, in the hinterland of Tripoli, others toward Egypt, particularly Alexandria and the Maghreb, where they joined existing settlements.[12] One of the hypotheses of a Jewish push toward the Saharan oases, as far as the river Niger, is that it was a consequence of the dispersion that followed the Jewish defeat in AD 115. This hypothesis could be combined with the legends of Jewish kingdoms in Africa and numerous variations about the destiny of the Lost Tribes in the African desert. As we have seen, Delafosse, situated in western Africa, one of the phases of the great extension of the Jews-Syrians, ancestors of the Peul. Legends attributed the origin of the great empire of Ghana to these refugees.[13]

For years, the scholarly consensus was that the Falasha were the descendants of Agaw, who came to Ethiopia through Egypt or South Arabia.[14] The case for diffusion through Egypt rests upon the known presence of Jews in Egypt prior to the Exodus and the existence of the Jewish contingent at Elephantine. This settlement allegedly marked the beginning of the extension of Jewish influences toward the interior of the continent. Among the different theories on the question of Falasha origins, the Lost Tribes view also usually assumes that the path of migration was through Egypt.[15] If the time and the modes of the appearance of a form of Judaizing religion in Ethiopia among the Falasha remain indeterminable, researchers agree on some elements at the origin of one version of the myth.[16] There were certainly Jews in the south of Egypt whose presence could suggest hypotheses of a diffusion of the Falasha from this region. Historians date the settling of Jewish soldiers in the region of Elephantine back to the middle of the seventh century BC, at the time when Menasseh was freed from his Assyrian overlord and was able to provide mercenaries to Egypt in order to obtain their support.[17] The attractiveness of a theory of diffusion of Jews from Egypt is enhanced by the papyri of Elephantine, which provide information on the type of syncretistic Judaism practiced by the Aramaic-speaking community at Elephantine, comparable to aspects of Falasha practice. But, in fact, there is little information on their movements toward the interior of the continent.[18] We know that the garrison of Elephantine was in charge of keeping watch on the southern border, and soldiers were, according to the few available sources, appointed to the escort of caravans toward Nubia, which provided gold, ebony, ivory, animal skins, spices, ostrich feathers, minerals, and slaves.[19] A document mentioned by Porten recounts an expedition in Nubia from Elephantine, just before the Persian conquest, whose convoy included thirty rowers, sixty "Palestinians"—perhaps Jews—fifteen Syrians, and several Egyptians and Nubians.[20]

In conclusion, there is no real evidence either that the Elephantine community was authentically "Israelite" or that it had any bearing at all upon the development of the Falasha community or any other African community. At most it may suggest a new chapter in that history.

From the eleventh century on, Arab travelers spoke of the existence of Jewish groups in Africa, but the *Bilad al-Sudan* and the *Tarikh al-Fattash*, collections of Arab sources on medieval western Africa, give little direct information about the Jews. The existence of black Jews, as suggested by Arab authors, would give some historical support, tenuous as it may be, to the legends of a Jewish kingdom in Africa. Although Arab authors more or less ignored these minorities, which had no specific significance from their point of view, these are the only documents available before the conquest by the French of the Touat area at the beginning of the twentieth century. Then, Arab-speaking French military officers or missionaries collected old documents and attempted to reconstruct local history by questioning the inhabitants.

In *Bilad al-Sudan*, Father Cuoq gathered Arab texts from the eighth to the sixteenth century, covering the area of western Africa to the west of the Nile and the south of the Sahara.[21] Among the Arab authors, al-Bakri (ca. 1014–1094) is considered the greatest geographer of the Muslim West, alongside al-Idrissi (ca. 1100–1165), the best known Arab geographer of the Middle Ages. *Kitab al-Masalik wa l-Mamalik*, the work al-Bakri finished in 1068, is regarded as one of the best sources on the history of these regions during this period.[22] The work was taken up again in the first third of the twelfth century by al-Zurhi's *Djughrafiya*.[23] Later on, in 1154, al-Idrissi wrote *Kitab Radjar* at the request of Roger II of Sicily.[24] This work, in addition to the information on itineraries it provided, established an inventory of peoples and their practices from west to east. Incontestably, the best known of the Arab historians and geographers of Africa was Leo Africanus (ca. 1492–1550), who was born of Arab Muslim parents in Granada and traveled in Africa, visiting Timbuktu and the empires of Mali and Bornu. For many years, his *Description of Africa* was the only source on sub-Saharan Africa and became the major geographical source of knowledge on the continent.[25] Translated in 1556 into both Latin and French, the book had a number of editions in several European languages and carried great authority; it makes frequent mention of Jews in Africa. Leo Africanus tells us that Africans, before being Muslims, had observed the Jewish religion, that there were warrior tribes in the Atlas Mountains claiming descent from King David, that the Canaanites traveled to Africa and were followed later by the Sabeans, and that the ruler of Timbuktu was "the mortal enemy of Jews."[26] According to some Arab historians, when Arab armies penetrated Berber lands in the seventh century, many of the tribes were Jewish or strongly influenced by Judaism. Ibn Khaldun, another great Arab historian, wrote in the fifteenth century:

> It is possible, moreover, that others among those Berber tribes believed in the Jewish religion, which they have received from the Israelites at the time of the expansion of their kingdom to the

neighborhood of Syria and their rule over it. This was true of the Jarawa in the Aures Mountains, the tribe of the Kahina, who was killed by the Arabs at the beginning of the Conquest. This was true also of the Nafusa in Africa, Quandalawqa, Madyuna, Bahlula and Ghiyata and the Banu Bazaz in the outermost Maghreb, until the great Idris (a descendant of Hasan ibn Hasan), who shone forth in the Maghreb, wiped out all the remnants of religions and communities that were in this area.... One of the most respected of them was the Kahina, Daya the daughter of Matyah the son of Tifan, queen of the Aures Mountains; her people were of the Jarawa tribe, kings and leaders of the Butr (a group of Berber Tribes).[27]

Legend recounts that the Kahina was a Jewish Berber queen and a priestess with supernatural powers who was crowned queen of the Maghreb when, at the head of her soldiers mounted on camels, she compelled the Arab general Hassan ibn Numan to retreat. When ibn Numan came back with enormous reinforcements, the Kahina's prophetic talent allowed her to predict the defeat of her people; she ordered her sons to go over to the enemy, and she chose to be killed in action.[28] Later historians all follow ibn Khaldun's footsteps; opinions on the historical value of the Kahina's story and the Judaization of Berbers are divided.

The contribution of these antique sources to research carried out by French colonial agents from the end of the nineteenth century encouraged the perception of traces of a Jewish presence in western Africa. Here we can observe how the myths regarding this presence took root.

Jewish Groups of the Saharan Margins during the Middle Ages

Since ancient times, in the long strip of pre-Saharan territories, which spread from Alexandria to the mouth of the Wadi Draa, "local traditions can be found everywhere that attest the ancient existence of sedentary Jewish populations, to whom the introduction of certain techniques might be linked (metallurgy and well boring)."[29] Jews were able to reach the regions of western Africa, Ghana, Mali, Bornu, and Songhai by settling in important places, trading posts, and markets, through which transited the trade from Maghreb to Sudan.[30] The *triq lemtouni*, the earliest trans-Saharan trail, established a link from Fez and Marrakesh to Walata and Timbuktu through the western Sahara and Mauritania; it eventually created a network that connected with all the great North African centers to Timbuktu. As the new crossroads attracted settlements, it seems that Jews were among them from the first.[31] The usual occupations of these Jews from the southern Maghreb, that is, traders and goldsmiths or silversmiths, brought them into contact with West African populations who provided gold dust. Because black Africa lacked salt, horses, and manufactured goods, its people exchanged gold and slaves for goods brought by North African traders. Gold extracted from the mines of Senegal, Mali, and the northeast of the Gold Coast was the main object of trans-Saharan trade. In Muslim lands, Muslims were theoretically prohibited from owning or trading in gold.[32] It seems that this is why the Jews were present near production centers, why they took part in the caravans that carried gold, and why coin makers and goldsmiths who worked and sold the gold were often Jews.[33]

Michel Abitbol pointed to the presence of various Jewish groups on the Saharan confines before the Middle Ages: some Jews lived in Taghawust and Goulimine, the last two Moroccan posts on the trans-Saharan Atlantic route before entering the desert. Farther to the east, a small Caraite Jewish "kingdom" is said to have existed in the Draa valley, until the beginning of the eleventh century. Its existence is plausible, given the fragmented political situation of the region at the time and the anteriority of Jewish traditions in the area.[34] If these Jewish "states" existed, their economic viability rested on trade with Sudan. If one believes the local tradition, one of the earliest Jewish communities of the area lived in Ifran, where the caravan of the Moroccan Sous left for Senegal. According to legends gathered by travelers, the members of this community claimed that their ancestors came from Palestine, via the edge of the Sahara, at the time of Nebuchadnezzar.[35] In the Tafilalelt, Sijilmassa, located at the crossroads between central Maghreb and western Sudan, was a city of rich merchants, a hub for trans-Saharan trade. It was fought over by North African dynasties. Before the destruction of its Jewish community by the Almohads (1050), it was an important center of Jewish civilization; this is confirmed by the well known Andalusian poet and rabbi Abraham Ibn Ezra (1092–1167), who wrote that it was a "city of sages and *Gueonim*, who maintained constant contact with the Talmudic schools of Mesopotamia, Egypt, North Morocco and Spain."[36] From the eleventh to the thirteenth century, under Almoravid (1070–1147) and Almohad (1130–1269) rule, the political unification of the western Maghreb was followed by the establishment of rigid Islamic law and the creation of a homogeneous religious society that gradually extinguished any particularism.[37] The Almohads were merciless toward the Jews who refused to convert to Islam. After a century of Almohad persecution, numerous Jewish communities had ceased to exist. Abraham Ibn Ezra recounted in his elegy, *Aha Yarad*, the extent of the disaster that fell on the Jews of Kairwan, Sfax, Gabes, and Meknes, who were massacred just before those of Fez and Marrakesh.[38] Even though the deterioration of the Jewish condition was not entirely uniform, from the time Almoravid authorities took control of North African trade by supervising all axes of communication, the situation was particularly unfavorable to the commerce of North African Jews, who turned to trade with India without entirely abandoning Saharan routes.[39]

On the Algerian-Moroccan border, according to a local chronicle discovered at the beginning of the twentieth century by the French A. G. P. Martin, the very earliest Jewish inhabitants of Touat and Gurara settled in the first century AD coming from Cyrenaica, and were followed by a second wave of settlers who arrived with Arab traders from Mossul.[40] The making of *foggara* (underground water pipes) in Touat, based on a model that previously existed in Mesopotamia, confirms that this know-how "seems to have originated from Persia and to date back to very ancient antiquity. They were mentioned as far back as the fifth century BC in Herodotus."[41] Another tradition from the region of Tuggurt, in the northeast of Touat, reveals that the Jewish population is so ancient that they are considered the earliest white inhabitants of the area:

> In the most ancient period whose tradition was conserved by memory, the country was inhabited by Jews who employed Negro workers and who owned *ksours* and palm groves.... One day, a man of the Beni-Merine named al-Hagj Slimane al-Merini al-Djellabi came from the Maghreb... it was around the 7th century (14th century AD). Several years after his arrival, he issued an edict stipulating that, within three days, all of the Jews had to become Muslims or leave the country. Most of them emigrated and those who remained were named *Mehadjerin* (expatriates).... The *Mehadjerin* are of Jewish race; they are the last descendants of the ancient Jews of Touat, and although they became Muslims, they continue to live and marry among themselves.[42]

This supports the allegation of G. Rohlfs, a German explorer who met this people in the nineteenth century and specified that "they say that they are descendants of Jews, but there is no evidence to confirm this origin,"[43] one can believe it because of the mixing with black populations.

In Touat, the gateway to Sudan, the Jewish community was very active up to the fifteenth century, as the Tlemcen-Touat-Niger trail was one of the main routes for Saharan trade. Touat was also linked to central Maghreb by the Mzab trail, with its Jewish communities of Wargla and Tuggurt.[44] In 1447, Antonio Malfante, a Genovese Christian, undertook a voyage to Touat. The letter he

North and West African regions concerned by a Jewish presence in the Middle Ages

wrote during his stay, between Tlemcen and Tamentit, is of great interest as regards the presence and prosperity of Jews in these regions at that time:

> Here Jews abound, they live in peace, under the rule of various masters each of whom defends his subordinates; they thus have a very peaceful social life. Trade is practiced here through their

intermediary and there are several who can be wholly trusted. This territory is a stopover point in Moorish country, where merchants bring and sell their goods; the gold brought here is purchased from those who come from the coast.... The Arabs... bring grain and barley here, which is sold all year long... but they have fierce enemies whose territory they do not dare cross, the Philistines.[45]

Philistines is the name given by Malfante to the Touareg, whose attacks reduced the number of caravans heading south, and it is possible to deduce that the Jews, who attempted to cross Touareg territories, were heading for Sudan.

Leo Africanus's testimony is the best source of information on the status of the Jews in the provinces bordering western Africa, as well as on their travels. He tells us that, at the beginning of the sixteenth century, Jewish merchants and craftsmen were living in the Wadi Nun, where the great annual gathering of Moroccan caravans took place: "[the caravans] that go to Timbuktu and Walatta in the country of the Blacks," as in Tiyout and Tedsi, where the importance of Jews in economic life is such that "they are not submitted to any tribute (*djizya*), they simply have to give some gifts to the noblemen." He also specified that in the neighboring city of Tedsi, about twenty kilometers from Taroudant, there lived "many Jewish workers such as goldsmiths, and ironsmiths," and that this city welcomed "the people who practice trade with the country of the Blacks."[46] Leo Africanus also noted the presence in the Draa of many Jewish traders, craftsmen, and goldsmiths, "on the route from Fez to Tombutto," as well as in the Filalian *ksours* of Tabu'samt and al-Ma'mum, and provided interesting indications about their travels: "There are ... some rich gentlemen (Jews) and many of them go to the country of the blacks whence they bring back goods from Berberia which they trade for gold and slaves."[47] In the Gheris, Jewish traders passing through were the only ones who had to pay a tax of a fourth of one gold *mithcal* per person, which tells us something about the mobility of Jewish traders in this region.[48]

We know, too, from the visit of Leo Africanus to Gurara around 1506, that "many Jews had lived there," and that "they were victims of a strange persecution in the year of the fall of Granada."[49] This Jewish community would have been condemned in 1492 by the decision of Cheikh Abd-al-Karim al-Meghili, who offered seven *mithcals* of gold to whoever would kill a Jew and ordered the destruction of the synagogue of Tamentit and the other synagogues of Touat. While some Jews could have fled northward or westward, some of the survivors would have been able to go farther south to the Sahara, toward the kingdom of

Gao, along the caravan routes. Soon after, we learn from Leo Africanus that, under the influence of the same al-Meghili, the Askya Muhammad the Great, ruler of Songhai, made an edict to expel the Jews from his kingdom and that Jews were obliged to either apostatize or die.[50] It seems that the policy of the Askya Muhammad was to put an end to all Jewish presence in the Niger basin,[51] but such measures against the Jews make sense only if Jews were numerous in the area.

There is evidence for the presence of Jews from ancient times in the Djerid, in Tozeur, Nafwasa, and Matmata. On the border between Tunisia and Tripolitania, Ghadames accommodated an ancient Jewish community whose existence is referred to in rabbinic texts.[52] In the Djebel Nafusa, vestiges of a Jewish quarter were discovered in the city of Sharus, which was crossed by the Tripoli-Sudan caravan trail. According to al-Bakri, in the eleventh century, in Djaddu, the starting point of the trail to the Kanem via the Fezzan, there lived "a large population of Jews."[53] Another piece of information is provided by Benjamin of Tudela, who left us a few lines, dating from around 1173, about their caravan journeys to black Africa: "It is a twelve-day journey from Aswan to Haluan, where there are some 300 Jews. From there they travel for 50 days by caravan, through the great desert called Sahara, to the city of Zavila, called Havilah in the Scriptures, into the land of Ghana....This land is located on the western side of Kush, which is called al-Hasbah."[54]

All this plausibly suggests an uninterrupted chain of Jewish colonies up to the border of the Sahara, scattered from the Atlantic Ocean to the Libyan Desert, whose economic life and longevity depended at least in part on the trans-Saharan trade. One can suppose that the Jews of Saharan caravans who traveled down toward Senegal and Niger were certain to meet communities of coreligionists, which enabled them to endure the insecurity of their travels and separation from their traditions. The importance of the trans-Saharan trade, which, as in the Touat, constituted the main resource of its Jewish inhabitants, led them to ask the rabbis of Algiers to study the religious problems with which the peddlers were confronted as regards the question of the risk of profanation of the Shabbat. The rabbinic jurisprudence in matters of trans-Saharan trade, the *responsa*, constitutes an important testimony of a Jewish presence in the Saharan confines, because the rabbis were required to create specific rulings on the risk of desecration of the Sabbath due to desert crossings. For those who could not leave the caravan on the weekly day of rest, Rabbi Isaac Bar-Sheshet Barfat (1326–1408) made the decision, which became law, to authorize caravaneers to continue their travel during Sabbath, under the condition that they began their travel at least three days before.[55]

If Jews participated in the trans-Saharan trade, did they have access to Sudanese trade centers, and did they found a lineage? Arab sources and certain traditions of western Africa, suggest that they did.

A Jewish Presence in Mauritania and Sudan in the Middle Ages

In Mauritania, according to Arab sources and certain oral traditions of western Africa, the first inhabitants of western Africa were the Bafour, whose Jewish origin is enigmatic and controversial. Following a process of organization, functioning, and decline of all Sudanese empires described by Charles Monteil,[56] one might assume that a Bafour empire existed several centuries before Islam.[57] These Bafour seemed to have introduced the cultivation of palm trees, horse breeding, new irrigation methods, and metallurgy. According to a tradition reported by André J. Lucas, "The Bafour were the first ones to plant palm trees and to dig deep and large wells. The *Mu'almin* (craftsmen) make, and have always made, works of art. They are called *Yahoud* because, according to legend, only Jews in Mauritania were craftsmen. And you know that the *Mu'almin* have neither homeland nor tribe."[58]

This tradition is also mentioned in the *Qartas* of Ibn Abi Zar (?–1320), who noted the presence of Jews of Arab origin in a place called Teklessyn, which resisted the Almoravids. In the Middle Ages, according to Ibn Abi Zar, the name of Baghara (Wangara) designated both the region located on the upper Senegal and its inhabitants. These people waged war against their Sanhâja neighbors, who were Berbers converted to Islam; "these tribes lived in the neighbourhood of Teklessyn; they were Arabs and practiced the Jewish religion."[59]

Al-Idrissi's testimony informs us that the Bafour spread out in the west of Mauritania and on the Atlantic coast when they were persecuted by the Almoravids: "To this important Bafor dispersion of the Judaized Blacks of Adrar and Tagant, one must add the Bafor fraction that lives on fish on the coast."[60] Al-Idrissi summarized the situation of some of these groups at the time following the Almoravids, "Only a small group of people from Kamnuria remain, scattered between these deserts and near the coast and living off dairy products or fish. They lead a hard and precarious life, they wander in this territory."[61]

According to Charles Monteil, the repression first by the Almoravids, then more pronouncedly in the sixteenth century, pushed a part of the Judaized Bafour to the south of the Senegal River, where they are thought to have merged with the Wolof populations and were named Sebe Baor by the Peul.[62] The oral tradition that presents the fishermen of the Mauritanian coast, the

Imraguen, Shnagla, and Ouled Ahmed ben Dahman, as descendants of the ancient Bafour, corroborates al-Idrissi's account, and observers noted that they concealed their Jewish origin.[63]

Al-Idrissi provides us substantial information about the presence of Jews, near the country of gold in western Sudan, or present-day Mali: "There are only two cities in this land of Lamlam, which are not larger than villages. One is called Malla and the other Daw.... According to the people of this region, the inhabitants are Jews, but most of them are submerged in impiety and ignorance."[64] He adds, "The inhabitants of Kamnuria following the sayings of merchants claim to be Jews ... their beliefs are a mixture of everything, they are nothing and have no well established belief."[65] Information from his contemporary al-Zuhri, who probably quoted his predecessors' work, supports the account of al-Idrissi: "The inhabitants of Karafun (in the region of Timbuktu) follow the Jewish religion. One can get there from Gao and Wargla. They read the *Tawrat* (Thora). They import silk cloth, saffron, tinted goods, tar, cauris, pearls."[66]

It is tempting to merge this information about a Jewish presence in the south of Sahara with the tradition of Eldad the Danite, who, in the ninth century, claimed that Jewish tribes ruled these regions. However, this claim has been strongly challenged by Raymond Mauny, who considers that these black groups were probably Soninke, who were conquered and dispersed by the neighboring Berbers and who were not really Islamized in the time of al-Idrissi:

> It is therefore not surprising that, a century later, they are presented as professing a religion that was a mixture of all sorts of things and that as they were not considered as Muslims by the Arabs, and not wanting to be called heathens so as to avoid the fate reserved by Islam for idolaters; these Soninke simply declared themselves as Jews, thus People of the Book, and as such were only subject to a special tax, the *Kharâj*, whereas had they been called heathens, and they would sooner or later have been condemned to slavery.[67]

One remark is nonetheless necessary regarding Mauny's reflections: to call themselves Jews suggests that the Soninke must have had some knowledge of Jews in the south of the Sahara.

The *Ta'rikh al-Fattash* also mentions the existence of a colony of Banu' Isra'il, living at Tendirma, in the southeast of Timbuktu: "In the place where the city of Tendirma was founded in 1496, an Israelite population had formerly lived whose wells and tombs still remained. These Jews, who inhabited the place until the fifteenth century, lived on agriculture and had dug wells because they grew vegetables which they sold, and for which merchants paid them considerable amounts of money."[68]

This small Jewish colony would have been condemned in the fifteenth century by the decision taken at the instigation of al-Meghili, who already exterminated the Jews from Touat and convinced the Askya Muhammad, the ruler of Timbuktu, forbidding Jews to enter his territory, which at that time covered the entire Sahelian region.[69]

The evidence of later travelers supports the existence of a Jewish presence in West Africa. At the end of the eighteenth century, the Scottish explorer Mungo Park noted the presence of Jews in the region of Timbuktu. Under the protection of the Touareg and Moors, from whom they were indistinguishable, it seems that they practiced Islam in appearance only and that they ensured their ethnic continuity through endogamy.[70] Mungo Park's testimony is supported by a later nineteenth-century source. Mardochée Aby Serour, a travelling rabbi and a travel companion of Charles de Foucauld, was offered hospitality by a tribe, the Daggatun, who lived among the Awllimiden Touareg and who claimed Jewish origin.[71] This group, which was settled in a territory extending from the Air to the Niger River by way of the Adrar of Ifora, did not mix with the other subjects of the Awllimiden Touareg. They freely asserted their ancient Jewish identity before the Awllimiden, of whom they were vassals. The testimony of the Daggatun, whose customs otherwise showed no trace of Jewish traditions, recalls the epic of the Touati Jews and their possible dispersal in the desert. Aside from the picturesqueness of Mardochée's account, nothing enables us to determine their origin,[72] any more than the origin of other groups living among the Touareg, such as the Ida Oushaq (or Dawsahak, sons of Isaac), the Igdalen, the Inhaden reputed to be of Jewish origin.[73] According to Henri Lhote, "The Inhaden are descendants of the Jews of Touat, where they practiced the craft of smiths and jewellers....The Inhaden are the artisan cast of the Touareg. Enad means 'the other' and, by extension, the one who is not named. The Touareg fear them also because of the supernatural powers, witchcraft and magic they attribute to them."[74]

These tribes could stem from portions of the Jewish Touati people, who found refuge with the Touareg; or is it possible that they were descendants of Jewish caravaneers raided in the desert? We shall see later that the massacre of the Touati Jews and the refuge that some survivors found in the region of Timbuktu shaped the popular consciousness and gave rise to local myths of groups who claim to be descendants of Touati Jews.

Farther south, in Sudan, the existence of a small Jewish community is noted by Valentim Fernandes in the beginning of the sixteenth century, in his

Descripçao: "In Walata, there were very rich and oppressed Jews, who are either peddlers, or goldsmiths or jewellers."[75] In another passage, Fernandes also tells of the presence of Jews farther west: "In this country (Gyloffa or Wolof country) and in Mandinga there are Jews, and they are called Gaul and they are black like the people of the country; however they do not have synagogues and do not practice the ceremonies of other Jews. They live separately from the other Blacks in their villages; these Gaul are often jesters."[76] Then follows a description of the griots, a marginal caste in western Africa, which suggests a confusion of Fernandes between Jews and griots. Mauny tells us that the term for *griot* is *gaulo* in Peul, which supports the confusion, even if Fernandes's testimony found an echo in the writings of J. Münzer, who affirmed in 1500: "Some of them, Blacks, are Jewish. They are called Garol in their language and are much hated."[77]

The most obvious evidence, however, of the economic activity of the North African Jews, of their role in trans-Saharan trade, and their presence in sub-Saharan Africa is found in the Majorcan Jewish geographers' portolans of the fourteenth and fifteenth centuries. In the fourteenth and fifteenth centuries in the Balearic Islands a center of studies flourished that provided scientific equipment for navigators such as astrolabes, compasses, and world maps. Majorcan cartographers Angelino Dulcert, Abraham and Yehuda Cresques, Mecia of Viladestes, and Petrus Roselli were all Jewish or of Jewish origin.[78] It seems likely that links existed between Spanish Jews, particularly those of the Balearic Islands, and their coreligionists of the Saharan edge of Africa. Charles de la Roncière informs us, "When the Majorcans began to make maps in the fourteenth century, they had firsthand information on the interior of the black continent, where other Jews were trading from south Moroccan (or Algerian) cities, with the countries situated in the south of Sahara and particularly, the empire of Mali."[79]

In 1339, Angelo Dulcert's map revealed the location of Mali and Walata, as well as the existence of a "*Rex Melli*, rich in gold,"[80] while the Catalan atlas of Abraham Cresques (1375) indicated the location of Tenbuch (Timbuktu). For de la Roncière, who devoted himself to a comparison of the maps developed during the Middle Ages, the astonishing precision of details provided by Majorcan geographers could only come from their Saharan informers, the Jewish caravaneers who traveled back and forth across the desert. Their maps were not limited to a political description of the countries located south of the Sahara, based on Arab geographers:"When we examine the maps of Africa produced (by Majorcan workshops), and compare them with Arabian maps, we can immediately see an essential difference, the former detail caravan routes and routes familiar (to Jews) whereas the latter are designed for political purposes.... Majorcan maps have a flexibility of expression that attests to close contact with reality."[81]

Exhibiting very clear advances in comparison with former maps, Majorcan portolans gave detailed information about the main caravan routes and the names of the main Saharan and Sudanese sites. Thus, in 1439, Angelino Dulcert was able to locate Mali (Melli), as well as the Walata (Huletem). His planisphere also indicates the trail connecting Sijilmassa to Walata, via Buda in Touat, which was used only as of the fourteenth century for safety reasons.[82] The high point of knowledge on the interior of the African continent was reached with the Catalan atlas by Abraham Cresques, which was used in large part by Mecia of Viladestes (1413) and Gabriel of Vallescha Ibn Krish (1439). Departing from the Draa, "which is crossed by the traders who enter the land of the Guinea's Negroes," Cresques went down to Sahara, "a region inhabited by people with covered mouths" and who "make caravans with camels."[83] Taghawust (Tagaost) "is the first step of the voyage towards the country of Mousamelli (Mali), lord of the Negroes of Guinea, the richest and noblest king of the whole region, so abounds the gold in his country." [84] This Catalan atlas also indicates the stopping points of the Sijilmassa-Timbuktu (Tenbuth) trail, via Taghazza (Tagazza), and the location of Gao and Sokoto (Zoghde).[85]

When the Jewish cartographic school of the Balearic Islands flourished, it seems that the Jews knew the Sahara and Sudan quite well and had traveled throughout their territories; this is confirmed by the testimony of Arab travelers. The involvement of Jews in trans-Saharan trade appears undeniable, even if it is not possible to assess whether small groups of isolated individuals could have founded a line of descent in Sahara or Sudan. Their banishment from the region of Songhai at the end of the fifteenth century, mentioned by Leo Africanus, seems to provide confirmation of their presence in Sudan, in a territory that would now include the southern part of Mauritania, the Niger basin, and the east of Senegal.

Conclusions about earlier periods are highly speculative. One might hypothesize that part of the Judeo-Berber populations were Judaized before the arrival of Arab-Muslims in the seventh century, and that these groups did not all adhere to Islam. One might also consider that Jewish groups, having imprecise contours, had a long-standing presence in Ghana and Mali until their destruction by the Almoravids in the eleventh century. Furthermore, if we take into account sources showing that Jewish traders and caravaneers did indeed crisscross the Sahara, we can imagine how a kind of mythology of African Judaism might have been created. Further, it is possible that centuries of Islamization would not necessarily obliterate some legacy of Judaism among the groups descended from these ancient Jews. In this case, some traces of Jewish culture might have survived in the subterranean memory of individuals or groups, as suggested in general by Freud. This mental process, which is similar to Freud's "return of the repressed," by which repressed elements are never entirely destroyed and reappear in a distorted way, might be at work and reveal surviving elements linked to ancient and repressed Jewish traditions.[86] Traces of Judaism were found in the 1950s among these populations by Charles Monteil, who asserts that the marabouts possessed Jewish books translated into Arabic, which they used as a source of occult science. Monteil also collected a number of legends, which, according to him, have a direct Hebrew origin, and he noted that the most noble and most humble fractions of the Sudanese people still assert that they are descendants of Jews.[87] Knowing the inclination of colonial agents to perceive Judaism in unlikely places, it is advisable to remain cautious about such assertions.

This debate has recently been reopened. Dierk Lange, a professor of African history at the University of Bayreuth (Germany), in *Ancient Kingdoms of West Africa: Africa-Centred and Canaanite-Israelite Perspective* (2004), using hitherto unexplored sources, presents the development of the West African empires of Ghana, Mali, and Songhay from a new perspective of ethnogenesis.[88] He maintains that the main clan and state structures of several West African kingdoms are based on the same dualistic pattern as that of the Canaanite-Israelite and hence also Phoenician societies. Supported by written records, oral traditions, and cult-dramatic performances, these similarities suggest the existence of early trans-Saharan contacts reaching back to the pre-Roman period.[89] The Phoenician trade appears to have been the single most important factor explaining the transfer of these organizational forms from North Africa to the sub-Saharan region,[90] where they could be particularly prominent in the Hausa and Yoruba societies. The Hausa and Yoruba traditions are considered by Lange as a phenomenon of *longue durée* that can be traced back to an Israelite model based on Canaanite antecedents. According to Lange, similar social institutions were transmitted from the Semitic world to the Horn of Africa, as a result of the ancient myrrh and frankincense trade, and some of these polities grew so powerful that they conquered and controlled a number of kingdoms in West and East Africa.[91]

Although these ideas have been branded as diffusionist and Hamitic, Lange's approach to Africa's regional history is a bold attempt to place East and West Africa kingdoms in the context of ancient Near Eastern history and culture. Lange's hypotheses represent a real challenge to the present paradigm of African history and open up new perspectives for research.

A Jewish Presence on the West African Coast and Islands

The Cape Verde Islands, which had been discovered between 1455 and 1462, were from 1472 essentially a slave-trading place, restricted to an exclusive monopoly of the Portuguese Crown. Despite the important role of Portuguese Jews in commerce, navigation, and cartography of Africa, as early as 1480 they faced profound oppression during the Spanish and Portuguese Inquisitions, when they became termed Marranos, or Judeos Segredos (Secret Jews). It was, however, in 1492 that the Spanish Inquisition developed its fullest expression of anti-Semitism, which quickly spread to Portugal. In 1496, King Manuel I of Portugal decided to exile thousands of Jews to São Tomé, Príncipe, and Cape Verde. Those who were not expelled were converted by force or executed. In the sixteenth century, during the persecution of the Jews in Portugal, an entire colony came to settle in Cape Verde, despite the opposition of Philip III of Spain, then king of Portugal.[92]

Despite their exile or *degredado* (convict) status, the small number of Europeans and Jews residing in Cape Verde were allowed to engage in trade, as long as they did not compete with the royal trading monopolies. The Crown, in the sixteenth and seventeenth centuries, encouraged the traders, converts or expelled Jews from Portugal, to settle along the Senegambia and upper Guinea coast to trade for ivory, hides, slaves, gold, gum, wax, and amber while based in Cape Verde.[93] Those traders, usually called *lançados*, were often but not always of Jewish origin. The term *lançados* derives from the Portuguese verb for "to throw out" and is related to outcast or fugitive roles in Portuguese-African coastal commerce. Christian *lançados* were also known, most of them being fugitives for some political crime. By the early 1600s, Cape Verdean *lançados* had trading centers all along the Senegambian coast at places such as Goree and Joal a Portuguese town in Gambia, and Ziguinchor in the Casamance and farther down the Guinea Coast.[94] In 1614, the governor of Cape Verde recorded that the greatest number of *lançados* were Jews. Jews from Cape Verde and Portugal were already known in Joal as early as 1591, and a synagogue was noted there in 1641 by Jorge de Castilho, governor of Cape Verde.[95] In 1606, in Portudal, and according to Father Baltazar Barreira on the Senegalese coast, there were 100 Portuguese "following the law of Moses."[96] In 1622, the Cape Verdean governor, Dom Fransisco de Mourra, reported to the Portuguese king that the Guinea coastal rivers "were full of Jews who were masters of the local regions and were quite independent of the Crown."[97] In the seventeenth century, while retaining their bases in the Cape Verde Islands and in Guinea, the Portugueses withdrew from Senegambia. During this period, the term *ganagoga*, which named people who were able to speak many local languages, was used in the Upper Guinea and Cape Verde region to imply Jewish *lançados*.[98]

Even if the anti-Semitism of Spain and Portugal and the financial interests of the Portuguese Crown were constantly trying to restrict their success, Jewish *lançados* played a central role in the economy and society. Because of their collaborative relation with African cultures and the fact that they had African wives, their multiracial and multicultural identity contributed widely to the cultural-linguistic mixture that constitutes the Cape Verdean Creole culture.[99] In 1698, a testimony of the French traveler Lemaire confirmed the intermixing of Jews with the local population, the second generation being more mixed and superficially converted to Catholicism: "Other than these three groups, there is one that is a kind of Portuguese, mulattos; people call them so because they had served them in the past and because they are descendants of the first inhabitants of this coast.... From the Negro women they married Mulattos were born.... As they followed the religion of their former masters, they are part Jew, part Catholic... not more one than the other."[100]

Historically, Jews first came to the island of São Tiago during the Inquisition and were confined to a separate community in Praia. From the nineteenth century, other Jews of Moroccan origin joined this colony.[101] There are still traces of their presence in the village of Santo Antao, located on the northern coast, where a village named Sinagoga evokes an ancient Jewish presence. A number of steles with Hebrew inscriptions, discovered in the Boa Vista and the Ponta da Sol cemeteries, indicate that Jews, probably emigrants from Morocco, lived on this island in the nineteenth century. Some of their descendants left it after the creation of the State of Israel in 1948, leaving behind a mixed population with Jewish-Moroccan patronymics.[102]

Traces of a Jewish presence are to be found, too, in São Tomé. The São Tomé islands were discovered in 1472, probably devoid of native populations, during an expedition by two Portuguese pilots, Joao de Santarem and Pero de Escobar. It was only in 1485 that the Portuguese king became interested in them and took measures to encourage settlers.[103] It seems that King John II then offered the Jews of his kingdom the alternative of converting to Catholicism or immigrating to São Tomé. Reade wrote, "John II of Portugal in 1484, finding that the climate (of San Thormé) [sic] was so unhealthy, gave the Jews in his kingdom the agreeable choice of being baptised, or of colonising San Thormé and marrying women brought over from Angola. From this union arose a mixed race, which the Portuguese firmly perpetuated."[104]

King Manuel of Portugal, seeking funds to finance his program of colonial expansion, imposed huge taxes on the Jews, with very little time to pay. When it was seen that there was very little likelihood that the majority of the Jews would pay the tax, the king deported their young children to São Tomé and Príncipe.[105] Two thousand Jewish children, boys and girls no more than eight years old, were separated from their parents and deported there, where the majority of them died from starvation and illnesses. We learn from some sources that Alvaro de Caminha, the governor of São Tomé, managed to save 600 children by sending them with African nannies to the island of Príncipe and to Rio Reale.[106] Nevertheless, a testimony of Francisco Coelho, in 1669, asserts that, afterward, the Jews who lived in these islands enjoyed a certain freedom: "They are assigned the introduction of cocoa (coming from Brazil) in Prince Island and São Tomé... and..., without real evidence (they practice) some local dietary restrictions... they use the six branches star as a magic sign of Nigeria and some features of cabalistic numerology, some ritual details."[107]

The presence of descendants of Jews in São Tomé up to the twentieth century is supported by the testimony of M. D. W. Jeffreys, an official who completed an assignment in the region in 1936. Jeffrey reported that there existed "a small group, indistinguishable from the others, but who claimed a separate origin. They claimed to be of Jewish descent....Their names were not particularly Jewish and though their males were circumcised, that did not set them apart because the males of the other groups were also circumcised. They were also light complexioned."[108] He added, "The story of these natives... had a substratum of truth. They no doubt were descendants of the Jewish colonists settled on São Tomé some three hundred and fifty years earlier."[109]

Several evidences confirm, too, the presence of Jewish *lançados* or of their descendants on the coast of western Africa. A seventeenth-century text by Francisco de Lemos Coelho on the description of the coasts of Guinea indicates that "many Jews, born in Portugal, lived there, owning very large houses and went there to practice their religion because the kings of the country protected them and in fact because they could not be punished."[110] Coehlo also reports that in Rufisque, Senegal, many Jews, some of whom came from the north, owned trading houses, and that they were rather disdained by both Africans and residents. They also paid more taxes than the other whites, "but they were resigned to do so in order to live according to their laws. They left descendants in this country, resulting from relations with Negresses, who were Jewish like themselves, but, thanks to divine mercy, they converted to the Catholic Church in my time."[111]

Among the travelers who noted a Jewish presence on the Coast of Guinea, John Ogilby wrote in a book on Africa published in 1679, "Many Jews are also scattered over this region: Some natives, boasting themselves of Abraham's seed, inhabit both parts of the River Niger; others are Asian strangers, who fled thither either from the desolation of Jerusalem by Vespasian, or from Judea wasted and depopulated by Romans, Persians, Saracens and Christians; or else such as came out of Europe, whence they were banished."[112]

In the nineteenth century, David Livingstone reported a colony of "educated" blacks 200 miles in the interior of Saint Paul of Loanda, in Ambaka, whom he called "Jews of Angola."[113] This region, like São Tomé, had the function of being a colony for undesirable Portuguese of all kinds. These "Jews of Angola" were remarkable traders, esteemed as clerks and writers, and they knew well the history of Portugal and Portuguese laws. Their commercial expeditions took them hundred of miles into the interior of the country, and they knew the region long before the arrival of the Jesuits, who paid little attention to the presence of Jews in this area. On the Cabinda coast in Portuguese West Africa, another black group called "Mavumba," recognized as renowned potters, was considered by Ratzel as descendants of Jews expelled from Portugal and deported to São Tomé.[114]

In his work on the groups claiming a Lost Tribes origin, Godbey mentioned that Adolf Bastian, who participated in the German Loango Expedition of 1873–1876 on the coast of Congo, observed blacks who were called Judeos by the Portuguese. He found among them certain characteristics generally assigned to Jews and described them as "grave and reserved when compared to other Blacks and wealthy because they control most of the trade."[115] Nonetheless, Godbey stresses what he calls "the aberrations of ethnologists" in search of Semitic or white characteristics in African populations. In particular, he recalls the medieval legislation whereby a slave could, at that time, earn his freedom by acquiring the religion of his owner. Anti-Jewish legislation in Spain and Portugal, the "Siete Partidas," or Seven Codes of Alphonse X (1250–1280), aimed, among other things, to limit Jewish proselytism: "Moreover, we forbid any Jew should dare to make his slave turn Jew, although the slave be a Moor or of any other barbarous people. But should it be done, the slave who has been made a Jew or Jewess shall become free and withdrawn from the owner."[116] Any slave could thus earn his freedom by adopting the Jewish religion. The interpretation of this ban and its consequences supports the hypothesis of the existence of Africans who became Jewish, emancipated and without white ancestry, who would have later spread toward neighboring coasts.[117]

A compilation of testimonies gathered by a certain Lucien Wolf seems to demonstrate the same custom of proselytism in the Canary Islands. In the minutes of trials taking place between 1499 and 1667, one can find the testimony of a black slave claiming that "the employers tried to terrify her into adopting their (Jewish) customs"; another slave asserts that when he "was asked why he did not work on Saturday as other days, he replied that his master had ordered him to do nothing." And he adds that his master "took his two young brothers, one fifteen and the other between sixteen and eighteen... and that they were taught Jewish laws." Another indication comes from the sentence of a Guinean black, named Pedro Alvares, who was tried at the age of 100 because "he asserted that all men should be circumcised." The judgment handed down in this case was: "Such an error in a Negro, and of the age of one hundred, deserved exemplary punishment had he not died during the process and thus escaped punishment."[118]

The presence of Jewish traders and mixed-race traders living with African communities in the islands and on the West African coast seems to be a short chapter in the history of these regions. In the context of the merging and blending of Iberian, Moorish, Jewish, and African peoples, Portuguese *lançados* Jews may have introduced a certain degree of knowledge of Judaism in the Creole culture of subsequent generations. Half-caste descendants of the *lançados* used free servants or slaves to help them. Considering the "Siete Partidas" of Alphonse X, Judaism could have steadily spread by proselytizing African slaves.

This suggests long historical roots, which can continue to play a role in the survival of Jewish cultural identity in these regions and elsewhere. Due to the Atlantic slave trade, there could probably be African-Portuguese populations in the Caribbean islands, similar to and linked with those in Africa. The wealth, religious freedom, higher instruction level, and "proselytism" of the Jews may have been interacting influences that nurtured the myth of Jewish ancestry among some African American Jewish societies and sowed the seeds of black Jew movements.

Possible References to Hebrew-Semitic Traces in Southeast Africa

Traditions built around the biblical story of King Solomon and the queen of Sheba have frequently been invoked to explain the history of southern Africa. According to the Bible, the wealth of Solomon was acquired through a trading venture he undertook with Hiram, the king of Phoenicia. We already know that the idea that Solomon acquired gold and wealth from Africa contributed to the notion that Ophir, the land of biblical gold, was located at the tip of Africa. The legends of the maritime undertakings of Solomon and the Phoenicians established links between the Semitic world and East Africa, which played a decisive role in determining how Europeans viewed Southeast Africa.

The idea that all African achievements were the product of outside Hamitic influence was widely propagated by several European explorers and colonial officials. The monumental stone structures of Great Zimbabwe haunted British imaginations, which simply refused to believe that this achievement could be the work of black Africans. Early European discoverers of Great Zimbabwe proposed a wide variety of external origins for the building of this magnificent construction. The favorite theory was that the builders of this impressive city had been Phoenician, and that the monuments were connected with the biblical tales of King Solomon's goldmines and the queen of Sheba. When J. T. Bent carried out the first excavations in 1891—damaging large parts of the site in the process, and thus making the job of later archaeologists extremely difficult—the objects uncovered suggested to him tenuous comparisons and parallels with Assyria, Cyprus, Egypt, and Arabia. As Garlake comments about Bent, "He approached the problem of Great Zimbabwe firmly believing, like almost everyone else, that its origins must lie with a civilised ancient people, who must therefore necessarily have come from outside Africa."[119]

It is the claim of "Jewishness" of the Lemba people of southern Africa, intriguing in historical terms, that recently revived an issue that was dependent on myths and legends or diffusionism. The Lemba are a black southern African Bantu-speaking group of 50,000 to 70,000 people who live in the southern, central, and eastern parts of Zimbabwe and in northeast South Africa.[120] According to oral history, the Lemba came from Judea, Egypt, Yemen, or Ethiopia.[121] Professor M.E.R. Mathivha, the late president of the Lemba Cultural Association (LCA), suggested that the Jewish ancestors of the Lemba migrated as traders, in the seventh century BC, from the north to Yemen, where they established their community in Sena.[122] The Jewish community of Sena, or Basena, was supposedly expanded by Jews who escaped the Babylonian exile in 586 BC and traded with Phoenician merchants in the Orient and Africa.[123] From Sena, they crossed into Africa through the indefinable "Pusela," moving down the coast, building great cities in Zimbabwe until finally settling the northern part of South Africa.[124] Additionally, the Lemba assert Jewish identity through their customs of circumcision, food prohibitions, and ritual slaughter of animals. The tradition of an origin outside Africa differs from clan to clan, but all those who have observed them agree that they have undergone Hebrew-Jewish influences and that, in the past, they had contact with Muslims.[125]

British colonists, who had a political interest in dismissing the role of black populations in the building of Great Zimbabwe, considered the Lemba as descending from the Jewish builders of the stone city. In 1967, Gayre of Gayre, who had been the editor of the racist journal the *Mankind Quarterly*, in Bulawayo (Zimbabwe), affirmed that the Lemba's history can specifically be traced back to the pre-Islamic Sheba of Yemen, who was converted to Judaism. In his book *The Origin of the Great Zimbabwe Civilisation* (1972), he further argued that the Lemba have Jewish cultural and genetic traits that can only have been acquired from Judaized Sabeans, who settled in the region thousands of years ago: "The probability against coincidence is so great that we have to accept the fact that the Lembas observe the Mosaic code and that we have to explain its occurrence among this small tribe of traders who have the 'Caucasoid genes' and live in Northern Transvaal and some adjacent parts of Rhodesia. Moreover, only the Lembas bleed animals to death as enjoined by the Mosaic code and this act is restricted to the circumcised."[126]

A recent survey carried out by A. Ruwitah, the senior curator of ethnography at the Museum of Human Sciences of Harare in Zimbabwe, rejected this hypothesis of an extra-African origin of the Lemba, considering it was the product of invention by outsiders.[127] According to Parfitt, however, there are cogent grounds for considering that the Lemba's ancestors came from southern Arabia, perhaps the city of Sena in Hadramaut, which had a tradition of migrations to Africa.[128] Parfitt suggests that, later on, the history of the Lemba might have been linked to the Islamization of the eastern coast of Africa, particularly the civilization of the city referred to by medieval Arabian geographers as Sayuna, where religious syncretism was practiced and accepted.[129] Upon arrival of the Portuguese in the sixteenth century, the Lemba might have turned away from Islamic influence and developed their own religious and identity system, in particular by conserving the practice of endogamy and dietary taboos that still characterize them today. This is what certain indirect sources lead us to imagine.

Jews had been living in the Arabian Peninsula for centuries before the time of Muhammad. Hypotheses and speculations about the dates and circumstances surrounding their arrival date their presence to biblical times. Jewish settlers, probably established in the oasis communities of northern Arabia around the last part of the Second Temple period, were found in considerable numbers in Arabia.[130] They were well integrated into the life and culture of the peninsula, where they practiced caravan trade, date cultivation, and craft-making. These Jews, who spoke Arabic, were organized into clans and tribes, and although they probably constituted a relatively small percentage of the population, their influence was strong in pagan Yemen. We know that the fertile oasis of Yathrib in Arabia had been settled by Jews organized in tribes, who constituted the majority of the population and probably gave its name to al-Madina, that is, Medina. When Muhammad came to Medina, they were forced to sell their properties and leave the area. What became of them afterward is not at all clear.[131]

Jewish influence in the Arabian pre-Islamic period was significant enough to play an important role in classical Arabic historiography. A chain of traditions of a legendary nature, together with interpretations of epigraphy, gave rise to the not implausible hypothesis of a mass conversion to Judaism in the Himyarite kingdom (southern Arabia) until its conquest by the Ethiopians in 525.[132] Dhu Nuwas, king of Himyar, was allegedly converted to Judaism by his father, Abu Kariba (ca. AD 385–420). Abu Kariba himself had converted earlier, under the influence of some Jews who assisted him in a campaign against Persia and some Arabian provinces of Byzantium. According to these traditions, Dhu Nuwas, the last of the Himyarite kings, became a devoted Jew whose zeal alienated Christian merchants. A neighboring king, Aidug, defeated Dhu Nuwas, who retaliated by attacking another Christian city, Najran. He besieged the city, giving the inhabitants the alternative of accepting Judaism or dying, following which 20,000 of them chose death. An Abyssinian army defeated Dhu Nuwas, who died jumping into the sea with his horse. Even if these traditions admittedly have a legendary character, there are some reasons to believe that the legend of the conversion of the Himyarite kingdom to Judaism is founded on some historical elements.[133]

The anonymous work the *Periplus of the Erythrean Sea*, from the first century AD, provides information on a very early pre-Islamic Arab influence in East Africa.[134] The *Periplus* records that the Sabeans (pre-Islamic-Arabian-Yemenites) were one of the great Semitic powers in ancient times and were involved in all settlement and exploitation of the coasts of East Africa, where they exchanged spears, axes, knives, and glassware for ivory and tortoise-shell.[135]

In the search for Sena, the mythic city of the Lemba, a further important source of information is constituted by the accounts of Arab historians and traders. In fact, a number of unreliable traditions attempt to give a precise historical framework for the arrival of the Arabs on the east coast of Africa. One such tradition claims, "It is well known that, in the year 696, the two princes of Oman, Sulaiman and Said, were attacked by the forces of the Khalif 'Abd al-Malik ibn Marwan of Damascus, and forced to flee to the land of Zanj (East Africa). There we also find the tradition of the coming of the Arabs who settled along the coast, and the name of their chief who was Haji Said."[136]

In AD 943, the Arab historian Abu'l Hassan al-Masudi wrote that Muslims of Arabia sailed on the Indian Ocean as far south as Madagascar, and to Sofala

(Sufalah) in the lands of the Wakwak people.[137] According to al-Idrissi, in the tenth century, Sayuna was a "town connected to the land of Sofala, and peopled by groups of Indians and Zanj and others."[138] In the thirteenth century, another Arab writer, Hassan Ibn Said, who was also a philosopher and historian, described Sayuna as the capital of the kingdom of Sofala. It has been supposed that the fabulous Sayuna of the Arab geographers was indeed the Sena on the Zambezi. While it is interesting to recall that the name Sayuna is very similar to the normative Arabic word for Zion and identical to the Judeo-Arabic, the form of Arabic used by Jews, there is no proof other than the obvious similarity of names.[139] Some sort of a non-African population was again referred to in the fourteenth century by Ahmad ibn Majid, the Arab pilot who showed Vasco do Gama the way from the Sofala region to India. He mentioned that the population around Sofala included "men of the Egyptian Nile."[140]

The Portuguese historian Joao de Barros, writing in the sixteenth century, refers to the arrival of heretical Muslims who moved into the interior in the eighth or ninth century. He called them Emozaidji, which may be an attempt to formulate the Arabic *umma zaydiyya* (the Zaidi nation), referring to followers of the Shi'ite pretender to the throne, Said ibn Ali, who was killed in 739. The Lemba ancestor, "Said," is referred to by most of the observers who have described the tribe, and he may conceivably have a connection with de Barros's Emozaidji, but in any case there is no proof of this. However, Said is a common Arab name, and the presence of this name in the Lemba tradition is strongly suggestive of an Arab influence.[141]

Upon their arrival, the Portuguese described the inhabitants of Sofala, and those of the settlement at Sena on Zambezi, as Moors. According to Antonio de Saldanha in 1511, there were some 10,000 Moors living in the Sofala hinterland. D. N. Beach, the author of a history of the Shona, notes that Portuguese documents of the eighteenth century frequently referred to *mouros* who traded in the country, and that this term was often translated by "Arabs" or "Swahili"; in fact, to the Portuguese of that period, *mouro* simply meant Muslim, of whatever color or language, who could be distinguished by a Muslim name, a turban, and some degree of Islamic religion.[142] Duarte Barbarosa, writing in the sixteenth century, noted, "These Moors of Sofala are black men, some olive-skinned who use the tongue of the land which is that of the Gentiles. They speak some Arabic." Beach comments, "It seems highly probable that the Muslims of the Plateau, some five centuries after East African trade began to reach it, were simply Islamized Shona. It is of course possible that Swahili and even Arabs did visit the Plateau, but there is no definite proof of it."[143]

Dos Santos adds that, further inland, "they [these lands] are inhabited by heathen Kaffir and Moors, some black, some white, some of whom are rich, also they are the subjects of the Monomotapa, they live there almost independently, being at a great distance of the court of the king."[144]

Twentieth-century oral traditions reveal that these same areas were inhabited by a "red-skinned" race of traders, known as Amwenye Vashava. Ahmad ibn Majid also refers to these people and mentions that the area around Sofala belonged to the people of Muna Musavi, which is probably the singular form of Amwenye Vashava. According to Parfitt, these people were, no doubt, the ancestors of the Mwenye, or the Lemba of today.[145] The name Vashava is preserved in the tribal praise-name Musavi (or Mushavi), and its meaning can be explained from the Bantu root meaning "to trade," while Mwenye evokes feudal lord or master.[146] The Portuguese expedition under Antonio Barretto ended the political power of the Moors of the Sofala region, and Muslim traffic up to the Zambezi came to an end. As Parfitt wrote, "Those non-Bantu elements in the Sofala-Sena hinterland never made any attempt, as far as we know, to contact the strong Muslim community to the north. Nor they did acquire or re-acquire the Quran. As the Lemba so often maintained—their book was lost."[147]

There are various indications that, in the first half of the fourteenth century, the Mwenye occupied the northern part of present-day Zimbabwe. There is also substantial evidence that these Mwenye were present at the court of the Monomotapa and that they formed a political entity.[148] A report, from an African named Mahumane, provides more information about them and tells us that, from the beginning of the eighteenth century to the second half of the nineteenth, political and cultural changes came from outside:

> The Walembers [Lemba] who are always coming here with those of Inthowelle... are a nation which lives on top... of the country of Inthowelle, and they are a nation which some years ago got the worst of a struggle with those from Gole and then part of them went under the protection of the Inthowellers while the other part submitted to the victor. The aforementioned Walembers were said to be rich in gold, too, and this nation was also doing trade with the Portuguese in the direction of the aforementioned Sena and Manica.[149]

All traces of these putative Lemba's ancestors were lost thereafter; they probably integrated into other groups, where they filled the roles of goldsmiths, iron and copper workers, medicine men, and ritual experts.[150] These few hypotheses suggest that, since ancient times, there could have been links between southern Arabia and the southeast coast of Africa, including Madagascar.

Possible References to Jewish and Semitic Migrations in Madagascar

In respect to one or more Jewish colonies in ancient Madagascar, the subject has been much debated due to the accounts of Etienne de Flacourt, the French governor of Fort Dauphin. Flacourt, who spent the year 1652 in Madagascar, reported the discovery of remnants of an ancient Jewish colony on the eastern coast of Madagascar, on the island of Sainte-Marie and in Fenerive:

> The peoples who, I think, were the earliest to come to Madagascar were the Zaffre-Ibrahim, or Abraham lineage, who lived on the island of Sainte-Marie and neighboring lands; all the more so, since although they practice circumcision, they have no mark of Mohammedanism, know neither Mohammed nor his caliphs, and consider their followers as Caffres and men without law; they do not eat or conclude any alliance with them. They celebrate and do not work on Saturday, and not on Friday like the Moors and have no name similar to the ones they have; this leads me to think that their ancestors visited this island during the earliest migrations of the Jews, or that they descend from the most ancient Ismaelite families, as early as before the captivity in Babylon, or from those who could have remained in Egypt after Israel left the country. They have maintained the names of Moses, Isaac, Joseph, and Noah..., even if there are here women and children much whiter than the Matatanes and having hair as straight as them.[151]

Following on Flacourt, and referring frequently to his account, subsequent observers such as the Capitaine de Valgny identified an ancient background of ideas among some Malagasy populations—particularly the belief in only one God who cannot be represented by an image—which evokes a similarity with the Jewish pre-Solomonic civilization.[152] Another suggestion of a possible Jewish-Hebrew presence in Southeast Africa comes from Alfred Grandidier, the most important and influential authority on Madagascar of all times. Grandidier dedicated his life to filling the fifty-two volumes of his encyclopaedic *Histoire physique, naturelle et politique de Madagascar* (1901) and is considered the ultimate authority on this subject. About an ancient Semitic migration to Madagascar, Grandidier wrote, "The fleets sent by King Solomon toward the southeast coast of Africa had probably some of their ships lost on the coasts of Madagascar and it is not unlikely that, in ancient times, some

Jewish colonies had been founded, voluntarily or not, in this island known from the Comoros."[153]

Grandidier listed thirty-five traits common to all Malagasy and ancient Jews.[154] His considerations are largely inspired by an Arab text, written in Mayotte, quoted by Gevrey, that relates the history of the Comoros Islands and reveals that "in the times of Solomon-ben-Daoudou (Salomon son of David), Arabs or Idumean, coming from the Red Sea with their wives, children and slaves, settled in Ngazidya (Great Comoro) and after that, many men from Africa and the Zanguebar coast came to inhabit these islands."[155] Grandidier inspired numerous collaborators and disciples, such as Keane, who would write in *The Gold of Ophir* (1901) about the ancient links between Palestine and Madagascar "that people who preserve many Israelitish rites, usages and traditions, cherish the memory of Abraham, but have no knowledge of any of the prophets after the time of David," which implies that the Jewish immigrants left their home at a very remote date.[156]

Documents are quoted to show that the Comoros, a stopping point between Madagascar and Rhodesia, were peopled during the reign of Solomon "by Arabs or rather by Idumean Jews from the Red Sea." As explained herein above, elsewhere in Africa, borrowings from the myth of the Lost Tribes included in the interpretative movement of the earliest colonial enterprise contributed to the construction of the origins of the Malagasy by foreigners. In the nineteenth century, some missionaries of the London Missionary Society believed that all of the Malagasy religious antecedents derived from the Hebrew religion itself, and that "all Malagasy" were supposed to be the descendants of "Jews who came to Madagascar in Phoenician ships."[157]

Malagasy origins have long been the subject of much academic dispute, which is still only partially resolved. There is a consensus among modern scholars that navigators from Indonesia settled along the coast of East Africa, acquired some Bantu vocabulary, and then sailed to Madagascar already speaking a language that contains a mixture of Bantu words.[158] In fact, ancient accounts attest to the trading or migratory movements of Phoenicians, Chinese, Indians, Malays, Persians, Arabs, and Jews along the coasts of southern Arabia, eastern Africa, and the Indian subcontinent.[159] Any of these people could have reached Madagascar in outriggers, dhows, junks, or any other kind of seafaring craft, with the help of wind and currents. Maritime contacts do not allow for any automatic inference of any significant contribution to the peopling of Madagascar; however, it can be postulated that many migrations into Madagascar took place. Therefore, the presence of Idumean colonies or Arab Jews from Yemen in Madagascar may be considered. As explained earlier, since very ancient times, Yemenite Arabs have gone as far as Sofala on the eastern coast of Africa, and the Comoros archipelago was visited by their boats.

We know that Arabs traded down the eastern coast of Africa. In this context "Arab" is a convenient name covering various groups affected to a greater or lesser extent by Islam, originating in most cases in Arabia, but who could have spent several generations, in East Africa or elsewhere, en route to Madagascar. Local chronicles from the main islands of the eastern coast of Africa, as well as accounts of the great sea travels undertaken by the Portuguese in the sixteenth century, enable us to follow the major Arab and Persian migrations that could have reached eastern Africa, Comoros, and Madagascar.[160] Immigration of some groups belonging to minority religious sects and suffering persecution after the expansion of Islam in Arabia, Persia, and Egypt probably took place. Grandidier considered that the earliest Arab colons in Madagascar could have been "Zeidites, some of them having left the Sawad of Kawfa after having failed in their revolt against Caliph Hischam in 737 and the others after having overthrown the Ommayyad caliph Walid... had to leave Arabia according to Masudi's record and the accounts of Barros and Joao dos Santos."[161] The evidential value of these hypotheses is discussed adequately by Gabriel Ferrand, an important Arabist and student of Muslim communities in Asia, Africa, and Madagascar, in "Les migrations musulmanes et juives à Madagascar" (1905). The study of an undated manuscript, which refers to a caliph who reigned in the thirteenth century, leads Ferrand to consider that the Islamized Malagasy descended from Sunnite Muslims. Ferrand discovered in a *khotba,* a special Friday prayer that Islamized Malagasy recited in Madagascar, mention of the ultimate Abbassid caliph of Baghdad, Al-Mostas'im, who reigned from 1242 to 1258. The title of Prince of the Believers, given to the caliph in the *khotba,* shows that the Islamized Malagasy and their descendants still prayed for the one who was the ruler of their ancestors.[162] Ferrand also cited a text whose author is thought to be a member of the orthodox Shiite sect, or Imamites, and he envisaged that the Persian-Shiites could have migrated to the eastern coast of Madagascar between 800 and 818, while acknowledging that the discrepancy of information does not make it possible to clearly determine the date and origin of the earliest Arab arrivals on the island.[163]

A Portuguese record of the Jesuit priest Luiz Marianno, who visited the southeastern coast of Madagascar in 1613, evoked the hypothesis of a Muslim migration prior to the thirteenth century. According to the words that Father Marianno recorded from King Andriantsiambani, the king himself,

> [They] originated from Mangalor and Mekka where his ancestors were born. These ones [who had embarked] on one or several ships,

got lost, and from the coast of India, ran onto the coast of the north tip of Madagascar island. Little by little they multiplied and came as far as the south tip. This had happened many years (earlier). In one branch there had been seventeen generations and in the other fourteen. Thus, on the eastern coast of Madagascar people of this family are scattered.[164]

Father Marianno observed that the customs they kept were a testimony of their origin, that they were Moors, and that they called themselves Solimas, a derivation in modern Malagasy of Silamu/Islam. While pointing out that "they have the same colour as Indians, Arabs and Javanese," Father Marianno added that they have a Koran written in Arabic, observe Ramadan, do not eat pork, and practice circumcision.[165]

The first Arab ancestors are generally known in Madagascar as Antalaotra, or "people from across the sea."[166] It is likely that the first Arabs to cross the Mozambique Channel were some of these pre-Islamic traders who had been pushed out of Arabia or Africa. They could have been members of one of the sects that broke away from the orthodox Mohammedan faith during the turbulent times of Muhammad and his immediate successors, or Jews who had converted to Islam. Sometime in the eighth or ninth century, their boats reached the Malagasy coast, probably from the Comoros, and they set up trading posts along the northwest coast from where they expanded.[167] Elsewhere on the island, particularly along the east coast, there are numerous traces of Arab or Islamic cultural influence but no knowledge of the central features of the Muslim religion, the name Allah, the mosque, prayers, or the pilgrimage to Mecca. Where the name of Muhammad is distantly remembered, he represents one prophet among others rather than *the* Prophet, what would seem to indicate that the Arabs from whom the Antalaotra descended were pre-Islamic. The combined evidence from archaeology, oral traditions, and written sixteenth-century Portuguese accounts reveals that early Muslim traders had two important settlements on the western coasts of Madagascar.[168] Archaeological excavations at the northeastern site of Vohemar, known by its ancient name of Ihàrana, have yielded an entire culture complex based on external commerce and dominated by traders who wrote in Arabic since at least the twelfth century.[169]

A subsequent group was the Zafiraminia (descendants of Ramini), who probably arrived early in the fourteenth century and who, according to their traditions, came from Mecca or from Ramni, which was the medieval name for Sumatra, sometime after Islam had established itself in Indonesia in the thirteenth century.[170] The ancestors of the Antemoro arrived some two centuries after the Zafiraminia, around the end of the fifteenth century. They are of major interest as possessors of important historical manuscripts, the *Sorabé* (Great Writings or Sacred Books), probably originally written in Arabic, but adapted at an early stage to the Malagasy language.[171] The *Sorabé* are concerned with astrology, geomancy, divination, and medicine, the knowledge of which gave the possessors great prestige throughout Madagascar.[172] If they are historical records of major interest, the reliability of the *Sorabé* is uncertain because most of them appear to have been written relatively recently and copied with varying degrees of accuracy, from older documents. Even if the *Sorabé* do not really help us to be precise about the origins of the Antemoro, like the Zafiraminia, with whom their traditions are often confused, they claim noble descent from Mecca and mention sometime a stay in Africa on the way to Madagascar. Another hypothesis of the origin of the Antemoro was recently suggested by Brown: "It has been recently argued very plausibly that the origin of both the name and the people is to be found in the Somali country of south-eastern Ethiopia, where there was a tribe called *Temur* which disappeared from the area in the fifteenth century," which coincides with the date of the arrival of the Antemoro in Madagascar.[173] Such a trace has been found by Enrico Cerulli in Ethiopia's epic song, *Negus Yeshak*, which refers to a vanished people named Temur in connection with the Somali. Therefore it is not impossible to consider that the original ancestors of the Antemoro came from Arabia to the Somali area, which was traditionally a home for heretics and dissenters who were subsequently driven out by the expansion of the Galla people.[174]

The Islamic faith of the Antemoro, who practice both tribal and clan endogamy, seems to have declined rapidly, and little trace remains apart from a special taboo on eating pork, funerary rituals, and sacrifices.[175] It was mainly through the Antemoro that words borrowed from Arabic were absorbed into the Malagasy language, notably the days of the week and terms associated with astrology, arithmetic, and divination. The Antemoro carried a priestly prestige deriving from their "magical" arts, which enabled them to provide *ombiasy* (priest doctors) and *mpsikidy* (diviners) to the ruling clans in their own regions, as well as to many other tribes.[176] One might deduce that the Antemoro immigrants, like the Antalaotra in general, were predominantly male and married local Malagasy women.

If the Antemoro genealogical traditions allow for some reasonable speculation with respect to an initial Arab settlement, the Portuguese chronicles are more precise. In 1507–1508, a Portuguese captain, Ruy Pereira, mentioned a possible colony of Moors at Matitana, a place inhabited by the Antemoro, and reported that the local inhabitants were no strangers to external trade, having brought silver and beeswax to his ship.[177] Tristao da Cunha, admiral of the Portuguese fleet in the western Indian Ocean, was able to find in Mozambique a Moor named Bogima who had previously been to Matitana. In 1513, Lisbon sent Luis Figuera to establish a small fort and ginger-processing factory in Matitana. Luis Figuera wrote that, by that time "Matitana [was] a town densely inhabited by Moors."[178] It is therefore possible to say that Moors on the African mainland knew about the region of Matitana and traded occasionally with it before the Portuguese discovery of Madagascar in 1506.

Specific links with Africa can be found on the tombs at Sokoambé, on the western coast, where bird carvings appear on rectangular tombstones. Only the tombs of Sokoambé in Madagascar have bird effigies that are remarkably similar to soapstone carvings of birds found in Great Zimbabwe.[179] According to Dos Santos (1609), the term Sakoambé/Sakuambé/Sakumbe was related to the kingdom of Sacumbe on the Zambezi River, at a point marked by a cataract that impeded navigation.[180] While this link with Great Zimbabwe could be questioned, it coincides with numerous local traditions of a Malagasy dynasty in this area, the Maroseràna or Volamena, which appeared in the mid-sixteenth century.[181] This dynasty is considered by several traditions as formed by the marriage of new immigrants, described as "white men," with the daughters of local chiefs. The Maroseràna later took over leadership of the Sakalava society, and the first Sakalava conqueror was called Andriandahifotsy, which means "Prince White Man."

Throughout Madagascar, Grandidier observed that "nearly all of the chiefs and rulers [were of an] origin different from the mass of people," as attested by words of their mother tongue.[182] As an expression of the Hamitic myth, it has been generally accepted that an Arab or Indonesian origin might explain the legend of early white chiefs, but recently it has been argued that the founder of the Maroseràna came from black Africa, more specifically, the Zimbabwe Empire, around the Zambezi.[183] An African origin has also been suggested for the names of other early Maroseràna kings, particularly Andriamandazaoàla, whose name translates as "crusher of trees," which was one of the titles of Mwene Mutapa, the great Zimbabwe king. One Sakalava tradition is that precursors of the Maroseràna landed on the southwest coast of the island with a shipload of gold, which they used to gain supremacy over the local people.[184] The alternative name of the Maroseràna, Volamena, means "golden" in Malagasy, while Maroseràna itself may be derived from *mari*, which was the word for gold in Zimbabwe. If it is difficult to believe that Africans from Zimbabwe could be described as white, there is a possible explanation that would attribute a Zimbabwe origin of the dynasties with the "white men" tradition. In the late Middle Ages, the Zimbabwe gold may have been taken over by the Arabs.

Nineteenth-century travelers to Vendaland and Mashonaland had cited the local tradition that white men had once inhabited the interior. In *Twenty Five Years in a Wagon in the Gold Regions of Africa* (1887), Andrew Anderson wrote "The natives state that the gold was worked and the forts built by the white men that once occupied this country whom they called Abberlomba."[185] It is therefore imaginable that the ancestors of the Maroseràna were Arabs who could have landed on the southwest coast with a shipload of gold and that they set up kingdoms of their own based on the model of the Zimbabwe Empire.[186]

This hypothesis coincides with Murdock's opinion, which considers that a Venda-Zimbabwe link can be postulated for the Antanosy society inhabiting the southeast part of the island and who claim an Islamic descent. Murdock suggests interesting parallels between the Antanosy and the Venda-incorporated Lemba who possess "markedly Semitic" physical features, as well as cultural traits "that distinguish them sharply from their neighbours."[187] It seems that the Zimbabwe complex accounts for much African influence in Madagascar. Kent suggests that the Shona-like pottery discovered in southeastern Madagascar, dated circa AD 1100, may be "the indication of a terminal human migration of people or peoples familiar with some features of the Zimbabwe culture. Much later, no doubt, links between old Rhodesia and Madagascar proved to be both familiar and useful to the gold-bearing proto-Maroserana."[188]

One can establish a parallel between these hypotheses and the opinion of Wilmot, who states that "Moguedchou [Mozambique] was founded about 930 years after Christ, and there seems little doubt that the political establishment of Arabs at Sofala can be shown to have taken place about 1100 AD," in fact during the supposed period of Ihàrana settlement.[189] Most of the evidence thus suggests that the origin of some of the Malagasy dynasty could be connected with the Arab world, through Africa, since ancient times.[190] The White King myth, as well as the notion that dynastic change in Madagascar was imposed by a foreign culture, can be explained by repeated waves of Moorish migrations to the Great Island.[191]

While questionable, there are some interesting analogies between the Lemba of Venda and Zimbabwe and the Malagasy group descending from the Antalaotra, particularly with respect to the prestige conferred by divination and medicine, which differentiates them from their neighbors, and the tradition of their being "white men." A small group of Onjàtsy, to the north of Vohemar, which claims an Arab origin, has a reputation as *ombiasy* and *mpisikidy* that strikingly recalls the characteristic activities of the Lemba such as tradition and the earliest observers recorded them.[192] As discussed earlier, Parfitt suggested that the Arab traders of the Sofala hinterland known as Amwenye Vashava could probably be the ancestors of the Mwenye or the present-day Lemba. There are various indications that the "red-skinned" Mwenye traders occupied the northern part of today's Zimbabwe around the fourteenth century. There is also substantial evidence that these Mwenye were present at the court of Monomotapa and that they formed a political entity.[193] In advancing connections between Madagascar and Zimbabwe, it is possible to imagine that the original ancestors of the Antalaotra could be these Mwenye Arabs who could have come from Zimbabwe to Madagascar. This hypothesis suggests that the Antemoro and the Lemba, who both reveal substantial Arabian/Islamic influences, could share a common Semitic substratum. They both could have subsequently developed the basis of a characteristic identity and religious system, during which time they lost the instructions of the Koran but maintained certain traditions. However, this hypothesis, which suggests connections between some Malagasy ruling clans and the Lemba, calls for further research and can nowhere substantiate any single-origin or monolithic theory of the Malagasy past.

Most of the evidence thus suggests that the past of such groups as the Lemba in southern Africa, or the Antemoro descendants in Madagascar, is connected with the Arab world. But there are also suggestions that earlier immigrants from Yemen could have been associated with the aforementioned Muslim followers of Said ibn Ali, constituting altogether the "Moorish people," a kind of Judaic-Arabic people, described by historians and missionaries. Since pre-Islamic times, Arab-Hebrews or Judaized Arab merchants could have migrated to the shores of Africa for trade and then, after the arrival of the Prophet, for religious, political, or economical reasons. Thus a Sabean or Yemenite involvement and influence in Southeast Africa might have been possible. This seems to be confirmed by the recent genetic investigations carried out on the Lemba, discussed later, which suggest an extra-African origin, without entirely allowing us to distinguish between Jewish and Arab-Semitic ancestry.

Genetic research on the notions of origins, ancestry, and identity has during recent decades become interlaced with history, popular discourses, and myths.[194] Genetic archaeology—the study of the detailed structure of DNA—is being used to gain a better understanding of the relationships between populations separated by distance and time and to enhance the knowledge of history not enlightened by documentary evidence.[195] The way in which genetics has been perceived by African Americans, Native Americans, Jews, or other communities concerned by "historical" genetic research about their identity is part of a mythical reconstruction of history. The case of the Lemba is one of the most frequently cited because genetic investigations were an essential step in the elaboration of their Jewish myth of origins. In recent years, in respect to the construction of African Jewish identities, genetic findings have entered the discourse of history.[196] For societies whose claim of origins harbors a certain ambiguity, the notion of "imagined genetic communities" developed by Bob Simpson is one more element that intertwines with mythical realities and historical metaphors.[197]

9

African Jews in Western and Central Africa

As we examine the centuries of speculation concerning Jews in Africa, the myths that have been created in this respect, and the undoubted historical links that existed between Jews, Judaism, and black Africa at certain times and places, we are forced to reflect on the links between past myths and events and the manifestations of a series of religious movements revolving around Judaism in one form or another today. The hints of and clues to a Jewish presence in Africa, so seductive over time and so productive of images and constructions of the "other," fizzle out in the vast expanses of the African interior. Over the last century, manifestations of similar myths and religious directions have mushroomed on African soil connected with the past, through the subterranean world of the imagination. Who is to say whether the account of, say, Leo Africanus had an impact or not on the readiness of nineteenth-century English travelers to find Judaic populations in the Great Lakes area, or on that of French travelers and missionaries to find signs of a Judaic presence in the lush interior of Madagascar? In the previous chapter, we examined evidence for the existence and continued presence of Jews in western sub-Saharan Africa. There are no reliable historical records to hint at the presence of Jews in central, eastern, or southern Africa, but legends and myths of Jewish communities, and even kingdoms, abound in these areas.
We shall see that there is little historical continuity in these diverse manifestations of Judaism. The modern Judaizing movements

are often linked more to unexpected reactions to colonialism than to the implantation in Africa of Jewish ideas, practices or people, at some remote time.

As seen earlier, from the early colonization, Africans' sacred world was informed by characters and legends appropriated from the Hebrew Bible. Like their African American brethren, Africans found numerous analogies in the experience of Africans and of the Jewish people facilitating various adaptations of Judaism within their religion. In this chapter, we turn our attention to the numerous groups throughout black Africa that, for one reason or another, have adopted or claimed a Jewish or Hebrew identity.[1]

Before examining these groups, some attention must be given to the role of proselyte organizations that create a link between marginal Jewish groups and worldwide Jewry. The moral, religious, and financial support of these organizations contributes significantly to the existence and recognition of marginal Jewish societies. In April 2005, the historic decision by the chief rabbi of Israel, Rabbi Shlomo Amar, to recognize the Bene Menashe of India as "descendants of Israel" is largely the consequence of Amishav's—now called Shavei Israel—involvement.[2] Created in Jerusalem in 1975, Amishav is dedicated, under the directorship of its founder, Rabbi Eliyahu Avichail, to finding lost and dispersed remnants of the Jewish Diaspora and assisting individuals who wish to rejoin the Jewish community.[3] In recent decades, Avichail accepted the Jews of Kurdistan as the descendants of Dan and Nephtali, as well as the Jews of Daghestan, Azerbaijan, Georgia, Armenia, Turkmenistan, Uzbekistan, and Buchara, who have traditions similar to theirs.[4]

In Africa and elsewhere in the world, the prominent American-based Kulanu (i.e., "All of Us" in Hebrew) organization has undertaken a variety of activities on behalf of marginal "Jewish" groups, bringing them closer together and closer to mainstream Judaism. Its president, Jack Zeller, speaks of Jews around the world, from the Shinlung Jewish community in India, to the Marranos of Brazil or Santa Fe "even if...the other Jew is of a darker skin colour or different appearance, or practices a Judaism that is non-rabbinic in origin or is a newly arrived Jew by choice."[5] Aware of the "electrifying" effect of visits by Western Jews to isolated Jewish communities, Kulanu volunteers are numerous among remote communities, where they act as an interface in the exchange of information. Jack Zeller considers that "never before in Jewish history has it been easier to meet remote and virtually ignored or newly developing Jewish communities. We can do it by phone, fax, e-mail."[6] Kulanu's activities include research, contact, education, donation of religious books and articles, facilitation to conversion, if requested—as we shall see further for the Abayudaya of Uganda.[7]

Kulanu has aroused considerable interest in the Zakhor Jews of Mali. We shall begin our examination with this group, which, while forming part of a worldwide network of recent claimants to a Judaic ancestry, may simultaneously be viewed as actually having some justifiable historical claims.

The Zakhor Jews of Timbuktu, Mali

Created in 1993 in Timbuktu, the Zakhor association (Zakhor meaning "Remember" in Hebrew), comprises about 1,000 people. It is a movement organized around the Malian historian Ismael Daide Haidara, whose followers claim to be the direct descendants of Saharan Jews.[8] In the manifesto published in 1996 and sent to the presidents of Mali and Israel, diplomatic missions in Mali, and Jewish communities throughout the world, the members of Zakhor recognize themselves as Jews and proclaim, "The time has come for us to remember and this time is one of the most difficult of our history....We shall have to traverse the course of years, from generation to generation, to recall our Israelite origins that the fathers of our fathers kept silently and to accept this origin. Zakhor was created for this purpose."[9] The manifesto, which was published in its entirety in Malian newspapers, affirms in *Le Républicain* (May 29, 1996) that they want to reconnect with their ancestors: "We are Jews because our ancestors were Jews, whose genes are found in all our families. Our Judaism is based on ethnicity. We have to take it and the world has to accept it....We are Jewish as are the Falasha or Falashmura of Ethiopia. Our history can only be told as the destiny of *de-Judaized* Jews who nonetheless recognize themselves as being of Israelite origin."[10]

The manifesto lists, as the three obligations of the members of Zakhor to "become a *Banu-Israel* community again," first, by teaching their children about their heritage, second, by learning and using Hebrew as a second language (without rejecting Arabic), and third, by safeguarding their sociocultural heritage, the preservation of their cemeteries being a major element in this respect. The manifesto also refers to the Diaspora: "Where one Jew can be found in the world, there is Israel, Israel is throughout the world and Jerusalem and the Promised Land are its navel, because the Jewish Diaspora is throughout the world."[11] However, the founding members of the community consider that "[our] intention is not to return to Israel, but to assert our identity."[12]

Since 1996, news of the presence of some 1,000 "Jews" in Timbuktu spread throughout Mali and in the international press, where Zakhor became a widely discussed phenomenon. In March 1996, the Agence France Presse reported on a community of Jewish origin in the Timbuktu area, who had in the past "converted to Islam because of the hostility of local rulers to their own faith." In June 1996, Radio France Internationale reported, "Historians and researchers were surprised to discover the existence of a Jewish community of about 1,000 people in the Timbuktu region of Mali. These families decided to come out in the open and set up the Timbuktu Association of Friendship with the Jewish world." A BBC broadcast in June 1996 also reported on the community, and a historically documented article, "Juifs, Noirs et Maliens," was published by Sennen Andriamirado in *Jeune Afrique* (January 14, 1997). In the United States, Rick Gold's lecture on the "hidden" Jews of Timbuktu, held in December 1999 at Temple Shalom, Chevy Chase, Maryland, was published in the *Washington Jewish Week* (December 30, 1999).[13]

In what context did the Zakhor members' claim for Judaism arise? In 1992, after more than twenty years of military coups and insecure regimes, a new constitution was approved, providing a multiparty democracy.[14] As descendants of ancient African empires Ghanean, Malinke, and Songhai, Malians express great pride for their ancestry and ethnic membership.[15] Before 1993, the members of Zakhor did not speak of themselves as Jews. The recognition of their Jewishness was probably facilitated by the political liberalization in Mali. It was also triggered by the recent departures of the Falasha from Ethiopia to Israel, in the 1980s and again in 1991, and their subsequent history in the Jewish state. As Parfitt suggested, "One of the mechanisms whereby a use of Judaism has come to the fore and particularly in Africa and the United States has been through a discourse substantially generated by discussions about the Falasha, the so-called Jews of Ethiopia."[16] It seems that what appears as ethnic consciousness was revived by an incident in 1963 in the area of Timbuktu. An administrative document reports a serious dispute between descendants of Jews and Sorkos fishermen, who wanted to settle near the cemetery, where, according to oral tradition, the first Ismael al Yahudi, their eponymous ancestor, is buried. With a new awareness of their identity, the Timbuktu "Jews" rose up in strong opposition.[17]

From a religious point of view, today, one does not observe in Timbuktu any Jewish rites or customs, but rather crypto-Judaic practices. The religious life of the Jews of Timbuktu is highly syncretistic, that is, they claim a Jewish identity and practice Islam. They have been clear from the start that they were devoted only to the reestablishment of Jewish identity and not the conversion to Judaism. Indeed, in Mali, about 90 percent of the population is Muslim, with most of the remaining 10 percent following traditional religions. Nevertheless, despite their complete integration into Mali's Islamic culture, the alleged descendants of Touati Jews seem, almost always, to marry other Jewish descendants, and they still give Hebrew names to their children.[18] Some founding members of Zakhor, such as Abdessalman Al Kohin, sign their names with a Star of David, and it is said that Hebrew songs are still sung.[19]

The family leaders who founded Zakhor declared themselves to be descendants of Jews of the Touat. In the previous chapter, we examined evidence of the presence of Jews on the trans-Saharan trade routes and the centuries-old mention of the existence of Jewish groups in the Timbuktu region of western Africa, before and after Islamization and up to the fifteenth century. As early as in the twelfth century, al-Bakri, al-Zurhi, and al-Idrissi signaled a Jewish presence in the region of Timbuktu, and in the thirteenth century Ibn Said and Ibn Abi Zar gave similar information.[20] As seen earlier, the contribution of the cartographic school of Majorca in the fourteenth century provided convincing testimony on the precision of the knowledge of the Sahara of the Jews, who were authorized, by the *responsa*, to carry on their caravan trip during the Sabbath.

We know that the Jews of Touat, whose population increased since the end of the fourteenth century with Jews exiled from Spain, were exterminated in 1492 by Cheikh Abd-al-Karim al-Meghili, who ordered the destruction of the synagogues of Touat. After the destruction of the communities of Tamentit and Gurara, some of the survivors could have gone farther south to the Sahara and followed the caravans' route to find refuge with other Jews settled near the river Niger. Ismael Haidara, the leader of Zakhor, tells of the exile of the Touati Jews in these terms: "Many Jews died, the synagogue of Tamentit was destroyed and other Jews went farther away to the fringes of Sahara in the kingdom of Gao."[21] If so, the surviving Touati Jews experienced only a very temporary peace in the region of Gao. According to the Sudanese author Ahmed Baba, Askya Muhammad the Great, ruler of the Songhai, under the influence of the same al-Meghili who had left Touat for Sudan, issued an edict of expulsion of Jews from his kingdom around 1500.[22] The policy of Askya Muhammad was to put an end to any Jewish presence in the Niger loop. In the fifteenth century, Leo Africanus wrote, "The king was a mortal enemy of the Jews, none of them should inhabit the city, the people who entertain them have their belongings confiscated."[23] Five centuries later, Haidara concludes that "the Jews could not go farther, in front of the great Nile of the Arabs (the river Niger). They stop facing the Koran and the sword. They convert." And he adds, "It was thus that black Jews became Muslims."[24]

The families' leaders who founded Zakhor declare, "The three families who constitute our community are Levite Kehath (Kati), Cohen and Abana."[25] Haidara reveals that he learned from elders coming from Kirshamba, a village near Timbuktu, when his father died, that "there were things he ought to know, that they were not Haidara or Toure," which are common Songhai names. His uncles revealed to him that their family descended from Jews, "but we did not say it; we have taken our women's names, the knowledge of the family's Jewish identity being preserved, in secret, to protect ourselves from persecution." According to traditions, the Abana family, traders and dyers, came to Timbuktu sometime early in the nineteenth century and settled in Kirshamba.[26] This tradition seems to be in agreement with information from Oliel, who signals that Abani is the name, probably of Hebrew origin, of an ancient village in Touat and specifies that "the people of Touat reputed to be of Jewish origin kept the use of this patronymic."[27]

In 1996, Haidara possessed fourteen commercial and legal manuscripts, obtained from a set of family archives that refer to these families.[28] Most of the documents are written in Arabic, some are in Judeo-Arabic, some have handwritten notations in Hebrew script, and others are in Spanish. Haidara has undertaken a linguistic analysis of these texts to try to retrace an ancient Jewish presence in Timbuktu and to recall his own past.[29]

In his book *Les Juifs à Tombouctou* (1999), Haidara considers that the patronymic *Kâ'ti* is the result of an error of vocalization by the translators of the *Tarikh el-Fettash* and that the correct reading would be *Cota*, a name used by a number of converted Jews in Spain and Portugal.[30] According to his research, the Cota family was forced to convert to Catholicism, then left Spain for Ceuta, Morocco, around 1467. From there, they went to Algeria, then Mauritania, then Timbuktu. Sometime during this journey, the family converted to Islam and adopted the name Kati. The oral tradition of Kirshamba indicates Ismael al-Yahudi as the ancestor of the Kati of Kurmina. This Jew would have reached Cheyda through Morocco, Walatta, and Kumeyra. From him descended the famous Alfa-Kota or Kati who founded Kirshamba and undertook the writing of the *Tarikh el-Fettash*, the first historical work on the Niger loop, in 1519.[31] Boubakar Khalidi, the representative of Zakhor in Kirshamba, provides a variant to this account and notices that they all had the last name of *Djarumba*, which is not recognized as a Songhai name, and which has the same meaning as *Aliahudu-hu* (i.e., al-Yahudi, the Jew).[32]

Among these documents, an account of the year 1080 (1766) noted the death of al-Hâjj Abd al Salâm al-Kûhin, 9 Safar 1080 (July 17, 1766), without giving any information about him as an individual. The same chronicle also mentioned al-Hâjj Abd al-Karim al-Kûhin, who was captured by the Touareg during an attack on Timbuktu and released for a ransom of 1,000 *mithcals* of gold and two horses. Oral tradition holds that those in Tangassane, another village near Timbuktu with Jewish ancestors, are descendants of al-Hâjj Abd al Salâm al-Kûhin. Al-Hâjj al-Kûhin is remembered as a Jew by birth who made the pilgrimage to Mecca after his arrival and started a family in Tangassane.[33]

From this time on, the patronymic *al-Kûhin* appears often enough in archives so that the presence of these Kûhin in Timbuktu allows us to imagine a community of Jewish traders, very likely of Moroccan origin and converted to Islam, who had kept their Jewish patronymic.[34] This information seems to coincide with the account of Mungo Park, who in 1796, as we have seen, revealed the presence of Jews in the region of Timbuktu who were Arabic speaking, who recited the same prayers as the Moors, and who safeguarded their ethnicity through endogamy.[35]

The route to Timbuktu, which was closed to the Jews, apparently since Askya Muhammad's edict, was reopened in the nineteenth century by a traveling rabbi born in Morocco, Mardochée Aby Serour.[36] In 1860 Mardochée arrived with a caravan in Timbuktu, where he set up a commercial activity and where in 1863, some coreligionists joined him. A hundred or so deeds of sale and letters testify to the presence in Timbuktu[37] of a little more than ten Jews from Morocco who were able to constitute a minyan and establish a synagogue.[38] Recommended by Auguste Beaumier, the consul of France in Mogador, Mardochée subsequently became a correspondent of the Société de Géographie in France, on whose behalf he explored African lands. As such, he became the travel companion of Charles de Foucauld, and we recall that he signaled the existence of nomadic Jews, called "Daggatun," or "those who changed their faith," by the Touareg. According to Mardochée, in order to flee the Touat from the persecution of Abdel Malik, the Daggatun, whose numbers were estimated at 300,000 or more, "scattered everywhere in the desert. Some of them live near Timbuktu, others near Boudjehiba (or Bouzebiha ?), Mabrouk, Mamoun; some of them are on the bank of the river (Djoliba or Niger), in the city of Agades and in the city of Bamba; but most of them live in the great desert of Adgag, among the great family of Aulamiden, who are orthodox Touareg."[39] Mardochée specified that he himself learned the history of nomadic Jews living in the desert "from his father and his father's brothers and their father [who] were born in el Hammeda and... told us constantly of these events."[40]

We do not have any reliable historical material to decide if the founding members of Zakhor descend from Jews who fled al-Meghili. However, we may wonder how these Malians of Timbuktu began to think of themselves as Jews. As seen throughout this survey, claims to Hebrew descent among African people have a long history. Among African traditions there are many derivations from the biblical texts, and legends referring to the departure from Egypt are prominent. Thus, families who founded Gombou in Mali claim to originate from Canaan: their ancestors originated from Bani Israela, who left to settle in Egypt in the time of Pharaoh Aryan al-Walidi and who, when Joseph died, left the Nile valley for the Niger valley. According to the *Tarikh al-Sudan*, the magicians summoned by Pharaoh during his controversy with Moses came from Kukiya, the former Songhai capital city, in the south of present-day Mali.[41]

At the beginning of the nineteenth century, French colonial explorers of the Senegal and Niger rivers adopted the Hamitic hypothesis and merged it with fragments of these legends, which they used to create symbolic distances between groups. We know that Delafosse's hypothesis of a Judeo-Syrian origin of the Peul accompanied the search for the sources of the Senegal and Niger rivers and the exploration of the city of Timbuktu. His views were based on the descriptions and interpretations of Africa of his time.[42] As Felix Dubois observed in *Timbuktu the Mysterious*:

> The Songhois themselves furnish further proof that they were originally strangers in the country. Their speech is totally different from the numerous Sudanese dialects, and its roots are those of the language of the Nile. Moreover their physical type owns nothing in common with that of the West African Negro. In the most mixed group of Negroes a Songhoi may be identified at the first glance; his skin is as black as theirs, certainly, but nothing in his mask conforms to their well-known characteristics. The nose of the Songhois is straight and long, pointed rather than flat: the lips are comparatively thin, and the mouth wide rather than prominent and broad; while the eyes are deeply set and straight in their orbit; a cursory glance shows that the profile resembles that of the European, and one is struck by the remarkable intelligence of their physiognomy and expression.[43]

Among many others, Amaury Talbot's opinion was that "the mass of the Songhai are certainly Negroes, though there is little doubt that their ruling families had a strain of Hamitic or even Semitic blood."[44] During the colonial era almost every English-speaking anthropologist reflects this influence. In his book *History of the Colonisation of Africa by Alien Races* (1913), Sir Harry Johnston attributed an Egyptian origin to the Songhai as follows: "Though black-skinned and woolly haired, their features are often of the Caucasian cast, and their characteristics generally those of Negroids rather than Negroes."[45] Charles Meek noted among the Songhai in Timbuktu "a notable elegance of manners," while a traveler stressed the "Egyptian appearance" of the portico of their house.[46]

Among the influences on the crystallization of Jewish identities, the mythic image of the nomadic Daggatun Jews is probably one of the main elements that gave support to the reorganization of the Timbuktu Jews' identity.

At a certain point in its history, a little before the French annexation of Timbuktu (1893–1894), the inhabitants of this city met a traveling rabbi who appeared suddenly and put an end to their isolation. He also reintroduced the myth of the forgotten Jews. The mythic past of the Daggatun sustained the collective memory of Jewish legends of the south of the Maghreb and the search for kinship with ancestral Jewish traditions. This coincided with the introduction or reintroduction of Jewish practices in Timbuktu observed by Mardochée and his companions between 1860 and 1868, their presence inducing a renewal of ties with the rest of the Diaspora. Similarly, in the nineteenth century, the tiny caste of Bene Israel of West India built up a legend around David Rahabi, a Jewish *paradesi* traveling trader from Cochin, who was aware of the presence of the Konkan community but who never visited it. The Benei Israel collective memory, however, remembered his name and associated him with the reintroduction of some forgotten practices and the reorganization of their religious and community life.[47]

For this community, the reestablishment of a Jewish identity is well under way. Nowadays, instead of maintaining Jewish affiliation in secret among elders, Malian Jewish families are openly known by all the members of the community. Richard Gold, who worked for the U.S. Agency for International Development (AID) in Bamako from 1993 to 1997, has followed the process undertaken by the Zakhor and brought the Malian Jewish community to the attention of Americans, partly through the Internet. The listserv of Kulanu has carried Gold's messages and increased the importance of links forged with other Jewish communities outside Mali. Nowadays there are more than sixty listings for "Jews of Timbuktu" on the Internet. After the visit to Timbuktu in 1996 by Samantha Klein, a Peace Corps volunteer, the Malian newspaper *Le Républicain* recorded this first contact between American Jews and Malians, writing, "Everybody here knows that they are their long-standing relatives and that they all descend from the Twelve Tribes of Israel."[48]

Since its creation, Zakhor has been able to carry out a number of health-related and educational activities. Immediate projects requiring Western assistance include ethnographic and historic research on the Jews of Timbuktu. Other plans include the provision of grants to record oral histories and to organize further research on other sub-Saharan African descendants of Jews, the training of Hebrew-language teachers, and the restoration of the Jewish cemeteries of the area.[49]

Members of Zakhor seem increasingly conscious of their uniqueness and take pride in their Jewish heritage. Haidara revealed the existence in Timbuktu, on the other bank of the river, of a cemetery dedicated to the Touati Jews and their descendants, "the Touati's cemetery."[50] Thus, the members of

Zakhor now consider the tombs of Mardochée's family, in the sand near Timbuktu, as a part of their Jewish patrimony, thus appropriating all Jewish traces in the vicinity of Timbuktu.[51]

Since the release of the manifesto, Zakhor wrote a letter to the governor of the Timbuktu district protesting against anti-Semitic statements made by a radio station that operates from the governor's office building. The letter reads:

> On the 15th and 19th of August 1996, a programme referred to the Jews of *Alioudou-hou* considered as lost and cursed.... You cannot ignore that in the region of Timbuktu live about one thousand Malian Jews who, furthermore, are Muslim, like yourself. Your programmes are thus a moral persecution of a component of the population of the Republic of Mali.... Mali is constitutionally lay, that is, multidenominational, multiracial.... We have the right to assume our ancestry and cultural heritage, which is, in large part, this Judaism you disparage.[52]

On the basis of well-anchored founding myths, the members of Zakhor, by claiming the statute of a "dispersed Jewish community," updated the myth of the lost-and-the found tribe. The examination of their myth of origins reveals the way in which they are redefining their self-image. They explain their presence in Timbuktu as being the result of a connection with members of another ancient Jewish community living in Touat, themselves direct or indirect descendants of Jews from Solomonic Israel. The founding members of Zakhor portrayed themselves as a small, early prosecuted Jewish population said to have been superseded by a later Islamic community. As for the Falasha of Ethiopia, the attempts to explain their origins are of an essentially diffusionist nature, and we shall see that this is the case for the majority of the groups studied.[53] In constructing its Jewish identity, Zakhor depicted its history as one more fragment in the mosaic that constitutes the Jewish experience and produced familiar images that were easy to integrate with popular views. The story of the Malian Jews, as Kaplan suggested concerning the Falasha, is "the recapitulation in miniature of the universal history of Judaism."[54]

The Igbo of Nigeria

There are currently several self-proclaimed Jewish communities across Nigeria, and their growth is significant. Members of these Jewish communities mostly come from the Igbo group—the third-largest ethnic group in the country—who live in the southeastern region of Nigeria. There are more than twenty-five synagogues of different sizes across the country from Abuja to Port Harcourt, and some estimate the possibility of as many as 30,000 Igbo practicing some form of Judaism.[55] Several religions coexist in Nigeria, which accentuates regional and ethnic distinctions. Islam predominates in the north, among the Hausa and Fulani, and Protestantism and local syncretist Christianity are most evident in the Yoruba areas in the west, while Catholicism is prevalent in the Igbo and closely related areas.[56]

Today, three categories of Igbo have a link to Judaism: the Hebrewists, who consider themselves as "pre-talmudic" Jews on the basis of the alleged Hebraic traditions of their forefathers; the members of the various Jewish congregations who have been striving toward Jewish recognition for some years; and, finally, the Sabbatherians, who number more than 2 million and who practice a kind of Judaism while also reading the New Testament. A widespread belief among the Igbo is that prior to the arrival of British missionaries they practiced a form of Judaism.[57] The Igbo are currently developing versions of their tribal history that place it as part of the Jewish Diaspora or claim that their ancestors came from Israel via the old African trade routes. According to the Igbo lore of the Eri, Nri, and Ozubulu clans, Igbo groups traditionally claim descent from three particular Israelite tribes—Gad, Zevulun, and Menashe—and call them Benei Gath, Benei Zevulun, and Benei Menashe. The Igbo compare their traditional customs, burial rites, circumcision on the eight day, ritual slaughter of animals, exclusiveness, marriage customs, and agricultural practices with those of ancient Israelites.

Remi Ilona, a historian of the Igbo and an activist of the Gihon Jewish community, has studied the Igbo's customs, giving a detailed description of each and linking them to biblical traditions, including rules of hygiene, storage, prayers, and festivals. Although he accepts that "these traditions must have in many cases 'faded,' changed and metamorphosed somewhat, yet [they] are recognisable as Hebraic in origin and content. They are still unmistakable as vestiges of Hebrew practices ... seen in the Torah books of Leviticus, Numbers and Deuteronomy."[58]

The name Igbo/Ibo is widely considered as a corrupt form of Ivri/Ibri/Hebrew. The interpretation of the Igbo name for the Supreme Being, Chukwu Abiama, is God of Abraham (*Chukwu* means God, and *Abiama* may be a derivative of *Abraham*).[59] When asked, "Where do the Igbo come from?" Chief Onwa, who at ninety is the oldest man of the Nri clan in Igboland, answered without hesitation:

> The Igbo are a people called Hebrews. They were led by a man with the name Eri. There were troubles in their original home, so they

took a ship and sailed down the Omambala River [tributary of the Niger]. Eri was chief. On crossing the Omambala River into Igboland he settled and established his government. They came from the place where sacrifices are made.... They are related to Israel, Hebrews and Israel are brothers. Originally their name was Hebrew but after crossing the river they changed it to Igbo.[60]

The Nri are often described as the most important keepers of Igbo traditions, responsible for performing rituals of purification among other Igbo clans. The clan is considered to carry the Levite practices evoked by the English missionary George Basden in his book *Among the Ibos of Nigeria* (1921).[61] Basden, who stayed in Nigeria for many years, found all manner of signs of Judaism among the Nigerian people: "There are certain customs which rather point to Levitic influence at a more or less remote period. This is suggested in the underlying ideas concerning sacrifice and in the practice of circumcision. The language also bears parallels with Hebrew idiom."[62]

With regard to the encounter between some Nigerian groups and Judaism, one must consider the recurring theme of the Hamitic hypothesis. Among early anthropologists, colonists, and missionaries from the nineteenth century, one popular suggestion was that the Igbo and Yoruba, or at least major features of their religion and culture, originated from Egypt.[63] For example, Talbot asserted, "The statues which reached their greatest development in the Mbari temples of the Ibo, though in clay, and most primitive, are similar in feeling and design to some found in Tutoukhamem's tomb."[64]

White supremacist versions of the Hamitic myth, examined above, maintained their vivid influence up to the mid–twentieth century. As recently noted by the historian Philip Zachernuk, Nigerian authors of the late nineteenth century and early twentieth century, in rethinking their history, adopted the interactions of these influences and accepted the "degeneration of their ancestors" from more advanced civilizations, particularly as a result of migrations from Egypt.[65] In the 1960s, an Irish colonial administrator, Robert Collis, who spent several years in Nigeria, saw a clear difference between the Igbo and other West Africans, explicitly evoking stereotypes about the Jews: "There is no doubt that the Ibo men are the hardest workers in Nigeria, and their women among the most charming and the most intelligent... and have shown themselves to have IQ's as high as any race or group anywhere in the world."[66] This theory was involved by the priest and lampoonist J. Olumide Lucas in the 1940s to explain the progressive and intelligent character he attributed to his people.[67]

At the beginning of the twentieth century, Reverend Samuel Johnson, the first Yoruba historian to write the history of his people, adopted the idea of a migration from Nubia through the Arabian Peninsula, down to the present territory. According to Johnson, there was no doubt that the language and religion of the Yoruba derived from Upper Egypt.[68] Following this line of thought, S. O. Biobaku claimed in 1955 that the Yoruba originated from Meroe, the ancient kingdom of the Sudan, while Emmanuel Ughulu asserted the Jewish origin of the small tribe of Esan.[69] In his critical book about the Lost Tribes, Godbey established that in the 1930s, colonial cultural preconceptions were adopted by 400 families of around 2,000 Yoruba Jews in the district of Ondo in southwestern Nigeria (100 miles east of Abeokuta and 900 miles from Timbuktu). Their Muslim or fetishist neighbors gave them the name of Emo Yo Quaim, that is, Foreign People. This community claimed a Semitic descent, called themselves by the Hebrew name of B'nai Ephraim (Children of Ephraim), and asserted that their Moroccan ancestors were expelled from oasis to oasis by Muslim persecution, beyond Timbuktu.[70] However, the information about the existence of Emo Yo Quaim Jews appears to rely heavily on a novel by Lobagola, *An African Savage's Own Story*, which was rather successful in the 1930s.[71] Lobagola, who gave lectures in the United States, told of his surprising adventures as a black Jew from Dahomey who left the African bush for modern civilization. He wrote in his autobiographical novel, "I already said that my people observe the main practices of Judaism, because we believe that we descend from Jews who came to Africa many centuries ago. We have the Thora (the laws of Moses) and we follow it to the letter. We celebrate Passover, Pentecost, Rosch Haschana, Yom Kippour and Souccoth. We practice circumcision and we obey seven Rabbis [sic]."[72] The claim to ancient links with Hebrews seems shared even by some Christian Igbo. For example, Uche P. Ikeayibe, an Igbo Christian minister, wrote a booklet in 1999 on the origin of the Igbo people and posited that Igbo are Israelites. He backed his position by citing the book of Olaudah Equiano, an Igbo captured by slave merchants in the eighteenth century, who was transported to England and sold there. Equiano considered an icon by the Igbo, educated himself, and wrote *The Interesting Narratives of the Life of Olaudah Equiano or Gustavus Vassa the African*, in which he suggested that the Igbo were one of the Lost Tribes of Israel.[73]

More recently, Sir N. Okafor-Ogbaji, the coordinator of King Solomon Shepherd Federation, an African American Jewish association in New Jersey, claimed that the Aro-Igbo of eastern Nigeria are Bani Israel. He published a genealogical chart tracing the ancestry of the Aro-Igbo from Adam to Arodi, the founder of the Aro lineage, and attempted to demonstrate "quite interesting similarities in the morpho-syntactic and semantic structures of the Igbo and ancient Hebrew."[74]

The convergence of these conceptions probably contributed to the self-delineation of some Nigerian groups as Jews by heritage. In a context where the idea of a Hebrew origin was implicitly present, when did the Igbo's claim for Judaism arise? Analogies between the experience of Igbo and of Jews have produced other associations. Even before the economic cooperation that existed between the Igbo and Israel prior to the Biafra war (1967–1970), there was a widespread sentiment among the Igbo that they were part of the Jewish people. Suffering episodes in the Jewish past assumed particular significance for the Igbo, who suffered persecution during the Biafra-Nigeria war.[75] When, in May 1967, in southern Nigeria, the Igbo proclaimed their independence, the Nigerian government immediately put a blockade in place. A civil war began that lasted for two and one-half years and killed more than 1 million people. During the conflict, journalists used references to genocide and holy war to arouse international consciousness, and circulated pictures of emaciated children to denounce famine used as a political weapon.[76] In 1970, when the war ended, the Nigerian Finance Commissioner forced the Igbo who had money in banks to accept twenty Nigerian pounds in lieu of whatever amounts they had. The Abandoned Properties Edict of 1973, which enacted the seizure of Igbo's land properties by non-Igbo Nigerians, was likened to Nazi confiscation of Jews' possessions.[77] Since then the Igbo have regularly compared their experience to the modern experience of the Jews; this induced one member of the Abuja community to say, "I have noticed that when the Igbo talk about Biafra, they veer into discussions on Israel and Zionism. Unconsciously, our people have identified the return/*teshuvah* (repentance or return) to God/Judaism as the panacea for what some perceive as injustice from the British/Nigerians."[78]

The dire circumstances of the Igbo's postwar period were made even more precarious by famine and political instability. Since the oil boom of the 1970s, Nigeria's economy has been in a crisis. Without extraordinary help, the Igbo cannot under existing conditions generate access to well-being in the future. In such a dire situation, where food, shelter, and education are unaffordable for the majority of the population, the symbolic recognition they find by identifying their experience as a Jewish one also offers the possibility of inestimable outside help. After the ravages of the transatlantic slave trade, colonialism and the rejection of ancestral customs, the failure of Biafran aspirations, and repeated persecutions, the Igbo are in a quest for identity today. The historical experience and suffering of the Jewish people and the creation of the State of Israel seem to offer them a workable paradigm.

Today, one should not expect to encounter the majority of Igbo practicing Judaism. Most belong to various Christian churches and know relatively little about Judaism, but they have a deep sentiment that the Igbo come from Israel. Every congregation represented a way of connecting with Judaism, partly due to interactions with Western Jewry.[79] Some of the larger and significant communities include the Gihon Hebrew Centre, founded in September 2004 in Abuja, which could be described as somewhat orthodox, and the Tikvah Israel Congregation, led by Sar Habbabuk, which could be described as conservative.[80]

Since 2003, Kulanu and American and Israeli visitors have donated Torahs, books, and prayer items to the Gihon Hebrew Centre, which now has its own synagogue and library in Abuja and has created an academy where the Hebrew language and basic Judaism are studied.[81] The community now carefully observes all the formalities and prayers of the Jewish services and customs.[82] From a questionnaire I sent to the Gihon community in May 2005 concerning the oral tradition of the families, it appears, outside a palpable thirst for Jewish studies and life, that almost all of the respondents are convinced of their Jewish heritage and consider that they grew up with the idea of their Jewish origin, even if they formerly practiced Christianity.[83] Overall, the questionnaire showed that the majority of the community members consider that the traditional Igbo religion, which existed before the arrival of Christianity, was "like Judaism," and they explain their reconnection to Judaism as akin to a revelation. As concerns their expectations with respect to their Jewish affiliation, almost all the respondents expressed Jewish aspirations, such as the "return to Torah," the desire to visit Jerusalem, and the desire to reclaim a heritage that has been denied them for so long.

At the end of June 2005, with the support of the American Jewish World Service and Kulanu, an American rabbi from Illinois, Rabbi Rosen visited the Igbo in Nigeria for an entire month. A large number of the Igbo, including Sabbatherians, informed by word of mouth of the rabbi's arrival, came from far away to attend his lectures, to hear his comments on the Bible and his teachings on the Torah. The rabbi led or participated in the services of Sabbath in the three synagogues of Abuja and also worked with the Igbo who had begun *teshuvah* (repentance/return). According to Rabbi Gorin, as many as 10,000 people might be interested in a Halachic conversion.[84] The visit of Rabbi Rosen, which was considered a historic event among the Igbo of Nigeria, reinforced the Igbo's Jewish identity elsewhere, as indicated by the following e-mail sent by an Igbo living in England to the Abuja community: "I must thank you for everything, especially on the role you are playing for the reawakening of the truth on the Igbo Jews. This is a great achievement that only the great minds will discover."[85]

In recent years, as access to information via the Internet has grown, the Igbo's Jewish identity is acquiring new pieces every day, like an expanding jigsaw puzzle. The typological association of Igbo as descendants of the Ten Tribes of Israel has been recently sustained by the discovery in the region of Aguleri of an onyx stone with the name Gad engraved in a form of ancient Hebrew. This is believed to be the confirmation of Jewish ancestral origin according to an interpretation of Exodus 39:6: "And they wrought onyx stones enclosed in ouches of gold, graven as signets are graven, with the names of the children of Israel."

Various recent events have provided synergies and connections between Jewish African Americans and Igbo. The established model of African American Jewish communities who claim a Judaic descent can only facilitate and speed up the current process of religious identity elaboration of Igbo. In August 2003 in the United States, on the small island of St. Simons, Georgia, a Chicago-based group of Nigerians from the Igbo tribe, and others from Haiti and Canada, met to mark the sanctification of the place where Igbo men threw themselves into the sea rather than live as slaves. As part of the event, a member of the Chicago organization, Bruce Dan Judah Carey, presented a paper on the history of the Igbo, Ndi, and Hebrew people. Okpala Eze Nri Chukwuemeka I. Onyesoh, who represented the high priest of Igbo Land, gave a lecture on the conditions of the Igbo people under the current government of Nigeria. He wore a red *kippah* and a tallith described by the Kulanu article's author as "the garment worn by all Ibo priests when they officiate a cultural ceremony," these well-known attributes of Judaism being clearly given by an external observer the status of ancestral Igbo religious attire.[86] In January 2006, the Institute for Jewish and Community Research and Beth Shalom B'nai Zaken Ethiopian Hebrew Congregation, San Francisco, sponsored a trip to Nigeria. They were represented by individuals involved in the Alliance of Black Jews such as Rabbi Capers Funnye. The purpose of this trip was to visit the leaders of the various Igbo communities who claim to be of Jewish descent and to ascertain their interest in joining the recently formed American-based Pan African Jewish Alliance (PAJA).[87]

The Igbo Jews are now awaiting DNA testing that would find the Cohen DNA marker in both Igbo and Yoruba groups. While much more historical research needs to be done, it will be interesting to see what the long-term effects are on this community, in particular if or when the impact of scientific findings intervenes in their narratives.

The House of Israel of Ghana

Like the Igbo of Nigeria, another group, in the southwestern corner of Ghana, the House of Israel of Sefwi Wiaso and Sefwi Sui, is a new Jewish community.

Sefwi Wiaso is a village of 4,000 inhabitants where there is a new synagogue and a core group of around 800 people practicing Judaism.[88]

In 1976 a Ghanaian man named Aaron Ahotre Toakyirafa had a vision. He "spoke with the spirits," who inspired him to believe that he and his fellow villagers were actually descendants of the Lost Tribes of Israel. According to Toakyirafa, before the arrival of Christian missionaries, the Sefwi people had specific traditions deriving from Judaism. They strictly adhered to rest on Saturday, followed dietary restrictions that forbade them to eat pork, circumcised boys, and required women to go into isolation during their menstrual period, and so on. The founders of the community suggested that their ancestors originated from Jews in North Africa who had crossed the Sahara Desert centuries ago, perhaps from Timbuktu, ending up in the Ivory Coast. Over time, they lost connections to their Jewish roots but apparently maintained some Jewish customs. Then, the Jewish families of a district of the village called New Adiembra attempted to learn about Jewish practices and began to take Jewish observances very seriously. Nowadays members of the community say that they embraced Judaism because, to them, the Old Testament contained more truth than the New Testament. They reject Jesus Christ in all forms and consider themselves to be Jewish, although they would like to convert formally.[89]

This Jewish community is unique in Ghana. About one-third of Ghana's inhabitants are either Muslim or animist, and nearly everyone else is Christian.[90] As in many other countries in West Africa, evangelism has put down firm roots, and its fervor seems contagious.[91] Local religions also endure in Ghana and are often practiced in syncretism with the mainstream religions. Traditional cosmology expresses belief in a supreme being, referred to by the Akan as *Nyame*, or by the Ewe as *Mawu*. In precolonial times, the area of present-day Ghana comprised a number of independent kingdoms, including Gonja and Dagomba in the north, Ashanti in the interior, and the Fanti states along the coast. Modern Ghana takes its name from the ancient kingdom of Ghana, some 500 miles to the north of present-day Accra, which controlled the gold trade between the mining areas to the south and the Saharan trade routes to the north, and was also the focus for the export trade in Saharan copper and salt. Formed from the merger of the British colony of the Gold Coast and the Togoland trust territory in 1957, modern Ghana became the first sub-Saharan country in colonial Africa to gain its independence.[92] History and myths of the origin of modern Ghana are intimately linked with traditions of the ancient kingdom and biblical texts. Biblical references are found in various West African traditions, as the formation of the blacksmith caste, or the famous legend of Wagadu recorded by Charles Monteil, relating to the foundation of the ancient kingdom of Ghana. This tradition tells that the founder of this kingdom was "the chief of blacksmiths, Dinga, descending from King Solomon."[93] According to the tradition, when Dinga became blind and was transferring his power, he was tricked by his youngest son in the same way that Isaac tricked Jacob to deprive Esau of his right as the eldest son. There are different narrations of who Dinga was, but invariably they establish the fact that he was a stranger from afar, probably of white origin.[94] The lengthy components of the story of the exile of the Ten Tribes are found in this myth. African scholars consider the legend of Wagadu as "a condensation of stories which serve as archives for the entire ethnic group....First there is the long Soninke journey from Yemen or Palestine, then the crossing of North Africa through Egypt and what is presently the desert up to Adrar and Tagant, and the settlement in the fertile north region of Timbuktu."[95] It must be said that in the specific case of the smiths, biblical traditions and possible Jewish influences seem to be interrelated to the point that in some regions of Mauritania, for instance, smiths are called *Yahoud* and *Yibro*. In Somalia there is also evidence of the *samanyo*, an action by which a father "buys back" his son from the *Yibir* and then later receives a blessing, which simulates the buying back of the firstborn male child from the Levites, such as described in the book of Numbers (3:12, 13).

We know that since al-Idrissi, claims were made by Arabic writers of the Middle Ages that there were Jewish inhabitants in the south of the kingdom of Ghana. In the nineteenth century, the notion derived from the Hamitic hypothesis that, in this region, there were people of non-African extraction was widespread among Europeans due to the magnificent artworks of these regions.[96] No doubt the mechanism that, in the colonial context, fostered an imagined Hamitic origin had been active in this region. Thomas E. Bowdich, one of the first Europeans to have close contact with the Ashanti, after observing their customs, religious expressions, laws, architecture, art, and facial features, asserted that they were descendants of the "civilized Ethiopians of Herodotus."[97] While speaking of the Ashanti and kindred tribes, Ratzel affirmed without hesitation, "There are 12 stocks, the members of which are distributed promiscuously throughout these tribes, however remote they may be in situation or politically separated."[98] This culminated with Frobenius's theories affirming that the artworks of the Yoruba came from Plato's "Atlantis" and were thus essentially Greek.[99] These opinions were widely shared and conveyed by French anthropologists, such as Pr Eugène Pittard, who used anthropometry to claim that the Ashanti had the physical traits of populations that would have migrated from the northeast.[100] In *Hebrewisms of West Africa*, Williams theorized on the possible contacts between Hebrews and the tribes of West Africa. He even detected traces of Hebrew in the Ashanti's language, beginning with their name, which he broke down into *ti* for "children of" and *Ashan* for a city of Judea. Williams also identified a number of Jewish customs in the Ashanti rituals, from wedding rituals to purification ceremonies and menstrual isolation, and noted elements in common between the Ashanti and ancient Hebrews, such as the worship of Ob, the use of "Amen," endogamy, marriage between cousins, surnames, and above all, the worship of the Supreme Being.[101] Captain Rattray, the Ashanti district commissioner, a highly qualified official of the empire, who published a number of works about the Ashanti, shared Williams's point of view: "I am convinced that the conception, in the Ashanti mind, of a Supreme Being, has nothing whatever to do with missionary influence, nor could it be ascribed to contact with Christians or even, I believe, with Mahomedans.... In a sense, therefore, it is true that this great Supreme Being, the conception of whom has been innate in the minds of the Ashanti, is Jehovah of the Israelites."[102] While much more historical research needs to be done, part of the discourse of the new Jewish community in Ghana clearly has strong reminiscences of this background.

Let us see in what context the House of Israel members' claim of Jewish origin developed. Since the independence in 1957, corruption and internal military strife proved apparently intractable problems. In the 1960s and 1970s, Ghana went through an extended period of instability marked by military rule. By the early 1980s, Ghana's economy was in an advanced state of collapse; a military government under the leadership of Flight Lieutenant Jerry John Rawlings came to power and instituted the Economic Recovery Program (ERP). The effects of the ERP on the domestic economy, however, led to a lowered standard of living for most Ghanaians.[103] After Toakyirafa's death in 1991, it seems that the community had a difficult time, and that some of its members even attended church, since they were afraid of being further persecuted.[104] In 1993, David Akenorah, a close relation of Toakyirafa, became the primary leader of the House of Israel community and fostered its growth. Akenorah then contacted the Ghanaian community of the United States and asked for help from his African American coreligionists, who were active in Jewish causes. To develop the knowledge of Judaism of the members of the Sefwi Sui community, he appealed for the donation of prayer and Torah books and help in improving their farming activities.[105] Since 1996, following these contacts and contacts with Kulanu, teachers and rabbis began to visit the community, teaching its members Hebrew and Torah and bringing with them educational and religious material. The synagogue Tifereth Israel, named after a generous congregation in Des Moines, Iowa, was built. Kulanu helped the community for economic development, and the Sefwi people started a business making embroidered challah covers.[106] More recently, the community has been receiving a steady flow of Jewish visitors from the worldwide Jewish community. Many have been writing about the community, bringing them to the attention of Jews worldwide.

The story of the Sefwi communities is significant of the typological associations of African peoples with the Lost Tribes of Israel. Sefwi communities subscribed to the common history of the global dispersion of the Jews among the nations deriving from the myth of origins of Ghana. Mythical traditions such as the legend of Wagadu brought the Hebrew Bible to life in their African-based practices and had been considered as a Jewish heritage within some communities. The group appropriation of Judaism characterized a Hebraic-African formation in which aspects of Old Testament traditions were integrated with African elements. In the 1990s, inspired by Toakyirafa's vision, the communities of Sefwi Wiaso seemed to consider Judaism as a living religion that they must interpret according to the needs of their community. Their link to Judaism was through a lost Israelite claim associated with millenarian beliefs, which may have been introduced to them through colonialism and Christianity or alternatively may have been inherited from their indigenous religious beliefs. Recently, following exchanges with the African American Diaspora, it seems that the community's discourse on identity is evolving. A certain Daniel Baiden of Ghanaian origin, who lived in the United States, went back to Ghana in 1996 and visited the community. He introduced himself as follows:

> I am a Jew who was born in Ghana ... my family's oral history says that our ancestors are from Ethiopia, and that our family originally had come from Israel. As a child I heard many times that we were part of one of the Ten Lost tribes of Israel. Like many Ethiopians, we moved a lot. Hundreds of years ago, to flee the conquerors of Ethiopia, my ancestors migrated west, eventually settling in Ghana.... When I heard from Kulanu about the village of Sefwi Wiaso, I was sure that my family must somehow be responsible for the village's turn toward our faith. I grew up always aware of my Jewish heritage. My father Emmanuel had learned much about modern Judaism from a friend, Rabbi Weiss, a Polish refugee who lived in Ghana in the late 1940s and early 1950s.... My family [in Ghana] possesses various Jewish ritual objects that are quite old, including tallitot, Stars of David, and prayers written in Amharic, the Ethiopian language.... I moved to the United States in 1979, I joined the Congregation *Os eh Shalom*, in Laurel, Maryland, where Rabbi Gary Fink has served as my spiritual teacher.... I regularly attend

Shabbat services, keep a kosher home and I am active in Jewish causes.[107]

We already know that African Americans gave rise to myths of origin in which Ethiopia became a common birthplace. Recent remarks of Baiden signal the perpetuation of the Ethiopia/Judaism/Africa amalgamation, as it was constituted among African American Jewish groups in the 1950s. Hitherto, the community of Ghana was not particularly connected to Ethiopia as regards its myth of origin. The visit of Baiden mythologized Ethiopia as a place of origin for African Jews. In claiming ties to a Jewish lineage whose roots are in Africa, Baiden provided the Sefwi community with the assertion that Africa was the geographical foundation of Judaism—the land that had produced the Jewish religion. Baiden's intervention offers a good example of a subsystem of reciprocal representation, between the new Jewish community in Ghana and African American Jews of Ghanaian ancestry.[108]

In bringing to Ghana the version of the standing myth of origin of African American Jews, Baiden went full circle by providing a new piece in the symbolical identity process of the community of Ghana.

The Tutsi-Hebrews of Havilah

From the late 1980s, a group of Tutsi, who have their origin in the Great Lakes area, claim that this region was the home of a Hebraic community in ancient times, and they assert a Jewish identity. They refer to their homeland, which allegedly extends far beyond the regions where the Tutsi now reside as Havilah, according to the name given in Genesis 2:11 to the legendary territory irrigated by the Pishon River. Since 1999, the movement's headquarters is in Brussels, Belgium, where intellectual Tutsi expatriates in Europe have founded the Havilah organization. According to their ideology, they focus their efforts on the Hebraic remnants of pre-Talmudic tribes of Israel, isolated on "the other side of the rivers of Ethiopia" (Zephania 3:10). During a festival held in 1990 in Nigeria, Tutsi intellectuals celebrated "the physical reunification of the lost tribes of Havilah, Guihon and Futa Djalon" at a date that, in order to show the symbolical reference, corresponded to Pesach, the Jewish festival celebrating the end of slavery and the departure from Egypt.[109]

In 1999, during an inaugural conference of the Havilah Institute, its president, Professor Bwejeri, proclaimed from Brussels the Judaization of all Tutsi. This conference was structured around revealing themes such as "Under the sign of the armorial bearings of Havilah: the Star of David, a characteristic of the modern States of Israel and Burundi" or "Solomon's drums of which the Shebatic sovereigns of Havilah are the guardians."[110] The Havilah Institute is an organization that claims to assemble "seven centres of research, intervention and influence settled on nearly every continent." These centers bring together high-level Tutsi expatriates, who are experts in the economic, financial, political, and military sectors. In the words of Professor Bwejeri, the charismatic leader of Havilah, these centers are dedicated to "restoring and reviving the lost memory of the twelve Hebraic codes, which for thousands of years, characterized the civilization of Cushitic peoples of southern Abyssinia (Rwanda, Burundi, Ankole, Buhavu), settled on the fringes of the White Nile and guardians of King Solomon's mines."[111]

Today, in claiming their Hebrew identity, the Tutsi combine the Hamitic myth and Afrocentrist arguments.[112] From a theological point of view, Professor Bwejeri affirms that the cultural and religious references of the Batutsi have perpetuated either pharaonic monotheism from the eighteenth dynasty of Egypt or the Mosaic prescriptions transcribed in the Hebraic Torah.[113] He states that the political organization of the Batutsi kingdoms (from the Kush kingdom until post-Zagwe kingdoms: 1270–1960) are strictly related to the Solomonic system.[114] He considers that "the ancient material civilization of the Batutsi, their language, their mythology, their religion and their political legacy and their general way of life, all those matters can be described exactly as related by Eldad Ha Dani."[115]

The self-image of the Tutsi is largely the creation of outsiders, which is to say that it is fundamentally an identity that has been imagined into existence. The first explorers to reach the region of Rwanda and Burundi were immediately struck by the differences they observed between the three groups of Hutu, Tutsi, and Twa. The "tall, lithe and angular" Tutsi were perceived as being quite different from the Hutu and Twa. In his *Journal of the Discovery of the Nile* (1863), the explorer John Hanning Speke proposed an explanation of these differences by a theory, according to which the Tutsi, after having migrated from the north, subjugated the groups around them and became the ruling caste. He considered them closely allied to the pastoral Galla of southern Ethiopia, and the idea that the Tutsi were superior to the other groups of the region persisted.[116] In comparing them to the Hutu and the Twa, with whom they shared the same territory, Mary H. Bradley, during a 1926 visit to Tanganyika, wrote of "the sophisticated Watutsi of Rwanda . . . who have a precise theology and elaborate account of the creation of the world." She asserted, "Their stories came from the north with these tribes of pronounced Hamitic and Semitic origins."[117]

In the twentieth century, long after Speke's and Bradley's assertions, colonial administrators, whose judgment had been formed by these clichés, undertook to convince the Great Lakes region's elite of their innate superiority. Pierre Rychmans, who for ten years was resident administrator in Burundi, states, "The Batutsi were destined to rule. Their very appearance is enough to assure them of a considerable prestige among the inferior races that surround them."[118]

The Catholic Church, which has long been one of Rwanda's most powerful institutions, generated substantial discourse and additional evidence of the Tutsi origins. In 1933, Father Pagès asserted that the Tutsi, as well as the Peul, were Hamites-Semites who had come from Egypt and Abyssinia in caravans accompanied by black porters.[119] The Rwandan priest Alexis Kagame, in addition to his prestige as a man of the church, played an important role in enabling the Hamitic ideology to take root within the indigenous population, through his contribution to the writing of the history of Rwanda.[120] Mgr Léon Classe, archbishop of Rwanda, wrote in 1922:

> The population of Rwanda is composed of three races: the Batutsi, which is the noble class, the Bahutu or common people, and the Batwa or Pygmies....The Batutsi are not Bantu, they are, if you prefer Negroids and they are the people in Africa who have the highest Hamitic index. A long time ago, before the Christian era, there were in Asia Minor important migrations of peoples who went to Egypt, then populated Abyssinia and progressively spread southward. This is the likely origin of our Batutsi.[121]

The perenniality of the Hamitic myth is striking. In 1978, Paul del Perugia, who had been French ambassador in Rwanda, wrote in his book *Les derniers rois mages*, "The Hamite...came very late, at the end of the thirteenth century, to the inter-lake area.... Everything made them irreducible to the Bantu. The Hamites are neither Negroid, nor Europoid. The origins of their splendid race remain still mysterious."[122] He concluded that they were, in a way, "Magi."

In what context did the Tutsi's claim of a Jewish identity arise? Although there had always been class divisions, the colonial Belgian government decided in the 1930s to officially categorize the Hutu and Tutsi, by drawing artificial distinctions between the two, based on their ethnic background and distribution of power.[123] When the Belgians declared the country independent in 1962, a system of inequality and violence instituted by Rwanda's first elected president, Gregoire Kayiamba, leader of the sole Parmehutu Party, ensued.

The policy of labeling people with ethnic identity cards, begun by the Belgian government, was continued and used to discourage mixed marriages. Beginning in the 1970s, thousands of Tutsi were forced to resign from medical or educational positions or forced into exile or, worse, killed. For the subsequent governments, the issue of ethnicity remained a source of tensions, each ethnic group holding onto the memory of past massacres. New waves of ethnic clashes were unleashed in the 1990s. The main causes included a sagging economy and food shortages, and a subsequent mass flight of refugees that contributed to create a dangerous political climate. Violence escalated up until 1994, when a genocide of unprecedented swiftness officially left 937,000 Tutsis and moderate Hutus dead at the hands of organized bands of militia.[124]

Since their terrible suffering, the Tutsi describe their history as a microcosm of worldwide Jewish history, using key words such as *genocide, pogrom, Shoah, persecution*, and *anti-Semitism*.[125] Professor Bwejeri wrote: "For the last 40 years, the *Batutsi* have been exterminated and till now they are being exterminated, because of their Hebraic identity and their Solomonic legacy."[126] Following this, the spokesmen of Tutsi Hebrews called out to Israel and the international community to condemn and take measures against the anti-Semitic violence in Africa toward the 500,000 Tutsi of Rwanda. They also turned to the Jewish organizations of the Diaspora, and particularly of the United States, asking for their support. There is no doubt that the theory of the existence of an ethnic kinship between Tutsi and Hebrews carries an important emotional and historical charge for themselves and also for the descendants of victims of the Holocaust who provided significant support for the Tutsi cause.[127] In the autumn of 2004, the Kulanu president observed:

> The deterioration of the status of a remnant of the biblical people of Kush so far up the Nile from the more familiar Beta Israel of Ethiopia challenges us in more ways than is tolerable. We can ask that there is no more trouble for these proud upholders of an ancient national and religious tradition....US members of Congress have been alerted, and now they must be encouraged to transform their concern into action.[128]

In Europe, Jewish organizations took charge of demonstrations against the Tutsi genocide, such as that which was held on June 8, 2005, in Brussels, under the auspices of the Committee of Coordination of Jewish Organisations of Belgium (CCOJB), under the banner "No impunity for the negation of the genocide of Armenians, Jews and Tutsi."[129]

Nonetheless, it may be that considerations other than religious, that is, strategic and political, encourage the approach of the Tutsi-Hebrews to their identity. Denouncing the breakdown of the Arusha Accords,[130] Havilah decided in 2002, through the voice of Bwejeri, who now holds the title of Prince of Nkoronko, to launch a political attack they named Geulah (Redemption), whereby the Batutsi are reclaiming "their sovereignty, their lands and the principles of their multi-millenary civilization, inherited from their ancestors, the Kushites from South-Abyssinia."[131] These arguments fall within the scope of a Jewish-Zionist model, but the Tutsi's claims are analyzed by some people as a political ideology of domination. In an article entitled "Judaïsation des Tutsi: Identité ou stratégie de conquête" (2000), Erik Kennes considers that "the opportunist thesis of the existence of an ethnic kinship between Tutsi and Hebrews, which was built inside secret lairs, is presently spreading out... a maneuver brilliantly orchestrated by the former and intended to impose their metamorphosis to 'Hebrew-Tutsi' on the rest of mankind worldwide."[132] According to Kennes, this political manipulation coincides with the wars that shake the African Great Lakes region, and its only aim is to get support from Jewish groups and Western partners.

Between the Hamitic myth and Afrocentrist theses, and through the absorption of ideologies, as successive elaborations took place, we have a striking example of the way the myth of "Tutsi-Hamite" origins has been transformed into a recent "Tutsi-Jewish" identity. In May 1999, the Canadian newspaper *National Post* published an article on the Hema, another black people of the Great Lakes area who, following genetic analysis, claim that they are black Jews who descend from Aaron, Moses' brother.[133] This statement coincided with the beginning of the Havilah movement's finding its voice in Brussels and the spread, by the media, of the first scientific information on the Jewish origin of the Lemba and the Cohen Modal Haplotype, to be developed in the next section.[134]

This process by which the Tutsi developed a Jewish identity is very similar to the history of the Baluba in the Congo, whose upper classes were viewed as special, and therefore extraneous, in colonial times. This process, which has continued to the present day, might have been encouraged by a book, *In the Heart of Bantuland*, written in 1969 by D. Campbell, in which the author noted, "Northward [of Katanga] lives one of the greatest tribes of Central Africa, the Baluba, who are undoubtedly of Semitic origin. The name Baluba means 'the lost tribe,' and their language and customs have many Hebrew affinities. Their name for an idea of God, with their word for water, and people, and many other words and ideas, show their Semitic strain."[135] More recently, the idea of the Jewish identity of the Luba was mentioned in a publication of the United States Institute of Peace. The report observes that, since the early 1960s, "the Luba administrative, social, and commercial elite have spread all over the Congo country to form an ethnic Diaspora that has been viewed with suspicion by the rest of the political class." The report, which confuses identity elements and political arguments, as was observed with respect to the Tutsi, defines the situation of the Luba as follows:

> As early as the 1960s, the Baluba regarded themselves as the "Jews of the Congo" and some of their notorious leaders (for example, J. Nagalula) were called "Moses." They felt persecuted by most other ethnic constituencies, who disliked the privileges the Baluba allegedly garnered under the white administration. During the Second Republic they remained highly visible in politics: President Mobutu's strategy was to consistently absorb the Luba elite into the highest level of the political hierarchy in order to better control it. Since 1978 one of the harshest opponents of the regime among the Luba has been Etienne Tshisekedi, later named the "Zairian Moses," who together with ten fellow Kasaians, led a protracted struggle against Mobutu.... In almost all of the regions and provinces, the Luba Diaspora was implicitly accused of wanting power only for its own people. Like the Shabans, the Luba are threatened with expulsion by the "native sons." The grievance of the Jews of Zaire once again resonates.[136]

It seems today that the Luba are fully aware of this discourse, which they have espoused, particularly the consideration that the etymology of the name Luba conveys the sense of a Lost Tribe.[137]

Cape Verde–Israel Friendship Society

Recently, in the Republic of Cape Verde, some Afro-Portuguese who assert that they are descendants of Jews who settled there as part of the colonization by Portugal have openly reclaimed their identity. They recall an ancient Jewish presence, which they trace back to an emigration related to the Inquisition. Following Cape Verde's independence from Portugal almost twenty years ago, more Cape Verdeans are taking interest in their history and ancestry.

Although none of them seem to be practicing Jews, many are aware of both their own Jewish ancestry and the history of a Jewish presence in Cape Verde, or a Jewish settlement on other islands. Some, who have North African Jewish patronymics, are descendants of Moroccan emigrants who settled on this island in the nineteenth century and traded hides and pelts or were engaged in other commercial activity.[138] Considerably more is known about the Cape Verdeans of Moroccan Jewish ancestry than those of Portuguese ancestry. In Praia, the capital of Santiago Island, these people have banded together to form the Cape Verde–Israel Friendship Society. The society is headed up by Dr. Januario Nascimento, a descendant of a family from Tangiers that arrived around 1850–1880 and founded a synagogue.[139]

Although little has been written on this subject, fascinating oral accounts have been provided by Cape Verdeans as fragments of individual or collective memory. One man affirms that his father was Jewish because he and some other men would get together, cover their heads, and read a language that looked like Arabic, adding that his father told him to be skeptical about what the Catholic priests might tell him. Another man remembers a family story about a great-grandfather, a "new Christian" who was forced to join the clergy. He mutilated his hand on a sewing machine so as to be unable to conduct Mass and thus escaped.[140] In a public meeting, one young woman spoke of her family's aversion to pork and wanted to know about other practices that might link her to Judaism.[141]

Among the various objectives of the Cape Verde–Israel Friendship Society is the restoration of three Jewish cemeteries, in particular that of Penha Franca, on Santo Antao Island.[142] For the time being, these people essentially want to rediscover their Jewish past, not to convert to Judaism. They want to know more about their background, ask for scholars to come to Cape Verde to conduct research on the subject, and exchange ideas with Israelis and American Jews.

In the same way, in Angola, probable African descendants of sixteenth-century *lançados*, who bear Jewish names, recently discovered their Jewish ancestry without knowing anything of Jewish traditions. The Israeli ambassador Tamar Golan, during her visit to Angola, stated, "They do not know about the law of Return and they have no intention of immigrating to Israel. We are not trying to force religion or tradition on them, but we have noticed that since representatives of Israel came to Angola in 1995, there is growing pride among them. Everywhere they go they say that they are cousins of the Embassy. Even the former foreign minister Paulo Jorge said to me, 'I have Jewish blood.'"[143]

Since then, the embassy has invited some of them to receptions and to the Passover Seder. Thus, in present times, Jewish roots that have been so tightly interwoven with African or Creole cultures are emerging and celebrated in the context of building a new sense of collective pride.

Among these groups concerned with Judaism, some justifiable historical claims are intertwined with the myth of the Lost Tribes and revised versions of the Hamitic myth adapted to their own ends. We shall next examine an East African group, the Abayudaya of Uganda, which, in a sense, defies the overall conclusion posited above in that, while forming part of a worldwide network of recent claimants to a Judaic ancestry, they may be viewed as a phenomenon of spontaneous adhesion to Judaism.

10

African Jews in Eastern and Southern Africa

The Abayudaya of Uganda

For more than eighty years, a religious group in Uganda has considered itself Jewish and practiced Judaism. Following numerous contacts with Jewish organizations, in February 2002, around 400 members of the Abayudaya community[1] (which includes around 800 people) were formally converted to Judaism by U.S. and Israeli conservative rabbis.[2] The case of the Abayudaya is not unique: this phenomenon of spontaneous adherence to Judaism, without any direct contact with a Jewish community, reminds us of the case of the Italian village of San Nicandro, Italy, where a small group of people adhered to Judaism between the two world wars. In the Puglia region, a group of individuals followed a certain Donato Manduzio (1885–1948), who introduced them to the Old Testament. Later on they came into contact with Jews, and most of them migrated to Israel after the war.[3]

At the origin of the Abayudaya community was a charismatic person, Samei Lwakilenzi Kakungulu, a brilliant military chief who converted to Protestantism during the 1880s. Kakungulu cooperated with the British and aspired to establish his own kingdom and to be recognized as *kabaka* (king) of the eastern region of Uganda.[4] His hopes, however, were dashed. In 1913, he abandoned his military and political activities and began to concentrate on matters of faith and religion. In the unstable conditions after the imposition of the

Protectorate, new groupings of a politico-religious kind crystallized.⁵ Kakungulu started out being close to a local Protestant church, the Bamalaki, whose faith rested on devotion to the Bible and who regarded Saturday as the Sabbath. The Bamalaki appeared in Uganda in 1913 and contested the British authorities on religious grounds.

The followers of this sect were Protestants whose faith rested on a fundamentalist devotion to the Bible. Relying on the Old Testament, an important principle of this new faith was violent opposition to the use of medicines and immunizations for human beings and animals, referring, among many other verses, to Jeremiah. "In vain shalt thou use many medicines; for thou shalt not be cured" (Jeremiah 46:11). Kakungulu began to study and meditate on the Old Testament for long periods and was stricter than the Bamalaki in the observance of all Moses' commandments. He then opposed the Bamalaki on the issue of circumcision.⁶ As the Bamalaki claimed that circumcision of eight-day old male children was practiced only by Jews, Kakungulu declared himself *Muyudaya*, which means Jew in Luganda. Nevertheless, although he declared himself a Jew, he still believed at that time in the New Testament and in Jesus Christ. In 1919, Kakungulu started a separated sect known as The Community of Jews Who Trust in the Lord (Kibina Kya Bayudaya Absesiga Katonda) and then demanded that his followers adhere to all of the laws of the Bible, without exception. Kakungulu was circumcised, as were his sons, and he urged the members of his family and his followers to do the same.

Some Christian leaders tried to influence Kakungulu to return to Christianity. Kakungulu used many verses of the Old Testament to show that one must join the Jews. His religious convictions, including his objection to medicine, brought him into ever increasing conflict with the British administrators, and he was obliged to retire from his last official post as chief of Bukedi. The missionary John Roscoe, who visited Kakungulu and his followers in the 1920s in Mbale, describes Kakungulu's switch to Judaism, saying:

> The zeal of his party is considerable and they show a great desire to learn, read and write. Kakungulu is a chief of considerable means and much influence so that he is able to build schools and employ teachers in his own district where the teaching is regular and daily services are held....The teachers wear turbans like the Jews of old times, in fact the headdress is copied from pictures. They observe Saturday as a day of rest and keep it much more strictly than the Christians do their Sunday....They have formulated for themselves a religion out of this strange medley of ideas and their conduct is in complete accordance with their beliefs.⁷

From sections in the Bible that seemed to him important, Kakungulu compiled a guidebook of rules and prayers in Luganda for the members of his community, which was printed in 1922. In it, Kakungulu demanded complete faith in the Old Testament and all its commandments. In 1923, he built up a small place of worship near his house in Gangana which he named "Jewish Church."[8]

When, in 1926, he met a Jewish trader called Joseph, another phase began in the Abayudaya's appropriation of Judaism. Joseph agreed to Kakungulu's request to educate him in the Jewish faith. Great changes took place in the religious life of the Abayudaya: they stopped believing in the New Testament and in Jesus Christ. Joseph taught the Abayudaya both Jewish blessings and customary prayers, and they began to observe the Sabbath strictly. They practiced ritual head covering and ate the meat only of animals they had slaughtered. All Jewish festivals and feasts were celebrated. Kakungulu even divorced his wife because she refused to abandon Christianity and become Jewish.[9] Before he left, Joseph gave Kakungulu a voluminous Bible written in Hebrew and English. Kakungulu began to compile a new book of prayers devoid of quotations from the New Testament, but he died before he could have it published.[10] A few months before Kakungulu's death, another European Jew whom Kakungulu had encountered in Kampala visited the region and told the community that "[they] should follow Moses completely."[11]

In what context did the Abayudaya's faith arise? After all, a community faithfully practicing self-instructed mainstream Judaism at the far end of Africa, having discovered the religion on their own, seems a peculiar phenomenon. But what brought about this "miracle"? Kakungulu's establishment of the Abayudaya community was the typical act of a spiritually restless man whose religious views were constantly evolving. Before 1914, he supported many evangelists from the Christian Missionary Society (CMS) in Bukedi. After 1914, he was the Bamalaki's religion most generous supporter in eastern Uganda.[12] But why was Kakungulu's final faith Jewish? In addition to the vivid assimilation of the Old Testament of Kakungulu and his followers, a number of influences, both direct and indirect, incited the Abayudaya's self-delineation as Jews. Time and time again, we have seen how Christian and colonial discourse, drawing on evangelical hopes and expectations, were rooted in British imperial needs and attitudes and disseminated the concept of the Lost Tribes of Israel.[13] Sir Harry Johnston, the first British administrator of the Uganda Protectorate and a great defender of the Hamitic myth, said that Phoenicians or Canaanites carried Jewish ideas of religion as far as the eastern part of the black Continent.[14] One characteristic of early CMS preaching in Uganda, as well as Evangelical Anglican preaching in Britain in the late nineteenth century, was the appropriation of ancient Judaism. Henry Nevinson, one of these missionaries, recalled, "This strictly Biblical education produced, among those who like myself belong to the last century, the peculiar illusion that both the promises and the threatening of the Jewish lawgivers and prophets were especially designed for ourselves by a foreseeing Power. We never doubted that we English Evangelicals were the Chosen People."[15]

O'Flaherty, a CMS missionary, added to this discourse and stressed at the Ganda court that "Jesus Christ was a Jew...[and] we Europeans did not follow one of our race, we looked for the truth where it was to be found and we found it among the Jews."[16] Robert Walker, another CMS missionary, noted during the 1890s that "the customs and manners" of the Jews were of "greatest interest in Buganda."[17] After meeting Kakungulu and his followers at Mbale in 1904, J. J. Willis proclaimed, "In the economy of Missions in this part of Africa, Buganda are called upon to play a part not dissimilar to that played by the Jews in the first age of Christianity. Where ever the apostles went in their missionary travels, they found Jews of their own race and language, possessing and acknowledging the same Scriptures and animated by the same faith and hope."[18]

It is clear that these views added to the profound influence of the Hebrew Bible itself in the lives of certain Ugandan people nurtured the adhesion of the Abayudaya to Judaism. With respect to political and sociocultural factors, Kakungulu's shift to Judaism was largely the result of his disenchantment with British rule. A dispute over land in the Makerere region became a focus for the development of anti-British sentiment in Buganda. Kakungulu's final dismissal as Mbale county chief in 1923 was understood as one more example of arbitrary British protectorate behavior. After Kakungulu's death in 1928, the community, which had grown to 2,000 people at its peak, declined as a result of internal rivalries for the leadership of the group, not to mention the problems specific to any isolated minority.[19] By the 1960s, the group was reduced to 300 people and languished for lack of contact with the Jewish world; the vigorous activities of the Christian missionaries and their great influence in Uganda also had an impact. In the 1960s and 1970s, many of the community children became Christian while attending mission schools, and the community then consisted mainly of elderly people, women, and small children.[20]

In this context in the 1960s, an Israeli diplomat, Arye Oded, who held a post in Uganda and who published several articles in Israel, England, and the United States, was instrumental in establishing connections with world Jewry. By his permanent contacts with the Abayudaya, after he had left Uganda, Oded began the process of adopting internationally recognized standards of Jewish practice. He succeeded in interesting several Israeli personalities in the Abayudaya, among them the president of Israel, Yitzhak Ben-Zvi, and the chairman of the World Union for the Propagation of Judaism (WUPJ), Dr. Israel Ben-Ze'ev.[21] Ben-Ze'ev showed much enthusiasm, regarding the connections with the Abayudaya as an important turning point in the WUPJ's activities and the start of the conversion of Africans to Judaism. The community received *mezuzot,* prayer shawls, and other religious articles from Oded and from the WUP. The Abayudaya began to observe all the festivals mentioned in the Bible; they built *succot* (tabernacles) on the festival of the same name they did not eat *hametz* (leavened bread) during Passover; and during Pentecost, the harvest festival, they brought in the first fruits of the season and sold them to meet the needs of the synagogue.[22] As a result, contacts with Israel and the world Jewry contributed spiritually and morally to the community, and in 1962 the community was officially recognized by the government of Uganda. The community again grew to about 800, partly due to the return of some who had previously left it, but during Idi Amin's dictatorship the Abayudaya were outlawed and had to stop their activities, concealing their Jewishness lest they be arrested or murdered. Some converted to Islam or Christianity.[23] It was only in 1979, after Idi Amin's fall, that contacts and correspondence with the outside world were renewed. In the early 1980s, Gershom Sizomu, a grandson of Kakungulu's successor, reclaimed the land to build a synagogue, which restored the community's focus.

In 1995, the visit of the American-based Jewish organization Kulanu, which helped the community religiously and financially, particularly the children's schooling, marked a new step in the process that led to the formal integration of the Abayudaya in the Jewish world. The community now has university students and graduates and a Jewish high school, and the main synagogue has been enlarged and improved. Later on, with the financial help of the Institute for Jewish and Community Research in San Francisco, the spiritual leader of the community, Rabbi Sizomu, attended the Ziegler School of Rabbinic Studies at the University of Judaism, with the goal of opening a yeshiva in Uganda.[24] As the Abayudaya has developed significant relationships with Jews around the world, life is changing for the community. So, in February 2002, rabbis from the United States and Israel formally converted the Abayudaya.[25] This was agreed upon by two-thirds of the community, more than eighty years after Kakungulu embraced Judaism. After the first conversion, Rabbi Gorin noted, "Today's ceremony is not a conversion, but a strengthening of what you have always believed."[26] In an article in *Totally Jewish* (2002) that points out the growing interaction between the Abayudaya and outside Jewish visitors, Oded stressed that the Israeli Ministry of the Interior seemed determined to consider the Abayudaya as Jews with regard to the benefit of *aliyah*, which means the settlement in Israel.²⁷

The Abayudaya's affiliation with Judaism seems to appeal to Jewish universalism, opening up the definitions of the category of the dispersed, what Parfitt names "a kind of transnational community."²⁸ One can say that the Abayudaya have experienced, albeit in a limited way, the messianic process of gathering the "dispersed" that began in the fertile ground of the creation of the State of Israel, which permitted a further relaxing of ethnic barriers. Their vivid thirst for Judaism combined with the universalistic vision of the associations supporting the *nidhei Yisrael* gave their aspirations reality.

The Lemba of South Africa and Zimbabwe

The Lemba of southern, central, and eastern Zimbabwe, and northeastern South Africa, barely differ from the neighboring Venda or Shona groups, with whom they share the same language.²⁹ In July 1986, an article in the *Pretoria News* proclaimed, "Tribe claims Jewish link" and went on to say:

> As Israel struggles to absorb about 15,000 black Ethiopians into a modern, Western society, tens of thousands of blacks in South Africa, Zimbabwe and Mozambique are claiming descent from lost Biblical tribes. Spokesmen for the Lemba people say they originated around AD 600 from a Jewish tribe in what is today Yemen.... Professor Mathivha, president of the Lemba Cultural Organisation, said his people traced their source to Sanaa. They believe their forefathers were among people who crossed the Strait of Hormuz, some heading for Ethiopia with the others moving south. They trekked around the Horn of Africa and down the Indian Ocean coast to form an arc of settlements between Mozambique and the northern Transvaal.³⁰

Professor Mathivha commented: "Our entire outlook on life is Jewish. The few males who reject circumcision by the age of 15 will not be able to marry a Lemba girl." He then added that his people were following with interest the progress of the Falasha in Israel.³¹ Since this period, the Lemba have used their oral history and traditional customs associated with the Semitic identity propagated by the colonial officials to claim a modern Jewish identity. Often referring to themselves as "the white men who came from Sena," the Lemba are also known as the *Varemba*, "people who refuse"; *Vanwenye*, "foreigner," "guest," "Arab"; *Vhalungu*, that is, "Europeans," "non-Negroes." or "strangers"; or *Mushavi*, that is, "traders." The meaning or origin of these different names gives rise to various explanations, each of which can be linked to their oral tradition and suggests external influences in their past.[32]

It seems that ethnographers and missionaries from the early twentieth century propagated the Semitic identity of the Lemba, placing emphasis on their differences from groups among whom they lived. For instance, the famous ethnologist Henri Junod noted customs that suggested a Jewish link, such as circumcision, endogamy, observing a holy day each week, eating away from others, and obeying strict laws of purity. He noted that pork was excluded from the Lemba's diet, and that the meat they ate was subject to slaughtering rituals.[33] While commenting on the strong Semitic characteristics of the Lemba, and the fact that they lived "scattered among the Basuto and Bathonga of those parts, exactly as the Jews amongst Europeans nations," Junod deduced that this behavior was intended to protect a pure tribal identity.[34]

Hugh Stayt also noted that the Lemba had "marked Semitic characteristics," absorbed the language of the people among whom they settled, and maintained by endogamy "the purity of their race." He goes on to argue that the "life and customs of these peculiar people are strangely reminiscent of the wandering Jews of mediaeval times," by which he evokes the Lemba habit of living by trading rather than farming.[35] Stayt also observed that the Lemba "were feared for their superior intelligence"; this may have been connected to their metalworking skill, but also to their knowledge of medicine and their position as surgeons in the circumcision schools.[36] Both Junod and Stayt suggested that the Lemba were endogamous in much the same way that Jewish communities should have been, and Junod records that the Lemba do not give their daughters to the Venda, but have no objection to taking foreign women as wives, integrating them into their tribe as Lemba.[37]

Observers and travelers who identified Lemba as Jews found phenotypical aspects "attesting" to their racial origin. In the 1930s, some of the early ethnographic works of Stayt or Warmelo on the Lemba included profile photographs of the Lemba that established that they are "Semitic-looking" and that they have "Jewish" noses. Jacques considered that "many Lemba have straight noses, rather fine features and an intelligent expression which distinguish them from the ordinary run of natives... one does occasionally meet with a Lemba who possesses strikingly Semitic features. One of my informants, old Mosheh, even had what might be termed a typical Jewish nose, a rare occurrence in any real Bantu."[38]

In fact, among all the arguments put forward by earlier observers of the Lemba, the idea emerged that they constituted a separate group distinct from the other surrounding Bantu groups, and cared for preserving their tribal and ritual purity. The Semitic-Hebrew-Jewish account of the Lemba had been introduced in addition to the speculations of their non-Bantu origins. Following on this, Van Warmelo, in the 1930s, described their dietary rules, particularly those regarding the slaughter of animals and endogamy, as being of Semitic origin and was convinced that they had progressively migrated southward.[39] While the Lemba certainly pursued a different lifestyle from that of the people among whom they lived, these differences were perhaps exaggerated by ethnographers, including Frobenius, Jacques, Bullock, Thompson, and Von Sicard,[40] who propagated similar ideas, as did missionaries of the Swiss and Berlin missions.[41]

In fact, from a theological point of view, the Lemba's customs and rituals reveal religious pluralism and interdependence of these various practices.[42] If most of them belong to Christian churches, for example, the Zion Christian Church and Pentecostal groups, Muslim Lemba can also be found in Zimbabwe; the members of these groups tend to consider that they belong to Christianity or Islam in cultural rather than religious terms. These apparently religious identities do not prevent them from declaring themselves Jews through religious practice and ethnic identification. As Parfitt reported, "Those Lemba, who perceive themselves as ethnically Jewish, find no contradiction in regularly attending a Christian Church. By and large the Lemba who are most stridently 'Jewish' are often those with the closest Christian attachments."[43]

In what context did the Lemba's claim to Judaism arise? When the Lemba Cultural Association (LCA) was created around 1947, multiple ethnic interests in the northern Transvaal evolved, competing for access to increasingly scarce resources.[44] The founding of the association seems to express an ethnic consciousness in the context of government determination to divide communities along ethnic lines. The aims of the LCA's founder, Mr Bulengwa, may well have been to prevent assimilation. To preserve the Lemba culture, Mr Bulengwa incited them to maintain their eating habits (no pork) and endogamous practices, which recalled their Jewish connections. Gina Buijs comments: "The founding of the association was an attempt, through creating or recreating a separate and distinct cultural identity for the Lemba people, to proclaim the value and importance of the Lemba in the northern Transvaal and at the same time to identify them with a non-African community at a time when European domination seemed irreversible."[45] This process of self-identification with Judaism has not been linear. On the contrary, among the Lemba who participated in Le Roux's study, some observed that during the Black Liberation struggle in South Africa, they preserved their culture but were not so willing to be associated with a non-African white race.[46] After the democratic elections of 1994, they again wanted to remain exclusive and preserve for posterity their "separate and distinct cultural identity." This leads one to think that it represents a wider and more profound sentiment than a mere reaction to colonization.

Discovering the Lemba's Past through Their Genes

The Lemba's oral tradition recounts that the first Lemba coming from Sena, in the north, were men who married African women. Professors Spurdle and Jenkins of the South African Institute for Medical Research and the University of Witwatersrand, Johannesburg, using this information as a basis, had the idea of trying to solve the mystery of the Lemba's origin by collecting and analyzing their genetic material. Spurdle and Jenkins reasoned as follows: by identifying the Y chromosomes of the Lemba and establishing similarities with Jewish groups around the world, it might be possible to support a hypothesis of Jewish origin for the male lineage of the Lemba. On the basis of sixty-four DNA samples taken from male Lemba, Spurdle and Jenkins carried out a first analysis in which they established that 50 percent of the Lemba's Y chromosomes were of Semitic origin and 40 percent were Negroid, with the remaining 10 percent unidentified.[47] The conclusion of the two researchers suggested a genetic history quite consistent with the Lemba's oral tradition, and the results of their study found a wide audience in the 1990s. Parfitt's involvement in studying ethnic groups purporting to be descended of the Lost Tribes led him to spend several months among them, as related in his *Journey to the Vanished City* (1991). The publication of Parfitt's book was followed by numerous television and radio broadcasts. Such coverage by the media brought the Lemba to the attention of a large international public, whereas, until then, their existence was virtually unknown even in their own country.[48] The BBC subsequently broadcast a series entitled *Origins,* and Professor Steven Jones, a geneticist at University College in London, published a book, *In the Blood: God, Genes and Destiny* (1996), based on this series, which included a section on the Lemba.[49] While the terminology "Semitic genes" lacks precision as such, the genetic "bomb" of the "black Jews of South Africa" had exploded.

Some time later, to test the hypothesis of a possible South Arabian origin of the Lemba, and to check similarities between the structure of Lemba clans and their names against Hadramaut clans and their family names, Parfitt undertook a comparison between South Arabians' and Lemba's DNA. He collected DNA from 136 male Lemba for the Centre for Genetic Anthropology at the University College of London in 1997. In order to establish a comparison, the next step consisted of collecting DNA from South Arabians, in the region of the Hadramaut.[50] To establish a more precise evaluation of the paternal heritage of the Lemba, this team of researchers envisaged that the Jewish origins of the Lemba could be corroborated by a similarity between the Lemba's Y chromosomes and those of Jewish men living in other parts of the world. In a study published in the *American Journal of Human Genetics* in 2000, the Y chromosomes of 136 Lemba were compared to the Y chromosomes of Ashkenazic and Sephardic Jews, as well as Yemeni and non-Lemba Bantu speakers from southern Africa. The researchers found evidence of Semitic origins in the Lemba, although it was not clear whether this origin was Jewish, Arab, or both.

Interestingly, the study showed that one of the Lemba clans carried a high occurrence of a particular Y chromosome, the Cohen Modal Haplotype (CMH), "which is known to be characteristic of the paternally inherited Jewish priesthood and is thought, more generally, to be a potential signature of Judaic origin."[51] According to the Bible, Moses and Aaron were members of the tribe of Levi, selected for certain religious duties. Ever since, male descendants of Aaron have been designated "Cohanim," or priests, and the designation of Jewish males to this priestly status continues to this day. Through the male line, and determined by strict patrilineal descent, one might expect that male members of the Cohanim would carry similar Y chromosomes. An earlier study, based on a sample of 306 Jewish males from Israel, Canada, and the United Kingdom, had shown the diversity of the Levites' Y chromosomes and the homogeneity of the Cohanim's Y chromosomes, and that this particular haplotype was spread among both Ashkenazic and Sephardic Cohanim. Following this study, the identification of the CMH among men belonging to various allegedly Jewish groups appeared to provide evidence for claims of Jewish ancestry. The frequency of the CMH was high in the subclan of the Buba—that interestingly is composed of Lemba priests—where more than 50 percent of the men tested have this haplotype. In comparison, Levites carried only 3 percent, and among the general Jewish population, about 10 percent. The fact that the Lemba share some of the markers found in other Jewish populations could indicate that, in the past, one or more Jews introduced this gene without, however, making it possible to specify the geographical origin or time period in which this occurred.[52]

Finally, the results of a study carried out by an international team of scientists led by Michel Hammer, from the University of Arizona, and Barsheva Boné-Tamir, from the University of Tel-Aviv, published in *Proceedings of the National Academy of Science* in 1999. The study, using genetic samples taken from 1,371 men in seven different Jewish populations (Ashkenazi, Roman, North African, Kurd, Near Eastern, Yemenite, and Ethiopian) and sixteen non-Jewish groups, including the Lemba, indicated that the Lemba's Y chromosomes were closer to those of the Jews than were those of any other sub-Saharan African group.[53]

What did these surveys really teach us with respect to the Lemba's genealogy? In fact, the genetic studies simply established a non-African paternal descent for the Lemba; the intriguing presence of the CMH supported to some extent the hypothesis of their possible Jewish origin without, nonetheless, providing any absolute proof. If there were no doubts about the highly technical procedures of genetic studies, it clearly appeared that the shock wave caused by the revelation of a Bantu-Jewish population obviously dominated the scientific popularization elsewhere, not just among the various Jewish communities throughout the world. In May 9, 1999 a *New York Times* headline that read, "DNA Backs a Tribe's Tradition of Early Descent from the Jews" was followed by the French science magazine *Science et Vie* (August 1999, August 2000), which asserted that the Lemba were Jews, while *Hadassah Magazine* in January 2001 considered that the Jewish ancestry of the Lemba, on the male side, seems assured.[54] Media accounts reported the tracing of the genetic ancestry of the Lemba as if genetic tests had authoritatively settled the question, although the actual answers to these questions are far more complex. It was against this murky background, linking different and contradictory levels of racial thought, and scientific explanations, mingled with the vivid legend of the Twelve Tribes, that the genetic studies on the Lemba were received. Given the vast potential for misunderstanding or misuse of these categorizations, it was comforting for Jews and non-Jews to believe that there was some comparatively simple way to identify Jews. In simultaneously consolidating and undermining traditional notions, the media headlines spreading news of the genetic studies linking the Lemba to Jews, with photos showing them wearing Jewish religious attributes (skullcaps, prayer shawls, and *tallith*), presented striking images.

The DNA results provided proof of their Jewishness for the Lemba themselves and for Jewry in general, thus initiating redevelopment of their social and religious identity. Immediately thereafter, Kulanu sent a Jewish teacher, Yaacov Levi, whose mission was to bring the Lemba normative Judaism.[55] Two missions of Rabbi Leo Abrami, an American rabbi of French origin, were also sent by Kulanu in January and September 2002. In January 2002, I was present in Venda at a conference during Rabbi Abrami's first mission and was able to watch how he taught the history of Judaism to the Lemba, encouraging them to choose Judaism and to exclude Christian elements. He also taught them rudiments of the Hebrew alphabet, using his own personal method; above all, he organized with the members of the community gathered at this conference a Sabbath according to Jewish norms. Rabbi Abrami brought the Lemba copies of various books on theology, a copy of the new JPS Hebrew-English Bible, Hebrew handbooks, hundreds of leaflets about the practice of the Sabbath, and other instructional materials for the Lemba Cultural Association's library and the future synagogue.

In September 2002, when Parfitt attended the annual meeting of the Lemba Cultural Association, he noticed that, for the first time, the Lemba made it coincide with the Jewish New Year and, also for the first time, used a number of Hebrew expressions, such as "Shana Tovah" (For a good year). Fully aware of the importance of media coverage of genetic tests on the Lemba, Parfitt decided in 2003 to assess the reception and integration of the results of the genetic tests in Zimbabwe and South Africa. His method of evaluation included in-depth conversations based on 120 detailed questionnaires. Seventy percent of the Lemba were surveyed. Of those, 93 percent of the educated participants and 53 percent of the unskilled knew about the tests; only 11 percent of those who knew about the tests knew the results. When asked about the purpose of the tests, 48 percent of those who knew about the tests answered that it concerned "blood," 30 percent thought that "blood" was the link between Lemba and Jews, and only a few persons answered that it was about genes or DNA. As regards questions about how the tests had influenced the life of their community, the majority did not answer, and some answered that they did not know about the results. Those who answered that they knew about the tests stated that it was now established that the Lemba were Jews.[56]

Prior to the genetic tests, the Lemba asserted their identity through oral tradition and religious and/or cultural practices. The preliminary interviews carried out in 1997 by Le Roux revealed vague remarks: "We are different from other tribes....we are a holy people....our God is different....[these things] remind us who we are."[57] Since the genetic tests and the relationships established with members of the international Jewish community, one can see the awareness in their group of a new ethnic and religious identity that is based largely on their understanding of the genetic research passed on by the media.

What do we know about the consequences of this genetic research on other Judaizing African societies? Most of the leaders of other African Judaizing communities dispose of modern means of communication. Some of them, geographically close to the Lemba, knew about the research and had integrated it into their own affiliation to Judaism. For example, Kosintahi Nyathi Mbolekwa, from the community of Zimbabwe, expressed himself as follows:

> I am so pleased and proud to see such great efforts finally being made in addressing the significant genetic finds made by Parfitt and others. These are rather interesting and ground-shaking discoveries, but this information has been known for centuries.... I have relatives and friends from the Lemba tribe and we have always known

that all Bantus are Israelites but more than just the Lemba are Jews. The Lemba are just one major group of Jews that settled in southern Africa, but a much larger picture can be drawn of our entire inheritance. The Yoruba, Hausa, Ashanti, Buganda and many other tribes in Africa have made public and open their Jewish roots, but on deaf— or can I say outright racist—ears who find these claims outlandish.[58]

In 2003, a delegation from the community of Zimbabwe participated in the Lemba annual conference held in Venda. Ernest Nandhi Sadiki, one of the members of the Zimbabwean delegation, took this opportunity to announce that, "in our endeavour to bring the Lemba of Zimbabwe to their true identity, we will be holding our inaugural National Conference at Tadsembwa, in the Masvingo Province, close to the historical MaDzimbabwe, now known as Great Zimbabwe, which I understand was built by our forefathers."[59]

"Out of the blue"—for in no Jewish or non-Jewish source are they even hinted at—the Lemba have been proposed as Jews by virtue of a genetic tie to Jews elsewhere and by the mass media's oversimplification of the results of genetic tests. The way in which these results have been presented by the media and the way in which these presentations have been transformed into group narratives have played a major role in the impact of genetics on group identity issues from Africa to Asia. While we have no direct information enabling us to evaluate the consequences of the genetic tests of the Lemba on Judaizing communities located farther away, particularly those of central and western Africa, we must realize that the complete Lemba history has become accessible on the Internet through a multitude of search possibilities. For instance, Herman Taylor, the minister of the Shalom Hebrew Israelite Congregation of Jackson, Mississippi, following the media coverage of the findings on Lemba DNA, expressed his satisfaction that the kinship between his group and Israelite populations of Ethiopia, Rwanda, Burundi, Sudan, Nigeria, Uganda, and Malawi had been proven in such a conclusive way.[60] It is highly likely that the impact of the scientific findings has affected other peoples' own narratives and sense of their own origins. Given the increased technological access to information throughout the world, it is fairly certain that DNA research on group origins is one of the contemporary elements likely to modify the consciousness of such groups.

Zionist and Israelite Churches in South Africa

Most of the Lemba informants indicated that they belonged to some kind of Christian church, essentially the Zion Apostolic Church (ZAC) or the Zion

Christian Church (ZCC),[61] which now constitute the majority of so-called African independent churches (AICs) in South Africa and elsewhere in Africa.[62] Among these churches, which were founded in the 1910 and 1920s, some describe themselves as Zionist without having much in common with Jewish Zionism. In fact, they represent "Black Zion," a charismatic religious movement of Africans.[63] The name was taken from biblical references to Mount Zion in Jerusalem, based in part on the inspiration of a similar community in Illinois. These churches are a prominent part of African Christianity and emerged in a context in which Africans were denied social-economic and religious power, while mission churches dominated by Europeans often represented colonial oppression.[64] In general, the beliefs of these Zionist churches are eclectic. They have exercised mutatis mutandis a choice from among cults and sacred books, added fasts, immersion, and possession and purification rites and praise the founder, depending on the personality of the prophet who guides them. The principal sacred reference figures are Moses and John the Baptist. Their churches' practices are often rigorous. They forbid alcoholic beverages, smoking, or eating pork and have, in a way, assimilated dietary and purification elements from the Old Testament.[65]

From the same sphere of influence came the movement of *The Israelites*, which developed in South Africa in the 1920s under the leadership of Enoch Mgijima. Mgijima was an evangelist in the Methodist Church who began to have millennial visions and felt called to proclaim a return to the ancient religion of the Israelites.[66] He then joined the Church of God and Saints of Christ (CGSC), founded in the United States by the African American William Crowdy in 1896. As seen earlier, Crowdy claimed to have received a visitation from God and was told to re-create the religion of the biblical Jews for the black people. He is considered a founder of the first African American Jewish movement.[67] When he was asked to leave the CGSC in 1919, Mgijima was the undisputed leader among *The Israelites*, and many of them moved to Ntabelanga, where he lived, to draw near to the prophet.[68] For the authorities, however, this was illegal squatting on Crown land, and a dispute over land rights arose and continued throughout the 1920s. *The Israelites* argued their case with the authorities on a number of occasions, always maintaining that they were answerable only to God. After several incidents of defiance, *The Israelites* became more and more aggressive, began to arm themselves, and seemed resigned to the inevitable. In the tragic outcome of the confrontation with authorities, known as the "Bulhoek Tragedy" (1921), 163 *Israelites* died, 129 were wounded, and the others, including Mgijima, were made prisoners.[69] *The Israelites* movement, however, still exists in the Queenstown area.

Some sociopolitical factors of the time—the quantity and quality of land available to black people—were to play a part in the community set up by *The Israelites*, but overall its members who suffered perpetual discrimination, were in search of a status and ontological aura based on the model of the black Jewish American communities, from which they sprang. They consider themselves as the chosen people of Jehovah, whom their prophet came to free from the yoke of the whites. In the South Africa of discrimination, they needed to choose their own religious commitment, not one imposed by whites or anyone else.

The Black Philadelphia Church of Soweto, a similar religious group, was founded in the 1960s by Vayisile Joshua Msitshana, born into a Xhosa family and raised as a Methodist.[70] After meeting two Palestinians Jews while serving with the British during World War II, Msitshana noticed similarities between the Jewish and Xhosa cultures and felt that "what was not similar I found I really admired."[71] Subsequently, he intensified his study of Judaism and, as the name Philadelphia came to him in a dream, he founded the Black Philadelphia Church, first in Bloemfontein. In 1963, after undergoing conversion by an Orthodox rabbi, Msitshana led his followers to Judaism, saying, "I finally decided that we must have faith that we have chosen voluntarily, not one the white man or anyone else has forced upon us." He added, "In Judaism, I see the opportunity to unite and pull ourselves up as a people."[72] In the ghetto township of Soweto, this was how 1,000 people were groping for Judaism, learning badly pronounced Hebrew, and worshiping on Saturday. Aside from Msitshana himself, no member of the Black Philadelphia Church in Soweto has undergone any form of recognized conversion. All that can be said of them is that they wanted to be Jews, saw themselves as such, and practiced a very elementary form of Judaism. Although he has been soliciting white Jewry for several years with no success, Msitshana's attempts to have his movement accepted have failed. His application to the Johannesburg city council for a site for a synagogue was also turned down. When he requested assistance from both the Orthodox and reformed South African Jewish communities, he received no reply.[73] Nevertheless, it seems that anyone who met Msitshana could only be impressed by his sincerity in pursuing Judaism. Unlike his counterparts in Chicago, the people of Black Philadelphia make no ancestral claims, basing their faith purely on free choice, and they were at that time willing to undergo conversion or anything else Jewish authorities require, in order to be recognized as Jews.[74]

Msitshana's religious past provides interesting information on the course of the choice or construction of a Jewish identity among the various independent churches. Since he left the Methodist Church, Msitshana has been a Roman Catholic, Dutch Reformed, Anglican, Seventh Day Adventist, Twelfth Apostle, Jehovah's Witness, and a member of the Jerusalem in Christ Church, the Jewish Church in Zion, and the Independent Order of True Templars.[75] In the South Africa of discrimination, the voluntary choice of a religious commitment linked to Judaism clearly expresses the search for autonomy. The search for a status liberated from colonial oppression certainly appealed to people attempting to redefine themselves and to find a source of pride in the white supremacist South Africa.

The Jews of Rusape, Zimbabwe

The community of self-proclaimed Jews centered in Rusape, a small city in northeast Zimbabwe, claims both ancient and contemporary origins. They are convinced that all the Bantu people of Africa descend spiritually and genetically from the Lost Tribes that migrated from the kingdom of Israel. To the Rusape community, there is little difference between ancient African observances and ancient Jewish culture. The community favorably compares traditional Bantu symbols, burial rites, circumcision patterns, marriage customs, and agricultural practices to those of ancient Israelites. This led Solomon Guzawah, the current leader of the community, to say: "We believe most African (Black) descendants are in fact the ancient Hebrews and in fact most Blacks are the descendants of the twelve children of Israel....We believe the true faith of the African descendants is Judaism."[76]

Actually, the adhesion to Judaism of the Rusape Jews dates back to the 1900s. They consider, as do *The Israelites* who developed in South Africa in the 1920s under the leadership of Mgijima, the African American William Crowdy as their prophet. One can note that the Rusape movement followed the same line on the African continent as did Crowdy's Church of God and the Saints of the Christ in Lawrence, Kansas. According to the collective memory of the community, around 1903, a man named Albert Christian brought Crowdy's teachings to South Africa. Sister Elder Tabeth, a member of the community, gives more information on the formation of the community of Rusape, which seems to coincide with the emergence of Africans' consciousness as of the 1930s: "Around 1935, a village near Rusape, Zimbabwe, felt spiritually empty and sent an emissary to South Africa to learn about the teachings of Prophet Crowdy, whom they had heard about. Their emissary brought these teachings back to Zimbabwe. After several generations of development in Zimbabwe, Rabbi Ambrose Mukawaza arose to become the chief Rabbi of the movement for Central Africa, Zimbabwe, Malawi and Zambia."[77]

Today, there are several thousand members in the Rusape community who practice a "prophetic" Judaism. They define prophetic in the sense that each one of us is truly or potentially a prophet of God. The community members, who believe that Jesus was not the Messiah, but a prophet like Crowdy, observe all Jewish holidays. Prayer services in English, patterned after the standard rabbinic prayer service, together with daily observances such as kashrut, are practiced. The Rusape Jews also perform circumcision on boys of ten years old, as do the local Muslims.[78] The Rusape congregation is affiliated with the prophetic congregation Beth El from northern Virginia and has developed its culture of observance based, at least partly, on American Southern Baptist–inspired roots. Every Sabbath, the Jews of Rusape practice their own form of Judaism in the Temple Beth El of the Church of God and the Saints of Christ, reading the Torah and singing a new version of the Shema Israel (the most sacred prayer of Judaism, asserting the Oneness of God), in a combined version of Hebrew, English, and Shona.[79]

Let us now turn to the context in which this group's claim to Judaism arises. Following the agreement organized by Cecil Rhodes with the British South Africa Company in 1888, allowing them to mine gold, both the Ndebele and the Shona staged unsuccessful revolts against the British (1896–1897). After the referendum of 1922, when the whites chose to become a self-governing colony rather than part of the Union of South Africa, most blacks were excluded from the vote, despite the colony's theoretically nonracial constitution. In 1930, a land act was passed that excluded Africans from ownership of the best farming land, thus enhancing white supremacy. The labor law, adopted in 1934, prohibited the Africans from entering skilled trades and professions. As a consequence of all these actions, Africans were forced to work for subsistence wages on whites' farms, and in mines and factories.[80]

Nowadays, Solomon Guzawah, the active leader of the community, is happy to give information about his odyssey through Rastafarianism, Christianity, and Judaism over the years. He describes how he and the Rusape Jews feel a deep connection with Judaism that harmonizes with their historical Shona heritage of a belief in one God. Solomon also describes the need to reconnect to their ancient past, in order to find the strength to take control of their lives and fulfill the vision of the African Renaissance.[81] In a resolutely positive discourse, Guzawah believes that Judaism is the path to reject centuries of oppression, colonialism, and modern-day cultural imperialism.[82] Rabbi Makuwaza explained that the totems of their forefathers connected them with the various tribes of Israel and affirms that he himself is a Levite. He emphasized that all of them must fight for their Jewish identity in Africa and in the world. Each Saturday, at the end of the service, Rabbi Makuwaza asks anyone wanting to become a Jew to come forward and sit in the few chairs placed in the center of the congregation. Today there are half a dozen churches/synagogues affiliated throughout the country, with around 5,000 followers. Many of the believers were second- or third-generation Jews; for them, Judaism is essentially a faith in God, not a culture or a race. This is why they contest both a matrilineal descent and a definition of Judaism that they consider much too Eurocentrist.[83]

Throughout its history, the Rusape community has defined itself as clearly stemming from the first American black Jewish movement founded by Crowdy in Kansas. The syncretic Judaism they practice, which, theologically speaking, mixes Judaism and Christianity, appears to be well in line with numerous African American Jewish movements. The Rusape society appears as the direct emanation of these movements in Africa. In the same way, the community's ideology is impregnated with Pan-Africanism and notions of struggle against the cultural domination of the West, which, as we have seen, is one of the bases of African American Jewish identity. Today, the personal experience of the leader, Solomon Guwazah, and in particular his Rastafarian past, exhibit the same ideological and political characteristics. Without devaluing what is considered to be proper to the West, the discourse of the Rusape community exalts a certain idea of "Africanity" liberated from subjection to the Western world. Clearly this movement, explicitly born from the African American Jewish movements of the early twentieth century, now falls within the scope of the new religious movements, as a late African expression of the construction of a new identity, in simultaneous confrontation with modernity.[84]

The "Descendants of David" of Madagascar

The scores of existing traditions (*lovan-tsofina* in the Malagasy language) that tell, sometimes openly, but often obliquely, of ancestral origins from ancient Israel in the culture of innumerable Malagasy clans, constitute what some of them consider to be the "Malagasy secret." According to Kathie Quanbeck, who lived for thirty-five years among the Malagasy people and collected archives of oral testimonies, it seems that many Malagasy authorities (i.e., kings, priests, clan elders, many professionals and pastors, as well as some historians) do not want anything written or produced on their oral histories. At present, a Jewish identity within an institutional framework does not exist in Madagascar, but the belief clearly does exist among certain groups, movements, or individuals that many Malagasy have Hebrew blood.[85]

A young Malagasy man of the Sevohitse clan nicknamed "Que de Neuf," after several meetings, cautiously mentioned the existence of a place from where he came, Foibe Joisy, which means "the headquarters of the Jews," near Ambovombe. He commented, "We marry only within our clan. No one likes to come to our town. People do not like us. You have to hide the fact that you are Jewish."[86] Here, too, is what a member of the Tavaratra clan, who supposes that he is of Jewish descent, chose to reveal in 2000: "There is more about our clan that only our elders determine how much should be shared. Much is kept secret, only known by a very few leaders. Another fact is that there is something buried near my own land at Sandravinay. I do not know precisely what it is, but it seems to be a secret of grand significance. It is the issue of our true origins that my brother is researching now while working in Europe."[87]

Ascertaining the specific boundaries between groups in Madagascar is problematic, since they overlap and merge into one another.[88] Hence the boundaries between clans are nebulous, and anyone can identify with more than one clan.[89] Despite regional differences, members of numerous clans, mainly originating from the southeast and southwest regions of the island, [90] claim to be descendants of royal dynasties whose traditions are clearly of Semitic origin, such as Antemoro and Zafiraminia, descendants of Raminia.[91] This seems to be a consequence of certain European theories that appeared in the seventeenth century among French observers and were largely taken up again and developed by missionaries in the nineteenth century. As seen earlier, Flacourt, during his stay in Madagascar in 1652, had encountered on Ile Sainte Marie (also called Nosy Ibrahim), and at Vohipeno on the southeast coast, small groups who called themselves Zaffy-Ibrahim (descendants of Abraham or Ibrahim), who claimed to be Jews.[92] Flacourt's testimony was repeated by the French colonists who settled in the region during the time of Louis XIV. François Martin met natives at Analambolo, in the province of Fenerive, where he lived from 1665 to 1668, who "do not practise any exercise of religion; they, nevertheless admit that there is a God whom they acknowledge to be the author of all beings.... They respect Saturday, they do not work on that day in their plantations; the specific observance of that day, their circumcision and the loathing of some of them for eating pork, tell us that a few Jews or persons of this religion visited this region in the past, that they instructed the people and that some customs have remained."[93]

Although Christian missions were established in the sixteenth century, their greatest impact on Malagasy culture and politics began during the early nineteenth century, when missionaries were allowed to settle in the Highland Kingdom of Imerina.[94] By the beginning of the 1820s, the missionaries of the London Missionary Society (LMS), who had arrived in 1795, not only had created a considerable network of schools but also had completed the translation of the New Testament and substantial sections of the Old.[95] A number of studies show how inextricably Christianity and Christian values became interwoven with beliefs and practices concerning ancestors, especially in the Highlands.[96] In 1870, James Sibree, a missionary from the LMS, visited the group at Vohipeno who called themselves Zaffy-Ibrahim and recorded that they said to him during a conversation, "We are altogether Jews." He adds: "But I could not detect any difference in colour, features, or dialect between them and the other people of the eastern coast, while observing that they emphasized their Jewish origins." He thus recorded that one "intelligent-seeming" man said that his father had been a magician or sorcerer among the Jews, but during a general burning of idols and fetishes in 1869, his father had burned his books.[97] Sibree also recorded that in 1876, he met an Anakara who had helped Grandidier to copy fragments of *Sorabé*. This Anakara told him that he was a Zaffy-Ibrahim, descendant of Abraham, and added *Jiosy Mihitsy*, which means "entirely Jewish." *Jiosy* is the Malagasy transcription of *Jew* in English, and it was probably after hearing the preaching of English missionaries that this idea came to him, Abraham being included among Antemoro's ancestors, together with Noah and Moses.

Biblical characters and themes did not wait for the nineteenth-century missionary movement to penetrate Malagasy traditions. They have been known for a much longer time, through Muslim intermediaries. The legend of Noah, in particular, whose Arabic name *Nûh* has been rendered in Malagasy as *Noho* or *Ranoho*, was mentioned by Flacourt, who himself had met scribes who owned Arabic-Malagasy documents.[98] The very same Malagasy legends contain figures that also traveled through Muslim traditions, as well as others deriving from biblical sources transmitted by missionaries.[99] Within a process of dynamic reorganization, local indigenous mythographies appropriated symbols from the seventeenth century. They had been considerably added to by the nineteenth-century Christian missions while simultaneously recasting older mythic themes, to fashion a symbolic instrument. One recognizes a mix of references to events and struggles marking the early centuries of the Hegira, and at times teachings from the Koran.[100] Antemoro legends combine in unexpected ways the names of Islamic leaders and biblical figures from the most ancient times, in search of a kind of spiritual kinship. One of these legends contracts and synthesizes the question of the origin of various races or ethnic groups by recounting that Mahomet had five sons, who all became kings in Arabia: these were Abraham, Noah, Joseph, Moses, and Jesus, the last four of them having fathered Tsimeto, Kazimambo, Anakara, and Raminia.[101] The free-running use or reuse of myths of origin seems to serve an immense array of ideological and spiritual needs, and many of the elements that Malagasy societies cast as traditions are in fact the product of ongoing processes of cultural innovation.[102] Numerous characters from biblical episodes are taken into a syncretic framework without any direct link to a specific passage in the Bible. The biblical account serves as an available model to be reemployed for an imagined Semitic or Judaic identity. Following Benedict Anderson's term "imagined community," we can see that the emergence of the Malagasy Jewish identity is a long-standing phenomenon.[103]

The specificities recorded by Flacourt and the French colonists in the seventeenth century were taken up again in the nineteenth and twentieth centuries by Grandidier, in his monumental work *Histoire Physique, Naturelle et Politique de Madagascar*. In this work, Grandidier concluded that Malagasy peoples are derived from a pre-Solomonic Jewish civilization, and he established a listing of thirty-five traits common to all Malagasy peoples and to the ancient Jews.[104] The whole of this monumental work institutionalized knowledge about Madagascar and subsequently came to have an impact on the native populations.[105] I have a document recently written by Pastor F.S., an Andrevola descendant of a Sakalava king, who describes the Jiosy (Jewish) origins of his clan and makes a comparison of more than two dozen of the Andrevola traditional practices with those in Grandidier's listing.[106]

Such views continued to be expressed throughout the twentieth century. In the 1940s Reverend Father Briand, a French missionary, dedicated a strange book to the influence of Hebrew on the Malagasy language, asserting that "the Malagasy language is a peculiarity, and the source of this peculiarity is in the Hebrew language."[107] As the earliest comparativists in North America, for instance, proposed conjectural histories that trace the Indians back to ancient Israel, European comparativists in Madagascar reported that the Malagasy still observed aspects of the biblical Law of Moses. Strongly criticizing what he calls the "theory of borrowing," Arnold Van Gennep opposed the colonial comparativist approaches:

> The beliefs of the inhabitants of Madagascar have been alternatively compared to those of Malayans, Polynesians, Jews, Muslims.... From these similarities, ethnic kinship or the existence of long-lasting intimate relationships was inferred.... The reasoning was not only wrong because it identified the relation of causality, but particularly because attention was not paid to the common

characteristics of all custom or belief.... The missionaries have been responsible for this judgment that became a dogma about Malagasy's ancient monotheism, that would afterward have been darkened and broken up and so transformed into polytheism and sorcery. The primitive monotheism of the Malagasy is like the one of Semites, Germans or Bantus, a pure invention.[108]

What of the impact of all this on the Malagasy themselves? Of the religious traditions that have shaped contemporary Malagasy cosmologies and social practice, Islamic culture, brought by traders and immigrants since at least the tenth century, has had a profound impact throughout the island.[109] The influence is well documented in the case of theories and practices of divination, destiny, and temporal and spatial categories, and in the sacred manuscripts of the Antemoro of the southeast. Today, the Islamic elements have become local Malagasy cultural practice.[110]

According to what appears to be the dominant tradition, those Malagasy who refer to themselves as Jews assert that their ancestors are descendants of David, who came from a place outside Madagascar, that is, Arabia or Africa. They were shipwrecked off the coast of Africa and arrived in dhows on the shores of Madagascar, wearing long white robes and always accompanied by a red cow. Those who claim to be descendants of David assert that their ancestors believed in one God and never had idols. There are a number of variants of this myth of origin, for example, Mr. B's description of the origin of his clan, the Tavaratra from Sandravinany (located somewhere in the south of the city of Vagaindrano, on the southeast coast of Madagascar), who

> came from somewhere in the area of Medina, or somewhere on the sea coast of Saudi Arabia, in scores of botries full of families to the northern coast of Madagascar. Some of them, the Tantakara, stayed in the area of that northern coast, others continued southward along the eastern coast of Madagascar. The dhow of our family contained one red zebu and when the dhow reached the Vohipeno area, the zebu brayed, so they stopped here temporarily. But then they continued southward, past what is known as Fort Dauphin, and continued on around the southern coast, even going as far as Androka. At the mouth of that river, the zebu brayed again, two times; so they stopped there but eventually left again, and returned the way they had come. After travelling back eastward along Madagascar's southern coast, then northward along part of the eastern coast, at the Vohipeno area, the red zebu brayed three times. So they stopped there, and our family eventually moved as far south as Sandravinany, a region which

was open totally, with no persons having settled it. We were the original Malagasy people in that area around what is now known as Sandravinany.[111]

He continues: "Thus we are Tavaratra, and we circumcise the boys. What we do not know is if we were Muslims and Arabs and we do not know for sure from what kind of people we originated. If our elders do know, they may or may not tell the rest of the story to us."[112]

Certain parts of this saga of origin do suggest a Semitic ancestry that could be rooted in historical experience. We know that the fertile oasis of Yathrib in Arabia had been settled by Jews organized in tribes, who formed the majority of the population and who, under Muhammad, were forced to sell their properties and leave the area.[113] Thereafter, the history of these Arab Jews, who felt constrained to leave their oases, was perhaps linked with the Islamization of the east coast of Africa and the shores of Madagascar by the Arabs. The descendants of David appropriated these historical elements, which served the particular vision of their origins, and they consider that they are the descendants of these Jewish tribes subjugated or expelled by Muhammad. Their explanations abundantly refer to this, by establishing numerous connections with Medina and South Yemen. Mr. B. stresses that a clue to the origins of his clan, the Tavaratra, must be the names of two lakes near Sandravanany, Lake Erian and Lake Esazalan, which are similar to the name of two cities on the southern coast of Yemen, Ar Riyan and As Said Azzan.[114]

The legend of the red zebu probably came from the biblical tradition of the Red Heifer (Numbers 19:1–22).[115] The Red Heifer was part of the sacrifice given to the Levites to perform and has a symbolic meaning of Levitical defilement and purification. However, as discussed earlier, the identification of Levitical customs was an obsession of the missionaries or early European anthropologists. One of these anthropologists detected Levirate survivals among the Bara, a Malagasy group seen as "Africans" of Madagascar, and hinted at an Ethiopian connection: "The Levirate still exists among several peoples, but it is basically Hebraic and it still exists in Abyssinia. Its presence in Madagascar seems to me obvious and of a much more ancient and deep influence than one could imagine, coming from Hebrews or Arabs who migrated there or from elements belonging to eastern Africa."[116]

Today, the Malagasy construction of ethnohistory has fully absorbed the identification of local tribes with the Lost Tribes introduced by the Christian missionaries. Pastor S., a professor of Old Testament studies at Boeny, asserts: "I know that there are many, many Malagasy who must be Levite priests; there is a specified clan elder, in each of these families, who has the special knife for killing the sacrificial animal, thus there is also a specified elder in the clan who has the privilege of killing the animal that is sacrificed."[117]

Is the selection of a Jewish ancestry by some Malagasy a mirror of some particular characteristic of some clans in precolonial times? Or is it the reflection of some Semitic influence from Arabia or Africa centuries before? Or is it the result of intervention by outsiders? Whatever the answers may be, significant historical "bricolage" (do-it-yourself) is clearly taking place. The previously mentioned examples illustrate Malagasy individuals, drawing on fragments of historical narratives as they reinterpret collective memory and identity. Today there are only limited echoes of the "Malagasy secret," and those who claim to know it appear somehow as crypto-Jews. If these Malagasy take pride in their Jewish heritage, there is no leader among them, nor any institution dedicated to promoting this identity. Up until now, these Malagasy individuals do not seem to have connections with other African Jewish organizations and movements, whether in Africa or elsewhere in the world. Moreover, the descendants of David have been widely ignored up to now, by Jews in general, and by Lost Tribes' research associations.[118] Nor have they been subjected to any ethnographic study about Judaism. What does the future hold? As seen earlier with the Lemba and other groups, the activity of missionaries, Jews or Christians, and researchers may well encourage cultural innovation or development. With globalization and the spread of the Internet, it will be interesting to see how this latent Jewish identity evolves once outside forces make their impact felt.

Throughout Africa, interpretations of the Hebrew Bible and analogies in the experiences of blacks and Jews have provided important models for Africans' identification with the descendants of the Lost Tribes of Israel. The different encounters between African religions and Judaism demonstrate both the creative spiritual capacities of the African people and the stimulating capacity of Judaism as a source of Africans' sacred life. Due to the interaction of internal and external influences, the twentieth century had a significant impact on the lives of these African groups. Through a complex process of events, they transformed their existence from a people whose history lay within Africa, to African Jews whose culture, religion, history, and identity became connected with the Jews of the Diaspora and with Israel. It is worth noting that the pace and degree of change of most of these African Judaizing groups rapidly increased all over Africa, as the number of Jewish visitors escalated. One can say that the transformation initiated by these groups to the status of African Jews was encouraged and shaped by Jews since the 1980s. The involvement of Jewish organizations and the actions of individuals within these groups have promoted rapid change in these African groups, with significant results. Visitors observed the apparently Jewish nature of their practices, customs, and way of life and accepted their affiliation within world Jewry. This was accompanied by a marked acceleration of cultural change. As Shelemay noted in respect to the Falasha during the 1960s and 1970s, among African Judaizing societies, traditional customs resembling those of normative Judaism were emphasized and elaborated on while unfamiliar Jewish practices were adopted.[119] To appeal to Jewish attention and highlight their own evolving religious orientation, as the Falasha did before them, most of these groups, such as the Abayudaya, or the House of Israel in Ghana, undertook a change in their production of crafts and began to produce figurines of Torah scrolls or Jewish stars, embroidered tallith and *kippas* (skullcaps), and CDs of Hebrew songs sung in an African style.[120]

In recent years, a myriad of other Judaizing societies, which are not included in this first survey, are burgeoning in West and East Africa and claim a Lost Tribes descent. I refer, for instance, to the Beit Avraham community in Kachene, Ethiopia, to a new movement of "Israelites" in Cameroon gathered around Rabbi Yisrael Oriel, and to a relatively small emergent community that has been formed in Laikipia, Kenya, that all have many deep connections with Judaism. These recent interesting developments of Judaism in Africa will stimulate further research.

Epilogue

Ancient Myths and Modern Phenomena

After the turn of the twentieth century, through a variety of religious encounters, some African societies began to transform their religious identity and claimed to be descendants of the ancient Israelites. These groups heralded the new phenomenon of an African Judaism within African religions. Indeed, the ground had been prepared for a long time. Spatial and metaphorical relationships historically connected them with ancient Israel. Throughout this study, starting from ancient myths, we have considered the development and growth of these phenomena among African groups, including their innovative adaptations. We now turn to a convergence of catalysts that, in this particular period of African history, have led African religious traditions mingled with Christianity, or sometimes Islam, to be superseded by a new Jewish cultural identity. As seen earlier, there is no normative model for the rich variety of Africans' encounters with Judaism. So, in this overview, I intend to understand the temporal parameters that encouraged some African groups' decision to turn to Judaism without sacrificing the richness of each group's particular history.

Why is it that this particular period of African history should witness the rise of Judaizing movements? Which factors must be taken into account to understand their dynamics?

This is happening at a time of rapid change in politics, culture, technology, and communications. As noted by James Beckford, globalization facilitates a transnational and transcultural diffusion of symbolic movements and meanings and enhances the "frequency, volume, and interconnections of movements of ideas." In doing so, globalization encourages the emergence of new movements in part by facilitating syncretism and the "recombination of fragments of experiences" from various traditions.[1] Globalization tends thus "to increase religious diversity within societies and to implicitly deregulate religious markets."[2] In the last decades, while space-age technologies have accelerated the break away from traditions, Africans are debating openly their constitutional rights to freedom of expression and freedom of religion.[3] Crucial social and technological developments have given the groups I have studied new opportunities and encouragement. The number of Web pages, which expanded rapidly and massively in the 1990s, enabled the myth of the Lost Tribes and the paradigm of Israelite identity to be spread to every corner of the globe. The Internet has had the effect of accelerating and extending the circulation of ideas, which fueled the crystallization of Jewish consciousness from one group to one another. A constant stream of communication by e-mail, as a means of publicizing their beliefs and activities, allowed emerging groups to be accepted by Western Jewry almost simultaneously with their own decision to think of themselves as Jews. This process, which took more than a century for the Falasha and around twenty years for the Lemba, was nearly instantaneous for groups such as Zakhor in Mali, the Igbo in Nigeria, or the House of Israel in Ghana.

Voluminous academic literature has emerged in recent years over the relationships between mass media and the intertwining of multiculturalism, ethnicity, and religion.[4] Teun Van Dijk has, in a number of works, pointed out that in the field of ethnic perceptions in particular, the role of the media is crucial in the sense that it is both ideological and structural: "For specific types of social and political events, including those in the field of ethnic relations, the news media are the main source of information and beliefs used to form the interpretation framework for such events."[5] Benedict Anderson's study stresses the power of collective representations, as well as the power of books, magazines, newspapers, and other media in multiplying and making the "reimagining" of communities possible through associations with other groups, which one might not have thought until then were "just like us."[6] Shohat and Stam's book *Unthinking Eurocentrism* (1997) associates the study of mass media with "race" discussions in an increasingly transnational world, in which the media sometimes refract and transform cultural identity.[7] Jennifer Gonzales comments on the World Wide Web:

> This relatively new domain for the phantasmatic projection of subjectivity (new in comparison to other media, such as film, television,

advertising and forms of cultural spectacle that produce patterns of identification), has also been championed as an innovative space for the re-inscription or redefinition of social relations as well as the re-conceptualisation of the traditional markers of race and ethnicity, sexuality and gender. There are currently thousands of online spaces that allow users to experiment with identity in an artificial world.[8]

The phenomenon of religious conversion in Africa has characteristically been discussed in relation to Christianity, being almost synonymous with "conversion to Christianity"; conversion to Judaism remains an unexplored field.[9] An attempt to come up with a general theory on conversions, from traditional religions to Christianity or Islam in Africa, was carried out by John Peel with the Aladura churches, created by the Yoruba in the nineteenth century. Regarding the question of what generates conversion from "traditional" to "world religions," Peel explains conversions in terms of the failing of indigenous beliefs vis-à-vis the social organization, which facilitates the introduction of new cults. The basic idea is that these changes, usually ascribed to the influence of Muslim and Christian proselytism, are active negotiations of new indigenous forms of Christianity or Islam.[10] This type of revitalization movement, which occurred to a lesser extent in Islam and, as observed by Rosalind Hackett, in traditional religions,[11] must be considered in the "mushrooming" of contemporary Judaizing movements in Africa.[12] However, understanding the precise issue of the religious shift to Judaism among certain African peoples requires some enlargement of the argument.

Instead of describing a single conversion process, which is the usual focus of studies on religious conversion, this work deals with the complex "phenomenon of dual conversion to a second world religion."[13] Most of the African groups I have described converted to Christianity before claiming an affiliation with Judaism. In the study of the conversion of the Indo-Burmese borderlands' Shinlung (Bene Menasseh) to Judaism, Shalva Weil points out that "research has usually focused upon a single conversion movement, irrespective of the fact that adherents to one religion may have undergone multiple radical transformations."[14] The African groups I refer to share a similar background to that of the Shinlung. Following a first conversion, they abandoned a set of norms and customs and changed their religious identification and participation. Cornelia Kammerer's model, which speaks of "replacement" instead of conversion, is a useful alternative to analyzing the contact between indigenous religion, Christianity, and then Judaism among African groups.[15]

Identity is linked with the political history of the country and the nation; Africans' identity was constructed upon the upheavals of history, from colonialism to independence, and from nationalism to the postcolonial present. As Said recognizes, the quest for identity is a general process by which a set of people seeks "to intensify its own sense of itself by dramatizing the distance and difference between what is closer to it and what is far away."[16] Among African Judaizing groups, exactly which circumstances triggered the religious identity shifts in question is not clear. These shifts may in some cases be related to a general dissatisfaction with Christianity as it was preached in the twentieth century, and to a desire to readopt elements of the pre-Christian religion and combine them in a modern framework. Justin Ukpong observed that "syncretism" in African Christianity is the expression of the fact that Christianity had not fully responded to African culturally based religious aspirations.[17] Prior to the rise of nationalism and the search for political autonomy in Africa, there were the so-called religious protest movements, which led to the rise of the "African Churches." African religious movements have for a long time attempted to restore their members' autonomy and integrity in their social and cultural life. G. Balandier puts it thus: "In Black Africa religious innovations constitute the prehistory of modern nationalism."[18] In the groups observed, specifically among the Jews of Rusape and the Zion Christian Church in South Africa, we have seen how conversion appears to be part of a wider reaction against Christianity and is associated with the demand for a religion not imposed upon them, and that would include their own pre-Christian beliefs. In respect to the Judaizing Shinlung, Weil writes, "The conversion to Judaism and the emergence of new religious forms are linked to the quest for by-passing Christianity and to the search for ethnic salience in novel form."[19] We remember that what triggered the affiliation to Judaism among the African groups has often been the dream of a mystic. Kakungulu in Uganda, Toakyirafa in Ghana, and Mgijima in South Africa began to have millennial visions and felt called to proclaim a return to the ancient religion of the Israelites, as a personal religious experience, "in protest against established church systems, that seemed excessively sacramental, priestly."[20] Weil stressed this phenomenon among the Shinlung:[21] "[They] managed to dovetail a claim of affiliation to lost Israelites together with indigenous legends about wandering tribes and to project millenarianism, which in some cases may have been inherent in their own religions, onto modern Judaism."[22] Following the affiliation of African Americans to Judaism at the beginning of the nineteenth century, the recent self-delineation of African groups as Jews underscored the significance of Judaism as a source of black identity.[23] In seeking to be relevant to this gap in the African existential world, the Judaizing movements' message aims to provide an alternative religious status validating Africans' own cultural roots and which, in some case, may counter the stigma of religious discrimination.

As for their brethren in the nineteenth-century United States, African Jews' encounter with Judaism is often related to resistance to white supremacy and frustration of blocked goal fulfilment. Indeed, the seeds of ethnic autonomy can be found in the rise of shifting religious identities as a quest for a politically effective cultural identity. We have seen earlier that, since the 1990s, identification with Judaism rose among the Tutsi of Rwanda, Burundi, and in Uganda, bringing with it its political, as well as ethnic and strategic, repercussions. This affiliation carries with it a heavy emotional burden, historical weight, political and strategic consequences, and religious connotations linked to Hebrew myths and the Jewish people. In this case, the emergence of a Jewish identity based on a perceived ancient ethnicity turns to ethnic autonomy and is linked to political national movements. One can find parallels with the Mizo National Front of the Shinlung, which mingled "Mizo Israelitism" with millenarianism in an attempt to demand national separation generated by combined dissatisfaction with local and national governments and past religion.[24] This view is also endorsed by C. L. Hminga, who affirms that affiliation to the Lost Tribes theory by the Lushai, in India in the 1970s, was part of an indigenous religion, and that the rise of Zionism can be explained as a revivalist reaction to Christianity.[25] The religious component of such form of "re-traditionalization," as described by Smith, is closely related to the quest for a politically effective cultural identity as seen surfacing even in the Western world.[26] This kind of ethnoreligious trend, which mobilizes populations against a foreign culture, seems to forge a new cultural identity, at least for the elite. To what extent the religious components of such trends could become an instrument for ethnopolitical claims in the context of these African groups is an open question. Presently, in their respective countries, with the exception of Rwanda, these movements are not viewed as representing a threat to political authority.[27]

However, focusing merely on colonialism and political antagonisms as the sole causative factor of these movements seems inadequate. For some of the African societies concerned in this survey, the adoption of a Jewish identity and rites, or the conversion to Judaism, appears as both an intellectual event and a sociological transformation akin to ethnogenesis. Thus, such religious movements must be understood as responses to psychological and cultural tensions and not only as expressions of political antagonisms. These religious shifts have occurred in a period of Africa's history when several indicators show that traditional religion has been eroded while people are experiencing a feeling of lost and vague identity. As for African Americans in the nineteenth century, the individuals who joined the African Jews movements had entered into a phase of "religious seekership," which Lofland and Stark have defined as the search for a religious system as a mean of interpreting and resolving conflicted life experience.[28] Specifically, Judaism has a rooted historicity that people with little or no recorded history may find compelling. In questioning Judaizing movements that have taken place in Africa, I am inclined to consider them rather as countersocieties that reflect important transitions in people's lives. Commitment to Judaism, as noted by Arthur Nock, "demanded renunciation and a new start...[not] merely acceptance of a rite but the adhesion of the will to a theology, in a word, faith, a new life in a new people."[29] Like other new religious movements emerging in the mid–twentieth century, African Judaizing societies' strategies "deliberately aspire to overcome national boundaries of ideology, religion, ethnicity, and citizenship in their drive toward a peaceful and harmonious world that is unified by what they consider to be universal values."[30] The affiliation of some African societies to the venerable Jewish religious tradition may thus legitimately be classified as "alternative spirituality," historically and sociologically connected with new religious movements.[31] In respect to the individuals in the African societies who are embarking on a new venture, which implies the acceptance of a radically different lifestyle and belief system in their quest for spiritual nourishment, I follow Smith, who considers that

> the significance of a rich "ethno-history" is both general and specific. To belong to a community of history and destiny and be part of a large cosmic purpose which is simultaneously terrestrial and even "kin-based," at least in theory, may well fulfil those hopes for immortality which other belief systems promised but failed to meet. Membership of a "super-family" that stretches back into time immemorial, and so formed into a remote posterity, helps to reassure as it defines a community and a wider purpose beyond individual mortality. More specifically, a rich "ethno-history" is a source of cultural power and a focus for cultural mobilisation....So the very unevenness of ethnic ties and ethnic history is an invitation to cultural emulation and competition, once the process of national transformation begins.[32]

In a world marked by political upheavals, ethnic conflicts, economic uncertainty, and ecological crises, the rise of Judaizing communities in Africa has incited me to try and understand the dynamics of external and internal forces that shape and reshape these modern Jewish identities. At a time when identities are sharply affected by the modernity crises, subtle gradations of Jewish identities indicate various attempts by Africans to bring creative and innovative responses into a bewildering and complex field of human behavior. What this study suggests is that the generation of an Africanized form of Judaism expresses the aspiration to oneness within an intellectual, moral, and spiritual universe. The groups under study seem to find in a Lost Tribes identity an important source for sustaining moral and political power. African Jews therefore seek change at a cosmic, social, and supraindividual level through the restoration of a real or imagined past social order.

Notes

INTRODUCTION

1. Sigmund Freud, translated from *Eine Kinderheiterinnerung des Leonardo da Vinci [A Childhood of Leonardo da Vinci]* (Paris: Folio, Gallimard, 1991), pp. 114–115. All translations are my own unless indicated otherwise.

2. Tudor Parfitt and Emanuela Trevisan Semi, *Judaising Movements* (London: Routledge Curzon, 2002), p. ix.

3. Stanford L. Lyman, "The Lost Tribes of Israel as a Problem in History and Sociology," *International Journal of Politics, Culture and Society* 12, no. 1 (1998): 34.

4. The surveys and publications on this community number in the thousands. In this study, the Falasha will be taken into account only in relation to the historical and cultural context of African Judaism, in order to apprehend other groups and understand their history. For a review on the literature on this subject, see *Bibliography on Ethiopian Jewry* (2001–2004), compiled by Shalva Weil (Addis-Ababa: SOSTEJE, 2004).

5. Parfitt and Trevisan Semi, *Judaising Movements*, p. ix.

6. Frederick Cooper, "Conflict and Connection: Rethinking Colonial African History," *American Historical Review* 99 (1997): 1515–1545.

7. See, e.g., Gyan Prakash, "Subaltern Studies as Postcolonial Criticism," *American Historical Review* 99, no. 5 (1994): 1475–1490. Much controversy has recently come to surround the status and value of postcolonial theory, which has been challenged on several fronts. See Bart Moore-Gilbert, *Postcolonial Theory: Contexts, Practices, Politics* (London: Verso, 1997).

8. Carlo Ginzburg, *Clues, Myths and the Historical Method* (Baltimore: Johns Hopkins University Press, 1989).

9. Renato Rosaldo, *Culture and Truth: The Remaking of Social Analysis* (Boston: Beacon Press, 1989), p. 217.

10. Melford E. Spiro, "Religion: Problems of Definition and Explanation," in *Cultural and Human Nature: Theoretical Papers of Melford E. Spiro,* ed. Benjamin Kilborne and L.L Langness (Chicago: University of Chicago Press, 1987): 187–222; Gary Porton, *The Stranger within Your Gates* (Chicago: University of Chicago Press, 1994).

11. Parfitt and Trevisan Semi, *Judaising Movements*, p. vii.

12. See, e.g., Steven Kaplan, "If There Are No Races: How Can Jews Be a 'Race'?" *Modern Jewish Studies* 2, no. 1 (2003): 79–96; Michael Corinaldi, *The Enigma of Jewish Identity: The Law of Return, Theory and Practice* (Jerusalem: Magnes Press, 2001); also Zvi Zohar and Avi Sagi, *The Circles of Jewish Identity in Halachic Literature* (Tel Aviv: HaKibbutz HaMeuchad, 2000); David T. Goldberg and Michael Kraus, eds., *Jewish Identity* (Philadelphia: Temple University Press, 1993).

13. Raphael Patai and Jennifer Patai, *The Myth of the Jewish Race* (Detroit, MI: Wayne State University Press, 1989). For a good survey of recent scholarship opinions on this topic from a variety of perspectives, including physical anthropology and genetics, see Faye V. Harrison, "The Persistent Power of Race," *Annual Review of Anthropology* 24 (1992): 47–74; Alain F. Corcos, *The Myth of the Jewish Race: A Biologist's Point of View* (Bethlehem, PA: Lehigh University Press, 2005). For a brief review on the literature on this subject, see Ari Kelman in *Reader's Guide to Judaism*, ed. M. Terry (Chicago: Fitzroy Dearborn, 2000), pp. 517–518.

14. Ephraim Isaac, "The Question of Jewish Identity and Ethiopian Jewish Origins," paper presented at the conference of the Society for Ethiopian Jewry, University of Addis Ababa, Ethiopia, October 14, 2004. The text is quoted in Diane Tobin, Gary A. Tobin, and Scott Rubin, *In Every Tongue* (San Francisco: Institute for Jewish and Community Research, 2005), p. 68.

15. M. McGiffer, "Editor's Preface" to "Constructing Race: Differentiating Peoples in the Early Modern Period," *William and Mary Quarterly* 54, no. 1 (1997): 3.

16. Kaplan, *If There Are No Races*, p. 85.

17. Indeed, the preferred self-designation of the Israelite community is that a Jew is a person who is either born of Jewish parents—that is, who has "Jewish blood"—or who converts to Judaism according to the law of an official branch of Judaism. See Shaye J. D. Cohen, "Conversion to Judaism in Historical Perspective from Biblical Israel to Post-Biblical Judaism," *Conservative Judaism* 36, no. 4 (Summer 1983): 31–45.

18. Yvonne Chireau and Nathaniel Deutsch eds., *Black Zion: African American Encounters with Judaism* (New York: Oxford University Press, 2000), p. 6.

19. Ken Blady, *Jewish Communities in Exotic Places* (Northvale, NJ: Jason Aronson, 2000), introduction by Steven Kaplan, p. xxv.

20. There are in Africa approximately 2,000 ethnic groups in more than fifteen nation-states.

21. Mircea Eliade, *Shamanism: Archaic Techniques of Ecstasy*, translated from the French by Willard E. Trask (Princeton, NJ: Princeton University Press, 1972), p. 15.

CHAPTER 1

1. Tudor Parfitt, *The Lost Tribes of Israel* (London: Weindenfeld and Nicolson, 2000), p. 47.
2. Ibid., pp. 36–57, 159.
3. Among whom I would quote: Parfitt, *Lost Tribes;* Shalva Weil, *Beyond the Sabatyon: The Myth of the Ten Tribes* (Tel Aviv: Beth Hatefutsoth, Museum of the Jewish Diaspora, 1991); Ronald Sanders, *Lost Tribes and Promised Lands* (Boston: Little, Brown, 1978); David A. Law, *From Samaria to Samarkand: The Ten Lost Tribes of Israel* (Lanham, MD: University Press of America, 1992); Yehoshua Benjamin, *Mystery of the Lost Tribes* (New Delhi: Gurja, 1989); Joseph Eidelberg, *The Japanese and the Ten Tribes of Israel* (Jerusalem: Givatayim, 1980); Karen Primack, *Jews in Places You Never Thought Of* (Hoboken, NJ: KTAV, 1998); Avraham Gross, "The Expulsion and the Search for the Ten Tribes," *Judaism* 41, no. 2 (1992): 130–147.
4. Parfitt, *Lost Tribes*, pp. 221–222.
5. Daniel Friedman, *Les enfants de la Reine de Saba* (Paris: Métaillé, 1994).
6. Michael Freund, "Let My People Go," Jerusalem Post Online, July 4, 2006, www.jpost.com/servlet/Satellite (accessed August 12, 2006).
7. Tudor Parfitt, "Place, Priestly Status and Purity: The Impact of Genetic Research on an Indian Jewish Community," *Developing World Bioethics* 3, no. 2 (2003), www.blackwellpublishing.com/journal; see also Mark G. Thomas, K. Skorecki, H. Ben-Ami, T. Parfitt, N. Bradman, and D. Goldstein, "Origin of Old Testament Priests," *Nature* 394 (July 1998): 138–140.
8. Allen H. Godbey, *The Lost Tribes a Myth: Suggestions towards Rewriting Hebrew History* (Durham, NC: Duke University Press, 1974).
9. Parfitt, *Lost Tribes*, pp. 22–23.
10. Andrew R. Anderson, *Alexander's Gate, Gog and Magog, and the Inclosed Nations* (Cambridge, MA: Mediaeval Academy of America, 1932), p. 80.
11. Ibid.
12. Ibid.
13. See, e.g., William G. Dever, *What Did the Biblical Writers Know, and When Did They Know It? What Archeology Can Tell Us about the Reality of Ancient Israel* (Grand Rapids, MI: Erdmans, 2001). Also Israel Finkelstein and Neil A. Silberman, *The Bible Unearthed: Archaeology's New Vision of Ancient Israel and the Origin of Its Sacred Texts* (New York: Free Press, 2001).
14. Bronislaw Malinowski, *Malinowski and the Work of Myth* (Princeton, NJ: Princeton University Press, 1992), p. 105.
15. The leading sources I used concerning the Ten Tribes (the Bible, the Talmud, and the Midrash) can be found in Rabbi Eliahu Avichail, *The Tribes of Israel: The Lost and the Dispersed* (Jerusalem: Zur-Ot Press, 5765). All quotations of the Bible come from *The Holy Bible,* containing the Old and New Testaments, Collins Bible. See also *Exile: Old Testament, Jewish and Christian Conceptions* (Leiden: Brill, 1997).
16. Lawson K. Younger, "The Deportations of the Israelites," *Journal of Biblical Literature* 117, no. 2 (Summer 1998): 201–227. Robert B. Coote and Keith W.

Whitelam, *The Emergence of Early Israel in Historical Perspective* (Sheffield: Almond Press, 1987); also "Leading Captivity Captive: The 'Exile' as History and Ideology," in *European Seminar on Methodology in Israel's History*, ed. Lester L. Grabbe (Sheffield: Sheffield Academy Press, 1998).

17. Ran Zadok, "Notes on the Early History of the Israelites and Judeans in Mesopotamia," *Orientalia* 51 (1982): 391–393.

18. Jacques Kohn, "A la recherche des Dix Tribus Perdues," *Kountrass* 48 (1994): 5–36.

19. Younger, "Deportations," p. 220.

20. Adolphe A. Neubauer, "Where Are the Ten Tribes?" *Jewish Quarterly Review* 1 (1889): 19.

21. Parfitt, *Lost Tribes*, p. 8.

22. Flavius Josephus (ca. AD 37–100), *Antiquities of the Jews*, Book 7, 5; Pliny the Elder (ca. AD 23–79), *Natural History*, Book 31.

23. Neubauer, "Ten Tribes," p. 20; Moses Edrehi, *An Historical Account of the Ten Tribes Settled beyond the River Sambatyon in the East* (London: printed for the author, 1836), pp. 20, 23, 77.

24. Rabbi Avichail, *Tribes*, p. 53.

25. Edward Ullendorf, *Ethiopia and the Bible* (London: Oxford University Press, 1968), p. 142. This would not be Ethiopia but the kingdom of Meroe. The term *Candace* refers to the function of queen in the ancient kingdom of Meroe. This state, located halfway between Egypt and Ethiopia, became an important center beginning in the eighth century BC and was conquered by the emperor of Axum, Ezana, in the fourth century AD.

CHAPTER 2

1. There are many versions of *Sepher Eldad*. See, e.g., *Eldad-ha-Dani*, ed. Abraham Epstein (Pressburg, 1891); Eliakim Carmoly, *Relation d'Eldad le Danite, voyageur du IXè siècle* (Paris: Dondé-Duprey, 1838); Elkan N. Adler, *Jewish Travellers: A Treasury of Travelogues from Nine Centuries* (London: Bloch Publishers, 1930); David Wasserstein, "Eldad ha-Dani and Prester John" in *Prester John, the Mongols and the Ten Lost Tribes*, ed. C. F. Beckingham and B. Hamilton (Aldershot: Variorum, 1996): 213–236.

2. Adler, *Jewish Travellers*, pp. 5, 15.

3. Ibid., pp. 12–13.

4. This information led recent scholars to locate the Halacha among Ethiopian Falasha, or Khazars, or North Yemen's Najran, without any general agreement on one of these assumptions. See Parfitt, *Lost Tribes*, p. 9. About Najran, see Tudor Parfitt, *The Road to Redemption: The Jews of Yemen, 1900–1950*, Brill's Series in Jewish Studies 17 (Leiden 1996), pp. 247ff. On the Falasha, see Steven Kaplan, *The Beta Israel (Falasha) in Ethiopia* (New York: New York University Press, 1992), p. 42; also Wasserstein, "Eldad," p. 214.

5. Neubauer, "Tribes," pp. 108, 109.

6. Adler, *Jewish Travellers*, p. xii.
7. Parfitt, *Lost Tribes*, p. 10.
8. Samuel Purchas, *Purchas in Pilgrimage* (London: W. Stansby, 1613).
9. Benjamin of Tudela in Adler, *Jewish Travellers*, pp. 83ff.; also Robert L. Hess, "The Itinerary of Benjamin of Tudela: A Twelfth-Century Jewish Description of North-East Africa," *Journal of African History* 6 (1965): 15–24.
10. Adler, *Jewish Travellers*, p. 55.
11. Maimonides does something similar, on one occasion identifying the inhabitants of the south as Hodim (Indians) and on another as Kushim (blacks) in *The Guide of the Perplexed*, translated with an introduction and notes by Shlomo Pines (Chicago: University of Chicago Press, 1963), vol.3, pp. 29, 51.
12. Adler, *Jewish Travellers*, pp. 58–59.
13. Menachem E. Artom and Abraham David, *From Italy to Jerusalem: Letters of Ovadiah of Bartenura from Eretz Israel* (C. G. Foundation Jerusalem project, Department of Land of Israel Studies, Bar-Ilan University, 5757, 1997), p. 74.
14. *The Journeys in Eretz Israel of R. Moses Basula in the Years 1421–1423*, p. 32, quoted in Abraham Melamed, *The Image of the Black in Jewish Culture* (London: Routledge Curzon, 2002), p. 150.
15. Moshe D. Cassuto, "Who Was David ha-Reubeni?" *Tarbiz* 32 (1963): 339–358.
16. Melamed points out that "it is no coincidence that the myth of the punishment of Ham (Canaan) appears in Christian literature only then, and grants theological legitimacy to economic interests." Before that, medieval slaves in southern Europe were white Slavs, from which in fact the word *slave* in various European languages derives. Melamed, *Image*, p. 151.
17. Abraham Melamed, "The Discovery of America in Jewish Literature of the Sixteenth and Seventeenth Centuries," in *Be-Ikvot Columbus: Amerika 1492–1992*, ed. M. Eliav-Feldon (Jerusalem: Merkaz Shazar and The Historical Society of Israel, 1997), pp. 443–462.
18. Menasseh ben Israel, *Hope of Israel*, introduction and notes by Henri Mechoulan and Gerard Nahon (New York: Oxford University Press, 1987), pp. 173–174.
19. Richard Popkin, "The Rise and Fall of the Jewish Indian Theory," in *Menasseh ben Israel and His World*, ed. Yosef Kaplan, Henri Mechoulan, and Richard Popkin (Leiden: Brill, 1989), pp. 63–82.
20. Thanks to the exchanges facilitated between Menasseh and the English theologians as a result of this story, an atmosphere was created that later facilitated the Jews' return to England. See *Menasseh Ben Israel's Mission to Oliver Cromwell* (London: Macmillan, 1901).
21. Arye Morgenstern, "R. Elijah, the Gaon of Vilna and His Historical Influence," in *Rahel Schnold* (Tel Aviv: Beth Hatefusot, 1998), pp. 67–73.
22. Walter J. Fischer, *Unknown Jews in Unknown Lands: The Travels of Rabbi D'Beth Hillel 1824–1832* (New York: KTAV, 1973).
23. Pierre-Gustave Brunet, "La légende du Prêtre Jean," in *Extrait des Actes de l'Académie des Sciences, Belles lettres et Arts de Bordeaux* (Bordeaux: C. Lefebvre, 1877), pp. 1–27; also Jean Doresse, *L'Empire du Prêtre Jean*, 2 vols (Paris: Plon, 1957).

24. François Fleuret, "La lettre du Prêtre Jean, Pseudo-Roi d'Abyssinie," *Mercure de France* 268 (1936): 298–309. For the search for Prester John, especially in Africa, see Dennison Ross, "Prester John and the Empire of Ethiopia," in *Travels and Travellers of the Middle Ages*, ed. Arthur P. Newton (New York: Barnes and Noble, 1968), pp. 174–194.

25. Brunet, "Légende," p. 15.

26. Neubauer, "Ten Tribes," p. 195.

27. Ibid.

28. Vincent Leblanc, *Les fameux voyages de Vincent Leblanc* (Paris, 1648), quoted in Tudor Parfitt, *Journey to the Vanished City* (New York: Vintage, 2000), p. 220. Among Christian travelers' accounts, the writings that constituted one of the driving myths of the time were those of a hypothetical traveler, Sir John Mandeville, who widely generalized the existence of the tribes of Israel, interpreted as Gog and Magog, in the mountains of the Caspian. See Sir John Mandeville, *Mandeville's Travels* (London: Hakluyt Society, 1953); Christiane Deluz, *Le livre de Jehan de Mandeville: Une géographie au XIV ème siècle* (Louvain: Institut d'Etudes Médiévales de l'Université de Louvain, 1988).

CHAPTER 3

1. Albert Kammerer proposed certain correspondences with contemporary geography: ancient Ethiopia, from Syene (Aswan) down to the southern tip, comprises all of Nubia, Sudan, and Abyssinia, although no one had a real notion of its autonomous existence. But, in the end he concludes with a large notion: "Subsequent to final analysis, Ethiopia corresponds to the whole of Africa, all the way to the Atlantic ocean and including the Sahara and the unknown countries in the south. Only Egypt, the Cyrenaic and northern Africa are excluded from this scope." See Albert Kammerer, *Essai sur l'histoire antique d'Abyssinie: Le royaume d'Aksum et ses voisins d'Arabie et de Méroé* (Paris: P. Geuthner, 1926), pp. 15–16.

2. Stéphane Gsell, *Histoire ancienne de l'Afrique du Nord*, 8 vols. (Osnabrück: O. Zeller, 1972), tome 7, pp. 5–6; also Emile F. Gauthier, *Le passé de l'Afrique du Nord, les siècles obscurs* (Paris: Payot, 1937), pp. 125–126.

3. François de Medeiros, *L'Occident et l'Afrique (XIIIe–XVe siècle)* (Paris: Karthala, 1985), p. 29. Medeiros underlined numerous references to the terms *Aethiops* and *Aethiopia* in *Thesaurus linguae latinae* (Berlin, 1900), vol. 1, fasc. 1, col. 1154 to 1157.

4. Malvern Van Wyk Smith, "Waters Flowing from Darkness: The Two Ethiopias in the Early European Image of Africa," *Theoria* 68 (1986): 67; Homère, *L'Odyssée*, trans. Victor Bérard (Paris: Les Belles Lettres, 1925).

5. Van Wyk Smith, "Waters Flowing," pp. 67–68.

6. Ibid., p. 67; Herodotus, *Thalie III*, ed. Philippe E. Legrand (Paris: Les Belles Lettres, 1967), pp. 17–26.

7. Van Wyk Smith, "Waters Flowing," p. 68; *Diodorus of Sicily*, 12 vols., ed. C. H. Oldfather (Cambridge, MA: Harvard University Press, 1935), vols. 1, 4. 9, and 11.

8. Van Wyk Smith, "Waters Flowing," p. 70; Salvanius of Marseilles, *De Gubernatione Dei*, trans. Eva M. Sanford (New York: Octagon Books, 1966), pp. 207–215.

9. Jacques Fontaine, *Isidore de Séville et la culture classique dans l'Espagne wisigothique* (Paris: Etudes augustiniennes, 1959), tome 2, p. 459. The maps created by Ptolemy were probably attempts to achieve realistic representations that were supposed to correspond to the coordinates he had carefully calculated for the main centers of the known world. Claudius Ptolemaus, *Cosmographia* (Bologna, 1447), with an introduction by R. A. Skelton (Amsterdam: N. Israel, 1963).

10. Van Wyk Smith, "Waters Flowing," pp. 71–72; Vicomte de Santarem, *Essai sur l'histoire de la cosmographie et de la cartographie* (Paris, 1850), pp. 288–434.

11. Van Wyk Smith, "Waters Flowing," pp. 73–75; Portulans in Youssef Kamal, *Monumenta Geographica Africae et Aegypti*, 16 vols. in 5; also Egon Klemp, *Africa on Maps* (Leipzig: Ed. Leipzig, 1968); Charles de La Roncière, *La découverte de l'Afrique au Moyen Age*, 3 vols. (Cairo, 1924), vol. 2, p. 1010.

12. About Monomotapa's empire, see Peter S. Garlake, *Great Zimbabwe* (New York: Stein and Day, 1974), pp. 174–181.

13. Van Wyk Smith, "Waters Flowing," p. 70.

14. Charles G. Seligman, *Races of Africa* (London: Oxford University Press, 1966), p. 96. The work of Seligman, first published in 1930 accepted as an authority, was republished in 1957 and 1966 and translated into French in 1953.

CHAPTER 4

1. Ullendorf, *Ethiopia*, pp. 138–145. See also, e.g., *The Legend of the Queen of Sheba in the Tradition of Axum*, ed. Enno Littmann (Leiden: Brill, 1904); *La légende de la reine de Saba* (Paris: Blotop, 2000).

2. The Gospels mainly retained the magnificence of Solomon's royal garments (Matthew 6:29; Luke 12:27) and mention that the queen of Sheba came from the limits of Earth to "listen to Solomon's wisdom" (Matthew 12:42; Luke 11:31).

3. Jacques Ryckmans, *L'institution monarchique en Arabie méridionale avant l'Islam* (Louvain: Publications Universitaires, 1951), p. 26.

4. Mathias Delcor, "La reine de Saba et Salomon. Quelques aspects de la légende et de sa formation principalement dans le monde juif et éthiopien, à partir des textes bibliques," in *Tradició I Traducció de la paraula: Miscel. Lània Giu Camps*, ed. F. Raurelt (Barcelona: Publicacions de lAbadia de Montserrat, 1993), pp. 309–310.

5. Delcor, "Saba," pp. 314–319. On the demonization of the queen of Sheba, see Low H. Silberman, "The Queen of Sheba in Judaic Tradition," in *Solomon and Sheba*, ed. James B. Pritchard (London: Phaidon, 1974), pp. 65–84.

6. The *Kebra Nagast*, "Glory of the Kings" consists of royal Ethiopian chronicles regarded as foundation myths and fantastic legends. *The Queen of Sheba and Her Only Son Meneyelek: Being the "Book of the Glory of Kings" (Kebra Nagast)*, trans. E. A. Wallis Budge (London: Kegan Paul, 2001).

7. The fable according to the Koran was borrowed from the Judeo-Christian concept of this time. According to Pirenne, it is in fact linked to the literary genre of the Jewish Haggadah, which is the narrative part of the Talmud written before AD 70. See Jacqueline Pirenne, "Bilqis et Salomon," *Dossiers de l'archéologie* 33 (1979): 6–10. Also Muhammad Tabari, *Les prophètes et les rois*, translated from the Persian by Hermann Zotenberg (Paris: Sindbad, 1984), vol. 2.

8. Scott T. Caroll, "Solomonic Legend: The Muslims and Great Zimbabwe," *International Journal of African Historical Studies* 21, no. 2 (1988): 233ff.

9. Pirenne, "Bilqis," p. 9.

10. *Sirah Antarah* is a fourteenth-century Arabian adventure tale. See Harry T. Norris, *The Adventures of Antar* (Warminster: Aris and Philips, 1980). Quotation from Harry T. Norris, "Did Antarah ibn Shad Conquer Zimbabwe?" in *A Miscellany of Middle Eastern Articles: In Memoriam Thomas Muir Johnston, 1924–83*, ed. A. K. Irvine, R. B. Serjeant, and G. Rex Smith (Harlow: Longman, 1988), p. 85, quoted in Parfitt, *Journey*, p. 215.

11. *Documents on the Portuguese in Mozambique and Central Africa, 1497–1840*, National Archives on Rhodesia and Nyasaland, Centro de Estudos Historicos and Ultramarinos, 6 vols. (Lisbon, 1962–1989), vol. 1, p. 395.

12. George M. Theal, *Records of South-eastern Africa, 1898–1903* (Cape Town: Struik, 1964), vol. 6, pp. 267–268.

13. Ibid., vol. 2, pp. 275–280.

14. Garlake, *Great Zimbabwe*, p. 62.

15. Ibid.

16. David Livingstone, *Missionary Travel and Researches in South Africa* (London: J. Murray, 1899), p. 29.

17. Thomas Baines, *The Gold Region of South Eastern Africa* (London: Stanford, 1877), p. v.

18. J. Theodore Bent, *The Ruined Cities of Mashonaland* (Freeport, NY: Books for Libraries Press, 1971), p. 242.

19. *The Journals of Karl Mauch*, ed. E. E. Burke (Salisbury: National Archives of Rhodesia, 1969), p. 117 (Mauch's diary, July 23, 1871), quoted in Garlake, *Great Zimbabwe*, p. 64.

20. Ibid.

21. Augustus H. Keane, *The Gold of Ophir, Whence Brought and by Whom* (New York: Negro University Press, 1969), p. 132. Also Ridder Haggard, *King Solomon's Mines* (New York: Oxford University Press, 1989).

CHAPTER 5

1. On travel literature and ethnography, see, e.g., Mary B. Campbell, *The Witness and the Other World: Exotic European Writing 1400–1600* (Ithaca, NY: Cornell University Press, 1988); Lorraine Daston, "Marvellous Facts and Miraculous Evidence in Early Europe," *Critical Inquiry* 18 (1991): 92–124; Daniel Defert, "The Collection of the World: Accounts of Voyages from the Sixteenth to the Eighteenth Centuries,"

Dialectical Anthropology 7, no. 1 (1982): 11–22; Ray W. Frantz, *The English Traveller and the Movement of Ideas, 1660–1732* (Lincoln: University of Nebraska Press, 1934); Stephen Greenblatt, *Marvellous Possessions: The Wonder of the New World* (Chicago: University of Chicago Press, 1991); Michael Harbsmeier, "Elementary Structures of Otherness: An Analysis of Sixteenth-Century German Travel Accounts," in *Voyager à la Renaissance*, ed. Jean Céard and Jean-Claude Margolin (Paris: Maison Neuve et Larose, 1987).

2. On the centering of Europe, see Loren Baritz, "The Idea of the West," *American Historical Review* 66 (1960–1961): 618–640; Denis Hay, *Europe: The Emergence of an Idea* (Edinburgh: Edinburgh University Press, 1957); Michel R. Trouillot, "Anthropology and the Savage Slot: The Poetics and Politics of Otherness," in *Recapturing Anthropology: Working in the Present*, ed. Richard G. Fox (Santa Fe: School of American Research Press, 1991).

3. Mary L. Pratt, "Scratches on the Face of the Country, or, What Mr Barrow Saw in the Land of the Bushmen," in *Race, Writing and Difference*, ed. Louis Gates Jr. (Chicago: University of Chicago Press, 1985), pp. 135–162.

4. Suzan Zantop, *Colonial Fantasies: Conquest, Family and Nation in Pre-colonial Germany, 1770–1880* (Durham, NC: Duke University Press, 1997), p. 14.

5. The different approaches to these questions have been analyzed and clarified in various, but not contradictory, ways and reflect the myths of society as applied to the basic structures of humanity. See Stuart Hall, *Representation: Cultural Representations and Signifying Practises* (Thousand Oaks: Sage, 1997), pp. 234–277. About the issue of representation, see also Winthrop Jordan, *White over Black* (Chapel Hill: University of North Carolina Press, 1986); Robert Young, *White Mythologies: Writing History and the West* (London: Routledge, 1990).

6. Michel Foucault, *The Order of Things: An Archaeology of the Human Science* (New York: Pantheon, 1971).

7. Edward Said, *Orientalism* (New York: Vintage, 1978), p. 7.

8. Mary Douglas, *Purity and Danger* (London: Routledge and Kegan Paul, 1966).

9. Anne McClintock, *Imperial Leather, Race, Gender, and Sexuality in the Colonial Context* (New York: Routledge, 1995), pp. 22–41; Robert Young, *Colonial Desire: Hybridity in Culture and Race* (London: Routledge, 1995).

10. Kwesi Dickson, *Theology in Africa* (New York: Orbis, 1984), p. 33.

11. Stefanus du Toit, "Missionaries, Anthropologists, and the Policies of the Dutch Reformed Church," *Journal of Modern African Studies* 22 (1984): 617–632; also Johannes Fabian, "Religious and Secular Colonisation: Common Ground," *History and Anthropology* 4 (1987): 37–49; Sjaak Van der Gest, "Anthropologists and Missionaries: Brothers under the Skin," *Man* 25 (1990): 588–601.

12. Maureen Henry, *The Intoxication of Power: An Analysis of Civil Religion in Relation to Ideology* (Dordrecht: D. Reidel, 1979), p. 25.

13. Johannes du Plessis, *History of Christian Missions in South Africa* (London: Longmans Green, 1911), p. 21.

14. Anthony J. Christopher, *Colonial Africa* (London: Croom Helm, 1984), p. 83.

15. David Chidester, *Savage Systems: Colonialism and Comparative Religion in Southern Africa* (Charlottesville: University Press of Virginia, 1996), pp. 2–17.

16. Said, *Orientalism*, pp. 7–8.

17. Valentin Y. Mudimbe, *The Invention of Africa: Gnosis, Philosophy and the Order of Knowledge* (Bloomington: Indiana University Press, 1988), p. 16.

18. Frank M. Snowden, *Blacks in Antiquity: Ethiopians in the Greco-Roman Experience* (Cambridge, MA: Belknap Press of Harvard University Press, 1970), p. 11. John P. V. D. Baldson, *Romans and Aliens* (Chapel Hill: University of North Carolina Press, 1979), p. 59.

19. Tudor Parfitt, "Hebrew in Colonial Discourse," *Journal of Modern Jewish Studies* 2, no 2 (2003): 160.

20. Tristan Todorov, *La découverte de l'Amérique: La question de l'autre* (Paris: Seuil, 1982), p. 11.

21. Guiliano Gliozzi, *Adam et le Nouveau Monde: La naissance de l'anthropologie comme idéologie coloniale: Des généalogies bibliques aux théories raciales*, trans. A. Estève and P. Gabelonne (Lecques: Théétète, 2000).

22. For examples of this school of thought, see Loren Eiseley, *Darwin's Century: Evolution and the Men Who Discovered It* (London: V. Gallancz, 1959), pp. 35–46. Also John C. Greene, "The American Debate on the Negro's Place in Nature, 1780–1815," *Journal of History of Ideas* 15 (1954): 384–396.

23. For some examples of this group, see, e.g., *The Works of Voltaire: A Contemporary Version*, notes by Tobias Smollet, translation by William Flemmings (New York: Gordon Press, 1975). Also Lord Kaines, *Sketches of the History of Man* (Edinburgh, 1780).

24. Hall, *Cultural Representations*, p. 244.

25. David Green, "Classified Subjects: Photography and Anthropology—the Technology of Power," *Ten* 18, no. 14 (1984): 31–32.

26. Frantz Fanon, *Peaux noires, masques blancs* (Paris: Seuil, 1971), pp. 154–155.

27. On the subject in general, see Robert Bennett, "Africa and the Biblical Period," *Harvard Theological Review* 64 (1971): 483–500, which gives an overview of scriptural references to Africa and the African, with linguistic, historical, and textual questions relevant to determining the place of Africa in the biblical period.

28. In most translations of the Bible the name Kush is written with a *C*: Cush. This is due to the influence of Latin; today, however, most scholars write *Kush*, which reflects the original spelling of the name in pre-Latin texts. Another general term for the sub-Saharan inhabitants of Africa is *black* or *black African*, terms commonly used in Greco-Roman studies. In this book, I use these terms interchangeably as called for by the context.

29. In Jeremy 46:9; Ezekiel 38:7; Nahum 3:9; in Isaiah 45:14; in Job 28:19.

30. Melamed, *Image*, pp. 54–55.

31. *Ham* in Hebrew means "hot" or "multitude" and thus does not necessarily express a racial difference.

32. Moshe Weinfeld, *The Promise of the Land: The Inheritance of the Land of Canaan by the Israelites* (Berkeley: University of California Press, 1993).

33. See David M. Goldenberg, *The Curse of Ham: Race and Slavery in Early Judaism, Christianity and Islam* (Princeton, NJ: Princeton University Press, 2005).

34. Melamed, *Image*, pp. 54–55. In the Bible, the black is sometimes seen to be in a different type of human situation, at least as to external appearance. Familiar quotations include "Can the black [*Kushi*] change his skin?" (Jer. 13:23) and "Are ye not as children of the black [*Kushi'im*]?" (Amos 9:7).

35. Robert Graves and Raphael Patai, *Hebrew Myths: The Book of Genesis* (London: Cassell, 1964), p. 121.

36. Hess, "Benjamin of Tudela," p. 17; also William G. L. Randles, *L'image du Sud-Est africain dans la littérature européenne du XVIè siècle* (Lisbon: Centro de estudos historicos ultramarinos, 1959), p. 152.

37. Snowden, *Blacks*, preface, pp. 8, 180. Also Jan N. Pieterse, *White on Black: Images of Africa and Blacks in Western Popular Culture* (New Haven, CT: Yale University Press, 1992). While Snowden tries to rehabilitate early Christianity, Pieterse seeks to absolve classical literature of racism. See also criticism of Snowden's claim in Lloyd A. Thompson, *Romans and Blacks* (London: Routledge, 1989), pp. 27, 42–43, 45, 54–55; and Westermann's argument on this question in William Westermann, *The Slave Systems of Greek and Roman Antiquity* (Philadelphia: American Philosophical Society, 1955). See also the important report of Jehan Desanges, *Revue des études latines* 48 (1970): 87–95, and his reserves about Snowden's naïveté.

38. Snowden, *Blacks in Antiquity*, pp. 2–3.

39. In Tacitus, *History*, book 5, pp. 2–4, in *Greek and Latin Authors on Jews and Judaism*, ed. Menahem Stern (Jerusalem: Israel Academy of Sciences and Humanities, 1980), vol. 2, pp. 1–6.

40. Thompson, *Romans*, pp. 104–105. From the eighth century, Islamic scholars found "scientific" backing in Greek literature, particularly in texts about the theory of climate, to identify the black negatively. See William M. Evans, "From the Land of Canaan to the Land of Guinea: The Strange Odyssey of the Sons of Ham," *American Historical Review* 85 (1980): 33; also Elisabeth Evans, *Physiognomics in the Ancient World* (Philadelphia: American Philosophical Society, 1969).

41. It appears that the symbolism of black-negative and white-positive is widespread among peoples of all colors. The same black-white color symbolism seen in Western traditions is found in China and South Asia. It has been found among the Chiang (a Sino-Tibetan people), the Mongour (a Mongolian people), the Chuckchees of Siberia, and the Creek Indians of North America. It occurs in Sanskrit, Caledonian, and Japanese, as well as Western, literature. Indeed, according to many anthropological reports, the phenomenon is common even in black Africa. See Goldenberg, *Curse of Ham*, p. 3.

42. Charles A. Auber, *Histoire et théorie du symbolisme religieux avant et depuis le christianisme* (Paris: A. Franck, 1870–1871), pp. 112–128; Athalya Brenner, *Colour Terms in the Old Testament* (Sheffield: JSOT Press, 1982).

43. Melamed, *Image*, p. 30.

44. Ibid., p. 64.

45. Snowden, *Blacks in Antiquity*, pp. 198–199. Also Najman Hindy, "Cain and Abel as Character Traits: A Study in the Allegorical Typology of Philo of Alexandria," in *Themes in Biblical Narrative: Jewish and Christian Traditions*, ed. Gerard Luttikhuizen (Leiden: Brill, 2003), pp. 107–118; *Vie des saints et des bienheureux*, by the Révérends Pères Bénédictins de Paris (Paris: Letouzey et Aney, 1946), tome II, pp. 131ff.

46. Medeiros, *Occident*, p. 247.

47. Augustine, *Ennarat*, in Psalms 40, 67, 71, 72, 73, quoted in Medeiros, *Occident*, p. 249.

48. Some examples of such prejudices were reported by the book of Proverbs, such as "Nigra petit nigrum: petit et monachum monialis," in *Proverbia sententiaeque latinitatis medii ac recentioris aevi*, by Hans Walther (Göttingen: Vandenhoeck, 1965), pt. 3, p. 123, no. 16624.

49. Flodoard, *De triomphis Christi sanctorumque Palestinae*, vol. 1, 13, pl. 135, col. 498.

50. Jean Devisse, *L'image du Noir dans l'art occidental* (Paris: Bibliothèque des Arts, 1979), pp. 62–63. This is a fading fresco on one of the pilasters that was copied by J. Wilpert, *Die römischen Mosaiken und Malereien der Kirchlichen Bauten*, Jahrhundert 2 (Anfl. Freiburg in Breisgau, 1917), vol. 4, pl. 168, 2.

51. Devisse, *Image*, pp. 62–63. Representation of three angels and one black demon of the same size, Patmos, Haghios Yoannis Theologos Monastery.

52. Devisse, *Image*, pp. 62–63.

53. Ibid., pp. 149–204.

54. Lynn Glaser, *Indians or Jews? An Introduction to a Reprint of Manasseh ben Israel's The Hope of Israel* (Gilroy, CA: Boswell, 1973), quoted in Parfitt, *Lost Tribes*, pp. 21–22.

55. What Cheyette names a "structural incoherence" obviously hit the Jews. Bryan Cheyette, *Construction of the Jews in English Literature and Society: Racial Representations, 1875–1945* (Cambridge: Cambridge University Press, 1993), p. 3.

56. Marco Polo, *La description du monde*, ed. Pierre-Yves Badel (La Flèche: Brodard et Taupin, 1998), pp. 79–81.

57. It seems that the issue was also taken up in the tenth century by Tabari in connection with the Koran and by Arabian authors such as Omara; see *Chronique de Tabari*, trans. Herman Zotenberg (Paris: Sindbad, 1989), vol.1, p. 523.

58. Anderson, *Alexander Gate*, p. 73.

59. Ibid., p. 69.

60. Ibid., p. 76.

61. Ibid., p. 74.

62. Ibid., p. 78.

63. Joseph Deniker, *The Races of Man* (New York: Scribner's, 1906), p. 50; Maurice Fishberg in *The Jews* (New York: W. Scott, 1911), p. 68.

64. In ancient Egyptian monuments, Canaanites are depicted as having red hair and beards; actors playing the role of Jews traditionally donned red wigs. Fishberg, *The Jews*, p. 68.

65. Sander L. Gilman, *Jewish Self-Hatred* (Baltimore: John Hopkins University Press, 1986), p. 6. For this section, I am deeply indebted to the rich information assembled by Gilman about the topic of the black skin of the Jews.

66. See discussion of motives for emphasizing the excessive sexuality of the black "other" in Pieterse, *White*, chap. 12. For an overview on the issue, see also Sander L. Gilman, *Difference and Pathology: Stereotypes of Madness* (Ithaca: Cornell University Press, 1985).

67. Since ancient times, not only in popular culture, but also in medical literature, an association was made between the length of one's nose and that of the male sex. See Sander L. Gilman, "The Jewish Nose: Are Jews White? Or the History of the Nose Job," in *The Other in Jewish Thought and History*, ed. Laurence Silberstein and Robert L. Cohen (New York: New York University Press, 1994), p. 7.

68. Manchester, John Rylands Library, ms. Lat. 24, Missal for the Use of Sarum (Salisbury), 13th, fol. 150 quoted in Devisse, *Image*, p. 76.

69. David Berger, *The Jewish Christian Debate in the High Middle Ages* (Philadelphia: Jewish Publication Society of America, 1979), p. 224, quoted in Sander L. Gilman, *L'autre et le moi: Stéréotypes occidentaux de la race, de la sexualité et de la maladie*, trans. C. Cantoni-Fort (Paris: PUF, 1996), p. 220.

70. Quotation of Prudencio de Sandoval in J. Friedman, *Jewish Conversion, the Spanish Pure Blood Law and Reformation: A Revisionist View of Racial and Religious Antisemitism*, pp. 16–17, quoted in James S. Shapiro, *Shakespeare and the Jews* (New York: Columbia University Press, 1996), p. 36.

71. On questions of cultural difference and racial discrimination, see, e.g., Edgar Rosenberg, *From Shylock to Svengali: Jewish Stereotypes in English Fiction* (London: Peter Owen, 1961). Also Hyam Maccoby, *The Sacred Executioner: Human Sacrifice and the Legacy of Guilt* (London: Thames and Hudson), 1982.

72. Sir William Brereton *Travels in Holland, the United Provinces, England, Scotland and Ireland, 1634–1635*, ed. E. Hawkins (1844), quoted in Shapiro, *Shakespeare*, p. 171.

73. Donald Maclean, ed., "London in 1689–90," *Transactions of the London and Middlesex Archaeological Society* 7 (1937): 151, quoted in Shapiro, *Shakespeare*, p. 171.

74. Adam G. de Gurowski, *America and Europe* (New York: D. Appleton, 1857), p. 177, quoted in Sander L. Gilman, *The Jew's Body* (London: Routledge, 1991), p. 175.

75. François M. Misson, *A New Voyage to Italy* (London: R. Bonwicke, 1714), vol. 2, p. 139.

76. Johann Pezzl, *Skizze von Wien: Ein Kultur- und Sittenbild as der josephinischen Zeit*, ed. Gustav Gugitz und Anton Shlossar (Graz: Leykam-Verlag, 1923), pp. 107–108, quoted in Gilman, *Jews' Body*, p. 210.

77. Howell, "Epistle Dedicatory the Wonderful and Most Deplorable History," quoted in Shapiro, *Shakespeare*, p. 36. See also allusions to Jewish smell in Isaac Levi, "Le juif de la légende," *Revue des Etudes juives* 20 (1890): 249–252.

78. James C. Prichard, *The Natural History of Man* (London: H. Baillère, 1845), p. 186; also Claudius Buchanan, *Christian Researches in Asia, with Notices of the Translation of the Scriptures into the Oriental Languages* (Boston: S. T. Armstrong, 1811), p. 169.

79. Houston S. Chamberlain, *Foundations of the Nineteenth Century*, trans. John Lees (London: John Lane, 1910), vol. 1, pp. 388–389; also Sander L. Gilman, *On Blackness without Blacks: Essays on the Image of the Black in Germany* (Boston: G. K. Hall, 1982), pp. 1–34.

80. Sander L. Gilman, "The Visibilty of the Jew in the Diaspora: Body Imagery and Its Cultural Context," The G. B. Rudolph Lectures in Judaic Studies, Syracuse University, May 1992, p. 29.

81. Petrus Camper, *Der natürliche Unterschied der Geschichtszüge in Menschen verschiedener Gegenden und verschiedenen Alters*, trans. S.T. Sömmering (Berlin: Voss, 1797), p. 7, quoted in Gilman, *Jew's Body*, p. 7.

82. Robert Knox, *Races of Men* (London: H. Renshaw, 1862), p. 134.

83. Friedrich Ratzel, *History of Mankind* (London: MacMillan, 1896–1898), pp. 112ff.

84. Samuel S. Smith, *An Essay on the Causes of the Variety of Complexion and Figure in the Human Species* (Cambridge, MA: Belknap Press, 1965), p. 42.

CHAPTER 6

1. On the theological roots of the Hamitic myth, see Louis Sala-Mollins, *Le code noir ou le calvaire de Canaan* (Paris: PUF, 2002); Rémi Brague, "Le déni d'humanité," *Lignes* 12 (1990): 217–232, and, more generally, Jean-Pierre Chrétien, "Les deux visages de Cham. Point de vue français du XIXè siècle sur les races africaines d'après l'exemple de l'Afrique Orientale," in *L'idée de race dans la pensée politique française contemporaine* (Paris: CNRS, 1977), pp. 171–199; John G. St. Clair Drake, "Détruire le mythe hamitique, devoir des hommes cultivés," *Présence Africaine* 24–25 (1959): 215–230; Wyatt McGaffey, "Concepts of Race in the Historiography of North East Africa," *Journal of African History* 7, no. 1 (1966): 1–17.

2. Seligman, *Races of Africa*, p. 96. The work of Seligman, first published in 1930, was accepted as an authority and was republished in 1939, 1957, and 1966 and translated into French in 1953.

3. John Pory, *Translation of Leo Africanus* (London: Hakluyt Society, 1896), xcii–xciv.

4. Chrétien, "Deux visages," p. 175.

5. For this section I am deeply indebted to Sanders's analysis and suggestions about the Hamitic myth. Edith R. Sanders, "The Hamitic Hypothesis: Its Origin and Functions in Time Perspective," *Journal of African History* 10, no. 4 (1969): 521–532.

6. For some authors the hypothesis of a primordial red race became a sort of universalistic racial mystique, mixing science and esotericism. Far from being cursed or degenerated, Hamites were the alleged survivors of original mankind, the real Adamites. See S. Zaborowski, "Méditerranéens et Nègres," *Revue de l'Ecole d'Anthropologie de Paris* A23 (1913): 149ff.

7. François-Xavier Fauvelle, *L'Afrique de Cheikh Anta Diop* (Paris: Karthala, 1996), pp. 132–133.

8. Léon Poliakov, "Les idées anthropologiques des philosophes du siècle des lumières," *Revue Française d'Histoire d'Outre-mer* 3 (1971): 258.

9. Vivant Denon, *Analyse et extraits du voyage dans la basse et haute Egypte pendant les campagnes du Général Bonaparte* (Paris: Legrand, 1802), pp. 108–109.

10. Constantin-F. Volney De Chasseboeuf, *Voyage en Syrie et en Egypte* (Paris: Mouton, 1959 [1787]).

11. William G. Browne, *Travels in Africa, Egypt and Syria* (London, 1806), quoted in Sanders, "Hamitic," p. 526.

12. Michael Russell, *View of Ancient and Modern Egypt* (New York, 1831), p. 27, quoted in Sanders, "Hamitic," pp. 526–527.

13. Sanders, "Hamitic," p. 527.

14. See, e.g., Josiah C. Nott, "The Negro Race," *Popular Magazine of Anthropology* 3 (1866): 102–118; Samuel L. Morton, *Crania American; or Comparative Views of the Skulls of Various Aboriginal Nations of North and South America,* to which is prefixed an "Essay on the Varieties of the Human Species" (London: Simpkin, Marshall, 1839).

15. Christian K. Bunsen, *Egypt's Place in Universal History: A Historical Investigation,* translated from German by C. H. Cotrell (London: Longman, 1859), pp. 847–867, quoted in Sanders, "Hamitic," p. 528.

16. See, e.g., Antoine d'Abbadie, *Notice sur les langues de Kam* (Paris, 1872); Rochet d'Héricourt, *Voyage de la Cote Orientale de la Mer Rouge dans le pays d'Adel et le royaume de Choa* (Paris, 1841–1842).

17. Joseph A. de Gobineau, *Essai sur l'inégalité des races humaines* (Paris, 1884, [1853–1855]), pp. 225–241. Saint-Vincent, often considered as one of the predecessors of Gobineau, expressed as early as 1827 ironic remarks about the theory of Hamitic blacks. "Kush," he wrote, "was the father of Nemrod, the founder of Assyria, Canaan the cursed was proto-Phoenician." See Bory de Saint-Vincent, *L'homme, essai zoologique sur le genre humain* (Paris, 1887), vol. 1, pp. 206–207, and vol. 2, pp. 150–156.

18. John H. Speke, *Journal of the Discovery of the Source of the Nile* (Edinburgh: Blackwood, 1863). See also Robert Cornevin, *Histoire de l'Afrique* (Paris: Payot, 1967), vol. 2, pp. 150–156.

19. Jacques Maquet, *The Premise of Inequality in Ruanda: A Study of Political Relations in a Central African Kingdom* (Ann Arbor, MI: UMI, 1994).

20. Pierre Trémeaux, *Voyage au Soudan Oriental et dans l'Afrique septentrionale pendant les années 1847 et 1848* (Paris: Lacour, 1853), vol. 2, p. 181.

21. Martial de Salviac, *Un peuple antique ou une colonie gauloise au pays de Ménélick: Les Galla, une grande nation africaine* (Cahors: Plantade, 1901).

22. Antoine de Préville, *Les sociétés africaines* (Paris, 1894), pp. 287–297; François Romanet du Caillaud, "Des chrétiens de Saint Matthieu existant en Afrique au commencement du XIVè siècle et de l'identification de l'Ouganda à l'empire chrétien du Magdasor," offprint of the *Actes du 8è Congrès International de Géographie de 1904,* pp. 930–939.

23. Chrétien, "Deux visages," p. 182.

24. Joseph Halévy, "Lettre à monsieur d'Abadie sur l'origine asiatique des langues du nord de l'Afrique," *Actes de la Société Philologique*, June 1–2 1869, pp. 29–46. See also Fulgence Fresnel, "Sur l'histoire des Arabes avant l'islamisme," *Journal Asiatique*, June 1838, pp. 497–544, quoted in Chrétien, "Deux visages," pp. 183, 188. Fresnel was an "orientalist" who defined the "language of Kush" used long ago in southern Arabia and Ethiopia, as a trace of an ancient civilization of the Euphrates, neither Semite, black, nor "red."

25. With regard to the role of such theories for the English colonial expansion, see Edgar Sanderson, *Africa in the Nineteenth Century* (London: Seeley, 1898); Frederick J. Lugard, *The Rise of Our East African Empire* (Edinburgh: Blackwood, 1893); William L. Langer, *The Diplomacy of Imperialism, 1890–1902* (New York: Knopf, 1951).

26. J. Barzun, *Race: A Modern Superstition* (New York: Harper and Row, 1965), p. 33, quoted in Sanders, "Hamitic," p. 529.

27. Giuseppe Sergi, *The Mediterranean Race* (London: Scoot, 1901), pp. 40–41.

28. Ratzel, *History*. St. Clair Drake denounced the responsibility of Ratzel and wrote: "Such concepts as Indo-Germanic, Semitic, Bantu races, are not only devoid of value, but must be rejected as a whole because they go astray," in "Détruire," p. 220. Delafosse also quotes the writings of P. Paulitschke; see Maurice Delafosse, "Les Hamites de l'Afrique Orientale," *L'Anthropologie* 5 (1894): 157–171.

29. St Clair Drake, "Détruire," p. 224; also Sir Harry H. Johnston, *A History of the Colonization of Africa by Alien Races* (Cambridge: the University Press, 1899); Charles C. Seligman, "Some Aspects of the Hamitic Problem in the Anglo- Egyptian Sudan," *Journal of the Royal Anthropological Institute* 41 (1913): 593–704.

30. Jean-Jacques Virey, *Histoire naturelle du genre humain* (Paris, 1824), vol. 2, p. 13.

31. Sanders, "Hamitic," p. 530.

32. See, e.g., Anson P. Atterbury, *Islam in Africa* (New York: Putnam's, 1899); John W. Gregory, *The Foundation of British East Africa* (London: Marshall, 1901).

33. Roland H. Oliver, *The Missionary Factor in East Africa* (London: Longmans, 1952); also Claude H. Perrot, "Premières années de l'implantation du christianisme au Lesotho, 1833–1847," *Cahiers d'Etudes Africaines* 1 (1963): 97–124; Jean-Pierre Chrétien, "Missions, pouvoir colonial et pouvoir africain," in *Christianisme et pouvoir politique* (Université de Lille III, 1971), pp. 139–154.

34. Armand de Quatrefages, *Histoire générale des races humaines* (Paris: H. Ennuyer, 1889), pp. 392–393. This did not prevent Quatrefages from writing: "The Negro is an intellectual monstrosity," in *Revue des Deux Mondes* (March 1843), quoted in Leon Poliakov, *Le mythe aryen* (Paris: Calmann-Lévy, 1971), p. 226.

35. Charles G. Seligman, *Egypt and Negro Africa: A Study in Divine Kinship* (London: Routledge, 1934); John R. Baker, *Race* (New York: Oxford University Press, 1974), pp. 401–417; Augustin Holl, "La question de l'age du fer ancien de l'Afrique occidentale: Essai de méthode" (paper presented at the meeting "Histoire et archéologie de la métallurgie du fer," March 21–27, 1983).

36. Garlake, *Great Zimbabwe*, pp. 66, 71–75. Garlake and Gertrude Caton-Thompson, *The Zimbabwe Culture: Ruins and Reactions* (Oxford: Clarendon Press, 1931), began to express doubts on the foreign origin of those achievements.

37. Henry Spencer, *Sociologie descriptive des races africaines*, introduction à l'édition de 1930, quoted in St. Clair Drake, "Détruire," p. 224.

38. St. Clair Drake, "Détruire," pp. 225–227. However, Greenberg shows that there are four languages or groups of languages that should "exhibit such morphological or lexical similarities, that one cannot doubt their kinship." This concerns Semitic, Berber, and ancient Egyptian languages and also Kushitic languages in eastern Africa (Galla, Sidamos, Bedauve, Somali, Kaffa, Alo), to which he would later add Hausa and Chad languages.

39. St. Clair Drake, "Détruire," p. 229.

40. Basil Davidson, *Old Africa Rediscovered* (London: Gallancz, 1959). See also the subsequent influence of the myth in Thurstan Shaw, *Nigeria: Its Archaeology and Early History* (London: Thames and Hudson, 1978), and its contributions to Peter Robershaw, *A History of African Archaeology* (London: Currey, 1990).

41. For a current overview of this issue, see, for instance, Graham Connah, *African Civilisations, Precolonial States and Cities in Tropical Africa: An Archaeological Perspective* (Cambridge: Cambridge University Press, 2001); Roland A. Oliver, *The African Experience* (New York: IconEditions, 1992).

42. Chrétien, "Deux visages," p. 182.

43. Quotation of Keupens, "Cours sur 'l'Urundi ancien et moderne," quoted in Chrétien, "Deux visages," p. 198.

44. *The Journal of Christopher Columbus*, ed. and trans. Cecil Jane (London: Blond, 1968), pp. 194–200; Amerigo Vespucci, *"Mundus Novus": Letters to Lorenzo Pietro di Medici 1504–1505*, in Elridge L. Huddleston, *Origins of the American Indians: European Concepts, 1492–1729* (Austin: University of Texas Press, 1967), pp. 5–6. Regarding the denial of religion in the Americas, see David Chidester, *Patterns of Power: Religion and Politics in American Culture* (Englewood Cliffs, NJ: Prentice-Hall, 1988).

45. Paul Roussier, *L'Establissement d'Issiny* (Paris: Larose, 1935), p. 213.

46. Emily Apter and William Pietz, *Fetishim as Cultural Discourse* (Ithaca, NY: Cornell University Press, 1993). Also Alfred C. Haddon, *Magic and Fetishism* (London: Archibald Constable, 1906).

47. Richard Burton, *The Lake Regions of Central Africa* (London: Longman Green, 1860), vol. 2, pp. 341–357.

48. James Grant, *A Walk across Africa: or Domestic Scenes from My Nile Journal* (Edinburgh: W. Blackwood, 1864), p. 145.

49. René Caillé, *Tombouctou ou le premier voyage à Djenné et Tombouctou, 1826–1828* (Paris: Epigones, 1991).

50. Chidester, *Savage*, pp. 11–20.

51. Snowden, *Blacks*, p. 146.

52. Lancelot Andrewes, *A Pattern of Catechistical Doctrine* (London, 1650; reprint, New York: AMS Press, 1967), quoted in Keith Thomas, *Man and the Natural World: Changing Attitudes in England 1500–1800* (London: Allen Lane, 1983), p. 21.

53. Edward Brerewood, *Enquiries Tracing the Diversity of Languages and Religions through the Chief Parts of the World, 1613* (London: printed for N. Ranew and J. Robinson, 1671), pp. 39–45.

54. Parfitt, "Hebrew," p. 160.

55. Louis André Vigneras, ed., *The Journal of Christopher Columbus*, trans. C. Jane (London: A. Blond and Orion Press, 1960).

56. John Reinhold Forster, *Observations Made during a Voyage round the World on Physical Geography, Natural History and Ethnic Philosophy* (London: G. Robinson, 1778), pp. 295–301.

57. Lewis Hanke, *The First Social Experiments in America* (Cambridge, MA: Harvard University Press, 1935), p. 72. Hanke pointed out the existence of Roldàn's manuscript in the Provincial y Universitaria library of Seville (ms., col. 333) and established the dating.

58. Ibid.

59. Diego Duràn, *Historia de las Indias de Nueva España e Islas de Tierra Firme*, ed. J. F. Ramirez (México City: Porrúa, 1967), vol. 1.

60. Gregorio Garcia, *Origen de los Indios del Nuevo Mondo* (Madrid: F. Martinez Abad, 1729), vol. 1, tome 3, pp. 177–317.

61. Quoted in Parfitt, "Hebrew," p. 164.

62. See also the version of de Antonio de la Calancha, *Cronica Moralizada de la Orden de San Agustin en el Perù*, 2 vols. (Barcelona, 1939), vol. 1, tome 1, chap. 5, pp. 39–41.

63. Huddleston, *Origins*, p. 34.

64. José de Acosta, *Historia Natural y Moral de las Indias* (Madrid: Cultura Hispánica, 1998), vol. 1, chap. 23, pp. 36–37.

65. Juan de Torquemada, *Primera (-tercera) parte de los veinte i uno libros rituales i Monarchia Indiana* (Seville: M. Clavijo, 1615), vol. 1, tome 1, chap.9, p. 25.

66. Gilbert Génébrard, *Chronographia in duos libros distincta (Lovanii: apud J.Foulerum, 1570)*. André Thévet, *La cosmographie universelle* (Paris, 1575), vol. 2, tome 1, Chap. 13, fol. 1022a.

67. John Eliot, *A Brief Narrative of the Progress of the Gospel amongst the Indians in New England in the Year 1670* (London: John Allen, 1671) in Howard Eilberg-Schwartz, *The Savage in Judaism: An Anthropology of Israelite Religion and Ancient Judaism* (Bloomington: Indiana University Press, 1990), p. 32.

68. Thomas Thorowgood, *Jews in America or Probabilities That Americans Are of That Race* (London: Slater, 1650), p. 3 in Eilberg-Schwartz, *Savage*, p. 33. Among English authors, see also William Strachey, *The Historie of Travell into Virginia Britania* (London: Hakluyt Society, 1953 [1849]), vol. 1, tome 1, chap. 3.

69. Hamon Lestrange, *Americans No Iewes, or Improbabilities That the Americans Are of That Race* (London, 1652), in Eilberg-Schwartz, *Savage*, p. 35.

70. Marc Lescarbot, *History of New France*, trans. W. R. Grant (Toronto: Champlain Society, 1914), vol. 3 in Eilberg-Schwartz, *Savage*, p. 35.

71. Joseph François Lafitau, *Customs of the American Indians Compared with the Customs of Primitive Times*, ed. and trans. William N. Fenton and Elisabeth L. Moore (Toronto: Champlain Society, 1974–1977 [1724]), vol. 1, p. 27.

72. Eilberg-Schwartz, *Savage*, pp. 36–38.

73. Renato Rosaldo, "The Rhetoric of Control: Illongots Viewed as Natural Bandits and Wild Indians," in *The Reversible World: Symbolic Inversion in Art and Society*, ed. Barbara Babcock (Ithaca, NY: Cornell University Press, 1978), pp. 240–257.

74. Chrétien, "Deux visages," p. 197.

75. David Chidester, *Christianity: A Global History* (San Francisco: Harper, 2000), p. 414.

76. E. L. Woodward, *The Age of the Reform, 1815–1870* (Oxford, 1938), in Parfitt, *Lost Tribes*, p. 181.

77. Father J. M. Van der Bugt, *Dictionnaire français-kurundi* (Bois-le-Duc, 1903), introduction, pp. LXXV, LXXXI.

78. Chrétien, "Deux visages," p. 190.

79. Ibid.

80. Adolf E. Jensen, "Beziehungen zwischen dem Alten Testament und der Nilotischen Kultur in Afrika," in *Culture in History: Essays in Honour of Paul Radin*, ed. Diamond Stanley (New York: Columbia University Press, 1960), pp. 452–453, quoted in Raphael Patai, "The Ritual Approach to Hebrew-African Culture Contact," *Jewish Social Studies* 24 (1962): 90; also Adolf E. Jensen, M. T. Cheldin, and W. Weissleder, *Myth and Cult among Primitive Peoples* (Chicago: University Press of Chicago, 1973).

81. Patai, "Ritual," p. 90.

82. M. Merker, *Die Masai* (Berlin: D. Reimer, 1904), pp. 290–332, in Patai, "Ritual," p. 87, quoted in Parfitt, *Lost Tribes*, p. 63.

83. Joseph J. Williams, *Hebrewisms of West Africa* (New York: Biblo and Tannen, 1930), pp. 7–14, 16–43, 51–93.

84. Ibid., p. 66.

85. In post-Napoleonic Europe, the idea of the unity of the Peul people who would have ruled important territories in western Africa was born. Anna Pondopoulo-Sanchez, "Comment les Peuls sont-ils devenus Juifs?" in "Généalogies rêvées," *Diasporas* 5 (2004), Centre national de recherche scientifique, pp. 87ff.

86. Ibid., pp. 88–89.

87. Maurice Delafosse, *Haut-Sénégal-Niger* (Paris: Larose, 1912), vol. 2, pp. 226–353; also Maurice Delafosse, "Les langues de l'Afrique," *L'Anthropologie* 30 (1920): 546.

88. For a recent critic of Delafosse's theory on the "Judaic-Syrians" in Ghana, see, e.g., Aboubacry M. Lam, *De l'origine égyptienne des Peuls* (Paris: Présence Africaine/Khepera, 1993), p. 51.

89. Delafosse, *Haut-Sénégal*, p. 234.

90. Charles de La Roncière, *La découverte de l'Afrique*, Vols. 1 and 2 (Cairo, Institut Français d'archéologie orientale, 1924–1925), vol. 1, pp. 102, 136. It has even

been said that the Peul could be considered as a branch of the Indonesian races or as descendants of the Annamites. See Maurice Abadie, *La colonie du Niger* (Paris: Société d'éditions géographiques, 1927), p. 57.

91. Edmond D. Morel, *Affairs of West Africa* (London: Heinemann, 1902), pp. 138ff.

92. Quoted in Williams, *Hebrewisms*, p. 246.

93. Herbert C. Hall, *Barrack and Bush in Northern Nigeria* (London, 1923), p. 9, quoted in Williams, *Hebrewisms*, p. 244.

94. Williams, *Hebrewisms*, p. 140.

95. Morel, *Affairs*, p. 139.

96. Williams, *Hebrewisms*, pp. 151–158. Among the various authors who considered that the Peul were of Hebrew origin, see Dr. Lasnet, Auguste Chevalier, and A. Cligny, *Une mission au Sénégal* (Paris: Challamel, 1900), p. 3; Abadie, *Colonie*, pp. 184ff.; Francis R. Rodd, *People of the Veil* (London: Macmillan, 1926), p. 57, quoted in Williams, *Hebrewisms*, p. 244.

97. John Philip, *Researches in South Africa* (New York: Negro University Press, 1969 [1828]), vol. 2, pp. 116, 364.

98. I am deeply indebted to David Chidester, the leading scholar involved in studying the distortion of southern African religions by colonialism. See Chidester, *Savage*.

99. Peter Kolb, *The Present State of the Cape of Good Hope: Or, A Particular Account of the Several Nations of the Hottentots: Their Religion, Government, Laws, Customs, Ceremonies and Opinions: Their Art of War, Professions, Languages, Genesis, etc.*, trans. Guido Medley (London: W. Innis, 1731), vol. 1, quoted in Chidester, *Savage*, pp. 47–72.

100. Chidester, *Savage*, p. 51.

101. Kolb, *Present State*, pp. 87–88, in Chidester, *Savage*, p. 52.

102. Kolb, *Present State*, pp. 99–102, in Chidester, *Savage*, pp. 51–53.

103. Kolb, *Present State*, pp. 105–107, in Chidester, *Savage*, p. 55.

104. Chidester, *Savage*, pp. 62–63.

105. Sidney Mendelssohn, "Judaic or Semitic Legends and Customs among South African Natives," Journal of the Royal African Society 14 (1914): 24–34.

106. J. H. Sogo, *The Ama-Xosa: Life and Customs* (Lovedale Mission Press: South Africa, 1932), quoted in Magdel Le Roux, "In Search of the Understanding of the Old Testament in Africa: The Case of the Lemba" (Ph.D. diss., University of South Africa, 1999), pp. 24–25.

107. Jews named those who abandoned their religion by the term *Cofar*; Muslims named those who ignored the true God or abandoned their Islamic religion by the terms *Coffers* or *Caffers*. See O. F. Mentzel, *A Geographical and Topographical Description of the Cape of Good Hope, 1785–87*, ed. H. J. Mandelbrote (Cape Town: Van Riebeeck Society, 1944), pp. 266–267, in Chidester, *Savage*, pp. 73–74.

108. Cowper Rose, *Four Years in Southern Africa* (London: Colburn and Bentley, 1829), vol. 2, pp. 116, 363, in Chidester, *Savage*, p. 91.

109. Chidester, *Savage*, p. 88.

110. Francis Fleming, *Southern Africa: A Geography and Natural History of the Country, Colonies and Its inhabitants* (London: Arthur Hall Virtue, 1856), p. 197, in Chidester, *Savage*, p. 93.

111. Thomas Philipps, *Philipps, 1820, Settler, His Letters*, ed. A. Keppel-Jones (Pietermaritzburg, South Africa: Shuter and Shooter, 1960), pp. 117–118; Robert Godlonton, *Narrative of the Irruption of the Kaffir Hordes into the Eastern Province of the Cape of Good Hope, 1834–1835* (Cape Town: C. Struik, 1965), pp. 229–231, in Chidester, *Savage*, pp. 95–96, 98.

112. See on this issue John Bird, *Annals of Natal* (Cape Town: C. Struik, 1965 [1888]), vol. 1, pp. 45; also Basil Leverton, *Records of Natal* (Pretoria: Government Printers, 1984), vol. 1, pp. 37–40, 247–248, in Chidester, *Savage*, p. 124. It is possible that a certain degree of prejudice against Islam played a role in this comparison, but it seems that the major element of this identification of the Zulu with ancient Israelites was due to the fact that Jews were considered as being able to be controlled and "ghettoized" under Christian rule.

113. Allen Gardiner, *Narrative of a Journey to the Zoolu Country in South Africa Undertaken in 1835* (London: William Crofts, 1836), p. 152, in Chidester, *Savage*, pp. 121.

114. Natal. *Native Affairs Commission: Proceedings of the Commission Appointed to Inquire into the Past and Present State of the Kaffirs in the District of Natal* (Pietermaritzburg, South Africa: Archbell, 1852–1853), vol. 3, pp. 62, 65, in Chidester, *Savage*, p. 132.

115. Ibid.

116. Natal. *Native Affairs Commission*, vol. 5, pp. 54–55, in Chidester, *Savage*, pp. 126–127.

117. John W. Colenso, "The Diocese of Natal," *Monthly Record of the Society of the Propagation of the Gospel in Foreign Parts* 4 (November 1853): 243–246; also John W. Colenso, "Church Missions among the Heathen in the Diocese of Natal," 1854 (Pietermaritzburg, South Africa: University of Natal Press, 1982), quoted in Chidester, *Savage*, pp. 129–140.

118. Chidester, *Savage*, pp. 129–140.

119. John W. Colenso, *The Pentateuch and Book of Joshua Critically Examined* (London: Longman, Robert and Green, 1862–1879), vol. 1, xxi, 4, p. 117, in Chidester, *Savage*, p. 137.

120. William R. Smith, *Lectures of the Religion of the Semites* (Edinburgh: A. and C. Black, 1889).

121. Chidester, *Savage*, pp. 171–172.

122. C. de B. Webb. and J. B. Wright, *The James Stuart Archive of Recorded Oral Evidence Relating to the History of Zulu and Neighbouring Peoples* (Pietermaritzburg, South Africa: University of Natal Press: Killie Campbell Africana Library, 1976, 1986), vol. 1, pp. 217, 243, 247, 261–262, in Chidester, *Savage*, p. 169.

123. After the Hottentots and the Zulu, the application by Europeans of this Jewish identification also extended to the Boers. One of the groups of Boers of the northern border was known in the 1860s as the "Jerusalemgangers" because they

thought they were approaching the Holy City. See Livingstone, *Missionaries Travels*, p. 27; also C. I. Latrobe, *Journal of a Visit to South Africa in 1815–1816, with Some Accounts of the Missionary Settlements of the United Brethren Near the Cape of Good Hope* (London: L. B. Seeley, 1818), in Chidester, *Savage*, p. 174.

124. Jean Comaroff and John Comaroff, *Of Revelation and Revolution: Christianity, Colonialism, and Consciousness in South Africa* (Chicago: University of Chicago Press, 1991), vol. 1. Also Chidester, *Savage*, pp. 36, 77–79, 116–118; Samwiri R. Karugire, *A History of the Kingdom of Nkore in Western Uganda to 1896* (Oxford: Clarendon Press, 1971), pp. 41–49.

125. Chidester, *Savage*, p. 261.

126. Molefi K. Asante, *The Afrocentric Idea* (Philadelphia: Temple University Press, 1987), p. 6.

CHAPTER 7

1. Among recent discussions about Afrocentrism, see Stephen Howe, *Afrocentrism: Mythical Pasts and Imagined Homes* (London: Verso, 1998); Mary Lefkowitz, *Not Out of Africa: How Afrocentrism Became an Excuse to Teach Myth as History* (New York: Basic Books, 1996); Stanley M. Burstein, "Egypt and Greece: Afrocentrism and Greek History," *Were the Achievements of Ancient Greece Borrowed from Africa?*, Proceedings from a Seminar in Georgetown University, Washington, DC, November 16, 1996 (publ. 1998), pp. 21–33; François-Xavier Fauvelle, "L'Afrocentrisme entre révision de l'histoire et quête d'identité," *Les Temps Modernes* 53, no 600 (1998): 285–302.

2. Volney, *Voyage*. Volney's work *Ruins of Empires* (1794) was reprinted up to 1990 by Afrocentrists, at the Black Classic Press.

3. In his contribution to Fauvelle's work *Afrocentrismes* (Paris: Karthala, 2000), p. 300, Stephen Howe indicates that the African American historian Wilson Jeremiah Moses discovered precursors of Afrocentrism in the 1790s. See Wilson Jeremiah Moses, *Afrotopia: The Roots of African American Popular History* (Cambridge: Cambridge University Press, 1998).

4. About the earliest and most comprehensive literature of this kind, see John C. de Graft-Johnson, *African Glory: The Story of Vanished Negro Civilizations* (New York: Walker, 1966); and Ayi Kwei Armah, *Osiris Rising: A Novel of Africa Past, Present and Future* (Popenguine, Senegal: Per Ankh, 1995).

5. A complex network of migrations certainly existed, but probably between areas within Africa and throughout the continent. See, for instance, Graham Connah, *African Civilizations*.

6. David Walker, *Appeal to the Coloured People* (1829), quoted in Ella Forbes, "African-American Resistance to Colonization," *Journal of Black Studies* 21, no. 2 (1990): 214. Also Hosea Easton, *A Treatise on the Intellectual Character and the Political Condition of the Coloured People of the United States and the Prejudice Exercised towards Them* (Philadelphia: Historic Publications, 1969), pp. 9–11.

7. James W. C. Pennington, *A Text Book of the Origin and History of the Coloured People* (Detroit, MI: Negro History Press, 1969 [1841]), pp. 3, 7, 9.

8. John W. Norris, *The Ethiopian's Place in History and His Contribution to the World's Civilization* (Baltimore: Afro-American, 1916), pp. 34–38.

9. See, e.g., William H. Councill, *Lamp of Wisdom; Or Race History Illuminated* (Nashville, TN: Haley, 1898); Harvey Johnson, *The Nations from a New Point of View* (Nashville, 1903).

10. Merriman-Labor quoted in Charles Marke, *Africa and the Africans* (1881), p. 127, in Howe, *Afrocentrism*, p. 42.

11. William H. Ferris, *The African Abroad or, His Evolution in Western Civilization* (New Haven, CT: Tuttle, 1913), p. 431.

12. J. F. Ade Ajayi, "Samuel Ajay Crowther of Oyo," in *Africa Remembered: Narratives by West Africans from the Era of the Slave Trade*, ed. Philip Curtin (Madison: University of Wisconsin Press, 1967); Martin R. Delany, *Principia of Ethnology: The Origins of Race and Colour...* (Philadelphia: Harper and Brothers, 1879); James Africanus Horton, *West African Countries and Peoples, British and Native... and a Vindication of the African Race* (London, 1868).

13. Quoted in Basil Davidson, *The African Past: Chronicles from Antiquity to Modern Times* (Boston: Little, Brown, 1964), p. 35.

14. Hollis R. Lynch, *Edward Wilmot Blyden: Pan-Negro Patriot* (New York: Oxford University Press, 1967), pp. 67–71, 73–77, 124.

15. Paul Gilroy, *The Black Atlantic: Modernity and Double Consciousness* (Cambridge, MA: Harvard University Press, 1993), pp. 210–211.

16. William E. B. Du Bois, *The Negro* (New York: Schocken Books, 1915).

17. William E. B. Du Bois, *Dusk of Dawn: An Essay towards the Autobiography of a Race Concept* (New York: Harcourt, 1940), p. 117. See also Anthony K. Appiah, "The Uncompleted Argument: Du Bois and the Illusion of Race," *Critical Inquiry* 12 (1977): 1.

18. About *noirisme*, see, e.g., J. Michael Dash, *Literature and Ideology in Haiti 1915–1961* (Totowa, NJ: Barnes and Noble, 1981).

19. Léopold Sedar Senghor, *Négritude et civilisation de l'universel* (Paris: Seuil, 1977); Aimé Césaire, *Cahier d'un retour au pays natal* (Paris: Présence Africaine, 1939). The theory of Senghor that "*Négritude* is Africa's contribution to the coming of a universal situation," with the contribution of the Belgian Father Placide Tempels's *La Philosophie bantou* (Paris: Présence Africaine, 1959) and the French René Griaule's *Dieu d'eau, entretiens avec Ogotemmeli* (Paris: Duchêne, 1948), crossed the Atlantic, where they had a considerable impact on African American thinkers, even if they subsequently became the target of violent attacks of African philosophers themselves. See, for instance, Paulin J. Hountondji, *African Philosophy: Myth and Reality* (Bloomington: Indiana University Press, 1996); also the Ghanaian philosopher Kwasi Wiredu, *Philosophy and an African Culture* (New York: Cambridge University Press, 1980). The critique of ethno-philosophy was taken up again by the Kenyan Dema Masolo in his *African Philosophy in Search of Identity* (Bloomington: Indiana University Press, 1994) and the Ghanaian Kwame A. Appiah, who led the most powerful attack against it in his controversial work *In My Father's House: Africa in the Philosophy of Culture* (New York: Oxford University Press, 1992).

20. Howe, *Afrocentrism*, pp. 73–79.

21. Ken Post, *Arise Ye Starvelings: The Jamaican Labour Rebellion of 1938 and Its Aftermath* (The Hague: Nijhoff, 1978), pp. 168–169.

22. Ibid., p. 171.

23. See, e.g., Edmund Cronon, *Black Moses: The Story of Marcus Garvey and the Universal Negro Improvement Association* (Madison: University of Wisconsin Press, 1969); Rupert Lewis, *Marcus Garvey: Anti-colonial Champion* (Trenton, NJ: Africa World Press, 1988).

24. James H. Boykin, *Black Jews: A Study in Minority Experience* (Miami: J. H. Boykin, 1996), p. 31.

25. UNIA claimed more than 6 million members worldwide.

26. Howe, *Afrocentrism*, p. 76.

27. Albert Cleage, *The Black Messiah* (New York: Sheed and Ward, 1968), pp. 3, 72, 243, 39–40.

28. See, e.g., Jack Salzman and Cornel West, *Struggles in the Promised Land: Towards a History of Black-Jewish Relations in the United States* (New York: Oxford University Press, 1997).

29. Kwaku Person-Lynn, *First Word: Black Scholars, Thinkers, Warriors* (New York: Harlem River Press, 1996), p. 72. About Jeffries, see Dinesh D' Souza, *Illiberal Education: The Politics on Race and Sex on Campus* (New York: Free Press, 1991), p. 7.

30. Akyaaba Addai-Sebo and Wong Ansel, *Our Story: A Handbook of African History and Contemporary Issues* (London: London Strategy Policy Unit, 1988), pp. 293–294.

31. Yosef Ben-Jochannen, *Africa: Mother of Western Civilization* (Baltimore: Black Classic Press, 1988), p. 589.

32. Yosef Ben-Jochannen, *We the Black Jews: Witness to the "Jewish Race" Myth* (Baltimore: Black Classic Press, 1993).

33. Jose V. Malcioln, *The African Origins of Modern Judaism: From Hebrews to Jews* (Trenton, NJ: Africa World Press, 1996).

34. Howe, *Afrocentrism*, p. 227.

35. Edwin Redkey, *Black Exodus, Black Nationalism and Back-to-Africa Movements, 1890–1910* (New Haven, CT: Yale University Press, 1969), p. 22.

36. Emanuela Trevisan Semi, "The 'Falashisation' of the Blacks of Harlem," in *Judaising Movements*, ed. Tudor Parfitt and Emanuela Trevisan Semi (London: Routledge Curzon, 2002), p. 90.

37. Elijah Muhammad, *Message to the Blackman in America* (Chicago: Muhammad Mosque of Islam no. 2, 1965), p. 31; Gilles Kepel, *A l'ouest d'Allah* (Paris: Seuil, 1996). See also Malcom X and Alex Haley, *The Autobiography of Malcom X* (New York: Chelsea House, 1996). Books and articles on the Black Muslims are numerous; see, e.g., Eric C. Lincoln, "The Black Muslims," in *Minority Problems*, ed. A. M. Rose and C. B. Rose (New York: Harper and Row, 1961), pp. 281–289; also Clifton E. Marsh, "Entretien avec W. D. Muhammad, septième fils d'Elijah," in *From Black Muslims to Muslims: The Transition from Separatism to Islam, 1930–1980*

(Lanham, MD: Scarecrow Press, 2000). It is currently thought that some 20 percent of the slaves sold in Africa (usually by Muslim slave traders) who reached American plantation were themselves Muslim, insofar as they came from Islamized areas of western coastal Africa.

38. Trevisan Semi, 'Falashisation,' p. 91.

39. Theodore Herzl, *Altneuland* (Paris: Editions de l'Eclat, 2005 [1931]), pp. 257–258.

40. Edward W. Blyden, *The Jewish Question* (Liverpool: Lionel Hart, 1898), p. 8. On the issue of "international religion," see Lynch, *Blyden*, pp. 63–65; also Hollis R. Lynch, "A Black Nineteenth-Century Response to Jews and Zionism: The Case of Edward Wilmot Blyden," in *Jews in Black Perspectives*, ed. Joseph Washington (Rutherford, NJ: Fairleigh Dickinson University Press, 1984), pp. 42–54.

41. Dominique Bobi, "Les nouveaux courants de pensée dans la diaspora noire: Un antisémitisme de type révisionniste," *Aleph Beth* 3 (March 1999): 67.

42. Bruce Felton, "The Origin of America's Black Jews," *Jewish Digest* 29 (November 1974): 12–16.

43. Yvonne Chireau, "Black Culture and Black Zion," in *Black Zion: African American Religious Encounters with Judaism, 1790–1930* (New York: Oxford University Press, 2000), pp. 17–18.

44. Melville Herskowitz, *The Myth of the Negro Past* (Boston: Beacon Press, 1941), p. 299. Also Graenum Berger, *Black Jews in America: A Documentary with Commentary* (New York: Federation of Jewish Philanthropies, 1978).

45. Albert J. Raboteau, *Slave Religion* (New York: Oxford University Press, 1978).

46. Chireau, "Black Culture," pp. 17–18.

47. St. Clair Drake, "African Diaspora and Jewish Diaspora: Convergence and Divergence," in Washington, *Jews in Black Perspectives*, p. 19.

48. Howard M. Brotz, *The Black Jews of Harlem* (New York: Schocken Books, 1970), p. 2; also Ulysses Santamaria, "Le judaïsme dans la culture négro-américaine," *Les Temps Modernes* 444 (July 1983): 63–64.

49. Harold Courlander, *Negro-Folk Music* (New York: Columbia University Press, 1963), pp. 36–43.

50. Brotz, *Black Jews*, p. 1.

51. About the situation of blacks and interracial relationships, it is interesting to refer to works written in the beginning of the twentieth century, such as Charles S. Johnson, *The Negro in American Civilization* (New York: Holt, 1930); James W. Johnson, *Black Manhattan* (New York: Knopf, 1930); and Sterling Spero and Abram L. Harris, *The Black Worker* (New York: Columbia University Press, 1931).

52. Okon Edet Uya, "Life in a Slave Community," *Afro-American Studies* 1 (1971): 289.

53. For example, an insurrection was led in Richmond, Virginia, at the beginning of the nineteenth century by Gabriel Posser, a slave who identified himself with Samson, his favorite hero, and who, like Samson, wore long hair. Posser had acquired some knowledge of the Bible and referred to it frequently in order to convince his colored brothers that they were descendants of Israelites and that God would free

them from slavery, as he did for their Jewish ancestors. Like Samson, Posser was convinced that God had chosen him to break the bonds of slavery and found a nation of free black men in America. See Edward F. Frazier, *The Negro in the United States* (New York: Macmillan, 1949), p. 87. See also Ralph Melnick, "Billy Simon: The Black Jew of Charleston," *American Jewish Archives* 1: 32 (April 1980): p. 3–8.

54. Booker T. Washington, *The Future of the American Negro* (Boston: Small Maynard, 1902), pp. 182ff. Washington was one who, alongside Blyden or Du Bois, contributed to the birth of black consciousness; see "Harlem's Black Jews Look to the Future," *People's Voice*, January 6, 1945, p. 20.

55. Chireau, "Black Culture," p. 19.

56. Howard M. Brotz, "The Negro Jewish Community and the Contemporary Race Crisis," *Jewish Social Studies* 1 (1965): 11–12; Chireau, "Black Culture," p. 20.

57. According to Leonard Barret, the notion of "Ethiopianism" appeared in Jamaica before it did in the United States: the term was adopted by George Liele, an American Baptist preacher who founded the island's first Baptist church in 1794. The cult of this church merged with African religions of the Jamaican slaves and developed outside Christian missions, strongly tinged with African practices. See Leonard Barret, *The Rastafarians: Sounds of Cultural Dissonance* (Boston: Beacon Press, 1988), p. 76, and chapter 2.

58. On the coming together of Ethiopianism and black nationalism, see Wilson J. Moses, *The Golden Age of Black Nationalism, 1850–1925* (New York: Oxford University Press, 1988); and also John G. St Clair Drake, *The Redemption of Africa and Black Religion* (Chicago: Third World University Press, 1970).

59. Arthur H. Fauset, *Black Gods of the Metropolis: Negro Religious Cults of the Urban North* (Philadelphia: University of Pennsylvania Press, 1944), pp. 31–40.

60. Ibid.

61. Ibid.; also Elly Wynia, *The Church of God and Saints of Christ: The Rise of Black Jews* (New York: Garland, 1994).

62. Ray K. Jones, "Negro Migration in New York State," *Opportunity*, September 1929, p. 270. It should be pointed out that the concentration of blacks in northern cities also signified access to political participation and representation: the Communist Party in New York and Chicago, which was particularly active within the African American community, then the Democratic Party, with Roosevelt and the great liberal coalition of the New Deal.

63. James Landing, "The Spatial Expression of Cultural Revitalization in Chicago," in *Proceedings of the Association of American Geographers* 6 (1974): 51.

64. About the relationships between Jews and blacks within the NAACP, see, for instance, Lewis D. Levering "Shortcuts to Mainstream: Afro-American Notables in the 1920s and 1930s," in Washington, *Jews in Black Perspectives*, pp. 83–94; also Hasia Diner, *In the Almost Promised Land: American Jews and Blacks, 1915–1935* (Baltimore: John Hopkins University Press, 1995).

65. Jeffrey S. Gurock, *When Harlem Was Jewish, 1870–1930* (New York: Columbia University Press, 1979), pp. 144–146. Also "Black Jews: There Are 125,000 of Them in the Country," *Our World* 3 (February 1948): 24–25.

66. Trevisan Semi, "'Falashisation,'" p. 96; Gurock, *Harlem*, pp. 144–146.
67. Chireau, "Black Culture," p. 21.
68. Ulysses Santamaria, "Black Jews: The Religious Challenge or Politics versus Religion,"*Archives Européennes de Sociologie* 28, no. 2 (1987): 226–227.
69. Brotz, *Black Jews of Harlem*, p. 10; Trevisan Semi, "'Falashisation', p. 96.
70. Santamaria, "Black Jews," pp. 226–227.
71. Chireau, "Black Culture," p. 22; Jacob Marcus, *The Colonial American Jew, 1492–1776* (Detroit: Wayne State University Press, 1970).
72. Albert Ehrman, "The Commandment Keepers: A Negro Jewish Cult in America Today," *Judaism* 8, no. 3 (1959): 267.
73. Brotz, *Black Jews*, p. 16, excerpt from a conversation with Matthew or another member of the group.
74. Jacques Faitlovitch (1881–1955) was born in Lodz and then lived in Paris, where he was a pupil of Joseph Halévy, the great specialist of Ethiopian languages at the Ecole des Hautes Etudes en Sciences Sociales. Faitlovitch's first journey among the Jews of Ethiopia took place in 1904–1905. See Emanuela Trevisan Semi, "Universalisme juif et prosélytisme. L'action de Jacques Faitlovitch, le 'père' des Beta Israel (Falashas)," *Revue de l'Histoire des Religions* 216, no. 2 (1999): 193–211.
75. Brotz, *Black Jews*, p. 49.
76. Trevisan Semi, "'Falashisation,'" p. 88.
77. Chireau, "Black Culture," p. 25.
78. Williams, *Hebrewisms*, pp. 66–92.
79. Ruth Landes, "Negro Jews in Harlem," *Jewish Journal of Sociology* 9, no. 2 (1967): 180–181.
80. Trevisan Semi, "'Falashisation,'" p. 94. On the evolution of the BNA (Beth B'nai Abraham), the personality of its leader, and Ford's behavior, see the article by Landes, who in the 1930s studied this movement in situ. Landes, "Negro Jews," pp. 175–189. Information about Ford's subsequent activities remains speculative. It is possible that he changed his name to Fard or Farrad, who founded Detroit's Islamic movement. See Lincoln "Black Muslims," p. 11.
81. It seems that Ford intended to compete with Garvey; see Landes, "Negro Jews," pp. 181–182.
82. Kenneth J. King, "Some Notes on Arnold J. Ford and the New World Black Attitudes to Ethiopia," *Journal of Ethiopian Studies* 10, no. 1 (1972): 81–87.
83. Ehrman, "Commandment," pp. 267–270; Trevisan Semi, "'Falashisation,'" p. 93. This congregation existed legally since 1930, when a decision of the Court of New York acknowledged its right to say its members were Jews. Branches of this movement were created in Philadelphia; Pittsburgh; Sharon, Virginia; Chicago; and Cullen, Virginia; as well as in St. Thomas, Virgin Islands; and Jamaica. See Santamaria, "Black Jews," p. 225.
84. Ehrman, "Commandment," pp. 267, 268.
85. Howard M. Brotz, "Negro Jews in the United States," *Phylon* 13 (December 1952): 325.
86. Ibid.

87. *Amsterdam News*, September 24, 1930, quoted in Ehrman, "Commandment," p. 267.

88. Bernard J. Wolfson, "Africa, American Jews: Dispelling Myths, Bridging the Divide," in *Black Zion*, p. 3, quotation p. 34.

89. Ibid., p. 48.

90. Ibid., p. 44.

91. These associations were created in the context of the extinction of Jewish communities during the Shoah and the simultaneous creation of a Jewish state in Israel. See Trevisan Semi's overview on these various associations in "Conversion and Judaisation: The Lost Tribes Committees at the Birth of the Jewish State," in Parfitt and Trevisan Semi, *Judaising Movements*, pp. 53–64. About Jewish missionary movements in the United States, see Lawrence J. Epstein, *Theory and Practice of Welcoming Converts* (Lewiston, NY: Mellen Press, 1992), pp. 81–96; about the debates on the issue of Jewish proselytism, see Steven Cohen, "Was Judaism in Antiquity a Missionary Religion in Ancient Times?" in *Jewish Assimilation*, ed. Menachem Mor (Lanham, MD: University Press of America, 1992), pp. 24–37.

92. Trevisan Semi, "Conversion," p. 53.

93. Ibid., p. 56.

94. E.g., Sino-Judaic Institute (California), China Judaic Association (Illinois), Society for Crypto-Judaic Studies (California), Washington Association for Ethiopian Jews, Kulanu, Shavei Israel (Amishav), and others.

95. Santamaria, "Black Jews," p. 226. An association of the same type, made up of black and white Jews, the Haza'ad Harishon, was created in 1967 in order to foster blacks' access to education.

96. Merrill Singer, "Symbolic Identity Formation in an African American Religious Sect: The Hebrew Israelites," in *African American Encounters with Judaism*, pp. 60–61.

97. A. D. Sice, "Libéria: Pour les Hébreux Israëlites, le Christ était noir," *Présence Africaine* 70 (1969): 233–240; Boykin, *Black Jews*, pp. 69–75; Robert G. Weisbord and Richard Kazarian, *Israel in the Black American Perspective* (Westport, CT: Greenwood Press, 1985), pp. 61–91.

98. Sice, "Liberia," pp. 233–240.

99. Ethan Michaeli, "Another Exodus: The Hebrew Israelites from Chicago to Dimona," in *African American Encounters with Judaism*, pp. 74, 80–81.

100. In Emmet Wigoder, "America's Black Jews in Israel," *Israel Magazine* 3 (1970): 43, quoted in Singer, "Symbolic," p. 67.

101. Michaeli, "Another Exodus," pp. 74–75.

102. Ibid.

103. Singer, "Symbolic," p. 68.

104. Ibid., p. 70.

105. Ibid.

106. Ibid., p. 87.

107. Jamaica was considered as the country with the highest rate of revolts and conspiracies. See Orlando Patterson, "Slavery and Slave Revolts: A Socio-historical

Analysis of the First Marron War, Jamaica, 1655–1740," *Social and Economic Studies* 19, no. 3 (1970): 289–325; also Barry Chevannes, *Rastafari and Other African Caribbean Worldviews* (London: Macmillan, 1995), p. 1.

108. Born in Ireland, the Great Revival reached Great Britain and the United States before reaching Jamaica during the 1860s, where it instilled the congregations with Christian obedience. But African practices of convulsion and other expressions of spirit possession that slipped into ceremonies led to its rejection by the congregations, after which it was practiced by a few isolated groups. Chevannes, *Rastafari*, p. 8.

109. Chevannes studied Revivalism and with Schuler attributed the development of religious ideas and the rebellion of slaves to a seemingly new Pan-African religion, called "Myal," the origin of the name being unknown. According to the interpretation of Schuler, this word has roots in Central Africa, expressing the capacity to absorb foreign influences that obviously characterizes the religion of these areas; see Chevannes, *Rastafari*, p. 369; also Monica Schuler, "Myalism and African Religious Traditions in Jamaica," in *Africa and the Caribbean: The Legacies of a Link*, ed. Margaret E. Crahan and Franklin Knight (Baltimore: Johns Hopkins University Press, 1979), pp. 65–79.

110. Boris Lutanie, *Introduction au mouvement Rastafari* (Paris: L'Esprit Frappeur, 1999), p. 20.

111. Barret, *The Rastafarians*, p. 76, and chap. 2.

112. Chevannes, *Rastafari*, pp. 10–11.

113. See the first studies carried out on this subject by G. Raton Simpson, "Political Cultism in West Kingston, Jamaica," *Social and Economic Studies* 4, no. 2 (1955): 133–149; then by Vittorio Lanternari, *Religions of the Oppressed: A Study of Modern Messianic Cults* (London: McGibbon, 1963).

114. According to legend, ganja is an herb that grew on Solomon's grave. Biblical references are invoked to justify the benefits of its use.

115. The rejection of the "Society of Babylon," that is, whites and their perversions, is expressed in a "Rasta-talk," an actual linguistic code. See Xavier Pollard, "Une contre-culture: La langue des Rastas," in *Notre Amérique métisse*, ed. Anne Remiche-Martinow and Graciela Schneier-Madanes (Paris: La Découverte, 1992), pp. 157–167.

116. Chevannes, *Rastafari*, p. 11. The religious symbolism of Rastafarianism uses music as the preferred tool for spreading the culture and participation in ceremonies. Bob Marley and other reggae musicians have contributed immensely to the spread of the Rastafarian culture worldwide.

117. Ibid. See the biography of Leonard Percival Howell by Hélène Lee, *Le premier Rasta* (Paris: Flammarion, 1999).

118. Quoted in Barret, *Rastafarians*, pp. 95–96.

119. Two organized groups considered themselves as members of the "House," a concept that emerged during the movement's second phase of development in the 1960s. The "House" was split into two other groups: the House of Dreadlocks and the House of Combsomes. The Combsomes have since disappeared, while the Dreadlocks have formed an assembly of elders who plan celebrations, form delegations for visiting foreign communities, and so on. Chevannes, *Rastafari*, p. 16.

120. Vittorio Morabito, "Au delà du fleuve de Koush," in *Afrocentrismes*, ed. François-Xavier Fauvelle-Aymar, Jean-P. Chrétien, and Claude-H. Perrot (Paris: Karthala, 2000), pp. 327–328.

121. The Ethiopian World Federation was founded in New York in 1937 by Haile Selassie to ensure the safety and integrity of Ethiopia. A branch was created in Jamaica as soon as 1938, and its relationships with Rastafarians were both close and strained regarding the question of which groups should take priority in the attribution of Ethiopian land. See Barret, *Rastafarians*, p. 228.

122. When an article in the *Daily Gleaner* of July 17, 1983, concluded that the Twelve Tribes was "the most Christian sect of the Rastafarian movement," a large number of the community members, displeased with this analysis, left Jamaica for England, the United States, or Canada rather than Ethiopia. Barret, *Rastafarians*, pp. 225–234.

123. A book has been published in the United States by a member of this community, K. P. Naphtali, *The Testimony of His Imperial Majesty Emperor Haile Selassie I, Defender of the Faith* (Washington, DC: Zewd Publishers, 1999).

124. Clifford Geertz, *The Interpretation of Cultures* (New York: Basic Books, 1973), p. 105.

125. Howe, *Afrocentrism*, pp. 2–3.

126. Trevisan Semi, "'Falashisation,'" p. 88.

CHAPTER 8

1. It does not seem possible to find a single definition to cover all the types and functions of myth. On the extremely complex cultural reality of myths and their multiple and complementary perspectives, see two works that analyze and link the thinking about myths of twentieth-century theorists. On Cassirer, Eliade, Lévi-Strauss, and Malinowski, see Ivan Strenski, *Four Theories of Myth in Twentieth-Century History* (London: Macmillan, 1987); on Barthes, Eliade, and Hillman, see Elisabeth Baeten, *The Magic Mirror* (Albany: State University of New York Press, 1996).

2. Mircea Eliade, *Aspects du Mythe* (Paris: Gallimard, 1963), pp. 11–12, quotation on p. 17. The work of Africanists and the validity of the oral tradition as historical source are summarized with methodological rigor and bibliography in Jan Vansina, *Oral Tradition: A Study in Historical Methodology* (Chicago: Aldine, 1965). On the historicity of myths, see Daniel F. McCall, *Africa in Time Perspective* (Boston: Boston University Press, 1964). Also T. O. Ranger, ed., *Emerging Themes of African History* (Nairobi: East Africa Publication House, 1974). For a totally opposed and factual approach, see, for instance, Geoffrey R. Elton, *The Practice of History* (London: Methuen, 1967); also Robin G. Collingwood, *The Idea of History* (Oxford: Clarendon Press, 1946).

3. Rollo May, *The Cry for Myth* (New York: Norton, 1991), p. 26.

4. Parfitt, *Lost Tribes*, pp. 206ff.

5. Godbey, *Lost Tribes a Myth*, p. 372.

6. Parfitt, *Lost Tribes*, pp. 157ff.

7. Haim S. Kehimkar, *The History of the Bene Israel of India* (Tel Aviv: Dayag Press, 1937).

8. J. Ki-Zerbo, ed., *Histoire générale de l'Afrique* (Paris: Présence Africaine/Edicef/UNESCO, 1986), vol. 1, p. 41.

9. Haim Z. Hirschberg, *History of the Jews in North Africa* (Leiden: Brill, 1974), p. 23.

10. The island got its name after the ivory trade that had taken place there since the earliest antiquity. Pierre Grelot, *Documents araméens d'Egypte: Littérature ancienne du Proche-Orient* (Paris: Editions du Cerf, 1972), p. 40.

11. Flavius Josephus, *Against Appion*, II, § 44, in Hirschberg, *History*, pp. 24, 53. Cyrenaica is present-day Libya and includes Tripolitana and Fezzan.

12. Raymond Mauny, "Le Judaïsme, les Juifs et l'Afrique occidentale," *IFAN* 11, no. 3 (1949): 359. Also Louis Leschi, "Rome et les nomades du Sahara central," in *Travaux de l'Institut de Recherches Sahariennes* (1942), vol. 1, pp. 47–62.

13. Delafosse, *Haut-Sénégal*, Vol.1, pp. 217ff.

14. James Quirin, *The Evolution of the Ethiopian Jews* (Philadelphia: University of Pennsylvania Press, 1992), pp. 7–15.

15. Ibid., p. 15.

16. It is interesting to note that this genealogy put forward by Ethiopian Jews to justify their Judaism does not correspond to the arguments on which the Great Rabbinate relies to recognize their Jewish identity. This Jewish identity was proclaimed by the Great Rabbi of Israel, from a rabbinic precedence dating back to several centuries, on the strength of a decision of the Great Rabbi of Cairo, stipulating in the sixteenth century that "these Falashas are, no doubt, issued from the tribe of Dan." See Michael Corinaldi, *Jewish Identity: The Case of the Ethiopian Jewry* (Jerusalem: Rubin Mass, 1998), p. 143.

17. Bezalel Porten, *Archives from Elephantine: The Life of an Ancient Jewish Military Colony* (Berkeley: University of California Press, 1968), pp. 8–12. Grelot and Vincent envisage a later arrival of Jewish mercenaries in the region. See Grelot, *Documents*, pp. 38ff.; also Albert Vincent, *La religion des Judéo-araméens d'Eléphantine* (Paris: Geuthner, 1937), pp. 8ff.

18. Among the works of reference, see Porten, *Archives*, pp. 37–39; Grelot, *Documents*, pp. 37–39; also Reuven Yaron, *Introduction to the Law of the Aramaic Papyri* (Oxford: Clarendon Press, 1961); André Dupont-Sommer, *Les Dieux et les hommes en l'île d'Eléphantine, près d'Assouan au temps de l'Empire des Perses*, Compte rendu de l'Académie des inscriptions des Belles Lettres 27 (Paris: Institut de France, 1978).

19. Grelot, *Documents*, p. 44; Raymond O. Faulkner, "Egyptian Military Organisation," *Journal of Egyptian Archaeology* 39 (1953): 33ff.; also Porten, *Archives*, p. 15. On the activity of the sailors cited by Strabo, see W. Erichsen, "Erwähnung eines Züges nach Nubien unter Amasis in einem demotischen Text," *Klio* 34 (1941): 56ff., quoted in Porten, *Archives*, p. 26.

20. Erichsen, quoted in Porten, *Archives*, p. 41.

21. Joseph Cuoq, *Recueil des sources Arabes concernant l'Afrique occidentale du VIII è au XVI è siècle. Bilad al-Sudan*, preface by Raymond Mauny (Paris: CNRS, 1975);

Octave Houdas and Maurice Delafosse, *Tarikh el-Fettach* (Paris: Adrien Maisonneuve, 1964). I shall use the spelling *Tarikh al-Fattash* herein. A similar study (that had attempted to achieve the same goal) already existed, which was a monumental work but was little used due to its limited diffusion. See Kamal Youssouf, *Monumenta Cartographica Africae et Aegypti*, 16 vols. (Cairo, 1926–1951).

22. Cuoq, *Bilad*, pp. 80–109. On al-Bakri's sources, see Tadeusz Lewicki, "L'Afrique noire dans le Kitab al-Masalik wa l-Mamedik d'al-Bakri (XIè siècle)," *Africana Bulletin* 2 (1965): 9–14. Also Vincent Monteil, "Al-Bakri, un routier de l'Afrique," IFAN 30 (1968): 39–116.

23. Cuoq, *Bilad*, pp. 115–123; also Mohammed Hadj-Sadok, "Le Kitab al-Dja'rafiyya de Abu 'Abd Allah Mohammad ben Abi Bakr al-Zuhri," *Bulletin d'Etudes Orientales* 21 (1968): 1–312.

24. Cuoq, *Bilad*, pp. 126–165; *Al-Idrissi*, trans. Reinhardt Dozy and Michael J. de Goeje (Alger: Maison des Livres, 1957).

25. Léon l'Africain, *Description de l'Afrique*, new edition translated by A. Epaulard and annotated by Theodore Monod, Henri Lhote, and Raymond Mauny, 2 vol. (Paris: A. Maisonneuve, 1980).

26. Ibid., vol. 1, pp. 45, 81, 11–12, 112; vol. 2, pp. 467–469.

27. Ibn Khaldun, *Histoire des Berbères et des dynasties musulmanes de l'Afrique septentrionale*, trans. Baron de Slane (Alger, 1852), tome 1, pp. 132, 208ff.

28. On the legends on the Kahina, apart from Ibn Khaldun, see Laurent C. Féraud, "Kitab el-Adouani, ou le Sahara de Constantine et de Tunis," in *Recueil des notices et mémoires de la Société Archéologique de Constantine* (1867). Also Emile Mercier, "Une page de l'histoire de l'invasion arabe: La Kahéna," *Recueil des notices et mémoires de la Société Archéologique de Constantine*, XII (Constantine: Arnolet, 1868), pp. 241–254. See also Masqueray's investigation on the survivals of this period in popular traditions; Emile Masqueray, "Traditions de l'Aouras oriental," *Bulletin de Correspondance Africaine* 3 (1855): 72.

29. Georges S. Colin, "Des Juifs nomades retrouvés dans le Sahara marocain au XVIè siècle," in *Mélanges Lopes-Cernival* (Lisbon: Portugalia Editora, 1945), p. 59.

30. On the great centers of trade of West Africa, Ghana, Songhai, Mali, and Bornu, see the studies by Antony G. Hopkins, *An Economic History of West Africa* (London: Longman, 1980). Also Jean Devisse, "Routes de commerce et échanges en Afrique occidentale en relation avec la méditerranée: Un essai sur le commerce africain médiéval du XI è au XVI è siècle," *Revue d'Histoire Economique et Sociale* 1, no. 10 (1972): 42–73.

31. I am greatly indebted to Michel Abitbol for his clarification on the presence of North African Jews on the edge of Sahara and their involvement in trans-Saharan trade. Michel Abitbol, "Juifs maghrébins et commerce transsaharien du VIII au XV è siècle," Etudes 5–6, in *2000 ans d'histoire africaine: Le sol, la parole et l'écrit* (Paris: Bibliothèque d'Histoire d'Outre-mer, 1981), pp. 229ff. Also Raymond Mauny, *Tableau géographique de l'ouest africain au moyen age d'après les sources écrites* (Dakar: IFAN, 1961).

32. It is made clear in a Hadith which mentions that the Prophet held a piece of gold in his right hand and a piece of silk in his left and said: "These two are forbidden to men of my community but permissible for women."

33. Louis Massignon, *Enquête sur les corporations musulmanes d'artisans et de commerçants au Maroc* (Paris: E. Leroux, 1925), p. 290.

34. Haim Z. Hirschberg, *History of the Jews in North Africa*, vol.1, 2d rev. ed. (Leiden: Brill, 1974), pp. 160–162; also Rabbi J. M. Toledano, *The Light of Maghrib* (Hebrew), quoted in Abitbol, "Juifs magrébins," p. 232; Ibn Khurdadbeh, *Description du Maghreb et de l'Europe au IIIè /IXè siècles*, publication and translation by Muhammad Hadj Sadock (Alger, 1949), pp. 117–118.

35. See Vincent Monteil, "Les Juifs d'Ifran," *Hespéris* 35 (1948): 151–160, who attempted to provide clarification on the origin of this community.

36. Hirschberg, *History*, vol. 1, p. 90. On religious life in Sijilmassa and contact with Babylon, see pp. 108–109. Also Djinn Jacques-Meunié, *Le Maroc saharien des origines à 1670* (Paris: Klincksieck, 1982), p. 44. Abraham ibn Ezra, who visited Africa and the Middle East, is also well known for his works as grammarian and exegete. See, e.g., Shlomo Sela, *Abraham ibn Ezra and the rise of medieval science* (Leiden: Brill, 2003).

37. On the fate of the Jews during Muslim dynasties, see Sarah Taïeb-Carlen, *Les juifs d'Afrique du Nord* (Paris: Editions Sepia, 2000), pp. 41–51 and note 67.

38. Ibid., p. 47; Hirschberg, *History*, vol. 1, p. 124.

39. Abitbol, "Juifs magrébins," p. 238. On the control of commercial routes by the Almoravids, see Devisse, "Routes," pp. 56–57. Also Paulo F. de Moraes Farias, "The Almoravids: Some Questions Concerning the Character of the Movement during Its Period of Closest Contact with the Western Sudan," *IFAN* 29 (1967): 859.

40. A. G. P. Martin, *A la frontière marocaine—les oasis sahariennes: Gourara, Touat, Tidikelt, Alger* (Paris: Challamel, 1908), p. 37. On the Jews of Touat, see Jacob Oliel, *Les Juifs au Sahara* (Paris: CNRS, 1994), pp. 21ff. and 45ff. Also Emile F. Gauthier, *Le Sahara* (Paris: Payot, 1928), p. 104.

41. Oliel, *Juifs au Sahara*, p. 41. Also Jean M. Solignac, "Travaux hydrauliques hafçides de Tunis," *Revue Africaine* 12 (1960): 560.

42. Martin, *Frontière*, pp. 39–40.

43. G. Rohlfs, *Reise and Globus* 17 (1893), quoted in Oliel, *Juifs au Sahara*, p. 117. Also Hadjib Ebn-ed-din el Eghwaati, *Notes of a Journey into the Interior of Northern Africa*, trans. W. B. Hogdson (London, 1831), p. 21.

44. On the Saharan routes of the Touat, see Mauny, *Tableau géographique*, pp. 432–440.

45. Antonio Malfante's letter was published by la Roncière, *Découverte*, pp. 146–147. This passage should be compared with the letter written in 1440 by the sultan of Bornu to the Merabtins of Touat in which the sultan complains that the inhabitants of Touat did not come to his country as they used to. Based on Malfante's writings according to which the trade of the region was governed by Jews, one can think that the sultan of Bornu refers to their absence. Martin, *Frontière*, p. 122.

46. Léon l'Africain, *Description*, vol.1, pp. 93–94, 71, 107, 59, 102.

47. Ibid., vol. 2, p. 429.

48. Ibid., vol. 2, p. 431.

49. Ibid., vol. 1, pp. 89, 93; vol. 2, pp. 423, 429.

50. Askya Muhammad had previously organized a pilgrimage to Mecca, whence he returned as caliph of all the Muslims of the Bilad al Sudan. See Ahmed Baba, *Naytl an Ibtihaj*, trans. Cuoq, *Bilad*, pp. 433–435.

51. Léon l'Africain, *Description*, vol. 2, p. 468.

52. Henri Duveyrier, *Sahara algérien et tunisien: Journal de route* (Paris: Challamel, 1905), pp. 48–58, 68; Nahum Slouschz, *Hébraeo-Phéniciens et Judéo-berbères* (Paris: Leroux, 1908), p. 446.

53. Al-Bakri, *Description de l'Afrique septentrionale*, trans. William de Slane (Alger, 1911), p. 25, quoted in Abitbol, " Juifs maghrébins," p. 234.

54. Cuoq, *Bilad*, p. 171.

55. "Réponses du rabbin Isaac Bar-Sheshet," *Tshubot Ha-ribash*, Constantine (1546–1547), quoted in Abitbol, "Juifs maghrébins," p. 245. It should be noted that, before 1491, when the Spanish rabbis expelled during the persecutions arrived in North Africa, community matters and controversies between Jews were submitted to Muslim judges. Subsequently, all matters of private law and unification of religious practice in the whole of North Africa were settled by rulings of rabbis in Algiers and relayed by correspondents living at each of the large Maghreb centers.

56. In the Middle Ages, Sudan included the present-day Sudan, Mali, Niger, and Chad.

57. Charles Monteil, "Problèmes du Soudan occidental: Juifs et judaïsés," *Hespéris* 38 (1938): 276–277. Under the rule and despotic authority of an aristocracy, often of foreign origin in a local Sudanese environment, the Sudanese empire invariably relied on a mass of slaves that was progressively adapted to conquest, domination, and enslavement to the benefit of the dominant fraction. Monteil supposes the existence of a Bafour empire that was split up as a result of both foreign attacks and defects inherent to this despotic regime.

58. André J. Lucas, "Considérations sur l'ethnique maure et en particulier sur une race ancienne: Les Bafours," *Journal de la Société des Africanistes* 1 (1931): 151–194.

59. *Roudh el-Qartàs, Histoire des Souverains du Maghreb*, trans. André Beaumier (Paris: Imprimerie Impériale, 1860), p. 165.

60. Cuoq, *Bilad*, p. 231.

61. Ibid., p. 146.

62. Monteil, "Problèmes," p. 281.

63. Reported by Jacob Oliel in *Au Sahara et en Afrique noire: Une présence ancienne des populations juives*, n.p.

64. Cuoq, *Bilad*, pp. 145–147.

65. Ibid.

66. Ibid., p. 122. Al-Idrissi places the Kamnuria in West Africa, in the south of present-day Mauritania, between the Draa to the north and Senegal to the south. According to Mauny, this enigmatic country with its mysterious name might exist, his

fictitious name drawn by al-Idrissi from Ptolemy's geography. Mauny, *Tableau géographique*, pp. 362–363.

67. Ibid., pp. 363–364.
68. Cuoq, *Ta'rikh al-Fattash*, p. 120.
69. Baba, *Nayl al Ibtihaj*, pp. 433–435.
70. Mungo Park, *Voyage dans l'intérieur de l'Afrique*, trans. Jean H. Castera (Paris: Maspero, 1980), p. 83.
71. See the study concentrated on Mardochée by Yosef. D. Sémach, "Un rabbin voyageur marocain: Mardochée Abi Serour," *Hesperis* 8 (1928): 385–399; see also Mardochée Aby Serour's text, annotated by Michel Abitbol, "Les Daggatoun, tribu d'origine juive demeurant dans le désert du Sahara," *Les Cahiers du Judaïsme* 10 (Autumn 2001): 79–82.
72. Abitbol asserts that the Daggatun are the descendants of a class of white slaves, the Amghad, who live among the Touareg; see Michel Abitbol, "Juifs et Noirs de part et d'autre du Sahara," *Les Cahiers du Judaisme* 10 (2001): 77. Oliel gathered an exchange of correspondence serving as a basis of the hypothesis that they are of Jewish-Moroccan origin in *Au Sahara et en Afrique noire*, n.p.
73. Oliel, *Au Sahara et en Afrique noire*.
74. Henri Lhote, *Les Touareg du Hoggar* (Paris: A. Colin, 1984), pp. 56ff. and 200ff.
75. Theodore Monod, A. Texeira da Mota, and Richard Mauny, *Valentim Fernandes(1506–1510): Description de la Côte d'Afrique* (Bissau, 1951), p. 85.
76. *O manuscrito Valentim Fernandes* (Lisbon, 1915), fol. 91–92, p. 66, quoted in Mauny, "Judaïsme," p. 373.
77. *Itinerario do Dr. Jeronimo Münzer* (exercetos) por Basilio de Vasconcellos, Coïmbra, 1932, p. 56, quoted in Mauny, "Judaïsme," p. 365.
78. La Roncière, *Découverte*, vol. 1, pp. 121–139.
79. Ibid., p. 129.
80. Ibid.
81. Ibid.
82. Ibid.
83. Ibid.
84. Ibid.
85. Ibid.
86. Sigmund Freud, *Die Traumdeuntung* (Leipzig: F.Deuticke, 1919), p. 538. Also Jean Laplanche and Jean-B. Pontalis, *Vocabulaire de la psychanalyse* (Paris: PUF, 1973), p. 424.
87. Monteil, "Problèmes," pp. 282–294.
88. Dierk Lange, *Ancient Kingdoms of West Africa: Africa-Centred and Canaanite-Israelite Perspective* (Dettelbach: Röll, 2004).
89. Ibid., pp. 215–296. From the in-depth study of the Bayajidda legend of the Hausa, Lange deduced that immigrants from Canaan founded Daura, the oldest town in Hausaland. According to Lange's considerations, the value of the Bayajidda narrative as a historical source lies first and foremost in its character as an oral

foundation charter for Hausa society based on an earlier broadly shared cult-mythological worldview that permeated all aspects of society. Lange, *Kingdoms*, pp. 215–228.

90. Lange, *Kingdoms*, pp. 13–39.

91. Ibid., pp. 307–340.

92. Elisa Siva Andrade, *Les Iles du Cap-Vert de la "découverte" à l'indépendance nationale* (Paris: l'Harmattan, 1996).

93. Jean Boulègue, *Les Luso-Africains de Sénégambie, XVI–XIX ème siècle* (Dakar: Université de Dakar, 1972), pp. 22–34.

94. Ibid., pp. 5, 56.

95. Ibid., p. 29.

96. Guy Thilmans and Izabel de Moraes, "La description de la Côte de Guinée du Père Baltazar Barreira," *IFAN* 34, série B, no 1 (1972): 1–50.

97. Boulègue, *Luso-Africains*, p. 56.

98. Ibid., p. 70 ff.

99. Richard Lobban, "Jews in Cape Verde and on the Guinea Coast" (paper presented at the University of Massachusetts–Dartmouth, February 11, 1996, www.umassd.edu/specialprograms/caboverde/jewslobban.html (accessed December 2, 2006).

100. *Les voyages du Sieur Le Maire aux îles Canaries, Cap Vert, Sénégal, Gambie par Dancourt* (Paris: J. Collombat, 1695), p. 96.

101. Lobban, "Jews in Cape Verde," p. 3.

102. Ibid.

103. J. Boto'Ora Ballong-Wen-Mewuda, "Le rôle de São Tomé dans l'établissement et le développement du commerce portugais dans le Golfe de Guinée au XVème et XVIème siècle," in *La Découverte, le Portugal et l'Europe*, Actes du colloque, Paris, May 26–28, 1988. Also Raimundo J. da Cunha Matos, *Ilhas de S. Tomé e Príncipe, Ano Bom e Fernando Po* (São Tomé: Impr. Nacional, 1916).

104. William W. Reade, *Savage Africa* (New York: Harper, 1864), p. 274.

105. Gloria Mound, "Judaic Research in the Balearic Islands and São Tomé," in Primack, *Jews in Places*, p. 61. See also Saul Usque, *Consolaçam às tribulaçoens de Israel*, 3 vols. (Coimbra: Franca Amado, 1906–1908).

106. See *Biblioteca de Ajuda*, 49-XI-38, fol. 145. Also *Monumenta Missionaria Africana*, vol. 4, p. 33; vol. 1, p. 177, quoted in Boto'Ora Ballong-Wen-Mewuda, "Rôle," p. 162.

107. P. Alexandre, *Les Africains* (Paris: Lidis, 1982), p. 169, quoted in Oliel, *Au Sahara et en Afrique noire*, n.p.

108. M. D. W. Jeffreys, "An Extinct Jewish Colony," *Jewish Affairs*, November 1954, p. 48.

109. Ibid.

110. Nize Izabel de Moraes, "La petite côte d'après Francisco de Lemos Coehlo (ca 1669)," *IFAN* B 35, no. 2 (1973): 239–268.

111. Francisco de Azev Coehlo, *Descripçao da Costa da Guiné* (Lisbon: Fundo General dos Manuscritos da Biblioteca Nacional, 1669), Ms. 319.

112. John Ogilby, *Africa, being an accurate description of Aegypt, Barbary, Lybia* (London: T. Johnson, 1670), p. 34.

113. Livingstone, *Missionary Travels*, pp. 414, 479, quoted in Godbey, *Lost Tribes a Myth*, p. 252.

114. Ratzel, *History*, vol. 3, p. 134.

115. Bastian, *Die Deutsche Expedition an der Loango Küste*, quoted in Godbey, *Lost Tribes a Myth*, p. 246.

116. James Finn, *Sephardim* (London, 1841), p. 324, quoted in Godbey, *Lost Tribes a Myth*, p. 247.

117. Godbey also relates these facts with the presence of Judaism among black Americans descended from partially Judaized black slaves. Godbey, *Lost Tribes a Myth*, pp. 248–249.

118. *Jews in the Canary Islands: Being a Calendar of Jewish Cases Extracted from the Records of the Canariote Inquisition in the Collection of Marquis of Bute*, translated from the Spanish and edited with an introduction and notes by Lucien Wolf (London: Jewish Historical Society of England, 1926), pp. 23, 90, 113, note 1.

119. Garlake, *Great Zimbabwe*, p. 66.

120. For the most recent works on the Lemba, see Parfitt, *Journey*; Parfitt, *Lost Tribes of Israel*, pp. 200–202; Parfitt and Trevisan Semi, *Judaising Movements*, pp. 39–51; Le Roux, "In Search."

121. The accounts of the migrations of the Lemba have been published by Professor Mathivha. See M. E. R. Mathivha, *The Basena/Vamwenye/Balemba* (South Africa: Morester Printers, 1992). Also Gina Buijs, "Black Jews in the Northern Province: A Study of Ethnic Identity in South Africa," *Ethnic and Racial Studies* 21 (1998): 661–662.

122. On the different locations of Sena and settlements of the Lemba, see Mathivha, *Basena*, p. 17; Henri A. Junod, *The Life of a South African Tribe* (London: MacMillan, 1927), pp. 72–74, 424; Parfitt, *Journey*, pp. 15, 21, 189, 193, 197, 308, 336.

123. Mathivha, *Basena*, pp. 1–7; Henri A. Junod, "The Balemba of Soutspanberg," *Folklore* 19, no. 3 (1908): 277; Parfitt, *Journey*, pp. 18, 19, 44.

124. There is no definition of the nature of "Pusela" in the Lemba tradition.

125. About the various hypotheses on an Islamic-Arabian origin of the Lemba, see Hugh A. Stayt, *The Bavenda* (New York: Oxford University Press, 1968); James E. Mullan, *The Arab Builders of Zimbabwe* (Salisbury: Rhodesia Mission, 1969); Nicolas J. Van Warmelo, *The Classification of Cultural Groups* in W.E. Hammond-Tooke, ed. (London: Routledge and Kegan Paul, 1974 [1937]), pp. 56–84; Parfitt, *Journey*, pp. 315ff.

126. Robert Gayre of Gayre, "The Lembas or Vendas of Vendaland," *Mankind Quarterly* 8 (1967): 6–7.

127. A. Ruwitah, "Lost Tribe, Lost Language? The Invention of False Remba Identity," *Zimbabwe* 53 (1997), quoted in Tudor Parfitt, "Genes, Religion and History," *Jurimetrics* 42, no. 22 (2002): 211.

128. Parfitt, *Journey*, pp. 336–337.

129. Ibid., p. 335.

130. Charles C. Torrey, *The Jewish Foundation of Islam* (New York: Jewish Institute of Religion Press, 1933), pp. 131–133, accepts the likelihood of an Israelite presence in southern Arabia from Solomonic times. See also David S. Margoliouth, *The Relations between Arabs and Israelites Prior to the Rise of Islam* (London: Oxford University Press, 1924).

131. Norman A. Stillman, *Jews of Arab Lands: A History and Source Book* (Philadelphia: Jewish Publication Society in America, 1979), pp. 1–22; Shlomo D. Goiten, *Jews and Arabs: Their Contacts through the Ages*, 3rd ed. (New York: Schocken Books, 1974), pp. 67ff; Watt W. Montgomery, *Muhammad at Medina* (Oxford: Clarendon Press, 1956), p. 219.

132. For the discoveries on the epigraphic sources during the last century, see Jacques Halévy, "Rapport sur une mission archéologique dans le Yémen," *Journal Asiatique* 9, IVth series (1872). On more recent important epigraphic discoveries, see Gonzague Ryckmans, "Inscriptions sud-arabes, " 10ème série, *Le Muséon* 66 (1953): 316–317; Albert Jamme, *Sabean and Hasean Inscriptions from Saudi Arabia* (Rome: Universita di Roma, 1966), pp. 39–55; also Giovanni Garbini, "Una bilingue sabeo-ebraica da Zafar," *AION* 30 (1970): 153–164.

133. On the reliable evidence about Judaism in the Himyarite kingdom, see Zeev Rubin, "Judaism and Rahmanite Monotheism in the Himyarite Kingdom in the Fifth Century," in *Israel and Ishmael: Studies in Muslim-Jewish Relations*, ed. Tudor Parfitt (New York: St. Martin's Press, 2000), pp. 32ff. For a skeptical approach, see Alfred F. L. Beeston, "Himyarite Monotheism," *Studies in the History of Arabia* 2 (1984): 149–154.

134. *Geographi, graeci minores. Périple de la Mer Erythrée*, translated into French by Ch. Muller (Paris: F. Didot, 1855).

135. Ibid., p. 267.

136. Van Warmelo quoted in William D. Hammond-Tooke, *The Bantu-Speaking Peoples of Southern Africa* (Johannesburg, 1937), p. 83. This version became more or less current in books about East Africa after 1871, with the publication of the Reverend G. P. Badgers's translation of the *History of the Imams and Seyyids of Oman* by Salil ibn Raziq, quoted in Parfitt, *Journey*, p. 198.

137. Probably Khoisan or Bushmen or Hottentots. See Theal, *Records*, vol. 4.

138. Parfitt, *Journey*, p. 312.

139. Lewicki, "Afrique," p. 93; A. Malecka, "La côte orientale de l'Afrique au Moyen Age de al Himyari (XVè siècle)," *Folia Orientalia* 4 (1962): 331ff., quoted in Parfitt, *Journey*, pp. 370, 313.

140. Parfitt, *Journey*, p. 370n.

141. Ibid., pp. 198–199, 367. Also H. Neville Chittick, "The Coast before the Arrival of the Portuguese," in *Zamani: A Survey of East African History*, ed. Bethwell A. Ogot (Nairobi: East African Publication House, 1974), p. 103; G. Mathew, "The East African Coast until the Coming of the Portuguese," in *The History of East Africa*, ed. Roland Oliver et al., vol. 1 (Oxford: Clarendon Press, 1963–1976), pp. 103–104.

142. D. N. Beach, *The Shona and Zimbabwe, 900–1850: An Outline of the Shona History* (London: Heinemann, 1980), p. 107.

143. Barbarosa was a sixteenth-century Portuguese diarist whose writings are included in *Documents on the Portuguese in Mocambique and Central Africa 1497–1840*, in Beach, *Shona*, p. 108.

144. Ibid.

145. The Lemba also call themselves Mwenye.

146. Parfitt, *Journey*, p. 314; Theal, *Records*, vol. 7, pp. 188, 199, 253, 530. Also D. P. Abraham, "Maramuca: An Exercise of the Combined Uses of Portuguese Records and Oral Traditions," *Journal of African History* 2 (1961): 212, quoted in Parfitt, *Journey*, p. 371.

147. Parfitt, *Journey*, p. 314; Eric Axelson, *Portuguese in South-East Africa, 1600–1700* (Johannesburg: Witwatersrand University Press, 1960), p. 27; Robert E. Gregson, "Trade and Politics in South-East Africa: The Moors, the Portuguese and the Kingdom of Mwenemutapa," *African Social Research* 116 (1973): 419.

148. Alan Smith, "Delagoa Bay and the Trade of South Africa," *Pre-colonial African Trade: Essays on Trade in Central and Eastern Africa...*, ed. Richard Gray and David Birmingham (New York: Oxford University Press, 1970), pp. 275–276.

149. Gerhard Liesegang, "New Light on Venda Traditions: Mahumane's Account of 1730," *History of Africa* 4 (1977): 167, 171.

150. Von Sicard and Van Warmelo corroborated the fact that, until recent times, the Lemba have been viewed as masters of magic arts and medicine. Harald Von Sicard, "Lemba Clans," *Native Affairs Department Annual* 39 (1962): 68–80; Van Warmelo, *Classification*, pp. 56–84. Junod described the crafts and industries of the Lemba and the remarkable metallurgical technique of their men. Junod "Balemba," pp. 276–287.

151. Etienne de Flacourt, *Histoire de la grande île de Madagascar* (Paris: A. Lesselin, 1658), avant-propos, pp. 3–4, and in subsequent edition (Paris: G. Clouzier, 1661), p. 308.

152. Capitaine de Valgny, *Bibliothèque, Muséum d'Histoire Naturelle* (1765), quoted in Alfred Grandidier, *Histoire physique, naturelle et politique de Madagascar, Ethnographie* (Paris: Imprimerie Nationale, 1908), vol. 4, tome 1, p. 99. This is also what the Abbé Rochon wrote in his *Voyage à Madagascar et aux Indes Orientales* (Paris: Prault, 1791).

153. Grandidier, *Histoire, Ethnographie*, vol. 4, tome 1, pp. 96–103, quotation on pp. 405–406.

154. Ibid.

155. Alfred Gevrey, *Essai sur les îles Comores* (Pondichéry: A. Saligny, 1870), p. 79.

156. Keane, *The Gold of Ophir*, pp. xiii, 151, quoted in Parfitt, *Journey*, p. 262.

157. Reverend J. Cameron, "On the Early Inhabitants of Madagascar," *Antananarivo Annual* 3 (1877): 257–265.

158. To summarize a vast amount of anthropological and ethnographic data, one can say that the Malagasy people are a mixture of African and Indonesian stock, with the African element predominating. However, they speak an essentially Indonesian language and possess a culture that probably owes more to Indonesia than to Africa but contains many elements common to both areas of origin. What is more

surprising is that the first human occupation in Madagascar did not take place until sometime after the beginning of the Christian era. The language clearly belongs to the family of Indonesian/Polynesian languages, as its grammar and structure are 100 percent and its vocabulary 80 percent identical, with the remainder being mainly Bantu, but also Arabic, French, English, and Sanskrit. See Mervyn Brown, *Madagascar Rediscovered* (London: D. Tunnaclife, 1978), chap. 2. Also Hubert Deschamps, *Histoire de Madagascar* (Paris: Berger-Levrault, 1960), pp. 24–30, 39–59, who recapitulated the various hypotheses and assertions about the origins of the Malagasy people.

159. On Phoenician migrations, see Antoine Court de Gebelin, *Le monde primitif* (1773–1782), vol. 1, pp. 52, 583, 553. Also I. Guët, *Les origines de l'Ile Bourbon et de la colonisation française à Madagascar* (Paris: L. Baudoin, 1885), pp. 34ff. Grandidier sees in the Malagasy, apart from their Semitic origin, Papuans and eastern blacks, mixed with Indonesians. See Grandidier, *Histoire, Ethnographie*, vol. 4, tome 1, pp. 16–71. Malayo-Polynesian and Malagasy customs were frequently compared; see, e.g., Robert S. Codrington, "Resemblances between Malagasy Words and Customs and Those of Western Polynesia," *Antananarivo Annual* 2 (1882): 122–127. Ferrand imagined arrivals of Bantus followed by Hinduized Indonesians who came from Sumatra, mixed with Arab and Persian migrations. See Gabriel Ferrand, *Essai des phonétiques comparées du Malais et des dialectes malgaches* (Paris: Geuthner, 1909).

160. Grandidier, *Histoire, Ethnographie*, vol. 4, tome 1, p. 105, who quoted the chronicles of Mogadiscio, Baroua, and the islands of Oungouya (Zanzibar) and of the Great Comoro.

161. Ibid., pp. 107–108.

162. Gabriel Ferrand, "Les migrations musulmanes et juives à Madagascar," *Revue de l'Histoire des Religions* 1, tome 52 (1905): 381–417.

163. Ibid., pp. 401–402.

164. *Explaçao portugueza de Madagascar em 1613. Relaçao inedita de padre Luiz Marianno (Boletim da Soc. De Geog. De Lisboa*, 1887), 3, II, 6, translation into French by Alfred Grandidier and Guillaume Grandidier, *Collection des ouvrages anciens concernant Madagascar* (Paris: Comité de Madagascar, 1903–1920), tome II.

165. Ibid.

166. On the Antalaotra, see Grandidier, *Histoire, Ethnographie*, vol. 4, tome 1, pp. 75–87, 157–165; Brown, *Madagascar*, pp. 21–22; Raymond Kent, *Early Kingdoms in Madagascar, 1500–1700* (New York: Holt, Rinehart and Winston, 1970), pp. 92, 323; Deschamps, *Histoire de Madagascar*, pp. 44ff. Also A. Jully "Origine des Andriana ou nobles," *Notes, Reconnaissances et Explorations* 4 (1898): 890–898, who considers that all of the Malagasy royal dynasties derive from Arab families.

167. Brown, *Madagascar*, pp. 20–21; Deschamps, *Histoire de Madagascar*, p. 57.

168. Charles Poirier, "Terre d'islam en Mer Malgache," *Bulletin de l'Académie Malgache*, special issue (1954): 71–116; Deschamps, *Histoire de Madagascar*, p. 55. Also J. Faublée, *L'ethnologie de Madagascar* (Paris, 1946).

169. Grandidier, *Histoire, Ethnographie*, vol. 4, tome 1, pp. 130–131, 139, 141–142; Kent, *Early Kingdoms*, pp. 102–103; A. Mouren and R. Rouaix, "Industrie ancienne des

objets en pierre de Vohemar," *Bulletin de l'Académie Malgache* 12, no. 2 (1913): 3–13 of reprinted edition; also P. Gaudebout and R. Vernier, "Notes sur une campagne de fouilles à Vohemar," *Bulletin de l'Académie Malgache* 24 (1941): 91–114.

170. Grandidier, *Histoire, Ethnographie*, vol. 4, tome 1, pp. 133, 147, 407.

171. On the Antemoro and the *Sorabé*, see Grandidier, *Histoire, Ethnographie*, vol. 4, tome 1, pp. 124–127, 143–157, 202–205; Kent, *Early Kingdoms*, chap. 3, "The Anteimoro." See also Gustave Mondain, *L'histoire des Tribus de l'Imoro au XVII siècle d'après un manuscrit arabico-malgache* (Paris: Leroux, 1910).

172. Kent, *Early Kingdoms*, p. 109.

173. Brown, *Madagascar*, pp. 23–24; Kent, *Early Kingdoms*, pp. 110–111.

174. Enrico Cerulli, *Somalia, scritti vari editi ed inediti*, vol. 1 (1957), p. 3, quoted in Kent, *Early Kingdoms*, p. 111.

175. Kent, *Early Kingdoms*, p. 106.

176. Deschamps, *Histoire de Madagascar*, pp. 57–58.

177. *Commentarios, de Afonso d'Albuquerque* (1576), in Grandidier, *Collection*, vol. 1, p. 18.

178. Barros, *Da Asia* (Decade II), in Grandidier, *Collection*, vol. 1, p. 24, and (Decade III), vol. 1, p. 53.

179. Brown, *Madagascar*, p. 26. About the Sakalava, the inhabitants of this region, see Kent, *Early Kingdoms*, pp. 160–204.

180. Axelson, *Portuguese*, pp. 5, 37.

181. On Maroseràna, see Raymond Kent, "The Sakalava, Maroserana, Dady and Tromba before 1700," *Journal of African History* 9, no. 4 (1963): 517–546.

182. Grandidier, *Histoire, Ethnographie*, vol. 4, tome 1, pp. 6–7 and note 2; Kent, *Early Kingdoms*, chap.1. The notion that the Antemoro could be "white" Arabs is contradicted by Flacourt, who reported in 1651 that members of the ten royal Antemoro ruling clan are "darker than the other Whites but are nonetheless their masters." Flacourt, *Histoire de la grande île*, vol. 8, p. 40.

183. Brown, *Madagascar*, pp. 26–27. Grandidier claimed that the Antemoro were Arabs from Arabia but considered that they could have reached Madagascar by way of East Africa instead of a direct route. Grandidier, *Histoire, Ethnographie*, vol. 1, tome 1, pp. 143–157 and notes, and vol. 1, tome 2, p. 639, note 139; in the 1917 edition, vol. 4, p. 508. See also Ferrand, "Migrations musulmanes," vol. 3, 1902, p. 114; Kent, *Early Kingdoms*, p. 167.

184. Brown, *Madagascar*, p. 27.

185. Andrew Anderson, *Twenty Five Years in a Wagon in the Gold Regions of Africa* (London, 1887), pp. ii, 144, quoted in Parfitt, *Journey*, p. 102.

186. Brown, *Madagascar*, p. 27; Oliver and Mathew, *History of East Africa*, vol. 1, p. 110.

187. George P. Murdock, *Africa, Its Peoples and Their Culture History* (New York: McGraw-Hill, 1959), p. 387; for Karanga-Shona links, see James G. Frazer, *The Native Races of Africa and Madagascar* (London: Lund, Humphries, 1938), pp. 14–16.

188. Kent, *Early Kingdoms*, pp. 254–255. Also Roland Oliver, "Discernible Developments in the Interior ca. 1500–1840," in *History of East Africa*, pp. 191–192.

189. Alexander Wilmot, *Monomotapa: Its Monuments and Its History* . . . (London: Fisher Unwin, 1896), p. 110.

190. Linguistic, ethnographic, and historical material cannot, however, be compressed into this preliminary work; parallels between Shona/Venda culture and the Antemoro could be the subject of further investigations.

191. Kent, *Early Kingdoms*, pp. 12–18, 20–22.

192. Brown, *Madagascar*, p. 22; Kent, *Early Kingdoms*, pp. 92–93.

193. Parfitt, *Journey*, pp. 241, 290–291, 314.

194. The use of the term *biological anthropology* for this discipline derives from its application in the early 1960s when the Society for the Study of Human Biology was inaugurated, the journal *Annals of Human Biology* was started, and the book *Human Biology: An Introduction to Human Evolution*, edited by Geoffrey A. Harrison et al. (New York: Oxford University Press, 1964), was first published. Pioneering work in this area was carried out by the Italian geneticist Luigi Luca Cavalli-Sforza, who designed a study using blood types to test the theory of genetic drift. Luigi L. Cavalli-Sforza, "Genetic Drift in Italian Population," *Scientific American* 221 (1969): 30–37. See also Steve Olson, *Mapping Human History: Discovering the Past through Our Genes* (New York: Houghton Mifflin, 2002), pp. 164–165; Josephine Johnston and Mark Thomas, "Summary: The Science of Genealogy by Genetics," *Developing World Bioethics* 3, no. 2 (December 2003): 103.

195. In the 1990s, the international Human Genome Diversity Project was created to address these issues. This project was designed to help us understand the genetic makeup of all humanity. The information it gathers may help clarify the history of specific human populations and the various human migrations. Its detractors argue that it could be used to define ethnic groups genetically, and therefore that it could lead to the creation of biological weapons targeted for specific populations. See, e.g.,www.stanford.edu/group/morrinst/hgdp/faq.html.

196. It is not within the scope of this work to consider the numerous critical considerations about the process making it possible to identify individuals on the basis of biological arguments and the possible misuse of genetics. For an overview, see, for instance, Richard Lewontin, *Biology as Ideology: The Doctrine of DNA* (New York: HarperPerennial, 1993); Sahotra Sarkar, *Genetics and Reductionism* (Cambridge: Cambridge University Press, 1996); Jonathan M. Kaplan, *The Limits and Lies of Human Genetic Research: Dangers of Social Policy* (New York: Routledge, 2000); Katia Gibel Azoulay, "Not an Innocent Pursuit: The Politics of a 'Jewish' Genetic Signature," *Developing World Bioethics* 3, no. 2: 119–126.

197. Bob Simpson, "Imagined Genetic Communities," *Anthropology Today* 16, no. 3 (June 2000): 5. See also, e.g., Troy Duster, *Backdoor to Eugenics* (New York: Routledge, 1990), p. 3.

CHAPTER 9

1. There will necessarily remain some small groups that deserve further research.

2. In 2004, Michael Freund founded Shavei Israel to expand the work of Rabbi Avichail. See Jerusalem Post Internet Edition, www.jpost.com (accessed April 2, 2005). About the Bene Menashe see Parfitt, "Place, Priestly Status," p. 3.

3. Hillel Halkin, "Wandering Jews—and Their Genes," *Commentary*, September 2000, pp. 58–60.

4. Avichail, *Tribes*, p. 51.

5. Primack, *Jews in Places*, p. xv.

6. Ibid., p. xvi.

7. Kulanu, www.kulanu.org/about-kulanu (accessed April 25, 2007).

8. From 1993 to 1996, Zakhor (the Timbuktu Association for Friendship with the Jewish World) was an informal, unpublicized association. It was formally registered in 1996 (*Journal Officiel du Mali*, April 30, 1996).

9. I. Maïga, "L'éveil de la communauté juive malienne," *Le Républicain*, March 27, 1996, p. 3.

10. Ibid.

11. Ibid.

12. Ibid.

13. Sennen Andriamirado, "Juifs, noirs et maliens," *Jeune Afrique* 1879 (January 8–14, 1997): 20–22. Also Rick Gold, "The Jews of Timbuktu," www.kulanu.org/timbuktu/zakhor.html (accessed April 25, 2007).

14. See, e.g., Anton Bebler, *Military Rule in Africa: Dahomey, Ghana, Sierra Leone and Mali* (New York: Praeger, 1973).

15. This is demonstrated by conflicts that took place at the time between the government and the Touareg ethnic group. The Touareg rebelled against the usurpation of their lands and the suppression of their culture and language.

16. Parfitt and Trevisan Semi, *Judaising Movements*, p. ix.

17. Maïga, "L'éveil," p. 3.

18. About the issue of biblical names in Africa, see the point of view of Abitbol, "Juifs et Noirs," pp. 77–78.

19. Jacob Oliel's private archives, document dated August 1996, Timbuktu. I am particularly indebted to Jacob Oliel, who kindly put his private archives on the Zakhor movement at my disposal.

20. Al-Bakri, in Cuoq, *Bilad*, pp. 80–109; al-Zurhi, in Cuoq, *Bilad*, pp. 122, 145–147; al-Idrissi, in Cuoq, *Bilad*, pp. 145–147; Ibn Said, in Cuoq, *Bilad*, pp. 201–219; Ibn Abi Zar, *Roudh el-Qartàs*, trans. by A. Beaumier (Paris: Imprimerie Impériale, 1860), p. 165.

21. Ismael D. Haidara, "La synagogue, le marché, le cimetière," *Tapama* 1 (December 1996): 3–5.

22. Ahmed Baba, "Naytl an Ibtihaj," in Cuoq, *Bilad*, pp. 433–435. On Askya Muhammad, see J. Spencer Trimingham, *A History of Islam in West Africa* (London: Oxford University Press, 1970), p. 97; John O. Hunwick, *Shari'a in Songhay: The Replies of al-Maghili to the Questions of Askia al-Hadj Muhammad* (New York: Oxford University Press, 1985).

23. Léon l'Africain, *Description,* vol. 2, p. 468; Martin, *A la frontière marocaine,* pp. 120–127.

24. Andriamirado, "Juifs, noirs," p. 21.

25. Ibid.

26. Oliel's archives, film, "Conversation avec Ismael Daidé Haidara à Tombouctou," August 1996.

27. Oliel, *Juifs au Sahara,* pp. 145–146.

28. Oliel's archives, photos, and films of Haidara family's documents, August 1996, Timbuktu.

29. Other documents, concerning the slave trade as well as the price of salt, spices, gold, or feathers, belonging to the Ahmed Baba documentation and research center of Timbuktu, have since been added to these manuscripts. The Centre de documentation et de recherches Ahmed Baba (CEDRAB) in Timbuktu was created by the Malian government in 1970 at UNESCO's initiative. On the gradual discovery of old manuscripts, see Jean-M. Djian, "Les manuscrits trouvés à Tombouctou," *Le Monde Diplomatique,* August 2004, p. 16.

30. Ismael D. Haidara, *Les Juifs à Tombouctou: Recueil des sources juives écrites relatives au commerce juif à Tombouctou au XIX è siècle* (Bamako: Editions Donniya, 1999). See also Irving Berg's account of his journey to Timbuktu and the discovery of the documents, "The Jewish Descendants of Timbuktu," *Kulanu Newsletter* 9, no. 3 (Fall 2002): 2.

31. Haidara, "La synagogue," p. 4.

32. Samantha M. Klein, "Finding the Jews of Timbuktu: An Account of the Voyage and Interviews with Members of Zakhor in Timbuktu," www.kulanu.org/timbuktu/ findingthejewsoftimbuktu (accessed March 7, 2007).

33. Berg, "The Jewish Descendants of Timbuktu," p. 13.

34. Haidara, *Juifs à Tombouctou,* pp. 26–29.

35. Mungo Park, *Voyage,* p. 83.

36. Jacob Oliel, *De Jérusalem à Tombouctou: l'Odysssée saharienne du rabbin Mardochée, 1826–1886* (Paris: Olbia, 1998).

37. Haidara considers that an extensive study of Aby Serour's trade remains to be carried out which will shed light on a large part of the Jewish presence in the Niger loop in the nineteenth century. Haidara, *Juifs à Tombouctou,* pp. 31–35.

38. The minyan is the quorum of ten males required before a full Jewish religious service can be held. The French consul in Mogador, Auguste Beaumier, who encouraged Mardochée's enterprise, and made it known to the Société de Géographie, was the first one to recount his journey. Auguste Beaumier, *Premier établissement des Israélites à Tombouctou* (Paris: Imprimerie E. Martinet, 1871).

39. Mardochée Aby Serour, "Les Daggatoun, tribu d'origine juive demeurant dans le désert du Sahara," translated from the Hebrew and annotated by I. Loeb, *Bulletin de l'Alliance Israélite Universelle,* supplément (January 1880): 6.

40. Ibid., p. 10.

41. Abitbol, "Juifs et Noirs," p. 75. For a general idea on local traditions, see Siré Abbas Soh, *Chroniques du Fouta sénégalais: Traduites de deux manuscrits arabes inédits*

de Siré-Abbâs-Soh et accompagnées de notes, documents annexes et commentaires et d'un glossaire et de cartes par M. Delafosse avec la collaboration de H. Gaden (Paris: E. Leroux, 1913).

42. Delafosse, *Haut-Sénégal*, vol. 1, pp. 217ff. About a Jewish origin of the Soninke, see also Monteil, "Problèmes," pp. 276–277. On the tendency of West African societies to claim prestigious genealogical links to Jewish ancestors, as well as a pre-Islamic pharaonic descent, and even ties to the Prophet's family, see, for instance, as regards Mali, C. Fay, ed., "Identité et appartenances dans les sociétés sahéliennes," *Cahiers des Sciences Humaines* 31, no. 2 (1995): 329–363. Also regarding the Fulbe of Ayre in central Mali, see Anneke Breedveld and Mirjam De Bruijn, "L'image des Fulbe: Analyse critique de la construction du concept de Pulaaku," *Cahier d'Etudes Africaines* 36, no. 4 (1996): 791–821.

43. Felix Dubois, *Tombouctou la mystérieuse* (Paris: Flammarion, 1900); English edition, *Timbuktu the Mysterious*, trans. Diana White (London, 1897), p 96ff.

44. Amaury P. Talbot, *Peoples of Southern Nigeria*, vol. 1 (London: Oxford University Press, 1926), p. 27.

45. Johnston, *History of the Colonisation* (ed. 1913), p. 13.

46. Charles K. Meek, *Northern Tribes of Nigeria* (London: Oxford University Press, 1925), vol. 2, p. 114; Leland Hall, *Timbuctoo* (New York, 1927), pp. 6 ff., quoted in Williams, *Hebrewisms*, p. 291.

47. Monique Zetlaoui, "Les Bene Israel, de la Côte de Konkan à la terre d'Israël," *Les Cahiers du Judaïsme* 10 (Autumn 2001): 19.

48. Mahamane Touré, "Tombouctou: Des Juifs américains rendent visite à ceux du Mali," *Le Républicain* 23 (January 19, 1997): 8; Karen Primack, "The Renewal of Jewish Identity in Timbuktu," www.kulanu.org/timbuktu/timbuktu.html (accessed July 9, 2006).

49. Gold, *Jews of Timbuktu*, par. 4.

50. Oliel's archives, Film "Tombouctou," August 1996.

51. Oliel's archives, Film "Conversation avec Ismael Daidé Haidara," August 1996.

52. Oliel's archives, letter from Zakhor, ref. 10/z.96, sent to the Directeur de Radio-Lafia.FM.

53. Steven Kaplan, "The Invention of Ethiopian Jews: Three Models," *Cahiers d'Etudes Africaines* 132 no. 33 (1994): 646; Lisa Antebi-Yemini, "De la périphérie de l'Afrique au centre du judaïsme européen," *Les cahiers du judaisme* 10 (Autumn 2001): 47.

54. Kaplan, "Invention," p. 646.

55. Concerning the two possible spellings of the word, *Igbo* is the term used by the members of this ethnic group themselves, whereas *Ibo*, being the anglicized spelling, is commonly used by Europeans and by Africans in their relationships with this group. I shall therefore use the term *Igbo* and the spelling used by the authors in all other cases.

56. Forty-seven percent of Nigerians are Muslims, 35 percent practice Christian religions, and the remaining 18 percent practice African syncretistic rites.

57. Meek, *Tribes*, vol. 1, p. 66.

58. Remi Ilona, *The Igbos: Jews in Africa?* with contributions from Ehav Ever Eliyahu (Abuja, Nigeria: Mega Press, 2004, reedited 2005), pp. 23–29, 64–73, 94–98, 108–123, quotation on p. 116. Remy Ilona, who is a lawyer, is supported in New York by the African American Jew Ehav Ever Eliyahu, who is a Kulanu member and former coordinator for Nigeria. Remy also created the Nigerian Jewish Friendship Association and the Igbo Israel Union. The basis of the primary material of this section comes from mail exchanges and personal communications with Remy Ilona, to whom I am grateful for his generous participation.

59. Ilona, *Igbos*, pp. 17–18.

60. Video interview of Chief Onwa by R. Ilona, November 2, 2002.

61. George T. Basden, *Among the Ibos of Nigeria* (Philadelphia: Lippincott, 1921), pp. 215–231.

62. Ibid., p. 31; Talbot, *Peoples*, vol. 1, p. 27.

63. Richard E. Dennett, *Nigerian Studies or the Religious and Political System of the Yoruba* (London: Macmillan, 1910), p. 11.

64. Talbot, *Peoples*, vol. 1, p. 21.

65. Philip S. Zachernuk, "Of Origins and Colonial Order: Southern Nigerian Historians and the 'Hamitic Hypothesis,'" *Journal of African History* 35, no. 3 (1994): 431–437. Also Joseph A. Atanda, "The Historian and the Problem of Origins of Peoples in Nigeria," *Journal of the Historical Society of Nigeria* 10, no. 3 (1980): 70–73.

66. Robert Collis, *Nigeria in Conflict* (Lagos, Nigeria: John West, 1970).

67. Zachernuk, "Origins," p. 447.

68. Samuel Johnson, *The History of the Yorubas* (London: Routledge, 1921), pp. 3–7; Howe, *Afrocentrism*, p. 120.

69. Zachernuk, "Origins," p. 447; Johnson, *History of the Yorubas*, pp. 3–7.

70. Godbey, *Lost Tribes*, pp. 244–245.

71. Lobagola, *Histoire d'un sauvage africain par lui-même*, translated from the English by G. M. Drucker (Paris: Albin Michel, 1932).

72. Ibid., p. 291. The essential importance of this account appears to be its likely dissemination and influence on black American populations in search of their roots and greater legitimacy, who founded African American Jewish communities.

73. Uche P. Ikeanyibe, *The Quest for the Origin of Igbo People* (Lagos, Nigeria: Aikmay, 1999); Olaudah Equiano, *The Interesting Narratives of the Life of Olaudah Equiano or Gustavus Vassa the African* (London, 1789).

74. N. Okafor-Ogbaji's interview, www.kwenu.com/publications/ojukwu/interview/okafor_ogbaju.htm (accessed March 30, 2007).

75. See Esther Benbassa, *La souffrance comme identité* (Paris: Fayard, 2007).

76. On the Biafra war, see, e.g., Douglas A. Anthony, *Poison and Medicine: Ethnicity, Power and Violence in a Nigerian City, 1966 to 1986* (Portsmouth, NH: Heinemann and others, 2002); Henri Boutet, *L'effroyable guerre du Biafra* (Paris: Chaka, 1992); Herbert Ekwe-Ekwe, *The Biafra War: Nigeria and the Aftermath* (New York: Lewinston, 1990).

77. Ejike Okpa, "20 Pounds to Igbos, Biafrans: Where's the Rest?" www.usafricaonline.com/twentypounds.html (accessed March 9, 2007).

78. Letters to Kulanu, "Kippot in Nigeria," *Kulanu Newsletter* 11, no. 2 (Summer 2004): 8.

79. Daniel Lis, "Swiss-Israeli Anthropologist Journeys to Nigeria" http://kulanu.org.nigeria/anthropologist.html (accessed March 30, 2007).

80. Jeff L. Lieberman, "Taking the Long Way Around: Nigerians Who Feel Connected to the Lost Tribes Return to Judaism," *Jewish Independent*, Vancouver, March 24, 2006.

81. Remi Ilona, "Ibo Greetings," *Kulanu Newsletter* 10, no. 1 (Spring 2003): 4.

82. Remi Ilona, "Mr. Green Comes to Nigeria," *Kulanu Newsletter* 10, no. 4 (Winter 2003–2004): 13; also Jeffery Davidson, "Shabbat with a Committed Group in Nigeria," *Kulanu Newsletter* 11, no. 1 (Spring 2004): 1, 12.

83. The questionnaire contained sixty-seven questions to thirty members. I am conscious of the methodological problem linked to the fact that this questionnaire was transmitted through R. Ilona, and that it is not possible to know exactly how it was presented to the members. In processing the results of the questionnaires, I treated them as narratives and applied a qualitative discourse analytical approach without considering it as a statistical study.

84. Joanne Palmer, "How a Nice Jewish Boy Became a Chief Rabbi in Nigeria," www/usjc.org/Becoming _Jewish6982.html (accessed April 25, 2007).

85. E-mail from Emeka Igwilo, from the United Kingdom to the Ibo-Benei-Israel group, July 25, 2005.

86. Rabbi Capers C. Funnye, "Awakening and In-Gathering of the Ibos," *Kulanu Newsletter* 10, no. 3 (Autumn 2003): 8.

87. Rabbi Shmuel Funnye, "Our People in Nigeria: An Israelite Journey," www.blackjews.org (accessed March 26, 2007).

88. Gabriel J. Gershowitz, "Gone to Ghana," www.kulanu.org/ghana/gonetoghana, [April, 5 2007].

89. "Ghana," http://kulanu.org/Ghana (accessed April 25, 2007).

90. Christianity prevails in the south, while Islam dominates the rural north.

91. Harris W. Mobley, *The Ghanaian's Image of the Missionary: An Analysis of the Published Critiques of Christian Missionaries by Ghanaians* (Leiden: Brill, 1970).

92. About the history of Ghana, see, e.g., William W. Claridge, *A History of the Gold Coast and Ashanti: From the Earliest Times to the Commencement of the Twentieth Century* (London: F. Cass, 1964); Davis E. Apter, *Ghana in Transition* (Princeton, NJ: Princeton University Press, 1972).

93. Charles Monteil, "La légende du Wagadu," *IFAN* 23 (1953): 24–26.

94. On the history of the invention of Ghana ruled by monarchs of white origin, see Jean-L. Triaud, "Le nom de Ghana, la mémoire en exil, mémoire importée, mémoire appropriée," in *Histoire d'Afrique: Les enjeux de mémoire*, ed. Jean-P. Chrétien and Jean-L. Triaud (Paris: Karthala, 1999), pp. 235–280.

95. See the myth of Wagadu in Lilyan Kesteloot, C. Barbey, and S. Ndongo, "Tyamaba, mythe Peul," *Notes Africaines* 185–186 (IFAN-Dakar, January–April 1985): 35–42.

96. Augustin Holl, "West African Archaeology: Colonialism and Nationalism," in *A History of African Archaeology*, ed. Peter Robertshaw (London: J. Currey, 1990), pp. 300ff.

97. Thomas E. Bowdich, *Mission from Cape Coast Castle to Ashantee* (London: J. Murray, 1819), p. 318.

98. Ratzel, *History*, vol. 3, p. 129.

99. Leo Frobenius, *Mythologie de l'Atlantide, le Poséidon de l'Afrique noire* (Paris: Payot, 1949).

100. Eugène Pittard, "Contribution à l'étude anthropologique des Ashanti," *L'Anthropologie* 35 (1910–1930): 464.

101. Williams, *Hebrewisms*, pp. 60, 66–92. Williams dedicated three chapters to the Semitic origins of the Ashanti, pp. 24–67; see also Patai, "Ritual," pp. 86–87.

102. Robert S. Rattray, *Religion and Art in Ashanti* (Oxford: Clarendon Press, 1927), pp. 140–141.

103. Zaya Yeebo, *Ghana, the Struggle for Popular Power: Rawlings, Saviour or Demagogue* (London: New Beacon Books, 1991).

104. Gershowitz, "Gone to Ghana," par. 4.

105. Letter of David Akenorah to Yacoov Gladstone, August 26, 1996, http://kulanu.org/ghana/ghana.html (accessed March 30, 2007).

106. See the different articles of Michael V. Gershowitz, "The Ghanaian Village That Wants to Be Jewish," *Kulanu Newsletter* 6, no. 3 (Autumn 1999): 3 and 14; 6, no. 4 (Winter 1999): 2 and 11; and 6, no. 5: 3 and 11(Spring 2000).

107. Daniel Baiden and Robert H. Lande, "The Ghanaian Village That Wants to Be Jewish," www.kulanu.org/ghanianvillage.html (accessed March 30, 2007).

108. Trevisan Semi, "Falashisation," p. 88.

109. Lazare Ndayongeje, "Mythe des origines, idéologie hamitique et violence en Afrique des Grands Lacs: Comprendre et agir," *Grands Lacs Confidentiel*, August 16, 2004.

110. "Chroniques de Havilah," Minutes of the Conference of October 10, 1999, www.abarundi.org/actualité/nationale/havila (accessed October 7, 2005).

111. Havilah, http://kulanu.org/africa, which also presents the activities of each center (accessed March 9, 2007).

112. Yochannan Bwejeri, "Havilah and the Tutsi Hebrews," www.kulanu.org/havila (accessed September 6, 2005).

113. In the local language, "ba" is a prefix indicating the plural.

114. Yochannan Bwejeri, *Les Batutsi: L'histoire confisquée* (Brussels: Editions de Havilah, 2001).

115. *Chroniques de Havila*, Minutes of the Conference of October 10, 1999.

116. Speke, *Journal of the Discovery*, quoted in T. Broadway Johnson, *Tramps around the Mountains of the Moon* (Boston, 1909), pp. 184ff., in Williams, *Hebrewisms*, p. 184.

117. Mary H. Bradley, *Caravans and Cannibals* (New York, 1926), pp. 65, 281.

118. Pierre Rychmans, *Grands Lacs Confidentiel* (1936), pp. 279–280, quoted in Jean-P. Chrétien, "Une révolte au Burundi in 1934," *Annales ESC* 26 (November–December 1970): 1707.

119. Révérend Père Pagès, *Un royaume Hamite au centre de l'Afrique* (Brussels: G. van Canpenhout, 1933), p. 5.

120. Alexis Kagame, "Les Hamites du Rwanda et du Burundi sont-ils des Galla?" *Académie Royale des Sciences d'Outre-Mer* 2 (1956): 314–356.

121. Mgr L. Classe, *Notice sur le Congo français*, Marcel Guillemot, ed. (Paris: J. André, 1900), pp. 677–693.

122. Paul Del Perugia, *Les derniers rois mages* (Paris: Phébus, 1978), pp. 35–36, quoted in Parfitt, *Lost Tribes*, p. 188.

123. See, e.g., William R. Louis, *Ruanda-Urundi, 1884–1919* (Oxford: Clarendon Press, 1963); Jean-C. Klotchkoff, *Rwanda Today* (Paris: Editions. JA, 1990).

124. Philip Gourevich, *We Wish to Inform You That Tomorrow We Will Be Killed with Our Families* (New York: Farrar, Straus and Giroux, 1998); Linda Melvern, *Conspiracy to Murder* (London: Verso, 2004).

125. William F. S. Miles, "Hamites—Hebrews: Problems in 'Judaizing' the Rwandan Genocide," *Journal of Genocide Research, Social Science and Politics and International Relations* 2, no. 1 (March 2000): 107–115.

126. Bwejeri, *Havilah*, par. 4, 5.

127. Rabbi David Kuperman, "Genocide Imminent Against Tutsi of Burundi," *Kulanu Newsletter* 11, no. 3 (Autumn 2004): 12; also Irwin M. Berg, "Jews in Central Africa," www.kulanu.org/tutsi/jews-africa.html (accessed April 26, 2007).

128. Jack Zeller, "An Appeal for Help from Kulanu's President," *Kulanu Newsletter* 11, no. 3 (Autumn 2004): 9.

129. E-mail from Shahanna on Kulanu-list, June 7, 2005.

130. The Arusha Accords were a set of five protocols signed by the Rwandese Patriotic Front (RPF) and the government of Rwanda in Arusha, Tanzania on August 4, 1993, ending the civil war. The talks were initially orchestrated by both the United States and France beginning in 1992 under the auspices of the Organization of African Unity. The protocols addressed several issues that were necessary for a lasting peace, including the rule of law, the repatriation of refugees, the reinstallation of people displaced by the war through power sharing, and the fusion of both armies. www.answers.com/topic/arusha-accords (accessed March 22, 2007).

131. "Havila renforce les liens avec les organisations juives des Etats-Unis," wwwnet.press.bi/Ago/havila2.htm (accessed June 4, 2005).

132. Erick Kennes, "Judaïsation des Tutsi: Identité ou stratégie de conquête," *Grands Lacs Confidentiel*, March 18, 2000.

133. *National Post Canada*, May 11, 1999, p. 17.

134. Mark G. Thomas, T. Parfitt, D. A. Weiss, A. Skorecki, J. A. Wilson, M. Le Roux, N. Bradman, and D. Y. Goldstein, "Y Chromosomes Travelling South: The Cohen Modal Haplotype and the Origins of the Lemba—the 'Black Jews of Southern Africa,'" *American Journal of Human Genetics* 66 (2000): 674–686.

135. Dugall Campbell, *In the Heart of Bantuland* (New York: Negro University Press, 1969), p. 226, quoted in Parfitt, *Lost Tribes*, p. 191.

136. www.usip.org/pubs/pworks/zaireII/chapI-II.html (accessed March 20, 2005), quoted in Parfitt, *Lost Tribes*, p. 191.

137. Parfitt, *Lost Tribes*, p. 191.

138. Carol Castiel, "Cape Verde Hosted Jews," *Washington Jewish Week*, January, 1995.

139. M. Mitchell Serells, "An Unusual Society in Cape Verde," www.kulanu.org/cape-verde/verde.html (accessed April 25, 2007).

140. Louise Werlin, "Jews in Cape Verde," www.kulanu.org/cape-verde/verde.html (accessed April 25, 2007).

141. Serells, "Unusual Society," par. 7.

142. Castiel, "Hosted Jews."

143. Yossi Melman, "Jewish Cousins," *Ha'Aretz*, March 30, 2001.

CHAPTER 10

1. *Yudaya* means "Jew" in Luganda, the local language; *ba* is a prefix indicating the plural.

2. Karen Primack, "Contemplating Miracles in Uganda," *Kulanu Newsletter* 9, no. 1 (Spring 2002): 6–9; Jean-F. Mayer, "Les Abayudaya de l'Ouganda enfin reconnus comme juifs," *Religioscope*, March 18, 2002.

3. See Emanuela Trevisan Semi, "A Conversion Movement in Italy," in *Judaising Movements*, pp. 65–86; Elena Cassin, *San Nicandro: Histoire d'une conversion* (Paris: Plon, 1957).

4. Arye Oded, *Religion and Politics in Uganda: A Study of Islam and Judaism* (Nairobi: East African Publishers, 1995), pp. 75–79; Michael Twaddle, *Kakungulu and the Creation of Uganda, 1868–1928* (London: James Currey, 1993), pp. 292–293.

5. Twaddle, *Kakungulu*, pp. 292, 299, 301; Oded, *Religion*, pp. 78ff.

6. Twaddle, *Kakungulu*, p. 283. Normally, the members of the Uganda tribes are the only Bantu tribe who forbade any mutilation of the body and regard circumcision as a violation of their tribal laws. See John Roscoe, *The Baganda: An Account of Their Native Customs and Beliefs* (New York: Barnes and Noble, 1966), p. 7.

7. John Roscoe, *The Soul of Central Africa* (New York: Negro Universities Press, 1969), pp. 264–265.

8. Oded, *Religion*, pp. 80–84.

9. Ibid., pp. 92–100.

10. Oded, *Religion*, pp. 84–87; Twaddle, *Kakungulu*, p. 284.

11. Twaddle, *Kakungulu*, p. 299; Oded, *Religion*, p. 86.

12. Oded, *Religion*, p. 80.

13. Parfitt, "Hebrew in Colonial Discourse," p. 159.

14. Johnston, *History*, pp. 40, 50, 51, 58.

15. Twaddle, *Kakungulu*, p. 281.

16. Ibid.

17. Ibid.
18. *Uganda Notes*, November 1904, pp. 159–160, quoted in Twaddle, *Kakungulu*, p. 281.
19. Twaddle, *Kakungulu*, pp. 92–93, 100–101.
20. Notably in 1960 when the new government of the Republic of Uganda nationalized the schools; see J. J. Kekki, "The Genesis of the Abayudaya Community," www.kulanu.org/abayudaya/kakungulu_bk.html (accessed March 20, 2007); also Oded, *Religion*, p. 101.
21. On the action of the proselyte organizations and the tendency toward a universal Judaism, see Trevisan Semi, "Conversion and Judaisation," pp. 53ff.
22. Oded, *Religion*, pp. 96–97, 102–103.
23. Ibid., pp. 101, 105–106.
24. Tobin, Tobin, and Rubin, *In Every Tongue*, pp. 85–86.
25. See details on the conversion procedure in Primack, "Contemplating Miracles," p. 6.
26. Ibid.
27. See the relation of the event in Rachel Pomerance, communiqué de *JTA (Jewish Telegraphic Agency)*, February 18, 2002, www.jewishsf.com/content/2-0-/module/displaystory/story_id/17854/edition_id/355/format/html/displaystory.html (accessed May 1, 2007).
28. Parfitt and Trevisan Semi, *Judaising Movements*, p. x.
29. Parfitt, "The Lemba, an African Judaising Tribe," in *Judaising Movements*, pp. 39–51; Le Roux, *In Search*, p. 26.
30. Buijs, "Black Jews," pp. 661–662.
31. Ibid.
32. Le Roux, *In Search*, p. 26.
33. Junod, *Life*, pp. 424, 72–73; Parfitt, *Journey*, pp. 21–22, 42, 87, 195, 311, 335–336.
34. Junod, "Balemba," p. 276. Also C. A. Wheelwright, "Native Circumcision Lodges in the Soutpansberg District," *Journal of the Royal Anthropological Institute* 35, no. 5 (1905): 251–255.
35. Stayt, *The Bavenda*, p. 18.
36. Ibid., pp. 52ff.
37. Junod, "Balemba," p. 286.
38. Quoted in Parfitt, *Journey*, p. 265.
39. Nikolas J. Van Warmelo, "A Preliminary Survey of the Bantu Tribes of South Africa," *Ethnological Publications* 5 (Pretoria: Government Printer, 1935), pp. 122ff.
40. Leo Frobenius, "Die Waremba. Träger einer Fossilen Kultur," *Zeitschrift für die Alttestamentliche Wissenschaft* 70 (1938): 162; A. A. Jacques, "Notes on the Lemba Tribe of the Northern Transvaal," *Anthropos* 26, no. 3 (1931): 248–250; Charles Bullock, *The Mashona and the Matabele* (London: Juta, 1950), p. 22; L. C. Thompson, "The Ba-Lemba of Southern Rhodesia," *Native Affairs Department Annual* 19 (1942): 78–86; Harald Von Sicard, *Ngoma Lugundu. Eine afrikanische Bundeslade* (Uppsala: Studia Ethnographica Upsaliensa, 1952).

41. See Buijs, "Black Jews," pp. 667–669, on the role of the missions and their influence on the division of the indigenous population along linguistic and geographical lines.

42. Magdel Le Roux, "African 'Jews' for Jesus," *Missionalia* 25, no. 4 (December 1997): 493–510.

43. Parfitt, "Genes, Religion," p. 213. Most Lemba combine circumcision and baptism ceremonies, while still practicing specifically African customs.

44. From 1913, the Native Land Act forced African sharecroppers off white farms and divided South Africa into black and white areas. Through this law, whites retained the best land, and blacks found it more and more difficult to earn a living from what was left. See Robert Edgar, *Because They Chose the Plan of God: The Story of the Bulhoek Massacre* (Johannesburg: Raven Press, 1988), pp. 6ff.

45. Buijs, "Black Jews," p. 671ff.

46. Le Roux, *In Search*, p. 69ff.

47. Amanda B. Spurdle and Trefor Jenkins, "The Origins of the Lemba, 'Black Jews' of Southern Africa: Evidence from p12F2 and Other Y-Chromosome Markers," *American Journal of Human Genetics* 59 (1996): 1126–1133.

48. Following the publication of the first edition of Parfitt's book, three representatives of the Lemba were received in October 1999 by the president of the South African Republic, Thabo Mbeki, who had seen the documentary based on this book and wanted to know more about them; see Parfitt, *Journey*, p. 343.

49. Parfitt, "Genes, Religion," p. 215.

50. Thomas, Parfitt, et al., "Chromosomes Travelling South," pp. 674–686.

51. Thomas, Skorecki, et al., "Origins of the Old Testament Priests," 138–140; also Avshalom Zoosmann-Diskin, "Are Today's Jewish Priests Descended from the Old Testament Old Ones?" *HOMO: Journal of Comparative Human Biology-Zeitschrift fuer vergleichende Biologie des Menschen* 51 (2000): 2–3.

52. Neil Bradman and M. G. Thomas, "Genetics: The Pursuit of Jewish History by Other Means," *Judaism Today* 10 (Autumn 1998): 4–7.

53. Halkin, "Wandering Jews," p. 55.

54. Nichols Wade, "DNA Backs a Tribe's Tradition of Early Descent from the Jews," *New York Times*, May 9, 1999 (late edition); Wendy Elliman, "Footprints in the Blood," *Hadassah Magazine*, January 2001, p. 19; Janine Lazarus, "At the Jewish Doorstep in Africa," *Hadassah Magazine*, January 2001, pp. 16–22.

55. "Levi Returns from South Africa," *Kulanu Newsletter* 7, no. 1 (2000): 1, 5.

56. Tudor Parfitt, "Constructing Black Jews: Genetic Tests and the Lemba—the Black Jews of South Africa," *Developing World Bioethics* 3, no. 2 (2003): 117.

57. Le Roux, "African Jews, " p. 510.

58. "Letter from Zimbabwe," *Kulanu Newsletter* 7, no. 4 (2000–2001): 5ff., quoted in Parfitt, *Judaising Movements*, p. 50.

59. Ernest Nandhi (Sadiki), "Lemba Convince Conference," *Kulanu Newsletter* 10, no. 3 (Autumn 2003): 1 ff.

60. Parfitt, *Judaising Movements*, p. 51.

61. They belong sometimes to the Lutheran Evangelical Church and the reformed churches, too. These churches are formed through separations and through new creations that adhere to a charismatic leader or the pressure of an ethnic group, which causes considerable fragmentation of the communities. In South Africa, the ZCC was established in 1917 when Elias Mahlangu founded the Zion Apostolic Church of South Africa, from which seceded Edward Lion's Zion Apostolic Faith Mission (ZAFM). Engenas Lekganyane's Zion Christian Church (ZCC) then seceded from the ZAFM around 1925 and is now the largest AIC in South Africa. See M. L. Daneel, *Old and New in Southern Shona Independent Churches* (The Hague: Mouton, 1971), vol. 1, p. 300; John Comaroff, *Body of Power, Spirit of Resistance: The Culture and History of South African People* (Chicago: University of Chicago Press, 1985), pp. 176 ff.

62. There are well over 10,000 independent Christian denominations. AICs have been variously described as "prophet-healing churches" by Turner, "spirit-type churches" by Daneel, "independent African Pentecostal Churches" by Hollenweger, "spiritual churches" by Baëta, and a Bible Church, Ethiopian Church, Zionist, messianic, millenarian, separatist church by the other sociologists, social anthropologists, and comparative religionists working in many African countries. See Harold W. Turner, *Religious Innovations in Africa* (Boston: G. K. Hall, 1979), p. 97; Walter Hollenweger, *The Pentecostals* (London: SCM, 1972), p. 151; C. H. Baëta, *Prophetism in Ghana* (London: SCM Press, 1962). Also John David Peel, *Aladura: A Religious Movement among the Yoruba* (London: Oxford University Press, 1968); Bohumil Holas, "Bref aperçu sur les cultes syncrétiques de la basse Côte d'Ivoire, " *Africa* 24, no. 1 (1954): 295–310.

63. Bengt Sundkler, *Zulu Zion and Some Swazi Zionists* (London: Oxford University Press, 1976), pp. 65–66.

64. This was especially true in South Africa, where, until relatively recently, churches were segregated. See Comaroff, *Body of Power*, pp. 168, 172.

65. Sundkler, *Zulu Zion*, pp. 313–315. In western Kenya churches exist that are similar to the African Israel Church Nineveh (AICN), founded in 1942 by a Luyia evangelist, Daudi Zakayo Kivuli, who died in 1974. The AICN, which claimed 800,000 members in Kenya in 1991, has many practices similar to those of other Pentecostal churches, but they observe Old Testament dietary and purification taboos, proscribing pork and fish without scales. See J. M. Kivuli, "The Modernization of an African Independent Church," *Organization of African Instituted Churches*, ed. J. Nussbaum (Nairobi: Freedom and Independence, 1994), pp. 58–63.

66. Joan Millard, "The Bulhoek Tragedy," *Missionalia*, http/:www.geocities.com/missionalia/bulhoek.htm (accessed March 26, 2007).

67. See, in chapter 7, The Black Jews in the United States.

68. Millard, *Bulhoek*, p. 5

69. Ibid., p. 6.

70. All the information in this section was taken from Alan M. Tigay, "Xhosa Rabbi," *Jewish Digest*, February 1975, pp. 71–75.

71. Ibid., p. 72. More recently, in Swaziland, a member of the royal family, Natan Gameze, who graduated from Oxford, decided to convert when he discovered "the beauty of Judaism." See *Jewish World Society Today*, www.aish.com/spirituality/odysseys/ The_Royal _Jew_ from_ Swaziland (accessed March 20, 2007).

72. Tigay, "Xhosa Rabbi," pp. 72–73.

73. Ibid., pp. 74, 73.

74. Ibid., p. 74.

75. Ibid., p. 75.

76. Jay P. Sand, "The Jews of Africa," www.mindspring.com/~jaypsand/rusape (accessed August 20, 2006).

77. Mark Ellyne, "The Black Jews of Zimbabwe," www.mindspring.com/~jaypsand/rusape (accessed July 26, 2006).

78. Mark Ellyne, "A Sabbath in Rusape, Zimbabwe," www.mindspring.com/~jaypsand/rusape.htm (accessed July 26, 2006).

79. Kulanu, "The Jews of Africa," www.kulanu.org/zimbawe.html (accessed March 2007).

80. See, e.g., Anthony J. Dachs and F. W. Rea, *The Catholic Church and Zimbabwe* (Salisbury: Mambo Press, 1979); Alois S. Mlambo, *White Immigration into Rhodesia* (Harare: University of Zimbabwe, 2002); David Martin, *The Struggle for Zimbabwe* (Johannesburg: Raven Press, 1981).

81. The African Renaissance originated in the various currents and tendencies of South African Afrocentrism and pan-Africanism, and from the Diaspora. See Lydia Samabakhsh-Liberge, "*L'African Renaissance* en Afrique du Sud," *Afrocentrismes*, pp. 382–399.

82. Mindi Cohen and Paul Zeitz, "A Visit with the Jews of Rusape," www.kulanu.org/ zimbabwe/visitrusape. [April 26, 2007].

83. Rabson Wuriga and Kohen Kossinathi, "Too Euro-centric." www.kulanu.org/zimbawe/tooeurocentric.html (accessed March 24, 2007); "Matrilineal or patrilineal descent" taken from a discussion on Kulanu's listserv, November 2001, www.kulanu.org/zimbawe/descent.html (accessed March 20, 2007).

84. On the construction of a religious identity able to confront modernity among African churches, see, for instance, Vittorio Lanternari, *Dei, profeti, contadini. Incontri nel Ghana* (Naples: Liguori, 1988); Claude-H. Perrot, "Prophétisme et modernité en Côte d'Ivoire. Un village éotilé et le culte de Gbahié," in *Religion et modernité en Afrique noire, Dieu pour tous, chacun pour soi*, ed. Jean-F. Bayart (Paris: Karthala, 1993), pp. 215–275.

85. The primary material for this section was taken from private archives constituted between 1970 and 2003 by Mrs. K. Quanbeck, to whom I am grateful for the communication of these documents through Tudor Parfitt.

86. Quanbeck's archives, Individuals' Discourses, no. 28, Antananarivo, August 1999.

87. Quanbeck's archives, Individuals' Discourses, no. 46, Mr. B. Faradofay, 2000.

88. Today some 45 percent of Malagasy are said to be Christians, divided more or less evenly between Catholics and Protestants. The Christian influence is far from homogeneous throughout the island. See Gillian Feeley-Harnik "Madagascar: Religious Systems," in *Encyclopaedia of Africa South of the Sahara*, ed. J. Middleton (New York: Scribner's, 1997), vol. 3, pp. 88–89.

89. Consequently, in order to avoid generalizing data or taking them out of context, I shall cite observations from an individual or a fragment of society without attempting to extend them to an entire ethnic group.

90. The societies and communities of Madagascar appear to be extremely diversified among themselves between social orders and suborders, ancestral differences, and subtle subdivisions. Literature reflects this diversity; see, e.g., Paul Ottino, *Les Champs de l'ancestralité à Madagascar* (Paris: Karthala et Orstom, 1998).

91. The Zafiraminia antedates the Antemoro in Madagascar by at least two centuries. Flacourt observed that two parallel societies existed among the Antanosy: the "whites" and the "blacks," the former being Zafiraminia and the latter known collectively as *marinh*. Flacourt, *Histoire*, vol. 8, pp. 25–27. Also Grandidier, *Histoire, Ethnographie*, vol. 1, tome 1, pp. 130–131 and notes.

92. Flacourt, *Histoire*, pp. 3–4 (ed. 1658).

93. François Martin, *Manuscrit des Archives Nationales* (1668), p. 311.

94. Jesuit missionaries from Portugal had appeared soon after the European discovery of the island, but their efforts bore no fruit. See Marianno, *Exploraçao*, pp. 315–354. Also Grandidier, *Histoire, Ethnographie*, vol. 1, tome 1, pp. 430–443. Lazarist missionaries had rather more success during the French occupation of Fort Dauphin in the seventeenth century, but after the abandonment of the colony, the Christian converts reverted to paganism; see *Mémoires de la congrégation de la mission (Lazaristes)*, ed. A. Milon (1866).

95. English contributions have been published in *Antananarivo Annual*. See also Bonar A. Gow, *Madagascar and the Protestant Impact: The Work of the British Missions 1815–1855* (London: Longman, 1979). The first Norwegian Protestant missionaries arrived in 1866; the North Americans followed in 1888 and have remained there since. The presence of French Catholic missionaries during the same period led to the establishment of Christian churches, generating ethnographic knowledge through their regular reports on local customs. On Norwegian missionaries, see Fierle Fuglestad, *Norwegian Missions in Africa History*, ed. Jarle Simensen (New York: Oxford University Press, 1986), vol. 2; among French missionaries, R. P. Callet is known for having written the royal traditions of the *Tantaran'ny Andriana* (History of the kings), ed. G. S. Chapus and E. Ratsimba (Tananarive: Académie Malgache, 1958).

96. See, e.g., Françoise Raison-Jourde, *Bible et Pouvoir à Madagascar au XIX è siècle. Invention d'une identité chrétienne et construction de l'état (1780–1880)* (Paris: Karthala, 1991); Maurice Bloch, *Placing the Dead: Tombs, Ancestral Villages and Kinship Organisation in Madagascar* (London: Seminar Press, 1971); Stephen Ellis, *The Rising of the Red Shawls: A Revolt in Madagascar 1895–1899* (London: Cambridge University Press, 1985).

97. James Sibree, *The Great African Island: Chapters on Madagascar, A Popular Account of Recent Researches in the Physical Geography, Geology, and Exploration of the Country and Its Natural History* (London: Trübner, 1880), pp. 108, 425.

98. Flacourt gives a Malagasy version of the history of the Deluge. Flacourt, *Histoire* (1661), pp. 58ff. See also the Malagasy version by Rajaonarimanana of the "Prophet Noah the Red." Narivelo Rajaonarimanana, *Savoirs arabico-malgaches: La tradition des devins Antemoro, Anakara* (Paris: Inalco, 1990), pp. 169ff.

99. See the texts gathered and studied by Noël J. Gueunier, "La Genèse de l'Homme Blanc, Récits d'origine du Sud-Ouest de Madagascar," *Etudes Ocean Indien* 15 (1992): 227–259.

100. Grandidier, *Histoire, Ethnographie*, vol. 4, tome 1, pp. 127–128.

101. Ibid., pp. 145, 150.

102. The best-documented example of this kind of process is the way in which Protestantism came to be regarded as a truly Malagasy ancestral "tradition," in the Highlands in the nineteenth century. See Bloch, *Placing*, pp. 14–15.

103. Benedict Anderson, *Imagined Communities: Reflections on the Origin and Spread of Nationalism* (London: Verso, 1991).

104. Grandidier, *Histoire, Ethnographie*, vol. 4, tome 1, pp. 96–103.

105. Ibid., pp. 100–103 and notes.

106. Quanbeck's archives, Individuals' Discourse, Pastor F.S., n.d.

107. Joseph Briand, *L'Hébreu à Madagascar* (Tananarive: Pitot de la Beaujardière, 1946), pp.13, 8–10. The analysis of language has been widely used in Madagascar to determine where the first Malagasy came from; see Augustus H. Keane, "The Himyarites in Rhodesia and in Madagascar," *Atheneoeum*, April 5, 1902, p. 435. Also Etienne de Flacourt, *Dictionnaire de la langue de Madagascar* (Paris: G. Josse, 1658); Gabriel Ferrand, *L'élément arabe et swahili en malgache ancien et moderne* (Paris: Imprimerie Nationale, 1904).

108. Arnold Van Gennep, *Tabou et totémisme à Madagascar* (Paris: E. Leroux, 1904), pp. 7, 3.

109. See, e.g., John Mack, *Madagascar, Island of the Ancestors* (London: British Museum Publications, 1986), pp. 32–38; Pierre Vérin, *The History of Civilisation in North Madagascar* (Rotterdam: A. A. Balkema, 1986); Noël Gueunier, *Les Chemins de l'Islam à Madagascar* (Paris: L'Harmattan, 1994).

110. Robert Jaovelo-Dzao, "Richesses culturelles d'une civilisation de l'oralité," in *Madagascar et le Christianisme*, ed. Bruno Hübsch (Paris: Karthala, 1993); Paul Vérin, "Austronesian Contribution to the Culture," in *East Africa and the Orient: Cultural Synthesis in Pre-Colonial Times*, ed. H. Neville Chittick and Robert I. Rotberg (New York: Africana, 1975). Between 9 and 15 percent of the Malagasy identify themselves as Muslims, while Hindus and Buddhists constitute about 1 percent of the population. Islam is overtly practiced as a religion only in some Islamized communities, mostly in the northwestern province.

111. Quanbeck's archives, Individuals' Discourses no. 46, Mr. B. Faradofay, 2000.

112. Ibid.

113. Stillman, *Jews of Arab Lands*, p. 16.

114. Quanbeck's archives, Individuals' Discourses no. 46, Mr. B. Faradofay, 2000.

115. The Red Heifer was to be sacrificed, with careful ceremony, and her ashes were to be carefully gathered, mixed with water, and used for certain cases of uncleanliness, particularly for those touching dead bodies.

116. S. Zaborowski, "A propos des Baras et des malgaches à cheveux crépus," *Bulletins et Mémoires de la Société d'Anthropologie de Paris* 8, no. 4 (1907): 398–399.

117. Quanbeck's archives, Individuals' discourse, Pastor F.S., n.d.

118. Personal e-mail from Karen Primack, Kulanu, May 17, 2005.

119. Natalia Berger and Kay Kaufman Shelemay, *The Jews in Ethiopia: A People in Transition*, ed. Yehuda Avner et al. (Tel Aviv: Beth Hatefusoth, 1986), pp. 43–45.

120. Steven Kaplan and Chaim Rosen, "Created in Their Own Image: A Comment on Beta Israel Figurines," *Cahiers d'Etudes Africaines* 36, nos. 141–142 (1996): 171–182.

EPILOGUE

1. James Beckford, "Religious Movements and Globalization," in *Global Social Movements*, ed. Robin Cohen and Shirin Rai (London: Athelone Press, 2000), p. 170; Irving Exham and Karla Poewe, *New Religions as Global Culture* (Boulder, CO: Westview, 1997).

2. Phillip Charles Lucas and Thomas Robin, eds., *New Religious Movements in the Twenty-first Century* (New York: Routledge, 2004), p. 6.

3. See Abdullahi Ahmed An-Na'im and Francis M. Deng, eds., *Human Rights in Africa: Cross-Cultural Perspectives* (Washington, DC: Brookings Institution, 1990). Also Louise Pirouet, "The Churches and Human Rights in Kenya and Uganda since Independence," in *Religion and Politics in East Africa: The Period since Independence*, ed. Holger Bernt Hansen and Michael Twaddle (Athens: Ohio University Press, 1995); Shanto Iyengar and Donald Kinder, *News That Matters* (Chicago: University of Chicago Press, 1987).

4. As is well known, the media play a central role in shaping the social cognition of the public at large, even if several and sometimes contradictory theories on mass communication influence exist. For an overview of these theories, see, e.g., Arthur A. Berger, ed., *Media USA: Process and Effect* (New York: Longman, 1991); Jennings Bryant and Dolf Zillman, eds., *Perspectives on Media Effects* (Hillsdale, NJ: Erlbaum, 1986); S. Hall, D. Hobson, A. Lowe, and P. Willis, eds., *Culture, Media, Language: Working Papers in Cultural Studies* (London: Hutchinson, 1980).

5. Teun A. Van Dijk, *Elite Discourse and Racism* (Newbury Park: Sage, 1993), p. 242. On the issues of reception and other sources of influence, see, e.g., John Downing, Ali Mohammadi, and Annabelle Sreberny-Mohammadi, *Questioning the Media: A Critical Introduction* (London: Sage, 1990); Doris A. Graber, *Media Power in Politics* (Washington, DC: Congressional Quarterly Press, 1984); Teun A. Van Dijk,

"News as Discourse," in *The New Handbook of Language and Social Psychology*, ed. Peter Robinson and Howard Giles (Chichester: Wiley, 1988), pp. 163–183.

6. Anderson, *Imagined Communities*, pp. 6–7.

7. Ella Shohat and Robert Stam, *Unthinking Eurocentrism: Multiculturalism and the Media* (London: Routledge, 1997).

8. Ibid., p. 299. Media theorists and communication scholars have provided extensive readings of this social collective practice. See, e.g., E. M. Hammonds, "New Technologies of Race," in *Processed Lives: Gender and Technology in Everyday Life*, ed. Jennifer Terry and Melodie Calvert (New York: Routledge, 1997); Allucquère R. Stone, *The War of Desire and Technology at the Close of the Mechanical Age* (Cambridge, MA: MIT Press, 1999).

9. For an overview on the issue of conversion in general, see, e.g., Peter G. Stromberg, *Language and Self-Transformation: A Study of the Christian Conversion Narrative* (Cambridge: Cambridge University Press, 1993). Also *De la conversion*, Centre d'Etudes des Religions du Livre, under the direction of J. C. Attias (Paris: Editions du Cerf, 1998); Anne H. Hawkins, *Archetypes of Conversion: The Autobiographies of Augustine* (Lewisburg, PA: Bucknell University Press, 1985); also Mark Heinrich, "Change of Heart: A Test of Some Widely Held Theories about Religious Conversion, " *American Journal of Sociology* 83 (1977),: 653–680; John Lofland and Rodney Stark, "Becoming a World Saver: A Theory of Conversion to a Deviant Perspective," *American Sociological Review* 30 (1965): 874.

10. John David Peel, *Aladura: A Religious Movement among the Yoruba* (London: Oxford University Press, 1968). B. A. Paw, *Christianity and Xhosa Tradition: Belief and Ritual among Xhosa-speaking Christians* (Oxford: Oxford University Press, 1975). For an overview of the different trends about this subject, see, e.g., Robert Horton, "African Conversion," *Africa* 41, no. 2 (1971): 85–108. See also, e.g., R. Godfrey Lienhardt, *Divinity and Experience: The Religion of the Dinka* (Oxford: Clarendon Press, 1961); Peter Rigby, "Pastors and Pastoralists: The Differential Penetration of Christianity among East African Cattle Herders," *Comparative Studies in Society and History* 23 (1981): 96–129.

11. Rosalind I. J. Hackett, "Revitalization in African Traditional Religion," in *African Traditional Religions in Contemporary Society*, ed. J. K. Olupona (New York: Paragon House, 1991), pp. 135–148.

12. Conversion to Islam has been documented in several contexts; on Yoruba Islam, see, e.g., John S. Trimingham, *History of Islam in West Africa* (London: Oxford University Press), pp. 25–33, 129, 221–222. On Nupe Islam, see Siegfried F. Nadel, *Nupe Religion* (London: Routledge and Kegan Paul, 1954), chap. 3. See also Lamin Sanneh, *The Crown and the Turban: Muslims and West African Pluralism* (Boulder, CO: Westview, 1997).

13. Shalva Weil, "Lost Israelites from the Indo-Burmese Borderlands: Retraditionalisation and Conversion among the Shinlung or Bene Menasseh," *Anthropologist* 6, no. 3 (July 2004): 219.

14. Ibid.

15. Cornelia A. Kammerer, "Customs and Christian Conversion among Zakha Highlanders of Burma and Thailand," *American Ethnologist* 17 (1990): 277–291, quoted in Weil, "Lost Israelites," p. 220.

16. Said, *Orientalism*, p. 55.

17. Justin S. Ukpong, "Current Theology: The Emergence of African Theologies," *Theological Studies* 45 (1986): 501–536.

18. Georges Balandier, *Sociologie actuelle de l'Afrique noire* (Paris: PUF, 1955), p. 9; James W. Fernandez, "African Religious Movements: Types and Dynamics," *Journal of Modern African Studies* 2, no. 4 (1964): 531–549. See also Melville J. Herskovits, *The Human Factor in Changing Africa* (London: Routledge and Kegan Paul, 1963).

19. Weil, "Lost Israelites," p. 230.

20. Robert Mc Henry, "Revivalism," in *New Encyclopaedia Britannica*, 15th ed. (1993), vol. 10, p. 9.

21. In April 2005, this tribe succeeded in its claim: a special team of rabbis from Israel will soon be sent to the Indian-Myanmar border to officially convert 1,000 members of this tribe, who have been recognized as Jews by Israel's chief Sephardic rabbi Shlomo Amar. The conversions will ensure that the group will be able to immigrate to Israel under the Jewish law of return. See I. MacKinnon, "Lost Tribe Dreams of Return to Israel after 2,700 Years of Exile," April 2, 2005, www.timesonline.co.uk/.

22. Weil, "Lost Israelites," p. 224. As with other millenarian movements, the conversion was triggered by a dream of a male mystic from Mizoram, which spread throughout the Mizoram, Manipur, and China states. This was in 1951. Weil points out that it is significant that this happened only three years after the establishment of the State of Israel, when pro-Israel sentiments were high internationally and the Indian people, in particular, admired the way the Jewish people had successfully gained their independence from the British. Weil, "Lost Israelites," p. 224.

23. Chireau and Deutsch, *Black Zion*, pp. 4, 7.

24. Weil, "Lost Israelites," pp. 221–222, 230.

25. Changte L. Hminga, *Christianity and the Lushai People* (1963), quoted in Weil, "Lost Israelites," p. 228.

26. Anthony D. Smith, "The Supersession of Nationalism," *International Journal of Comparative Sociology* 31 (1990): 10ff.

27. A more contextual analysis is needed within the prevailing discourse of democratization, civil society, and religious freedom that cannot be accomplished within the confines of the present book. In fact, no important nationalist movement has sprung directly out of an independent church or messianic movement: in South Africa, churches have led their trajectory in parallel to that of political nationalism, neither one supporting the other; in West Africa, where the colonial presence has been less oppressive, a direct expression of political nationalism has been possible, and "churches" not repressed by colonial authorities do not need political allies. See Terence O. Ranger, "Religious Movements and Politics in Sub-Saharan Africa," *African Studies Review* 29, no. 2 (1986): 1–63.

28. John Lofland and Rodney Stark, "Becoming a World-Saver: A Theory of Conversion to a Deviant Perspective," *American Sociological Review* 30 (1965): 862–875.

29. Arthur D. Nock, *Conversion: The Old and the New in Religion from Alexander the Great to Augustine of Hippo* (Oxford: Clarendon Press, 1933), p. 14. Also Gary Porton, *The Stranger within Your Gates* (Chicago: University of Chicago Press, 1994).

30. Beckford, "New Religious Movements and Globalization," p. 255.

31. The term *alternative spirituality* typically denotes an eclectic constellation of religious and spiritual phenomena situated outside the religious mainstream of a society's respective culture. Timothy Miller, "Introduction," in *America's Alternative Religions*, ed. Timothy Miller (Albany: State University of New York Press, 1995), pp. 1–10.

32. Smith, "Supersession," p. 15.

Bibliography

Abitbol, Michel. "Juifs maghrébins et commerce transsaharien du VIII au XV è siècle." Etudes 5–6, in *2000 ans d'histoire africaine: Le sol, la parole et l'écrit*. Paris: Bibliothèque d'Histoire d'Outre-mer, 1981.

———. "Les Daggatoun, tribu d'origine juive demeurant dans le désert du Sahara." *Les Cahiers du Judaïsme* 10 (Autumn 2001): 79–82.

Acosta, José de. *Historia Natural y Moral de las Indias*. Madrid: Cultura Hispánica, 1998. Vol. 1, chap. 23.

Addai-Sebo, Akyaaba, and Wong Ansel. *Our Story: A Handbook of African History and Contemporary Issues*. London: London Strategy Policy Unit, 1988.

Adler, Elkan N. *Jewish Travellers: A Treasury of Travelogues from Nine Centuries*. London: Bloch Publishers, 1930.

Al-Bakri. *Description de l'Afrique septentrionale*. Translated by Baron de Slane. Alger, 1913.

Anderson, Andrew R. *Alexander's Gate: Gog and Magog and the Inclosed Nations*. Cambridge: MA: Mediaeval Academy of America, 1932.

Anderson, Benedict. *Imagined Communities: Reflections on the Origin and Spread of Nationalism*. London: Verso, 1991.

Andriamirado, Sennen. "Juifs, noirs et maliens." *Jeune Afrique* 1879 (January 8–14, 1997): 20–22.

Appiah, Kwame A. *In My Father's House: Africa in the Philosophy of Culture*. New York: Oxford University Press, 1992.

Asante, Molefi K. *The Afrocentric Idea*. Philadelphia: Temple University Press, 1987.

Atanda, Joseph A. "The Historian and the Problem of Origins of Peoples in Nigeria." *Journal of the Historical Society of Nigeria* 10, no. 3 (1980): 70–73.

Auber, Charles A. *Histoire et théorie du symbolisme religieux avant et depuis le christianisme*. Paris: A. Frank, 1871.

Avichail, Rabbi Eliahu. *The Tribes of Israel: The Lost and the Dispersed*. Jerusalem: Zur-Ot Press, 5765.

Bader, Charles. *Les Yibro, mages Somali, les Juifs oubliés de la Corne de l'Afrique*. Paris: L'Harmattan, 2000.

Baeten, Elisabeth. *The Magic Mirror*. Albany: State University of New York Press, 1996.

Baines, Thomas. *The Gold Region of South Eastern Africa*. London: Stanford, 1877.

Baldson, John P. V. D. *Romans and Aliens*. Chapel Hill: University of North Carolina Press, 1979.

Baritz, Loren. "The Idea of the West." *American Historical Review* 66 (1960–1961): 618–640.

Barret, Leonard. *The Rastafarians: Sounds of Cultural Dissonance*. Boston: Beacon Press, 1988.

Basden, George T. *Among the Ibos of Nigeria*. Philadelphia: Lippincott, 1921.

Beach, D. N. *The Shona and Zimbabwe, 900–1850: An Outline of the Shona History*. London: Heinemann, 1980.

Beaumier, Auguste. *Premier établissement des Israélites à Tombouctou*. Paris: Imprimerie E. Martinet, 1871.

Beckford, James. "Religious Movements and Globalization." In *Global Social Movements*, edited by Robin Cohen and Shirin Rai, pp. 253–264. London: Athelone Press, 2000.

Ben Israël, Menasseh. *Hope of Israel*. Introduction and notes by Henri Mechoulan and Gerard Nahon. New York: Oxford University Press, 1987.

Ben-Jochannen, Yosef. *Africa: Mother of Western Civilization*. Baltimore: Black Classic Press, 1988.

———. *We the Black Jews: Witness to the "Jewish Race" Myth*. Baltimore: Black Classic Press, 1993.

Benbassa, Esther. *La souffrance comme identité*. Paris: Fayard, 2007.

Bennett, Robert. "Africa and the Biblical Period." *Harvard Theological Review* 64 (1971): 483–500.

Bent, J. Theodore. *The Ruined Cities of Mashonaland*. Freeport, NY: Books for Libraries Press, 1971.

Bibliography on Ethiopian Jewry (2001–2004) compiled by Shalva Weil. Addis-Ababa: SOSTEJE, 2004.

Berg, Irving. "The Jewish Descendants of Timbuktu." *Kulanu Newsletter* 9, no. 3 (Fall 2002): 2.

Berger, Graenum. *Black Jews in America: A Documentary with Commentary*. New York: Federation of Jewish Philanthropies, 1978.

Bird, John. *Annals of Natal*. Cape Town: C. Struik, 1965 [1888]. Vol. 1.

Blyden, Edward W. *The Jewish Question*. Liverpool: Lionel Hart, 1898.

Boto'Ora Ballong-Wen-Mewuda, J. "Le rôle de Sao Tome dans l'établissement et le développement du commerce portugais dans le Golfe de Guinée au XVème et XVIème siècle." In *La Découverte, le Portugal et l'Europe*. Actes du colloque, Paris, May 26–28, 1988.

Boulègue, Jean. *Les Luso-Africains de Sénégambie, XVI–XIX ème siècle*. Dakar: Université de Dakar, 1972.
Bowdich, Thomas E. *Mission from Cape Coast Castle to Ashantee*. London: J. Murray, 1819.
Boykin, James H. *Black Jews: A Study in Minority Experience*. Miami: J. H. Boykin, 1996.
Bradley, Mary H. *Caravans and Cannibals*. New York, 1926.
Bradman, Neil, and Mark G. Thomas. "Genetics: The Pursuit of Jewish History by Other Means." *Judaism Today* 10 (Autumn 1998): 4–7.
Brague, Rémi. "Le déni d'humanité." *Lignes* 12 (1990): 217–232.
Breedveld, Anneke, and Mirjam De Bruijn. "L'image des Fulbe: Analyse critique du concept de Pulaaku." *Cahier d'Etudes Africaines* 36, no. 4 (1996): 791–821.
Brenner, Athalya. *Colour Terms in the Old Testament*. Sheffield: JSOT Press, 1982.
Brerewood, Edward. *Enquiries Tracing the Diversity of Languages and Religions through the Chief Parts of the World, 1613*. London: printed for N. Ranew and J. Robinson, 1671.
Briand, Joseph. *L'Hébreu à Madagascar*. Tananarive: Pitot de la Beaujardière, 1946.
Brotz, Howard M. *The Black Jews of Harlem*. New York: Schocken Books, 1970.
———. "The Negro Jewish Community and the Contemporary Race Crisis." *Jewish Social Studies* 1 (1965): 10–17.
Brown, Mervyn. *Madagascar Rediscovered*. London: D. Tunnaclife, 1978.
Brunet, Pierre-Gustave. "La légende du Prêtre Jean." *Extrait des Actes de l'Académie des Sciences, Belles lettres et Arts de Bordeaux*. Bordeaux: C. Lefebvre (1877), pp. 1–27.
Buijs, Gina. "Black Jews in the Northern Province: A Study of Ethnic Identity in South Africa." *Ethnic and Racial Studies* 21 (1998): 661–682.
Bullock, Charles. *The Mashona and the Matabele*. London: Juta, 1950.
Bunsen, Christian K. *Egypt's Place in Universal History: A Historical Investigation*. Translated from the German by C. H. Cotrell. London: Longman, 1859.
Burton, Richard. *The Lake Regions of Central Africa*. Vol. 2. London: Longman Green, 1860.
Bwejeri, Yochannan. *Les Batutsi: L'histoire confisquée*. Brussels: Editions de Havilah, 2001.
Cameron, Reverend J. "On the Early Inhabitants of Madagascar." *Antananarivo Annual* 3 (1877): 257–265.
Campbell, Mary B. *The Witness and the Other World: Exotic European Writing 1400–1600*. Ithaca, NY: Cornell University Press, 1988.
Carmoly, Eliakim. *Relation d'Eldad le Danite, voyageur du IXè siècle*. Paris: Dondé-Duprey, 1838.
Caroll, Scott T. "Solomonic Legend: The Muslims and Great Zimbabwe." *International Journal of African Historical Studies* 21, no. 2 (1988): 233–246.
Cavalli-Sforza, Luigi L. "Genetic Drift in Italian Population." *Scientific American* 221 (1969): 30–37.
Chevannes, Barry. *Rastafari and Other African Caribbean Worldviews*. London: Macmillan, 1995.

Cheyette, Bryan. *Construction of the Jews in English Literature and Society: Racial Representations, 1875–1945*. Cambridge: Cambridge University Press, 1993.
Chidester, David. *Christianity: A Global History*. San Francisco: Harper, 2000.
———. *Patterns of Power: Religion and Politics in American Culture*. Englewood Cliffs, NJ: Prentice-Hall, 1988.
———. *Savage Systems, Colonialism and Comparative Religion in Southern Africa*. Charlottesville: University Press of Virginia, 1996.
Chireau, Yvonne and Nathaniel Deutsch eds. *Black Zion: African American Religious Encounters with Judaism, 1790–1930*. New York: Oxford University Press, 2000.
Chireau, Yvonne. "Black Culture and Black Zion." In *Black Zion: African American Religious Encounters with Judaism, 1790–1930*, edited by Yvonne Chireau and Nathaniel Deutsch, pp. 15–32. New York: Oxford University Press, 2000.
Chittick, H. Neville. "The Coast before the Arrival of the Portuguese." In *Zamani: A Survey of East African History*, edited by B. A. Ogot and J. A. Kieran, pp. 100–118. Nairobi: East African Publication House, 1974.
Chrétien, Jean-Pierre. "Les deux visages de Cham. Point de vue français du XIXè siècle sur les races africaines d'après l'exemple de l'Afrique Orientale." In *L'idée de race dans la pensée politique française contemporaine*, pp. 171–199. Paris: CNRS, 1977.
———. "Missions, pouvoir colonial et pouvoir africain." In *Christianisme et pouvoir politique*, pp. 139–154. Université de Lille III, 1971.
Cleage, Albert. The *Black Messiah*. New York: Sheed and Ward, 1968.
Coelho, Fransisco de Azev. *Descripçao da Costa da Guiné*. Lisbon: Fundo General dos Manuscritos da Biblioteca Nacional, 1669. Ms. 319.
Cohen, Shaye J. D. "Conversion to Judaism in Historical Perspective from Biblical Israel to Post-biblical Judaism." *Conservative Judaism* 36, no. 4 (Summer 1983): 31–45.
Cohen, Steven. "Was Judaism in Antiquity a Missionary Religion in Ancient Times?" In *Jewish Assimilation*, edited by Menachem Mor, pp. 13–33. Lanham, MD: University Press of America, 1992.
Colenso, John W. "Church Missions among the Heathen in the Diocese of Natal," 1854. Pietermaritzburg, South Africa: University of Natal Press, 1982.
———. "The Diocese of Natal." *Monthly Record of the Society of the Propagation of the Gospel in Foreign Parts* 4 (November 1853): 241–264.
———. *The Pentateuch and Book of Joshua Critically Examined*. Vol. 1. London: Longman, Robert and Green, 1862–1879.
Colin, Georges S. "Des Juifs nomades retrouvés dans le Sahara marocain au XVIè siècle." In *Mélanges Lopes-Cernival*. Lisbon: Portugalia Editora, 1945.
Comaroff, Jean, and John Comaroff. *Of Revelation and Revolution: Christianity, Colonialism, and Consciousness in South Africa*. Vol. 1. Chicago: University of Chicago Press, 1991.
Comaroff, John. *Body of Power, Spirit of Resistance: The Culture and History of South African People*. Chicago: University of Chicago Press, 1985.
Connah, Graham. *African Civilisations, Precolonial States and Cities in Tropical Africa: An Archaeological Perspective*. Cambridge: Cambridge University Press, 2001.

Cooper, Frederick. "Conflict and Connection: Rethinking Colonial African History." *American Historical Review* 99 (1997): 1515–1545.

Coote, Robert B., and Keith W. Whitelam. *The Emergence of Early Israel in Historical Perspective.* Sheffield: Almond Press, 1987.

Corcos, Alain F. *The Myth of the Jewish Race: A Biologist's Point of View.* Cransbury: Lehigh University Press, 2005.

Corinaldi, Michael. *The Enigma of Jewish Identity: The Law of Return, Theory and Practise.* Jerusalem: Magnes Press, 2001.

———. *Jewish Identity: The Case of the Ethiopian Jewry.* Jerusalem: Rubin Mass, 1998.

Cornevin, Robert. *Histoire de l'Afrique.* Vol. 2. Paris: Payot, 1967.

Councill, William H. *Lamp of Wisdom; Or Race History Illuminated.* Nashville, TN: Haley, 1898.

Courlander, Harold. *Negro-Folk Music.* New York: Columbia University Press, 1963.

Court de Gebelin, Antoine. *Le monde primitif.* Vol. 1. 1773–1782.

Cronon, Edmund. *Black Moses: The Story of Marcus Garvey and the Universal Negro Improvement Association.* Madison: University of Wisconsin Press, 1969.

Cuoq, Joseph. *Recueil des sources Arabes concernant l'Afrique occidentale du VIII è au XVI è siècle. Bilad al-Sudan.* Paris: CNRS, 1975.

Curtin, Philip ed. *Africa Remembered: Narratives by West Africans from the Era of the Slave Trade.* Madison: University of Wisconsin Press, 1967.

Daneel, M. L. *Old and New in Southern Shona Independent Churches.* Vol. 1. The Hague: Mouton, 1971.

Dash, J. Michael. *Literature and Ideology in Haiti 1915–1961.* Totowa. NJ: Barnes and Noble, 1981.

Daston, Lorraine. "Marvellous Facts and Miraculous Evidence in Early Europe." *Critical Inquiry* 18 (1991): 92–124.

Davidson, Basil. *The African Past: Chronicles from Antiquity to Modern Times.* Boston: Little, Brown, 1964.

———. *The Lost Cities of Africa.* Boston: Little, Brown, 1959.

Davidson, Jeffery. "Shabbat with a Committed Group in Nigeria." *Kulanu Newsletter* 11, no. 1 (Spring 2004): 1, 12.

Defert, Daniel. "The Collection of the World: Accounts of Voyages from the Sixteenth to the Eighteenth Centuries." *Dialectical Anthropology* 7, no. 1 (1982): 11–22.

Delafosse, Maurice. "Les Hamites de l'Afrique Orientale." *L'Anthropologie* 5 (1894): 157–171.

———. *Haut-Sénégal-Niger.* Vol. 1 and 2. Paris: Larose, 1912.

Delany, Martin R. *Principia of Ethnology: The Origins of Races and Colour....* Philadelphia: Harper and Brothers, 1879.

Delcor, Mathias. "La reine de Saba et Salomon. Quelques aspects de la légende et de sa formation principalement dans le monde juif et éthiopien, à partir des textes bibliques." In *Tradició I Traducció de la paraula: Miscel. Lània Giu Camps,* edited by F. Raurelt, pp. 309–310. Barcelona: Publicacions de l'Abadia de Montserrat, 1993.

Deluz, Christiane. *Le livre de Jehan de Mandeville: Une géographie au XIVème siècle.* Louvain: Institut d'Etudes Médiévales de l'Université de Louvain, 1988.

Deniker, Joseph. *The Races of Man.* New York: Scribner's, 1906.
Deschamps, Hubert. *Histoire de Madagascar.* Paris: Berger-Levrault, 1960.
Devisse, Jean. *L'image du Noir dans l'art occidental.* Paris: Bibliothèque des Arts, 1979.
———. "Routes de commerce et échanges en Afrique occidentale en relation avec la Méditerranée: Un essai sur le commerce africain médiéval du XIè au XVIè siècle." *Revue d'Histoire Economique et Sociale* 1, no. 10 (1972): 42–73.
Diner, Hasia. *In the Almost Promise- Land: American Jews and Blacks, 1915–1935.* Baltimore: John Hopkins University Press, 1995.
Doresse, Jean. *L'empire du Prêtre Jean.* 2 vols. Paris: Plon, 1957.
Douglas, Mary. *Purity and Danger.* London: Routledge and Kegan Paul, 1966.
Du Bois, William E. B. *Dusk of Dawn: An Essay towards the Autobiography of a Race Concept.* New York: Harcourt, 1940.
———. *The Negro.* New York: Schocken Books, 1915.
Duràn, Diego. *Historia de las Indias de Nueva España e Islas de Tierra Firme.* Vol. 1. Edited by J. F. Ramirez. Mexico City: Porrúa, 1967.
Duveyrier, Henri. *Sahara algérien et tunisien: Journal de route.* Paris: Challamel, 1905.
Easton, Hosea. *A Treatise on the Intellectual Character and the Political Condition of the Coloured People of the United States and the Prejudice Exercised towards Them.* Philadelphia: Historic Publications, 1969.
Edgar, Robert. *Because They Chose the Plan of God: The Story of the Bulhoek Massacre.* Johannesburg: Raven Press, 1988.
Ehrman, Albert. "The Commandment Keepers: A Negro Jewish Cult in America Today." *Judaism* 8, no. 3 (1959): 267–270.
Eilberg-Schwartz, Howard. *The Savage in Judaism: An Anthropology of Israelite Religion and Ancient Judaism.* Bloomington: Indiana University Press, 1990.
Eiseley, Loren. *Darwin's Century: Evolution and the Men Who Discovered It.* London: V. Gallancz, 1959.
Eliade, Mircea. *Aspects du Mythe.* Paris: Gallimard, 1963.
———. *Shamanism: Archaic Techniques of Ecstasy.* Translated from the French by Willard E. Trask. Princeton, NJ: Princeton University Press, 1972.
Epstein, Lawrence J. *Theory and Practice of Welcoming Converts.* Lewiston, NY: Mellen Press, 1992.
Equiano, Olauda. *The Interesting Narratives of the Life of Olaudah Equianao or Gustavus Vassa the African.* London, 1789.
Exham, Irving, and Karla Poewe. *New Religions as Global Culture.* Boulder, CO: Westview, 1997.
Fauset, Arthur H. *Black Gods of the Metropolis: Negro Religious Cults of the Urban North.* Philadelphia: University of Pennsylvania Press, 1944.
Fauvelle, François-Xavier. *L'Afrique de Cheikh Anta Diop.* Paris: Karthala, 1996.
———. "L'Afrocentrisme entre révision de l'histoire et quête d'identité." *Les Temps Modernes* 53, no. 600 (1998): 285–302.
Fay, C., ed. "Identité et appartenances dans les sociétés sahéliennes." *Cahiers des Sciences Humaines* 31, no. 2 (1995): 329–363.

Felton, Bruce. "The Origin of America's Black Jews." *Jewish Digest* 29 (November 1974): 12–16.
Féraud, Laurent C. "Kitab el-Adouani, ou le Sahara de Constantine et de Tunis." In *Recueil des notices et mémoires de la Société Archéologique de Constantine* (1867).
Ferrand, Gabriel. "Les migrations musulmanes et juives à Madagascar." *Revue de l'Histoire des Religions* I, tome 52 (1905): 381–417.
Ferris, William H. *The African Abroad or, His Evolution in Western Civilization*. New Haven, CT: Tuttle, 1913.
Fischer, Walter J. *Unknown Jews in Unknown Lands: The Travels of Rabbi D'Beth Hillel 1824–1832*. New York: KTAV, 1973.
Flacourt, Etienne de. *Histoire de la grande île de Madagascar*. Paris: A. Lesselin, 1658. Paris: G. Clouzier, 1661.
Fleming, Francis. *Southern Africa: A Geography and Natural History of the Country, Colonies and Its Inhabitants*. London: Arthur Hall Virtue, 1856.
Forbes, Ella. "African-American Resistance to Colonization." *Journal of Black Studies* 21, no. 2 (1990): 210–223.
Forster, John Reinhold. *Observations Made during a Voyage round the World on Physical Geography, Natural History and Ethnic Philosophy*. London: G. Robinson, 1778.
Foucault, Michel. *The Order of Things: An Archaeology of the Human Science*. New York: Pantheon, 1971.
Frazer, James G. *The Native Races of Africa and Madagascar*. London: Lund, Humphries, 1938.
Frazier, Edward F. *The Negro in the United States*. New York: Macmillan, 1949.
Funnye, Rabbi Capers C. "Awakening and In-Gathering of the Ibos." *Kulanu Newsletter* 10, no. 3 (Autumn 2003): 8.
Garcia, Gregorio. *Origen de los Indios del Nuevo Mondo*. Vol. I, III. Madrid: F. Martinez Abad, 1729.
Gardiner, Allen. *Narrative of a Journey to the Zoolu Country in South Africa Undertaken in 1835*. London: William Crofts, 1836.
Garlake, Peter S. *Great Zimbabwe*. New York: Stein and Day, 1974.
Gauthier, Emile F. *Le passé de l'Afrique du Nord, les siècles obscurs*. Paris: Payot, 1937.
———. *Le Sahara*. Paris: Payot, 1928.
Gayre of Gayre, Robert. "The Lembas or Vendas of Vendaland." *Mankind Quarterly* 8 (1967): 3–15.
Geertz, Clifford. *The Interpretation of Cultures*. New York: Basic Books, 1973.
Génébrard, Gilbert. *Chronographia in duos libros distincta*. Lovanii: apud J.Foulerum, 1570.
Gershowitz, Michael V. "The Ghanaian Village That Wants to Be Jewish." *Kulanu Newsletter* 6, no. 3 (Autumn 1999): 3, 14; 6, no. 4 (Winter 1999): 2, 11; and 6, no. 5 (Spring 2000): 3, 11.
Gevrey, Alfred. *Essai sur les Iles Comores*. Pondichéry: A. Saligny, 1870.
Gilman, Sander L. "The Jewish Nose: Are Jews White? Or the History of the Nose Job." Chap. 16 in *The Other in Jewish Thought and History*, edited by Laurence Silberstein and Robert L. Cohen. New York: New York University Press, 1994.

———. *Jewish Self-Hatred*. Baltimore: John Hopkins University Press, 1986.
———. *On Blackness without Blacks: Essays on the Image of the Black in Germany*. Boston: G. K. Hall, 1982.
Gilroy, Paul. *The Black Atlantic: Modernity and Double Consciousness*. Cambridge, MA: Harvard University Press, 1993.
Ginzburg, Carlo. *Clues, Myths and the Historical Method*. Baltimore: John Hopkins University Press, 1989.
Gliozzi, Guiliano. *Adam et le Nouveau Monde: La naissance de l'anthropologie comme idéologie coloniale: Des généalogies bibliques aux théories raciales*. Translated by A. Estève and P. Gabelonne. Lecques: Théétète, 2000.
Gobineau, Joseph A. de. *Essai sur l'inégalité des races humaines*. Paris, 1884, [1853–1855].
Godbey, Allen H. *The Lost Tribes a Myth: Suggestions towards Rewriting Hebrew History*. Durham, NC: Duke University Press, 1974.
Goiten, Shlomo D. *Jews and Arabs: Their Contacts through the Ages*. 3rd ed. New York: Schocken Books, 1974.
Gow, Bonar A. *Madagascar and the Protestant Impact: The Work of the British Missions 1815–1855*. London: Longman, 1979.
Grandidier, Alfred. *Histoire physique, naturelle et politique de Madagascar, Ethnographie*. Paris: Imprimerie Nationale, 1908.
Grandidier, Alfred, and Guillaume Grandidier. *Collection des ouvrages anciens concernant Madagascar*. Vol. 2. Paris: Comité de Madagascar, 1903–1920.
Graves, Robert, and Raphael Patai. *Hebrew Myths: The Book of Genesis*. London: Cassell, 1964.
Greenblatt, Stephen. *Marvellous Possessions: The Wonder of the New World*. Chicago: University of Chicago Press, 1991.
Grelot, Pierre. *Documents araméens d'Egypte, littérature ancienne du Proche-Orient*. Paris: Editions du Cerf, 1972.
Gsell, Stéphane. *Histoire ancienne de l'Afrique du Nord*. Vol. 7. Osnabrück: O. Zeller, 1972.
Gueunier, Noël J. "La Genèse de l'Homme Blanc: Récits d'origine du Sud-Ouest de Madagascar." *Etudes Ocean Indien* 15 (1992): 227–259.
Gurock, Jeffrey S. *When Harlem Was Jewish, 1870–1930*. New York: Columbia University Press, 1979.
Hackett, Rosalind I. J. "Revitalization in African Traditional Religion." In *African Traditional Religions in Contemporary Society*, edited by J. K. Olupona, pp. 135–148. New York: Paragon House, 1991.
Haidara, Ismael D. "La synagogue, le marché, le cimetière." *Tapama* 1 (December 1996): 3–5.
———. *Les Juifs à Tombouctou: Recueil des sources juives écrites relatives au commerce juif à Tombouctou au XIX è siècle*. Bamako: Ed. Donniya, 1999.
Halévy, Joseph. "Lettre à monsieur d'Abadie sur l'origine asiatique des langues du nord de l'Afrique." *Actes de la Société Philologique*, June 1–2, 1869, pp. 29–46.
Halkin, Hillel. "Wandering Jews—and Their Genes." *Commentary*, September 2000, pp. 58–60.

Hall, Stuart. *Representation: Cultural Representations and Signifying Practises*. Thousand Oaks: Sage, 1997.

Hanke, Lewis. *The First Social Experiments in America*. Cambridge, MA: Harvard University Press, 1935.

Harrison, Faye V. "The Persistent Power of Race." *Annual Review of Anthropology* 24 (1992): 47–74.

Harrison, Geoffrey A., et al. *Human Biology: An Introduction to Human Evolution*. New York: Oxford University Press, 1964.

Henry, Maureen. *The Intoxication of Power: An Analysis of Civil Religion in Relation to Ideology*. Dordrecht, Netherlands: D. Reidel, 1979.

Herskowitz, Melville. *The Myth of the Negro Past*. Boston: Beacon Press, 1941.

Hess, Robert L. "The Itinerary of Benjamin of Tudela: A Twelfth-Century Jewish Description of North-East Africa." *Journal of African History* 6 (1956): 15–24.

Hirschberg, Haim Z. *History of the Jews in North Africa*. Leiden: Brill, 1974.

Hirschberg, Haim Z. *History of the Jews in North Africa*. 2d rev. ed., 2 vols. Leiden: Brill, 1974.

Holl, Augustin. "West African Archaeology: Colonialism and Nationalism." In *A History of African Archaeology*, edited by Peter Robertshaw, pp. 296–308. London: J. Currey, 1990.

Hopkins, Antony G. *An Economic History of West Africa*. London: Longman, 1980.

Houdas, Octave, and Maurice Delafosse. *Tarikh el-Fettach*. Paris: Adrien Maisonneuve, 1964.

Howe, Stephen. *Afrocentrism: Mythical Pasts and Imagined Homes*. London: Verso, 1998.

Huddleston, Eldrige L. *Origins of the American Indians: European Concepts, 1492–1729*. Austin: University of Texas Press, 1967.

Hunwick, John O. *Shari'a in Songhay: The Replies of al-Maghili to the Questions of Askia al-Hadj Muhammad*. New York: Oxford University Press, 1985.

Hyamson, Albert M. "The Lost Tribes and the Influence of the Search for Them on the Return of the Jews to England." *Jewish Quarterly Review* 15 (1903): 640–645.

Ibn Khaldun. *Histoire des Berbères et des dynasties musulmanes de l'Afrique septentrionale*. Vol. 1. Translated by Baron de Slane. Alger, 1852.

Ibn Khurdadbeh. *Description du Maghreb et de l'Europe au IIIè/IXè siècles*. Published and translated by Muhammad Hadj Sadock. Alger, 1949.

Ikeanyibe, Uche P. *The Quest for the Origin of Igbo People*. Lagos, Nigeria: Aikmay, 1999.

Ilona, Remi. "Ibo Greetings." *Kulanu Newsletter* 10, no. 1 (Spring 2003): 4.

———. *The Igbos: Jews in Africa?* Abuja, Nigeria: Mega Press, 2004, reedited 2005.

———. "Mr. Green Comes to Nigeria." *Kulanu Newsletter* 10, no. 4 (Winter 2003–2004): 13.

Jacques, A. A. "Notes on the Lemba Tribe of the Northern Transvaal." *Anthropos* 26, no. 3 (1931): 248–260.

Jaovelo-Dzao, Robert. "Richesses culturelles d'une civilisation de l'oralité." In *Madagascar et le Christianisme*, edited by Bruno Hübsch, pp. 69–92. Paris: Karthala, 1993.

Jeffreys, M. D. W. "An Extinct Jewish Colony." *Jewish Affairs*, November 1954: 47–48.
Jensen, Adolf E. "Beziehungen zwischen dem Alten Testament und der Nilotischen Kultur in Afrika." In *Culture in History: Essays in Honour of Paul Radin*. Edited by Diamond Stanley. New York: Columbia University Press, 1960.
Johnson, Charles. S. *The Negro in American Civilization*. New York: Holt, 1930.
Johnson, Samuel. *The History of the Yorubas*. London: Routledge, 1921.
Johnston, Sir Harry H. *A History of the Colonisation of Africa by Alien Races*. Cambridge: The University Press, 1899.
Junod, Henri A. "The Balemba of Soutspanberg." *Folklore* 19, no. 3 (1908): 277–287.
———. *The Life of a South African Tribe*. London: MacMillan, 1927.
Kagame, Alexis. "Les Hamites du Rwanda et du Burundi sont-ils des Galla?" *Académie Royale des Sciences d'Outre-Mer* 2 (1956): 314–356.
Kammerer, Albert. *Essai sur l'histoire antique d'Abyssinie: Le royaume d'Aksum et ses voisins d'Arabie et de Méroé*. Paris: P. Geuthner, 1926.
Kaplan, Jonathan M. *The Limits and Lies of Human Genetic Research: Dangers of Social Policy*. New York: Routledge, 2000.
Kaplan, Steven. *The Beta Israel (Falasha) in Ethiopia*. New York: New York University Press, 1992.
———. "If There Are No Races: How Can Jews Be a 'Race'?" *Modern Jewish Studies* 2, no. 1 (2003): 79–96.
———. "The Invention of Ethiopian Jews: Three Models." *Cahiers d'Etudes Africaines* 132, no. 33 (1994): 645–658.
Kaplan, Steven, and Chaim Rosen. "Created in Their Own Image: A Comment on Beta Israel Figurines." *Cahiers d'Etudes Africaines* 36, nos. 141–142 (1996): 171–182.
Berger Natalia, and Kay Kaufman Shelemay. *The Jews in Ethiopia: A People in Transition*, edited by Yehuda Avner et al. Tel Aviv: Beth Hatefusoth, 1986.
Keane, Augustus H. *The Gold of Ophir, Whence Brought and by Whom*. New York: Negro University Press, 1969.
Kebra Nagast. The Queen of Sheba and Her Only Son Meneyelek: Being the "Book of the Glory of Kings." Translated by E. A. Wallis Budge. London: Kegan Paul, 2001.
Kehimkar, Haim S. *The History of the Bene Israel of India*. Tel Aviv: Dayag Press, 1937.
Kennes, Erick. "Judaïsation des Tutsi: Identité ou stratégie de conquête." *Grands Lacs Confidentiel*, March 18, 2000.
Kent, Raymond. *Early Kingdoms in Madagascar, 1500–1700*. New York: Holt, Rinehart and Winston, 1970.
———. "The Sakalava, Maroserana, Dady and Tromba before 1700." *Journal of African History* 9, no. 4 (1963): 517–546.
Kepel, Gilles. *A l'ouest d'Allah*. Paris: Seuil, 1996.
Kesteloot, Lilyan, C. Barbey, and S. Ndongo. "Tyamaba, mythe Peul." *Notes Africaines* 185–186 (IFAN-Dakar, January–April 1985): 35–42.
King, Kenneth J. "Some Notes on Arnold J. Ford and the New World Black Attitudes to Ethiopia." *Journal of Ethiopian Studies* 10, no. 1 (1972): 81–87.
Knox, Robert. *Races of Men*. London: H. Renshaw, 1862.

Kolb, Peter. *The Present State of the Cape of Good Hope: Or, A Particular Account of the Several Nations of the Hottentots: Their Religion, Government, Laws, Customs, Ceremonies and Opinions: Their Art of War, Professions, Languages, Genesis, etc.* Vol. 1. Translated by Guido Medley. London: W. Innis, 1731.

Kuperman, Rabbi David. "Genocide Imminent Against Tutsi of Burundi." *Kulanu Newsletter* 11, no. 3 (Autumn 2004): 12.

La Roncière, Charles de. *La découverte de l'Afrique au moyen age.* Vols. 1 and 2. Cairo, Institut Français d'archéologie orientale, 1924–1925.

Lafitau, Joseph François. *Customs of the American Indians Compared with the Customs of Primitive Times.* Vol. 1. Edited and translated by William N. Fenton and Elisabeth L. Moore. Toronto: Champlain Society, 1974–1977 [1724].

L'Africain, Léon. *Description de l'Afrique.* New edition translated by A. Epaulard and annotated by Theodore Monod, Henri Lhote, and Raymond Mauny. Paris: A. Maisonneuve, 1980.

Lam, Aboubacry M. *De l'origine égyptienne des Peuls.* Paris: Présence Africaine/Khepera, 1993.

Landes, Ruth. "Negro Jews in Harlem." *Jewish Journal of Sociology* 9, no. 2 (1967): 180–181.

Lange, Dierk. *Ancient Kingdoms of West Africa: Africa-Centred and Canaanite-Israelite Perspective.* Dettelbach: Röll, 2004.

Law, David A. *From Samaria to Samarkand: The Ten Lost Tribes of Israel.* Lanham, MD: University Press of America, 1992.

Lefkowitz, Mary. *Not Out of Africa: How Afrocentrism Became an Excuse to Teach Myth as History.* New York: Basic Books, 1996.

Levering, Lewis D. "Shortcuts to Mainstream: Afro-American Notables in the 1920s and 1930s." In *Jews in Black Perspectives,* edited by Joseph Washington, pp. 83–94. Rutherford, NJ: Farleigh Dickinson University Press, 1984.

Leverton, Basil. *Records of Natal.* Vol. 1. Pretoria: Government Printers, 1984.

Lewicki, Tadeusz. "L'Afrique noire dans le Kitab al-Masalik wa l-Mamedik d'al-Bakri (XIè siècle)." *Africana Bulletin* 2 (1965): 9–14.

Lewontin, Richard. *Biology as Ideology: The Doctrine of DNA.* New York: Harper-Perennial, 1993.

Lhote, Henri. *Les Touareg du Hoggar.* Paris: A. Colin, 1984.

Lieberman, Jeff L. "Taking the Long Way Around: Nigerians Who Feel Connected to the Lost Tribes Return to Judaism." *Jewish Independent,* Vancouver, March 24, 2006.

Littmann, Enno, ed. *The Legend of the Queen of Sheba in the Tradition of Axum.* Leiden: Brill, 1904.

Livingstone, David. *Missionary Travels and Researches in South Africa.* London: J. Murray, 1899.

Lobagola, *Histoire d'un sauvage africain par lui-même.* Translated from the English by G. M. Drucker. Paris: Albin Michel, 1932.

Lucas, André J. "Considérations sur l'ethnique maure et en particulier sur une race ancienne: Les Bafours." *Journal de la Société des Africanistes* 1 (1931): 151–194.

Lucas, Phillip C., and Thomas Robin, eds. *New Religious Movements in the Twenty-first Century*. New York: Routledge, 2004.
Lugard, Frederick J. *The Rise of Our East African Empire*. Edinburgh: Blackwood, 1893.
Lyman, Stanford L. "The Lost Tribes of Israel as a Problem in History and Sociology." *International Journal of Politics, Culture and Society* 12, no. 1 (1998): 7–42.
Lynch, Hollis R. "A Black Nineteenth- Century Response to Jews and Zionism: The Case of Edward Wilmot Blyden." In *Jews in Black Perspectives*, edited by Joseph Washington, pp. 42–54. Rutherford, NJ: Fairleigh Dickinson University Press, 1984.
———. *Edward Wilmot Blyden: Pan-Negro Patriot*. New York: Oxford University Press, 1967.
Maïga, I. "L'éveil de la communauté juive malienne" *Le Républicain*, March 27, 1996.
Mandeville, Sir John. *Mandeville's Travels*. London: Hakluyt Society, 1953.
Maquet, Jacques. *The Premise of Inequality in Ruanda: A Study of Political Relations in a Central African Kingdom*. Ann Arbor, MI: UMI, 1994.
Margoliouth, David S. *The Relations between Arabs and Israelites Prior to the Rise of Islam*. London: Oxford University Press, 1924.
Martin, A. G. P. *A la frontière marocaine—les oasis sahariennes: Gourara, Touat, Tidikelt, Alger*. Paris: Challamel, 1908.
Mathew, G. "The East African Coast until the Coming of the Portuguese." In *The History of East Africa*, edited by Roland Oliver et al., pp. 34–129. Oxford: Clarendon Press, 1963.
Mathivha, M. E. R. *The Basena/Vamwenye/Balemba*. South Africa: Morester Printers, 1992.
Mauny, Raymond. "Le Judaïsme, les Juifs et l'Afrique occidentale." *IFAN* 11, no. 3–4 (1949): 354–378.
———. *Tableau géographique de l'ouest africain au moyen age d'après les sources écrites*. Dakar: IFAN, 1961.
Mayer, Jean-F. "Les Abayudaya de l'Ouganda enfin reconnus comme juifs." *Religioscope*, March 18, 2002.
McCall, Daniel F. *Africa in Time Perspective*. Boston: Boston University Press, 1964.
McClintock, Anne. *Imperial Leather: Race, Gender, and Sexuality in the Colonial Context*. New York: Routledge, 1995.
McGaffey, Wyatt. "Concepts of Race in the Historiography of North East Africa." *Journal of African History* 7, no. 1 (1966): 1–17.
Medeiros, François de. *L'Occident et l'Afrique (XIIIe–XVe siècle)*. Paris: Karthala, 1985.
Meek, Charles K. *Northern Tribes of Nigeria*. Vol. 2. London: Oxford University Press, 1925.
Melamed, Abraham. "The Discovery of America in Jewish Literature of the Sixteenth and Seventeenth Centuries." In *Be-Ikvot Columbus: Amerika 1492–1992*, edited by M. Eliav-Feldon, pp. 443–462. Jerusalem: Merkaz Shazar and The Historical Society of Israel, 1997.
———. *The Image of the Black in Jewish Culture*. London: Routledge Curzon, 2002.
Melman, Yossi. "Jewish Cousins." *Ha'Aretz*, March 30, 2001.

Mendelssohn, Sidney. "Judaic or Semitic Legends and Customs among South African Natives." Journal of the Royal African Society 14 (1914): 24–34.

Mentzel, O. F. *A Geographical and Topographical Description of the Cape of Good Hope, 1785–87*. Edited by H. J. Mandelbrote. Cape Town: Van Riebeeck Society, 1944.

Michaeli, Ethan. "Another Exodus: The Hebrew Israelites from Chicago to Dimona." In *Black Zion: African American Encounters with Judaism*, edited by Yvonne Chireau and Nathaniel Deutsch, pp. 73–87. New York: Oxford University Press, 2000.

Miles, William F. S. "Hamites—Hebrews: Problems in 'Judaizing' the Rwandan Genocide." *Journal of Genocide Research, Social Science and Politics and International Relations* 1, no. 2 (March 2000): 107–115.

Miller, Timothy. "Introduction." In *America's Alternative Religions*, edited by Timothy Miller, pp. 1–10. Albany: State University of New York Press, 1995.

Mobley, Harris W. *The Ghanaian's Image of the Missionary: An Analysis of the Published Critiques of Christian Missionaries by Ghanaians*. Leiden: Brill, 1970.

Monod, Theodore, A. Texeira da Mota, and Richard Mauny. *Fernandes Valentim (1506–1510): Description de la Côte d'Afrique*. Bissau, 1951.

Monteil, Charles. "La légende du Wagadu." *IFAN* 23 (1953): 24–26.

———. "Problèmes du Soudan occidental: Juifs et judaïsés." *Hespéris* 38 (1938): 260–298.

Monteil, Vincent. "Les Juifs d'Ifran." *Hespéris* 35 (1948): 151–160.

Morabito, Vittorio. "Au delà du fleuve de Koush." In *Afrocentrismes*, edited by François-Xavier Fauvelle-Aymar, Jean-P. Chrétien, and Claude-H. Perrot, pp. 319–337. Paris: Karthala, 2000.

Moraes, Nize Izabel de. "La petite côte d'après Francisco de Lemos Coelho (ca 1669)." *IFAN*B 35, no. 2 (1973): 239–268.

Morel, Edmond D. *Affairs of West Africa*. London: Heinemann, 1902.

Morton, Samuel L. *Crania American; or Comparative Views of the Skulls of Various Aboriginal Nations of North and South America*, to which is prefixed an Essay on the Varieties of the Human Species. London: Simpkin, Marshall, 1839.

Moses, Wilson J. *The Golden Age of Black Nationalism, 1850–1925*. New York: Oxford University Press, 1988.

Mound, Gloria. "Judaic Research in the Balearic Islands and Sao Tome." In *Jews in Places You Never Thought Of*, edited by Karen Primack, pp. 60–63. Hoboken, NJ: KTAV, 1998.

Mudimbe, Valentin Y. *The Invention of Africa: Gnosis, Philosophy and the Order of Knowledge*. Bloomington: Indiana University Press, 1988.

Muhammad, Elijah. *Message to the Blackman in America*. Chicago: Muhammad Mosque of Islam no. 2, 1965.

Mullan, James E. *The Arab Builders of Zimbabwe*. Salisbury: Rhodesia Mission, 1969.

Murdock, George P. *Africa, Its Peoples and Their Culture History*. New York: McGraw-Hill, 1959.

Nandhi (Sadiki), Ernest. "Lemba Convince Conference." *Kulanu Newsletter* 10, no. 3 (Autumn 2003): 1.

Ndayongeje, Lazare. "Mythe des origines, idéologie hamitique et violence en Afrique des Grands Lacs: Comprendre et agir." *Grands Lacs Confidentiel*, August 16, 2004.

Neubauer, Adolphe A. "Where Are the Ten Tribes?" *Jewish Quarterly Review* 1 (1889): 14–28, 95–114, 185–201, 408–423.

Norris, Harry T. *The Adventures of Antar*. Warminster: Aris and Philips, 1980.

Norris, John W. *The Ethiopian's Place in the History and His Contribution to the World's Civilization*. Baltimore: Afro-American, 1916.

Nott, Josiah C. "The Negro Race." *Popular Magazine of Anthropology* 3 (1866): 102–118.

Oded, Arye. *Religion and Politics in Uganda: A Study of Islam and Judaism*. Nairobi: East African Publishers, 1995.

Oliel, Jacob. *De Jérusalem à Tombouctou: l'Odysssée saharienne du rabbin Mardochée, 1826–1886*. Paris: Olbia, 1998.

———. *Les Juifs au Sahara*. Paris: CNRS, 1994.

Oliver, Roland H. *The Missionary Factor in East Africa*. London: Longmans, 1952.

Olson, Steve. *Mapping Human History: Discovering the Past through Our Genes*. New York: Houghton Mifflin, 2002.

Pagès, Révérend Père. *Un royaume Hamite au centre de l'Afrique*. Brussels: G. van Campenhout, 1933.

Parfitt, Tudor. "Genes, Religion and History." *Jurimetrics* 42, no. 22 (2002): 209–219.

———. "Hebrew in Colonial Discourse." *Journal of Modern Jewish Studies* 2, no. 2 (2003): 159–173.

———. *Journey to the Vanished City*. 1992; New York: Vintage, 2000.

———. *The Lost Tribes of Israel*. London: Weindenfeld and Nicolson, 2000.

Parfitt, Tudor, and Emanuela Trevisan Semi. *Judaising Movements*. London: Routledge Curzon, 2002.

Park, Mungo. *Voyage dans l'intérieur de l'Afrique*. Translated by Jean H. Castera. Paris: Maspero, 1980.

Patai, Raphael, and Patai, Jennifer. *The Myth of the Jewish Race*. Detroit, MI: Wayne State University Press, 1989.

Patterson, Oliver. "Slavery and Slave Revolts: A Socio-historical Analysis of the First Marron War, Jamaica, 1655–1740." *Social and Economic Studies* 19, no. 3 (1970): 289–325.

Peel, John David. *Aladura: A Religious Movement among the Yoruba*. London: Oxford University Press, 1968.

Pennington, James W. C. *A Text Book of the Origin and History of the Coloured People…*. Detroit, MI: Negro History Press, 1969 [1841].

Perrot, Claude H. "Premières années de l'implantation du christianisme au Lesotho, 1833–1847." *Cahiers d'Etudes Africaines* 1 (1963): 97–124.

Person-Lynn, Kwaku. *First Word: Black Scholars, Thinkers, Warriors*. New York: Harlem River Press, 1996.

Philip, John. *Researches in South Africa*. Vol. 2. New York: Negro University Press, 1969 [1828].

Philipps, Thomas. *Philipps, 1820, Settler, His Letters*. Edited by A. Keppel-Jones. Pietermaritzburg, South Africa: Shuter and Shooter, 1960.
Pieterse, Jan N. *White on Black: Images of Africa and Blacks in Western Popular Culture*. New Haven, CT: Yale University Press, 1992.
Pirenne, Jacqueline. "Bilqis et Salomon." *Dossiers de l'Archéologie* 33 (1979): 6–10.
Pittard, Eugène. "Contribution à l'étude anthropologique des Ashanti." *L'Anthropologie* 35 (1910–1930): 464–472.
Plessis du, Johannes. *History of Christian Missions in South Africa*. London: Longmans Green, 1911.
Poirier, Charles. "Terre d'islam en Mer Malgache." *Bulletin de l'Académie Malgache*, special issue (1954): 71–116.
Pondopoulo-Sanchez, Anna. "Comment les Peuls sont-ils devenus Juifs?" In "Généalogies rêvées," *Diasporas* 5 (2004), Centre national de recherche scientifique, 87–97.
Popkin, Richard. "The Rise and Fall of the Jewish Indian Theory." In *Menasseh ben Israel and His World*, edited by Yosef Kaplan, Henri Mechoulan, and Richard Popkin, pp. 63–82. Leiden: Brill, 1989.
Porten, Bezalel. *Archives from Elephantine: The Life of an Ancient Jewish Military Colony*. Berkeley: University of California Press, 1968.
Pory, John. *Translation of Leo Africanus*. London: Hakluyt Society, 1896.
Post, Ken. *Arise Ye Starvelings: The Jamaican Labour Rebellion of 1938 and Its Aftermath*. The Hague: Nijhoff, 1978.
Prakash, Gyan. "Subaltern Studies as Post-colonial Criticism." *American Historical Review* 99, no. 5 (1994): 1475–1490.
Pratt, Mary L. "Scratches on the Face of the Country, or, What Mr Barrow Saw in the Land of the Bushmen." In *Race, Writing and Difference*, edited by Louis Gates Jr., pp. 135–162. Chicago: University of Chicago Press, 1985.
Préville, Antoine de. *Les sociétés africaines*. Paris, 1894.
Prichard, James C. *The Natural History of Man*. London: H. Baillère, 1845.
Primack, Karen. "Contemplating Miracles in Uganda." *Kulanu Newsletter* 9, no. 1 (Spring 2002): 6–9.
———. *Jews in Places You Never Thought Of*. Hoboken, NJ: KTAV, 1998.
Quatrefages, Armand de. *Histoire générale des races humaines*. Paris: H. Ennuyer, 1889.
Quirin, James. *The Evolution of the Ethiopian Jews*. Philadelphia: University of Pennsylvania Press, 1992.
Raboteau, Albert J. *Slave Religion*. New York: Oxford University Press, 1978.
Raison-Jourde, Françoise. *Bible et Pouvoir à Madagascar au XIX è siècle. Invention d'une identité chrétienne et construction de l'état (1780–1880)*. Paris: Karthala, 1991.
Rajaonarimanana, Narivelo. *Savoirs arabico-malgaches: La tradition des devins Antemoro, Anakara*. Paris: Inalco, 1990.
Raton Simpson, G. "Political Cultism in West Kingston, Jamaica." *Social and Economic Studies* 4, no. 2 (1955): 133–149.
Ratzel, Friedrich. *History of Mankind*. London: MacMillan, 1896–1898.

Redkey, Edwin. *Black Exodus, Black Nationalism and Back-to-Africa Movements, 1890–1910.* New Haven, CT: Yale University Press, 1969.
Rosaldo, Renato. *Culture and Truth: The Remaking of Social Analysis.* Boston: Beacon Press, 1989.
———. "The Rhetoric of Control: Illongots Viewed as Natural Bandits and Wild Indians." In *The Reversible World: Symbolic Inversion in Art and Society*, edited by Barbara Babcock, pp. 240–257. Ithaca, NY: Cornell University Press, 1978.
Rose, Cowper. *Four Years in Southern Africa.* Vol. 2. London: Colburn and Bentley, 1829.
Rosenberg, Edgar. *From Shylock to Svengali: Jewish Stereotypes in English Fiction.* London: Peter Owen, 1961.
Ross, Dennison. "Prester John and the Empire of Ethiopia." In *Travels and Travellers of the Middle Ages*, edited by Arthur P. Newton, pp. 174–194. New York: Barnes and Noble, 1968.
Rubin, Zeev. "Judaism and Rahmanite Monotheism in the Himyarite Kingdom in the Fifth Century." In *Israel and Ishmael: Studies in Muslim-Jewish Relations*, edited by Tudor Parfitt. New York: St. Martin's Press, 2000.
Ryckmans, Jacques. *L'institution monarchique en Arabie méridionale avant l'Islam.* Louvain: Publications Universitaires, 1951.
Said, Edward. *Orientalism.* New York: Vintage, 1978.
Sala-Mollins, Louis. *Le code noir ou le calvaire de Canaan.* Paris: PUF, 2002.
Salviac, Martial de. *Un peuple antique ou une colonie gauloise au pays de Ménélick: Les Galla, une grande nation africaine.* Cahors: Plantade, 1901.
Salzman, Jack and West Cornel. *Struggles in the Promised Land: Towards a History of Black-Jewish Relations in the United States.* New York: Oxford University Press, 1997.
Sanders, Edith R. "The Hamitic Hypothesis: Its Origin and Functions in Time Perspective." *Journal of African History* 10, no. 4 (1969): 521–532.
Sanders, Ronald. *Lost Tribes and Promised Lands.* Boston: Little, Brown, 1978.
Sanderson, Edgar. *Africa in the Nineteenth Century.* London: Seeley, 1898.
Santamaria, Ulysses. "Le judaïsme dans la culture négro-américaine." *Les Temps Modernes* 444 (July 1983): 62–88.
Santarem, Vicomte de. *Essai sur l'histoire de la cosmographie et de la cartographie.* Paris, 1850.
Schuler, Monica. "Myalism and African Religious Traditions in Jamaica." In *Africa and the Caribbean: The Legacies of a Link*, edited by Margaret E. Crahan and Franklin Knight, pp. 65–79. Baltimore: Johns Hopkins University Press, 1979.
Seligman, Charles G. *Egypt and Negro Africa: A Study in Divine Kinship.* London: Routledge, 1934.
———. *Races of Africa.* London: Oxford University Press, 1966.
———. "Some Aspects of the Hamitic Problem in the Anglo-Egyptian Sudan." *Journal of the Royal Anthropological Institute* 41 (1913): 593–704.
Sémach, Yosef D. "Un rabbin voyageur marocain: Mardochée Abi Serour." *Hesperis* 8 (1928): 385–399.

Senghor, Léopold Sedar. *Négritude et civilisation de l'universel.* Paris: Seuil, 1977.
Sergi, Giuseppe. *The Mediterranean Race.* London: Scoot, 1901.
Shapiro, James S. *Shakespeare and the Jews.* New York: Columbia University Press, 1996.
Sibree, James. *The Great African Island, Chapters on Madagascar, A Popular Account of Recent Researches in the Physical Geography, Geology, and Exploration of the Country and Its Natural History.* London: Trübner, 1880.
Sice, A. D. "Liberia: Pour les Hébreux Israëlites, le Christ était noir." *Présence Africaine* 70 (1969): 233–240.
Silberman, Low H. "The Queen of Sheba in Judaic Tradition." In *Solomon and Sheba*, edited by James B. Pritchard, pp. 65–84. London: Phaidon, 1974.
Simpson, Bob. "Imagined Genetic Communities." *Anthropology Today* 16, no. 3 (June 2000): 3–6.
Singer, Merrill. "Symbolic Identity Formation in an African American Religious Sect: The Hebrew Israelites." In *Black Zion: African American Encounters with Judaism*, edited by Yvonne Chireau and Nathaniel Deutsch, pp.55–72. New York: Oxford University Press, 2000.
Siva Andrade, Elisa. *Les Iles du Cap-Vert de la "Découverte" à l'Indépendance Nationale.* Paris: l'Harmattan, 1996.
Slouschz, Nahum. *Hébraeo-Phéniciens et Judéo-berbères.* Paris: Leroux, 1908.
Smith, Allan. "Delagoa Bay and the Trade of South Africa." In *Pre-colonial African Trade: Essays on Trade in Central and Eastern Africa...*, edited by Richard Gray and David Birmingham, pp. 265–289. New York: Oxford University Press, 1970.
Smith, William R. *Lectures of the Religion of the Semites.* Edinburgh: A. and C. Black, 1889.
Snowden, Frank M. *Blacks in Antiquity: Ethiopians in the Greco-Roman Experience.* Cambridge, MA: Belknap Press of Harvard University Press, 1970.
Siré Abbas Soh. *Chroniques du Fouta sénégalais: Traduites de deux manuscrits arabes inédits de Siré-Abbâs-Soh.* Paris: E. Leroux, 1913.
Speke, John H. *Journal of the Discovery of the Source of the Nile.* Edinburgh: Blackwood, 1863.
Spiro, Melford E. "Religion: Problems of Definition and Explanation." In *Cultural and Human Nature: Theoretical Papers of Melford E. Spiro*, edited by Benjamin Kilborne and L. L. Langness. Chicago: University of Chicago Press, 1987.
Spurdle, Amanda B., and Trefor Jenkins. "The Origins of the Lemba, 'Black Jews' of Southern Africa: Evidence from p12F2 and Other Y-Chromosome Markers." *American Journal of Human Genetics* 59 (1996): 1126–1133.
St, Clair Drake, John Gibbs. "African Diaspora and Jewish Diaspora: Convergence and Divergence." In *Jews in Black Perspectives*, edited by Joseph Washington. Rutherford, NJ: Farleigh Dickinson University Press, 1984.
———. "Détruire le mythe hamitique, devoir des hommes cultivés." *Présence Africaine* 24–25 (1959): 215–230.
———. *The Redemption of Africa and Black Religion.* Chicago: Third World University Press, 1970.

Stayt, Hugh A. *The Bavenda*. New York: Oxford University Press, 1968.
Stillman, Norman A. *Jews of Arab Lands: A History and Source Book*. Philadelphia: Jewish Publication Society in America, 1979.
Stoler, Ann. "Rethinking Colonial Categories: European Communities and the Boundaries of Rule." *Comparative Studies in Society and History* 31 (1989): 134–161.
Strenski, Ivan. *Four Theories of Myth in Twentieth-Century History*. London: Macmillan Press, 1987.
Sundkler, Bengt. *Zulu Zion and Some Swazi Zionists*. London: Oxford University Press, 1976.
Tabari, Muhammad. *Les prophètes et les rois*. Vol. 2. Translated from the Persian by Hermann Zotenberg. Paris: Sindbad, 1984.
Taïeb-Carlen, Sarah. *Les juifs d'Afrique du Nord*. Paris: Ed. Sepia, 2000.
Talbot, Amaury P. *Peoples of Southern Nigeria*. Vol. 1. London: Oxford University Press, 1926.
Theal, George M. *Records of South-eastern Africa, 1898–1903*. Vols. 2 and 6. Cape Town: Struik, 1964.
Thilmans Guy, and Izabel de Moraes. "La description de la Côte de Guinée du Père Baltazar Barreira." *IFAN* 34, série B, no. 1 (1972): 1–50.
Thomas, Keith. *Man and the Natural World: Changing Attitudes in England 1500–1800*. London: Allen Lane, 1983.
Thomas, Mark G., T. Parfitt, D. A. Weiss, A. Skorecki, J. A. Wilson, M. Le Roux, N. Bradman, and D. Y. Goldstein. "Y Chromosomes Travelling South: The Cohen Modal Haplotype and the Origins of the Lemba—the 'Black Jews of Southern Africa.'" *American Journal of Human Genetics* 66 (2000): 674–686.
Thomas, Mark G., Karl Skorecki, Haim Ben-Ami, Tudor Parfitt, Neil Bradman, and David Goldstein. "Origin of Old Testament Priests." *Nature* 394 (July 1998): 138–140.
Thompson, L. C. "The Ba-Lemba of Southern Rhodesia." *Native Affairs Department Annual* 19 (1942): 78–86.
Thompson, Lloyd A. *Romans and Blacks*. London: Routledge, 1989.
Thorowgood, Thomas. *Jews in America or Probabilities That Americans Are of That Race*. London: Slater, 1650.
Tigay, Alan M. "Xhosa Rabbi." *Jewish Digest*, February 1975, pp. 71–75.
Tobin, Diane, Gary A. Tobin, and Scott Rubin. *In Every Tongue*. San Francisco: Institute for Jewish and Community Research, 2005.
Todorov, Tristan. *La découverte de l'Amérique: La question de l'autre*. Paris: Seuil, 1982.
Toit, Stefanus du. "Missionaries, Anthropologists, and the Policies of the Dutch Reformed Church." *Journal of Modern African Studies* 22 (1984): 617–632.
Torquemada, Juan de. *Primera (-tercera) parte de los veinte i uno libros rituales i Monarchia Indiana*. Vol. 1, tome 1, chap. 9. Seville: M. Clavijo, 1615.
Torrey, Charles C. *The Jewish Foundation of Islam*. New York: Jewish Institute of Religion Press, 1933.

Touré, Mahamane. "Tombouctou: Des Juifs américains rendent visite à ceux du Mali." *Le Républicain* 23 (January 19, 1997): 8.

Trémeaux, Pierre. *Voyage au Soudan Oriental et dans l'Afrique septentrionale pendant les années 1847 et 1848*. Vol. 2. Paris: Lacour, 1853.

Trevisan Semi, Emanuela. "Conversion and Judaisation: The Lost Tribes Committees at the Birth of the Jewish State." In *Judaising Movements*, edited by Tudor Parfitt and Emanuela Trevisan Semi, pp. 53–64. London: Routledge Curzon, 2002.

———. "The 'Falashisation' of the Blacks of Harlem." In *Judaising Movements*, edited by Tudor Parfitt and Emanuela Trevisan Semi, pp. 87–110. London: Routledge Curzon, 2002.

———. "Universalisme juif et prosélytisme. L'action de Jacques Faitlovitch, le 'père' des Beta Israel (Falashas)." *Revue de l'Histoire des Religions* 216, no. 2 (1999): 193–211.

Triaud, Jean-L. "Le nom de Ghana, la mémoire en exil, mémoire importée, mémoire appropriée." In *Histoire d'Afrique, les enjeux de mémoire*, edited by Jean-P. Chrétien and Jean-L. Triaud, pp. 235–280. Paris: Karthala, 1999.

Trimingham, J. Spencer. *A History of Islam in West Africa*. London: Oxford University Press, 1970.

Turner, Harold W. *Religious Innovations in Africa*. Boston: G. K. Hall, 1979.

Twaddle, Michael. *Kakungulu and the Creation of Uganda, 1868–1928*. London: James Currey, 1993.

Ullendorf, Edward. *Ethiopia and the Bible*. London: Oxford University Press, 1968.

Van Gennep, Arnold. *Tabou et totémisme à Madagascar*. Paris: E. Leroux, 1904.

Van Warmelo, Nikolas J. *The Classification of Cultural Groups*. In W.E. Hammond-Tooke ed. London: Routledge and Kegan Paul, 1974 [1937].

———. "A Preliminary Survey of the Bantu Tribes of South Africa." *Ethnological Publications* 5 (Pretoria: Government Printer, 1935).

Van Wyk Smith, Malvern. "Waters Flowing from Darkness: The Two Ethiopias in the Early European Image of Africa." *Theoria* 68 (1986): 67–77.

Vansina, Jan. *Oral Tradition: A Study in Historical Methodology*. Chicago: Aldine, 1965.

Vespucci, Amerigo. *"Mundus Novus": Letters to Lorenzo Pietro di Medici 1504–1505*. Translated by George Tyler Northup. Princeton, NJ: Princeton University Press, 1916.

Volney De Chasseboeuf, Constantin-F. *Voyage en Syrie et en Egypte*. Paris: Mouton, 1959 [1787].

Von Sicard, Harald. "Lemba Clans." *Native Affairs Department Annual* 39 (1962): 68–80.

———. *Ngoma Lugundu. Eine afrikanische Bundeslade*. Uppsala: Studia Ethnographica Upsaliensa, 1952.

Webb, C. de B., and J. B. Wright. *The James Stuart Archive of Recorded Oral Evidence Relating to the History of Zulu and Neighbouring Peoples*. Vol. 1. Pietermaritzburg, South Africa: University of Natal Press, 1976, 1986.

Weil, Shalva. *Beyond the Sabatyon: The Myth of the Ten Tribes*. Tel Aviv: Beth Hatefutsoth, Museum of the Jewish Diaspora, 1991.

Wheelwright, C. A. "Native Circumcision Lodges in the Soutpansberg District." *Journal of the Royal Anthropological Institute* 35, no. 5 (1905): 251–255.

Williams, Joseph J. *Hebrewisms of West Africa*. New York: Biblo and Tannen, 1930.

Wilmot, Alexander. *Monomotapa: Its Monuments and Its History....* London: Fisher Unwin, 1896.

Wolf, Lucien, ed. *Jews in the Canary Islands: Being a Calendar of Jewish Cases Extracted from the Records of the Canariote Inquisition in the Collection of Marquis of Bute*. London: Jewish Historical Society of England, 1926.

Wolfson, Bernard J. "Africa, American Jews: Dispelling Myths, Bridging the Divide." In *Black Zion: African American Encounters with Judaism*, edited by Yvonne Chireau and Nathaniel Deutsch. New York: Oxford University Press, 2000.

Wynia, Elly. *The Church of God and Saints of Christ: The Rise of Black Jews*. New York: Garland, 1994.

Young, Robert. *Colonial Desire: Hybridity in Culture and Race*. London: Routledge, 1995.

———. *White Mythologies: Writing History and the West*. London: Routledge, 1990.

Younger, Lawson K. "The Deportations of the Israelites." *Journal of Biblical Literature* 117, no. 2 (Summer 1998): 201–227.

Zachernuk, Philip S. "Of Origins and Colonial Order: Southern Nigerian Historians and the 'Hamitic Hypothesis.'" *Journal of African History* 35, no. 3 (1994): 431–437.

Zadok, Ran. "Notes on the Early History of the Israelites and Judeans in Mesopotamia." *Orientalia* 51 (1982): 391–393.

Zantop, Suzan. *Colonial Fantasies: Conquest, Family and Nation in Pre-colonial Germany, 1770–1880*. Durham, NC: Duke University Press, 1997.

Zeller, Jack. "An Appeal for Help from Kulanu's President." *Kulanu Newsletter* 11, no. 3 (Autumn 2004): 9.

Zoosmann-Diskin, Avshalom. "Are Today's Jewish Priests Descended from the Old Testament Old Ones?" *HOMO: Journal of Comparative Human Biology-Zeitschrift fuer vergleichende Biologie des Menschen* 51 (2000): 2–3.

ONLINE BIBLIOGRAPHY

Baiden, Daniel, and Robert H. Lande. "The Ghanaian Village That Wants to Be Jewish." www.kulanu.org/ghanaghanianvillage.html. Accessed March 30, 2007.

Berg, Irwin M. "Jews in Central Africa." www.kulanu.org/tutsi/jews-africa.html. Accessed April 26, 2007.

Bwejeri, Yochannan. "Havilah and the Tutsi Hebrews." www.kulanu.org/havila. Accessed September 6, 2005.

Cohen, Mindi, and Paul Zeitz. "A Visit with the Jews of Rusape." www.kulanu.org/zimbabwe/visitrusape. Accessed April 26, 2007.

Ellyne, Mark. "The Black Jews of Zimbabwe." www.mindspring.com/~jaypsand/rusape. Accessed July 26, 2006.

———. "A Sabbath in Rusape, Zimbabwe." www.mindspring.com/~jaypsand/rusape.htm. Accessed July 26, 2006.

Funnye, Rabbi Shmuel. "Our People in Nigeria: An Israelite Journey." www.blackjews.org. Accessed March 26, 2007.

Gershowitz, Gabriel J. "Gone to Ghana." www.kulanu.org/ghana/gonetoghana. Accessed April, 5, 2007.

Gold, Rick. "The Jews of Timbuktu." www.kulanu.org/timbuktu/zakhor.html. Accessed April 25, 2007.

Kekki, J. J. "The Genesis of the Abayudaya Community." www.kulanu.org/abayudaya/kakungulu_bk.html. Accessed March 20, 2007.

Klein, Samantha M. "Finding the Jews of Timbuktu: An Account of the Voyage and Interviews with Members of Zakhor in Timbuktu." www.kulanu.org/timbuktu/findingthejewsoftimbuktu. Accessed March 7, 2007.

Millard, Joan. "The Bulhoek Tragedy." Missionalia. www.geocities.com/missionalia/bulhoek.htm. Accessed March 26, 2007.

Okafor-Ogbaji, N. Interview www.kwenu.com/publications/ ojukwu/interview/okafor_ogbaju.htm. Accessed March 30, 2007.

Okpa, Ejike. "20 Pounds to Igbos, Biafrans: Where Is the Rest?" www.usafricaonline.com/twentypounds.html. Accessed March 9, 2007.

Palmer, Joanne. "How a Nice Jewish Boy Became a Chief Rabbi in Nigeria." www/usjc.org/Becoming _Jewish6982.html. Accessed April 25, 2007.

Primack, Karen. "The Renewal of Jewish Identity in Timbuktu."www.kulanu.org/timbuktu/timbuktu.html. Accessed July 9, 2006.

Sand, Jay P. "The Jews of Africa."www.mindspring.com/~jaypsand/rusape. Accessed August 20, 2006.

Serells, M. Mitchell. "An Unusual Society in Cape Verde." www.kulanu.org/cape-verde/verde.html. Accessed April 25, 2007.

Werlin, Louise. "Jews in Cape Verde." [Online] http://www.kulanu.org/cape-verde/verde.html. Accessed April 25, 2007.

Wuriga, Rabson, and Kohen Kossinathi. "Too Euro-centric." www.kulanu.org/zimbawe/tooeurocentric.html. Accessed March 24, 2007.

Index

Abayudaya of Uganda, 161–166, 185
Aby Serour, Mardochée, 110, 139. *See also* Daggatun
Abyssinia. *See* Ethiopia
Aethiopia. *See* Ethiopia
Aethiops, 25, 39, 200n.3
African American Jews, 79–87, 88–89, 92–93, 101, 137, 157, 169
African character of the Jews, 41, 45–49
African genesis, 39
African Jewish identity, 4–6, 83–85, 93, 119, 137, 142, 147, 153, 155, 157, 167, 175, 178, 181, 184, 191–192
Afrocentrism, 8, 71, 73–79, 154, 157, 216n.1
Afrocentrist authors, 74–80
Akenorah, David, 151. *See also* Jews of Ghana
Aladura churches. *See* Peel, John
Alliance of Black Jews, 86, 148
Al-Meghili, 106, 107, 137, 139
American Indians as Jews, 12, 45, 59, 75. *See also* Levi de Montezinos
American Jewish World Service, 147

Amishav, 134
Anderson, Benedict, 181, 188
animism, 149
Antemoro, 128–129, 131, 179, 180, 182
anti-semitism, 114–156
Appiah, Anthony K., 75
Arabia/Arabian, 12, 20, 21–22, 27, 30, 34, 49, 52, 55, 63, 79, 98, 11, 119, 120–122, 126, 131
Arab authors, 100–102
  Al-Bakri, 101, 107
  Al-Idrissi, 101, 108–109, 122
Arab geographers, 27–28, 120
Arabs, 31, 33, 53, 58, 66, 68, 121, 122, 125, 127, 130–131
Almohads, 103
Almoravids, 108, 112
Ark of Covenant, 92
Arusha Accords, 157, 243n.130. *See also* Rwanda
Ashanti, 64, 149–151
Asia/Asians, 6, 22, 26, 45, 47
Askya Muhammad the Great, 107, 110, 137
Assyria/Assyrians, 14–16, 60

278   INDEX

Babylon/Babylonians, 14, 15, 91, 119, 124, 223n.115, 227n.136
Babylonian Talmud, 42
Bafour, 108–109, 228n.57
Baines, Theodor, 33. *See also* Great Zimbabwe
Baluba. *See* Jews of the Congo
Bani Israel, 139, 145
Bantu, 56, 49, 119, 123, 125, 155, 157
Basden, George T. 144
Ben Ammi, Carter, 87–89
ben Israel, Menasseh, 22
Bene Menashe of India, 12, 134
Benjamin of Tudela, 20–21, 43, 97, 107
Ben-Jochannen, Yosef, 76–78
Ben-Ze'ev, Israel, 165
Ben-Zvi, Yitzak, 165
Beit Avraham of Kachene (Ethiopia), 185
Berbers, 56, 74, 102, 108, 109
Beta Israel. *See* Falasha
Beth B'nai Abraham (the House of the Sons of Abraham), 85, 221n.80
Biafra-Nigeria war, 146
Bible, 14–16, 26, 33–34, 41–44, 69–70, 74, 76, 80–82, 84, 92–93, 118, 147, 152, 162–163, 170–184
Bilad al-Sudan, 100–101
Black Jews. *See* African American Jews
Black Philadelphia Church of Soweto, 175
Black-white symbolism, 46
Black Zion. *See* Zion Apostolic Church
Blackness of the Jews, 46–49, 53, 75, 134
Blyden, Edward W., 75–76, 80
Brotz, Howard M., 84
Buijs, Gina, 168
Bulhoek Tragedy, 174
Burundi. *See* Rwanda
Bwejeri, Professor Yochannan, 154, 156–157. *See also* Jews of Rwanda-Burundi

Canaan/Canaanites, 22, 42, 47, 53, 78, 83, 99, 101, 113

Cape Verde Islands, 114. *See also* Cape Verde Israel Friendship Society
Cape Verde Israel Friendship Society, 158–160
Caucasian, 52, 53, 56–57, 65
Cham/Chamites, 53, 55, 62, 66
Chamberlain, Houston S., 48
Chidester, David, 67
Chireau, Yvonne, 83
Christian Kingdom, 27, 32
Christopher Columbus, 58–59
Church Missionary Society. *See* Protestant missions
circumcision, 60, 68, 69, 78, 92, 124, 127, 144, 145, 162, 166, 167, 176, 177, 179
Cohanim, 170
Cohen Modal Haplotype (CMH). *See* genetic research
Colenso, John W., 69
colonial discourse, 38–39, 54
colonists, 38–39, 57, 58, 62, 65, 68, 116, 120, 144, 179, 181
Commandment Keepers Congregation of the Living God, 85–86
Committee for the Lost Tribes, 86–86
conversion/converts, 20, 30, 61, 83, 87, 90, 121, 134, 136, 165, 175, 189–190
Crowdy, William S., 82, 174, 176, 177, 178
Cuoq, Joseph, 101
Cyrenaica, 65, 99, 104

Daggatun, 110, 139–141
Davidson, Basil, 57
degeneration, 40, 52, 66–67, 144
degenerative Jewish nature, 47–48
Delafosse, Maurice, 65, 100–140
Descendants of David of Madagascar, 179, 182–184
Dhu Nuwas, 20, 121
Diaspora
    African, 73–93
    Jewish, 80, 93, 98, 133, 135, 143

Diodorus Sicilus, 26
discovery of America, 22, 45
Du Bois, William E. B., 75, 83

Egypt/Egyptians, 17, 21, 25, 26, 30, 41, 42, 43, 49, 51–54, 56, 65, 70
Eilberg-Schwartz, Howard, 61
Eldad the Danite, 19–21, 23, 62, 97, 109
Elephantine, 99–100
Eliade, Mircea, 98
endogamy, 64, 110, 120, 128, 139, 151, 167, 168
Equiano, Olauda, 145
Esther, 18, 30
Ethiopianism, 81–82, 90
Europe/Europeans, 8, 12, 13, 21–24
exile, 12–18, 22, 48, 87, 114, 137, 156
Ezekiel, 12, 15, 24, 42

Faitlovitch, Jacques, 84
Falasha, 3, 12, 21, 30, 83, 91, 93, 98, 100, 135, 136, 142, 166, 185, 188
 Falasha identity, 84–86
Falashisation, 84–93
Farrakhan, Louis, 76, 78, 79
Fauvelle, François-Xavier, 52
Ferrand, Gabriel, 126, 234n.159
Flacourt, Etienne de, 124, 179–181
Flavius Josephus, 16, 30, 99
Foetor judaicus, 48

Galla, 54, 63, 128, 154
Garvey, Marcus, 75, 76, 77, 80, 82, 90–92
genetic research, 157, 170–172
Ghana. See Jews of Ghana
Gihon Hebrew Centre, 147
Gilman, Sandor, 46, 48
globalization, 184, 187, 188
Gobineau, Joseph de, 54–55. See also Hamitic hypothesis
Godbey, Allen, 12, 13, 117, 145
Gog and Magog, 46, 200n.28
Grandidier, Alfred, 124–125, 129, 180, 181

Great Zimbabwe, 28, 31, 34, 57, 119–120, 129, 173
Greece, ancient 70, 73, 74, 77
Guinea, Coast, 114. See also Cape Verde Islands
Guzawah, Solomon, 176. See also Jews of Rusape

Haidara, Ismael D., 135, 137–138, 141. See also Jews of Timbuktu
Haile Selassie, 30, 84–85, 90, 91. See also Rastafarian movement
Halacha (Jewish law), 20, 21, 98n.4
Ham, curse of, 42–43, 44
Hamitic hypothesis /myth, 27, 28, 51–61, 62, 63, 66, 70, 74, 75, 92
Harlem, 78, 83, 84, 85, 86, 87. See also Jews of Harlem
Havilah, land of, 20, 34, 37
Hebrew Israelites, 87–89, 92
Hebrew language, 59, 62, 85, 141, 147, 181
Hebrewisms, 64, 85, 150
Hebrewists, 143
Herodotus, 26, 30, 104, 150
Himyar/Himyarites, 20, 34, 121
Hminga, Chantge L., 191
Homer, 26, 27
Hottentots, 12, 57, 67–68, 79
House of Israel of Ghana, 149–153

Ibn Khaldun, 101–102
Ida Oushaq or Dawsahak (Sons of Isaac), 110
Igbo of Nigeria, 143–148, 239n.55
inferiority
 of Blacks, 40–41, 52, 55
 of Jews, 47, 48, 49
Ilona, Remi, 143, 240n.58. See also Jews of Nigeria
Inhaden, 110
Inquisition, 114, 115, 158
Institute for Jewish and Community Research, 148, 165

internet, 141, 147, 173, 184, 188
Isaiah, prophecy of, 12, 15–18, 24, 41, 90
Ismael/Ismaelites, 65, 68, 124
Israel, ancient, 67–68, 69, 143, 176, 178, 181
Israelites, ancient, 12, 22, 42, 66, 69, 70, 83, 84, 102, 143, 145, 173, 176, 190
  of South Africa, 174–175
  in Cameroon, 185

Jeremiah, 12, 15, 17, 98, 99, 162
Jewish festivals, 89, 145, 163
Jewish Lançados, 114, 118
Jewish model, 81
Jewish organisations, 134, 147
Jewish travellers, 19–22
Jews of Angola, 117, 159
Jews of Cameroon, 185
Jews of the Congo, 157–158
Jews of Ghana. *See* House of Israel of Ghana
Jews of Kachene, Ethiopia. *See* Beit Avraham
Jews of Laikipia, Kenya, 185
Jews of Madagascar. *See* Descendants of David of Madagascar
Jews of Nigeria. *See* Igbo of Nigeria
Jews of Rusape, Zimbabwe, 176–178
Jews of Rwanda-Burundi. *See* Tutsi-Hebrews of Havilah
Jews of San Nicandro, 161
Jews of South Africa and Zimbabwe. *See* Lemba
Jews of Touat, 104–108, 110–112, 136–137, 138, 141–142
Jews of Timbuktu. *See* Zakhor
Jews of Uganda. *See* Abayudaya of Uganda
Jews of Yemen, 98, 119, 120–121, 125–126, 131, 150, 166, 178, 183
Johnston, Sir Harry, 56, 140, 163
Judeos Segredos (Secret Jews), 114
Junod, Henri A., 167

Kahina, 102–103
Kakungulu, Samei L., 162–164. *See also* Abayudaya of Uganda
Kaplan, Steven, 7, 142
Kebra Nagast, 30, 201n.6
King David, 31, 46, 101
King Solomon, legend of, 27, 29–33, 86, 90, 98, 99, 118–119, 150, 154
King Solomon Shepherd Federation, 145
Kolb, Peter, 67
Koran, 68, 127, 131, 137, 180, 202n.7, 206n.57
Kulanu, 134–135, 141, 147, 148, 152, 156, 165, 171
Kush, children of, 7, 16, 18, 20, 21, 24–25, 30, 41–42, 53, 63, 74, 92, 107, 156, 157, 204 n.28

Lafitau, Father, 61
Lange, Dierk, 113
La Roncière, Charles de, 65, 111
Lemba, 12, 119–123, 130–132. *See also* genetic research
Lemba Cultural Association, 119, 168, 172
Leo Africanus, 52, 101, 102, 106, 107, 137
Levi de Montezinos, Antonio, 22. *See also* American Indians
Levites, 92, 137, 144, 149, 170, 177, 183
Livingstone, David, 117
Lobagola, 145
London Missionary Society. *See* Protestant missions

McClintock, Anne, and Robert Young, 38
Majorcan Jewish geographers, 111
Malcioln, Jose, 77, 78
Malfante, Antonio, 104–105, 106, 227n.45
Malinowski, Bronislaw, 19
Mandeville, 200n.28

Maroserana, 130
Martin, A. G. P., 104
Masai, 56, 63–64, 66
Mathivha, Professor M.E.R., 119, 166
Matthew, Wentworth, 84, 85, 86
Mauny, Raymond, 109, 110, 111
Mauritania, 65, 102, 108–112, 138, 150
May, Rollo, 98
Medina, 121, 182, 183
Melamed, Abraham, 42, 199n.16
Mendelssohn, Sydney, 67
Meroe, 18, 26, 145
mimetic conversion, 83
Mizo National Front of the Shinlung. *See* Shinlung
monogenism, 40
Monomotapa, 23, 24
Monteil, Charles, 108, 113, 149, 228n.57
Moorish Zionist Church, 85
Mosaic Law for One World, 87
Msitshana, Vayisile. *See* Black Philadelphia Church of Soweto
Muhammad, 30, 79, 120, 121, 127
Myth, functions of, 14, 98. *See also* Eliade, M.; Malinowski, B.; May, R.

Nation of Islam, 79
National Association for the Advancement of Colored People (NAACP), 83
négritude, 76
Neubauer, Adolf, 15
nilotic, 62–63
Noah, curse of, 42, 44, 53, 67, 94
Nri clan, 143. *See also* Igbo of Nigeria
Nubians, 41, 74, 100

Obadiah of Bertinoro, 21, 62
Oded, Arye, 164–165
Old Testament, influence of, 61, 63–64, 66
  affiliation to by African Americans, 81–82, 92
  by Africans, 149, 152, 162–163, 174, 183
Ophir, 23, 26, 27, 29, 30, 32, 33, 34, 59, 118, 125
Orientalism, 38, 39
Origen, 44
Other/Otherness, 13, 37–38, 45–47, 49, 76, 97

Paganism, 43, 58
Pan African Jewish Alliance (PAJA), 148
Pan-Africanism, 77, 178
Parfitt, Tudor, 4, 39, 45, 59, 120, 123, 130, 136, 166, 168, 169, 172
Patai, Raphael, and J. Patai, 6
Periplus of the Erythrean Sea, 121
Peel, John, 189
Peul, 64–66, 100, 111, 140, 155, 213n.85
Philo of Alexandria, 44
Phoenicians, 30, 34, 53, 118, 125, 163
phylogenesis, 39
portolans, 27, 111–112
Portuguese navigators, 31–32
Prester John, 21, 23, 24, 27, 32
Príncipe, 114, 116
Prophet Cherry, 82
Protestant missions, 62, 66, 125
Ptolemy, 26, 32, 65, 101n.9

Quatrefages, Armand de, 55

Rabbi Capers Funnye, 86, 148
Rabbi Eliahu Avichail. 197n.15. *See also* Amishav
racialism, 39, 43, 48, 49
Rastafarian movement, 76, 84, 89–92, 178
Ratzel, Friedrich, 48, 56, 117, 150
Red Heifer, 183, 251n.115
Responsa, 107, 137
revivalist cults, 223n.109

ritual slaughter (of animals), 119, 143
River Niger, 100, 117, 137
Ruwitah, A., 120
Rwanda, 63, 154–156

Sabbatherians, 143, 147
Said, Edward. *See* Orientalism
Sambatyon, 16–17, 20, 23
Santamaria, Ulysses. *See* mimetic conversion
São Tomé, 113–116
Sefwi Wiaso. *See* House of Israel of Ghana
Seligman, Charles, 28, 52, 56, 201n.14
Semites, 63, 66, 68, 69, 75, 155, 182
Sena, 119, 120, 121, 122, 123
Sergi, Giuseppe, 55–56, 74
Sheba, Queen of, 25, 29–30, 32, 33, 34, 84, 86, 90, 98, 118, 119
Shinlung (Bene Menashe) of India, 189, 190
Shona, 122, 130
Sibree, James, 180
Siete Partidas (or Seven Codes of Alphonse X), 117, 118
Sizomu, Gershom, 165. *See also* Abayudaya of Uganda
slavery/slaves, 21, 42, 43, 62, 80–82, 84, 88, 100, 106, 114–118, 125, 148, 199n.16
Snowden, Frank, 43
Sofala, 27, 31, 32, 33, 121, 123, 129
Somalia, 150
Sons of Abraham, 12, 21, 68, 78, 85, 92, 97, 117, 124, 125, 143, 179, 180, 181
Sons of Asher, 14, 20
Sons of Benjamin, 14, 16
Sons of Dan, 4, 12, 14, 19, 20
Sons of Gad, 14, 19, 21, 143, 148
Sons of Issachar, 14, 19
Sons of Jacob, 14, 68, 84, 92, 97, 150
Sons of Joseph, 14, 124, 139
Sons of Judah, 14, 15, 16, 30, 46, 87, 90, 98
Sons of Levi, 12, 14, 170
Sons of Naphtali, 14, 15, 19, 20
Sons of Reuben, 14, 21
Sons of Simon, 14, 20
Sons of Zebulon, 14, 20
Sorabé, 128, 180
Speke, John H., 54, 154, 155
Stayt, Hugh, 167–168
St. Clair Drake, John, 57, 80, 210n.18
Sudan, 65, 99, 103, 104, 106, 107, 108–113, 137, 145, 173

Talmud/talmudic, 15, 17, 19, 21, 42, 43, 89, 103, 143, 154
Tarikh al-Fattash, 100, 138–139
Thorowgood, Thomas, 61
Toakyirafa, A., 149, 151, 152. *See also* House of Israel of Ghana
Torah, 86, 88, 143, 147, 154, 177, 185
Touareg, 106, 110, 138–139. *See also* Daggatun
Touat, 101–108, 110, 122. *See also* Jews of Touat
Trans-Saharan trade, 103–112, 137
Trevisan Semi, Emanuela, 4, 79, 84
Tutsi-Hebrews of Havilah, 153–158

Ukpong, Justin S., 190

Van Dijk, Teun, 188
Van Warmelo, Nicolas J., 168
Van Wyk Smith, Malvern, 27
Venda, 130, 166, 167, 171, 173

Wagadu, legend of, 141–150, 152
Weil, Shalva, 189, 190
Williams, Joseph J., 64, 85, 150–151

Xhosa, 67–68, 175

Yoruba, 28, 66, 113, 143, 144–145, 148

Zachernuk, Philip, 144
Zaffre-Ibrahim (or Zaffy-Ibrahim), 124, 179–180
Zafiraminia, 127–128, 249n.91
Zakhor of Timbuktu, 135–142, 188, 237n.8
Zantop, Susan, 38
Zion Apostolic Church (ZAC)/Zion Christian Church (ZCC), 173–174
Zion/Zionism, 17, 77, 79, 85, 87, 92, 122, 146, 157, 168, 173, 191
Zulu, 12, 68–70